ENDORSEMENTS

I just finished *Binding the Strongman Over America and the Nations*. This is one of the most amazing and rewarding books I have ever read. Twenty years ago, some of us planted the seeds of strategic-level spiritual warfare through books, conferences, and the Spiritual Warfare Network. John Benefiel's book, which brings beside him the voices of numbers of experienced field participants, provides an unbelievable display of the maturity, wisdom, discernment, commitment, measurable results, and superabundant fruit that the movement has now produced from those early seeds. This is the best book on spiritual warfare available today.

C. Peter Wagner
Vice President and Apostolic Ambassador
Global Spheres, Inc.

John Benefiel has written one of the most insightful, practical books on spiritual warfare that I have read in a long time. He gives perspective from a pastor who doesn't just talk about transforming his city and state; he has actually done it with measurable results!

Cindy Jacobs
Generals International

Binding the Strongman Over America and the Nations is a powerful manual for transforming regions and nations. Apostle John Benefiel helps the reader deal with hidden issues that hinder transformation. This powerful book brings understanding on how to deal with covenant breaking, gender issues, racial issues, innocent bloodshed, and ancient structures. Benefiel also uncovers revelation on dismantling the Baal structure in the nation. He documents tangible evidence that transformation is now occurring where these strategies have been implemented. Every person who has a desire to see their city or region look like heaven needs to read this book. Your life and your region will never be the same!

Barbara Wentroble
President, International Breakthrough Ministries
President, Business Owners for Christ International
Author, *Prophetic Intercession*, *Praying with Authority*, *Removing the Veil of Deception*, and others

Anything held in darkness is owned by the devil. This book shines a bright light that exposes much of the hidden darkness of our nation's history. Apostle Benefiel calls this book a roadmap to transformation. I believe it is more than that. It's an historical account of national sin, godly sorrow, and true repentance! It's actually a replicable blueprint to lasting change (true transformation), which is so needed in our nation. Be informed and be equipped by this great work.

Dr. Bill Sudduth
President, International Society of Deliverance Ministers

John Benefiel is a spiritual father in the kingdom of God. His leadership over the years and his heart for the nation have released an anointing that will affect generations. His ministry crosses all denominational, racial, and political boundaries. He has a vision for intercession and an eye in the spirit. Apostle Benefiel understands the times and seasons. He is a shaker and a mover in America. This book will give you prophetic insight and an apostolic impartation that will strengthen you in the end times.

Kimberly Daniels
Kimberly Daniels Ministries International

Dr. John Benefiel and his co-laborers have made a great contribution to the body of Christ. They clearly prove that there are spiritual forces that determine what happens in different parts of the earth. God has authorized His Church the spiritual insight and the delegated powers and authority to destroy evil principalities and power that cause problems on the earth. This book will inspire Christians around the world to bring transformation to their area, and even their nation. God bless you for sharing your revelation from the Holy Spirit and then proving it true in your life experiences. Every Christian who desires to be mightily used of God should read this book.

Dr. Bill Hamon
Bishop, Christian International Ministries Network (CIMN)
Christian International Apostolic Network, Ci Global Network
Author, *Day of the Saints*, *Prophetic Scriptures Yet to Be*, and others

In a war, nothing is more critical to victory than reliable intelligence. *Binding the Strongman Over America and the Nations* is a windfall of insight. Like a long-awaited dispatch from the frontlines, each page uncovers the enemy's position and unfolds a prophetic battle plan. You'll be inspired by the breathtaking story of God's work in Oklahoma as well as equipped to advance to a new place of triumph. This is a true gift to all of us who long to see transforming revival overtake our land.

Dr. David Cannistraci
GateWay City Church
San Jose, California

Dr. John Benefiel is on the cutting edge of understanding the power and authority given to the Church to transform cities, states, countries, and nations. I have read the original manuscript of this dynamic book, *Binding the Strongman Over America and the Nations*. In it is the secret to what Jesus said: "Whatsoever you bind on earth shall be bound in heaven and whatsoever you loose on earth, it will be loosed in heaven." John Benefiel promoted this and has led thousands to pray and bind the strong demonic forces that control neighborhoods, cities, and states.

In the 15 years I have known this humble, powerful pastor, he has raised up intercessors, spiritual warfare warriors, in all 50 states in the U.S. and several other countries. Read this book and practice this. I have seen results first-hand as I have watched the transformation of Oklahoma City. I am an eye witness. It really has happened and will happen in your city, too.

Dr. Emanuele Cannistraci
Apostle, Apostolic Missions International

In a time when it's easy to think that America is beyond human help with regard to transformation, Dr. Benefiel reminds us in a compelling way not to give up on this great nation, but rather to identify the key enemy and shift the Church into the "attack" position as we contend for the soul of this great nation. *Binding the Strongman Over America and the Nations* is a must read for every concerned citizen of God's kingdom.

Jackson Senyonga
Senior Pastor, Christian Life Church
Uganda, East Africa
Founder/President, Christian Life Ministries, USA

Revelation is the key to unlocking regions, territories, and nations. John Benefiel has definitely hit the bullseye with this book. His insight comes not only from the Word of God, but also from his experience in prayer and community transformation. The result is many believers embracing new understanding as the Holy Spirit teaches the Church how to move in more power and authority. Those who read this book will receive fresh insight and motivation to meet the challenges of their region. I encourage those who read it to believe God for transformation in your area. Don't be discouraged by the setbacks you seemingly have experienced in advancing the kingdom. The key of knowledge will unlock territories that have been closed for generations. John Benefiel gives us the key in the chapters of this book. I have seen what has happened in Oklahoma, and I have heard his teaching. Now, what others have seen and heard is in book form and can be read across our nation and around the world. The successes John and others experienced can be experienced by more of God's leaders and intercessors as they embrace the truths in this book.

I encourage you to read this book with an open heart and allow the Holy Spirit to impart wisdom to you. These truths have been forged through the crucible of experience and prayer. This makes them invaluable. John Benefiel has paid the price to obtain the knowledge of warfare and breakthrough. He has counted the cost and made the sacrifice to faithfully teach and practice what is in this book. Be blessed by his teaching, and share it with as many in the Church who will hear.

John Eckhardt
Apostle and Overseer, Crusaders Church Chicago
IMPACT Network Apostolic Institute of Ministry

Some say we have lost the war in this nation; it has deteriorated to a godless, sinful, chaotic state. While this may be partially true, something else is happening in our midst. People are arising who believe God and His Word. A state, a nation can be reformed. This book details how to think, believe, and act, not just theoretically but from an experiential standpoint. John Benefiel and team explain how they set out to change a state through sustained, united prayer and action. I was captivated, riveted by this book. John and team have pioneered a way to transform and reform a state, a nation. Reading this book will make you become a believer!

Barbara J. Yoder
Senior Pastor and Lead Apostle
Shekinah Regional Equipping and Revival Center
Breakthrough Apostolic Ministries Network
Shekinah Leadership Institute

BINDING THE STRONGMAN OVER AMERICA AND THE NATIONS

BINDING THE STRONGMAN over AMERICA AND THE NATIONS

HEALING THE LAND,
TRANSFERRING WEALTH,
AND ADVANCING THE KINGDOM OF GOD

DR. JOHN BENEFIEL

DESTINY IMAGE® PUBLISHERS, INC.
P.O. Box 310, Shippensburg, PA 17257-0310
"Promoting Inspired Lives."

This book and all other Destiny Image and Destiny Image Fiction books are available at Christian bookstores and distributors worldwide.

For more information on foreign distributors, call 717-532-3040.

Reach us on the Internet: www.destinyimage.com.

ISBN 13 TP: 978-0-7684-5322-5

ISBN 13 eBook: 978-0-7684-5323-2

ISBN 13 HC: 978-0-7684-5325-6

ISBN 13 LP: 978-0-7684-5324-9

For Worldwide Distribution, Printed in the U.S.A.

3 4 5 6 7 8 / 24 23 22 21 20

DEDICATION

This book is dedicated to my wonderful wife, Judith. We have been married 54 years, and other than Jesus, she is the love of my life. Without her love, encouragement, understanding, and wisdom I wouldn't still be here, much less have done all the things you will read about in this book. She is the most beautiful person on the inside as well as the outside that I know. I thank God for her every day because I love her more every day!

ACKNOWLEDGMENT

On March 2, 2015, my dear friend and covenant brother, Jay Swallow, went to his home in glory. In our years walking together, Jay, also known as Roaming Buffalo, adopted me into the Cheyenne tribe. During his 54 years serving the Lord, Jay ministered to more than 353 tribes in the United States, Canada, and South America. He also worked with First Nations people in Israel, Fiji, and Cuba. I know that he is among the great cloud of witnesses watching from heaven—cheering us on.

CONTENTS

FOREWORD

I still remember the week before the Oklahoma City bombing. I was ministering in a small church of one of the students I had been instructing at Southwestern Graduate School, an extension of Southwestern Christian University in Bethany, Oklahoma, on the outskirts of Oklahoma City, Oklahoma. I was about to speak when the Spirit of God spoke to me and said, "What you see this week, you will not see next week. The city will be at the door of the Church next week. The Church is not ready for the city to be there, but I will shake the city at your door."

I did not know what this meant, but as a prophetic voice, I just obeyed and prophesied what I had heard out loud to the congregation. One young lady began to shake violently. When we proceeded to minister to her, she went into weeping and travail. I said, "Lord, what is the meaning of all of this?" Prophets don't always understand. However, a true prophet obeys and says what needs to be said.

The next day I found myself in downtown Oklahoma City. Something was wrong! I could sense something foreboding in the atmosphere. A wrong spiritual force had a grip on the city. Who should I tell? What should I do? I left the city with a great burden that the Lord had allowed me to discern. However, I had no way to communicate what I was sensing.

The following Wednesday, Dr. Garnet Pike, dean of students for the graduate school, called and said, "Son, they tell me you are sensing something wrong in our city and you have a problem. Is that correct?" I said, "Garnet, there is something wrong in that city and the Body is too religious and fragmented to communicate and develop a strategy to change the situation!" Before he could ask, "What?" the explosion in downtown Oklahoma occurred! His next statement was, "A bomb has gone off downtown; I'll call you back!"

This terrible, historical instance changed the course of my life as a watchman prophet. It also changed the course of a city, affected a state, and is now changing a nation. *That is what this book is about!*

Dr. John Benefiel is a rare leader. He sees an opportunity and then develops a strategy. The above tragedy occurred in April 1995. The bombing of the Murrah Building created a footprint in America's history. Apostle John emerged as a leader to mobilize leaders, encourage intercession, become a change agent, and create a model that would change the course of a city, a state, and a nation. *That is what this book is about!*

What does the atmosphere have to do with a war over God's presence?

Actually, everything! We have an atmosphere about us that affects the way the earth operates. The atmosphere we carry affects the land we walk on. The more we are in union with God and His purpose for the earth, the more we create a right atmosphere around us. To usher in God's presence requires a change in the atmosphere, and we are assigned the task of bringing this about! *That is what this book is about!*

The Bible establishes that satan is the god of this world, the "prince of the power of the air" (Eph. 2:2). Yet, how is this so if Psalm 24:1 says, "The earth *is* the Lord's, and all it contains"? First, we must understand the terms used in those two verses. The Greek word for "earth" is *topos*, while the word for "world" is *cosmos*. This means that any structure that protrudes or is above the *topos* is subject to warfare. Second, we must realize the Bible establishes that there are three heavens. God and all His heavenly beings dwell in the third heaven. Satan, as the ruler of the air, attempts to rule from the second heaven to legislate illegally in the first heaven—that place where we physically stand above the earth.

Apostle Kimberly Daniels, in her book *Give It Back*, explains it this way:

> Ephesians 2:2 describes the assignment of the prince of the power of the air. One name for the Greek god of the second heaven is *Zeus*. The second heaven is a demonic headquarters that is strategically set up to control people like puppets on a string. In the spirit, that is exactly how it looks—like a puppet show! Every human being is connected to either the second or third heaven. People who are bound by second heaven activity are connected to the second heaven by demonic stings.
>
> The hydra is the god of recurring curses and is also seated in the heavens. It is one of the constellations or groups of stars that abide in the heavens. The power of the air (or unconscious cycle) is a subliminal bondage, which is controlled from the air. This spirit hides behind the cover of natural habits, and its victims never suspect that they are under its control. Before people are delivered from addictions and habits, demonic strings must be cut in the spirit to sever their alliances with the second heaven. After this, ground-level deliverance can take place.[1]

You will glean great insights into this structure as you read this book!

We must determine who is in charge of our atmosphere. Are we going to legislate God's rule in our atmosphere, or will our enemy control it? This is one of our greatest warfare dynamics to understand. In *Authority in Prayer,* Dutch Sheets writes:

> Where God and Satan are concerned, the issue has never been power, including control of the earth. God is all-powerful. ... It is always and only a question of authority. The same is true with us and our struggle with the kingdom of darkness. Satan didn't gain any power at the fall and didn't lose any at the cross. His power or ability didn't change at either event. His authority, or the right to use his power, *did.* In fact, though Christians often state otherwise, Scripture nowhere says that Christ delivered us from or dealt with Satan's power at Calvary. *He dealt with Satan's authority.*[2]

As you peruse the pages of this book, you will see a model develop concerning this truth!

A government wars to overthrow unjust rule. We must learn to legislate our realm of authority, while understanding that it is not the same thing as wielding power. Our realm of authority includes both heaven and earth. That is what makes up our atmosphere. Jesus broke satan's headship and removed his legal authority at the cross. He then overcame death, hell, and the grave. He liberated the captives. However, we must keep satan's power neutralized and defeated in the place in the earth where God has called us to be His stewards. That is what Elijah did when he commanded the heavens to withhold rain for three and a half years (see 1 Kings 17). Then, knowing it was God's perfect time for rain, he birthed a cloud into his atmosphere. The atmosphere was then filled with rain. *John Benefiel has developed an apostolic team and a strategy in this book to help you understand this principle!*

Dominion is always linked with boundaries. The question is, how will you occupy and rule in your sphere of authority? You see, boundaries are the personal property lines that each of us has been given. Boundaries help us to determine who may touch us and under what circumstances. Boundaries can be mental, emotional, or spiritual! There is and will continue to be a great war over boundaries. Individuals, people groups, and entire nations will be jostling for authority through expansion of their boundaries. Yet what we must realize is, most often the greatest impetus behind this is not a need for more *land*—it is the want of greater *supply*. It is easy to grow dissatisfied with the supply lines established within our own boundaries and decide we want to take something from someone else's boundary. This is how dominion wars began ages ago, and how they will continue to rage in the coming days. John Benefiel displays a model in this book over this issue!

Binding the Strongman Over America and the Nations will become a textbook to all intercessors, watchmen, prophets, and apostles. In days ahead, we will see many changing boundaries in the earth. There will be an attempt to rearrange the boundaries of nations illegally. Governments will align to overtake lands that were never destined to be overtaken. We must watch these wars carefully in the natural earth realm because they are linked with a quest for wealth.

Binding the Strongman Over America and the Nations is a model for raising up a Triumphant Reserve in days ahead! On May 31, 2008, the Lord showed *His Triumphant Reserve*. He raised me and showed me the nation of the United States of America. First, He revealed His remnant and where they were positioned. Next, He showed me their strength from state to state to state. He showed me how many were moving over into the enemy's camp of religion. He showed me how others were aligning around race and gender as opposed to mission call and gifting. Then He showed me high places. These were altars that had been built by the enemy and positioned strategically throughout the land. I saw how the sacrifices on these altars were empowering and keeping an atmosphere held captive by ruling hosts.

Next, the Lord showed me the atmosphere. In this vision, He showed me different layers of the atmosphere in relationship to His presence versus the demonic spiritual rule in that particular area or region. (Some areas have already been taken over, and darkness actually rules those areas.) There were 10 ruling centers already developed within the United States. Then He showed me the communication systems among these centers. I saw how one sacrifice empowered one dimension of an evil presence, and then that presence would communicate to another center as together they networked their plan of control. The Lord then showed me a Triumphant People who would rise up and overcome. They were positioned in the land and were waiting to be mobilized and gathered.

This book will be used as a prophetic model to redeem lands! Redemption was both a social and religious concept in the daily life of God's people. The Israelites were aware of their responsibility to one another to protect the weak and unprotected. Redemption secures the life of the people as a community, not just as individuals (see Deut. 25:5–10). In Israel, land had to stay in the family. A family could mortgage the land to ward off poverty. Biblically, there is a law of redemption in Leviticus 25:25, which states: "If one of your brethren becomes poor, and has sold some of his possession, and if his redeeming relative comes to redeem it, then he may redeem what his brother sold" (NKJV). A required kinsman could purchase back the land and bring back the inheritance to the family. If a family member died without an heir, the kinsman gave his name by marrying the widow and rearing a son to hand down his name (see Gen. 38:8; Deut. 25:5; Ruth 3–4). When death came at the hands of another man, the redeemer acted as the avenger of blood and pursued the killer (see Num. 35:12–34; Deut. 19:1–3). The redeemer principle was used of things consecrated to God (see Lev. 27:13–31). God used this principle in redeeming man (see Exod. 6:6; Isa. 43:1, 44:22, 48:20,

49:7). Those redeemed by God (see Job 19:25; Isa. 35:9, 51:10) were to learn to say "SO." *This book will help you say SO!*

Finally, this book will cause "the land to rejoice again!" Land takes on characteristics based on what we do on it, both good and bad. Land can be either defiled or blessed by the people who inhabit it. When we worship, we see a manifestation of God's justice into the iniquitous patterns on earth. Angelic visitation and glory are linked with people. Therefore, healing the land will be connected with individuals. When we worship, an extension of the kingdom of God in heaven begins to manifest on earth.

Binding the Strongman Over America and the Nations is a testimony to a land that was once captured, and which held a people of captivity, now rejoicing again!

Chuck D. Pierce
President, Global Spheres, Inc.
President, Glory of Zion International Ministries, Inc

CHAPTER 1

FORGIVING A NATION THAT NEVER ASKED

Dr. Negiel Bigpond
HAPN First Nations Director

The red nation shall rise again. It shall be a blessing for a sick world; a world filled with broken promises, selfishness and separation; a world longing for the light again.
—**Crazy Horse Prophecy, 1877**

THE sound of native drums beating swirled around Washington D.C. on October 6, 2016. I was there representing the Euchee with Willie Jock who represented the Mohawk Nation. We were doing something that hadn't been done before. Through All Tribes DC, we'd gathered at the Washington Monument with representatives from 27 Native American tribes to do business with God.

The platform we had permission to build sat in front of the Washington Monument. Worship leaders from various churches played instruments and sang. A huge crowd spread before us. Many sat on lawn chairs while others sat on blankets.

The journey to this day had been a long one. In truth, it may have begun in 1975 when Reverend Billy Graham loosed this prophetic word to Native American Christian leaders in Albuquerque, New Mexico. "You are a sleeping giant, the original American. You are now awakening. Just around the corner, you may become a spiritual super power in this country that could change not only America but the world."

Those words had released the move of God to restore evangelical Native Americans to the place in the body of Christ that had been forbidden since the white man introduced Jesus to them.

My personal journey with the prayer network began on July 13, 1997, at Church on the Rock in Oklahoma City. The convening apostle, John Benefiel, had been called by God to bring unity to the body of Christ. He'd gathered ministers and intercessors from across Oklahoma. A diverse group, they represented numerous denominations and cultures. Key leaders had humbled themselves before us for two hours that night. Kneeling, they'd repented to us for their sins, the sins of their fathers, and the sins of the nation.

They'd asked us to forgive. We did, making a covenant with them that has never been broken. Walking together as brothers, we'd embarked on a journey of forgiveness that had led to this day. The highlights of that journey have been reported in this book.

In January of 2003, 12 of us met in the office of Senator Sam Brownback. He'd allotted us 30 minutes, but he gave us two and a half hours. We showed him a thick book which we call the Book of Covenants. The book documented all 372 of the treaties that the U.S. government signed and ratified with the First Nations people.

Each and every one of them had been broken by that same government.

We put the Book of Covenants on the floor with a Bible on top of it. Together, we prayed. Afterward, Senator Brownback asked, "Is there anything else we need to do?"

"Senator," I said, "I think it's time for the United States to apologize to the First Nations people."

The senator got down on his knees. On behalf of the U.S. government, he asked for forgiveness for all the atrocities and broken covenants. We granted forgiveness and prayed for him. That meeting set us on a path of years spent working toward a Resolution of Apology from the President of the United States.

On December 10, 2010, President Obama signed the resolution. It was a small addition to the defense bill. Although signed, the apology was never activated by being released to the public.

In 2003, I worked alongside Jay Swallow to form the Inter-Tribal Prayer Network. This network included the chiefs of the five civilized tribes: Choctaw, Chickasaw, Seminole, Creek, and Cherokee. We signed a proclamation dedicating the month of November as the Inter-Tribal Prayer Month.

Nothing like this had ever been done before. Working through the Heartland Apostolic Prayer Network (HAPN), we traveled to Washington, DC to pray through the Baal Divorce Decree and do spiritual warfare.

I'm on the executive committee for the National Day of Prayer on behalf of the First Nations people. I know the authority we carry as First Nations people.

For instance, when a cab picks me up at an airport, I always ask the driver's nationality. They tell me, and I say, "Welcome to America."

"How can you say that?" they ask.

"I say it because I'm one of the First Nations people. Since I'm part of the first people of the land, I have the authority to welcome you."

As you will read later in this book, the reason that dealing with the First Nations issue is so critical is because of 372 broken treaties. All you have to do is read about the treaty that the Israelites made with the Gibeonites to know how God feels about broken covenants.

Israel came under severe judgment because of *one* broken covenant.

Those 372 broken covenants opened the door for the enemy to take our land.

Although African Americans didn't suffer broken covenants, they were brought here in chains, against their will. They were beaten, sold, and murdered at will.

All Tribes D.C. is working with Dr. Joseph Green to welcome African Americans to the country. That was never done. They're Americans. They're citizens. They have full rights in the nation, but they were never welcomed here.

We, the First People of the land, welcome African Americans.

An Unasked Apology

In 2016, we as a people knew that it was time for us to do something unprecedented in this land. February 4–6, 20 of us traveled to Washington, DC, to seek God for direction. We went in four directions asking God where He wanted us to pray and prophesy. Gabriel Madison Eagle came back and said God wanted us to pray at the Washington Monument. We prayed and agreed with that direction. That was just our trip to scout out the land.

The Lord told us that the Washington Monument, built to honor our first president, was a sacred place to pray according to 2 Chronicles 7:12-15.

> *Then the Lord appeared to Solomon at night and said to him, "I have heard your prayer and have chosen this place for Myself as a house of sacrifice. If I shut up the heavens so that there is no rain, or if I command the locust to devour the land, or if I send pestilence among My people, and My people who are called by*

My name humble themselves and pray and seek My face and turn from their wicked ways, then I will hear from heaven, will forgive their sin and will heal their land. Now My eyes will be open and My ears attentive to the prayer offered in this place."

That was why we gathered on October 6, 2016. With a platform built in front of the Washington Monument, we had a daylong event. Multiple worship teams led, with the sound of native drums echoing across the city. We gathered with representatives from 27 tribes, along with other Christians hungry to join the solemn assembly.

We believed that it was time for us as a people to forgive a nation that had never asked for forgiveness. That's what Jesus did on Calvary. He asked God to forgive the people who crucified Him, although they hadn't repented either.

We prayed the prayer written by Willie Jock:

We the people, the Host People of this Great Nation and the original lovers of this land, stand united with one heart and one mind, to bring the power of forgiveness to bear. As the Host People of Turtle Island, we forgive every atrocity and broken covenant ever designed to destroy us as a race of people. We break every curse, and renounce every lie, purposed to decimate us as human beings. We forgive the Government, the Church, and the educational system for the use of residential schools that attempted to destroy our culture and silence our voice as a people.

We stand in the gap for those who are unable or unwilling to forgive, and call upon the Master of Life to forgive us for harboring unforgiveness, resentment, hatred, bitterness, and rage. We repent of every curse that was spoken over America by our ancestors and we release the power of forgiveness to bring healing and the peace of Creator God to this land.

We declare and decree that our voice will no longer be silenced and that this nation and the world will hear our voice as we speak life and blessings over the Americas and the world.

We stand in faith believing that our citizenship lies in heaven, and we too all await the return of our Savior—the Lord Jesus Christ. Being all of one mind and heart, having compassion for one another, we declare our love as brothers; not returning evil for the evil perpetrated against us, but on the contrary we choose to release a blessing, knowing that the Father of us all has called us as His children to bless and not curse, that we may inherit a blessing. Amen!

Written by Apostle Willie Jock, Feb. 5, 2016
Declared at All Tribes D.C., Oct. 21, 2016

In John 20:23 we are told, "If you forgive the sins of any, their sins have been forgiven them; if you retain the sins of any, they have been retained." As a people, we remitted the country's sins against us.

We did it not only for the help and survival of this nation, but for ourselves. We're told in Mark 11:25, "Whenever you stand praying, forgive, if you have anything against anyone, so that your Father who is in heaven will also forgive you your transgressions."

We released the words of Crazy Horse's prophecy from 1877:

The red nation shall rise again. It shall be a blessing for a sick world; a world filled with broken promises, selfishness and separation; a world longing for the light again.

We released the words of Billy Graham's prophecy from 1975:

> You are a sleeping giant, the original American. You are now awakening. Just around the corner, you may become a spiritual super power in this country that could change not only America but the world.

We've had many great leaders stand with us along our journey to forgiveness. Among them was C. Peter Wagner, a man who always talked to Jay Swallow and me. He talked, pushing and prodding us in the way that we should go. Always cheering us on and celebrating all our victories.

At 2:45 that afternoon, a mighty wind blew through. A deluge of rain poured on us for about 10 or 15 minutes. That was the same time that Peter Wagner departed this life and entered glory. The natives believe that when someone dies, the rain will wash their footprints off the land as they cross to the other side. I think that Peter's departure at the same time we were forgiving this nation was his blessing our efforts.

I still believe that a President of the United States will one day activate the Resolution of Apology that President Obama signed. However, I know that as we as First Nations people forgave this land, something powerful happened. I wasn't sure what it would look like on the other side, but I knew it would be good.

We forgave the nation just prior to the 2016 presidential election. Had we not done it, the enemy would have had a legal case against our government in the Courts of Heaven. With forgiveness granted, that case was removed from the docket. Now we waited to see what God's will would be concerning our president.

CHAPTER 2

THIS ISN'T MUCH LIKE HEAVEN

*Revival is nothing else than a new beginning of obedience
to God, getting down in the dust before God with
deep humility and forsaking sin.*
—Charles Finney

IN the business world, if a model isn't working you either change your model or you go out of business. Not so in Christianity. For too long we've convinced ourselves that we know how to do church—even though our model wasn't working. For years, rather than admit that for some reason God *wasn't* answering our prayers for revival and awakening, we simply prayed harder, louder, and longer. Like the Pharisees, we acted as though God would eventually hear us for our long prayers. Maybe if we pray *this way,* He will hear us.

The only thing we haven't done is admit that perhaps we need to back up and ask God *why* our prayers for revival haven't been heard. Because you can't convince me that somewhere, somehow, someone with the right heart and right motive in the past hundred years didn't nail that prayer and get it right. And yet (can we finally admit what we know to be the truth?), God has not answered many of those prayers.

What we have today is a severe moral slump.

In the wake of a sexual revolution birthed in the 1960s, millions of babies have been aborted each year. We have gang violence in unprecedented numbers and kids killing kids at school and in the streets. Jesus instructed us to pray for His will to be done on earth as it is in heaven. But let's face it—we're *not* seeing heaven on earth. There's no sickness in heaven or blind eyes. There's no cancer, no AIDS, no terrorist attacks, or drive-by shootings. Heaven is not replete with rape and murder, mental wards filled with deranged people, or homeless and hungry people.

Of course, these problems aren't isolated to the United States. In her excellent book *Reformation Manifesto*, Cindy Jacobs, founder of Generals International and core leader for the U.S. Reformation Prayer Network, sums up the 20th century:

> As we stand at the dawn of the third millennium since Jesus came to the earth, we again see a world where sin and corruption are running rampant, destroying lives in whole new ways. The twentieth century was the bloodiest era in human history. We saw our first two world wars, the Holocaust, the rise of Communism and Fascism, and the reign of totalitarian regimes that turned children against their parents in the name of Cultural Revolution. The Killing Fields of Southeast Asia, attempted genocide in the Balkans and Rwanda, and the birth of Islamic extremism are just a few examples of how little progress humanity has made since the wickedness that caused the Great Flood. Twice as many Christians died as martyrs in the twentieth century as did in the previous nineteen hundred years. Will the twenty-first century be any different?[1]

Will the 21st century be any different here in America? I believe without a doubt that it will be. But it won't happen if the Church doesn't repent and change the way it operates. Old paradigms will not work in this new season any more than an old wineskin can hold new wine without rupturing.

That means that we have to go back to the Bible with fresh eyes and see how the Church was designed to function. Jesus said that we were to pray, "Thy kingdom come" (Matt. 6:10 KJV). But most of us understand very little about God's kingdom. I'm not talking about the one in heaven—we get that. Our problem has been grasping the reality that it is our job to establish God's kingdom *on earth*.

We've been praying for revival, but what God desires is that His kingdom rule over all the kingdoms of the world. We've been willing to settle for an awakening, but God's kingdom requires both transformation and *reformation*.

THAT OLD-TIME RELIGION

To understand these concepts, let's begin with the idea of revival.

At the turn of the 20th century, the country of Wales knew rapes, robberies, murders, embezzlement, and drunkenness as the norm. However, in response to prayer, a revival swept through Wales that resulted in 100,000 conversions in five months.

A man attempting to discredit the revival complained that after five years, only 80,000 of the converts still stood openly for Christ. To me, that sounds pretty good!

The revival's impact on Welsh society was astonishing. As a result, there were no more rapes, no robberies, murders, or embezzlements. The judges had no cases to try. A special meeting was held to discuss what to do with the police, who were now unemployed. Drunkenness was down by one half, and the illegitimate birth rate dropped by 44 percent.

In the U.S., the great Kentucky revival was sparked by James McGrady, a Scotch-Irish Presbyterian who led a Concert of Prayer the first Monday of each month. McGrady also got his people to pray with him on Saturday evening and at sunrise on Sunday morning. In the summer of 1800, 11,000 people gathered at a communion service launching a camp-meeting revival that swept over Kentucky, Tennessee, North Carolina, and the frontier.

In the middle of the 19th century, Jeremiah Lamphier advertised a prayer meeting to be held in the Dutch Reformed Church in Manhattan. Of New York City's population of one million people, only six showed up. The next week there were 14 in attendance, and the following week 23 came. Soon, they were meeting daily to pray, filling both the Dutch Reformed Church and the Methodist Church. And soon afterward, every public building in downtown New York City was filled.

Horace Greely, an editor of that day, explained that in the span of just one hour his reporter counted 6,100 men in 12 meetings praying. And then it swept through the city. An estimated 10,000 people were converted in New York City each week. Church bells rang, bringing people to prayer each morning, noon, and evening.

Through similar concerted prayer in 1905, the ministers in Atlantic City, New Jersey, reported that out of a population of 50,000 people, only five adults had *not* given their lives to the Lord Jesus.

During that same time in Portland, Oregon, 240 department stores closed from 11 until 2 each day for prayer. The merchants signed an agreement that no one would cheat and stay open.[2]

One of the definitions of *revival* is "an evangelistic service or a series of services for the purpose of affecting a religious awakening."[3] An *awakening* is defined as "a recognition, realization, or coming into awareness of something."[4] This "something" can describe a sinner coming to the realization of his need for a Savior. Another definition of awakening is "the act of awaking from sleep."[5] This is an apt description of an awakening by Christians to the presence of the Lord.

The revivals and awakenings described were wonderful and much needed moves of God, but I don't believe they should be our end goal, because they didn't bring lasting change to the culture. Most revivals extend for weeks, months, or even a few years at most. To see lasting change, we need transformation *and* reformation.

MODELS OF TRANSFORMATION

One of the leading experts on societal transformation is George Otis Jr. Through his research, Otis has identified and documented hundreds of largely transformed communities on three continents. The power of prayer and repentance can deliver similar results in our own neighborhoods, cities, states, and nations. One of those transformed cities is Almolonga, Guatemala. Until 28 years ago, this city of 20,000 citizens, many of whom referred to themselves as Christians, was not a place where people thrived. The fields produced such pitiful crops that there was rampant poverty. An estimated 92 percent of the adult population was addicted to alcohol. This small city boasted six jails that were so crowded the local police chief routinely had to export prisoners to the next city. Besides the jails, the only thriving businesses were the city's 36 bars.

A local pastor, miraculously spared from being murdered in an atmosphere hostile to the gospel, took a hard look at his city and realized that their prayers did not seem to be reaching heaven. He gathered a small remnant of Christians to pray and ask, "Why, God?"

IDOL WORSHIP IN ALMOLONGA

It wasn't hard to find the root of the iniquity in Almolonga. Although there were churches and people who professed to be Christians, most of the population also worshiped a demonic idol known as Maximón, which we now understand to be one of the manifestations of Baal.

The group of intercessors chose to believe God's Word in 2 Chronicles 7:14: "If My people who are called by My name will humble themselves, and pray and seek My face, and turn from their wicked ways, then I will hear from heaven, and will forgive their sin and heal their land" (NKJV).

None of this small group of true believers worshiped Maximón. Their ways weren't wicked, and they understood what Isaiah 53:12 had prophesied about Jesus: "Therefore, I will allot Him a portion with the great, and He will divide the booty with the strong; because He poured out Himself to death, and was *numbered with the transgressors*; yet He Himself bore the sin of many, and interceded for the transgressors."

Jesus, who bore no sin, numbered Himself among the transgressors to make intercession for many. By numbering themselves among the idolaters in Almolonga, the intercessors repented of the iniquity.

GOD HEALED THEIR LAND

Nothing happened overnight. As they prayed, God added to their group. Years passed, but because they believed God would heal their land, they refused to quit. And God honored His promise. If you were to visit Almolonga today it would not resemble the city that had been under the curse of idolatry.

At the time George Otis Jr. filmed a documentary about the transformation in Almolonga, there were only four of the original 36 bars remaining in the city. Instead of an alcoholism rate of 92 percent, less than 5 percent of the city was addicted to alcohol. Instead of six jails brimming with inmates, there were none. The police chief had nothing to do because there was no crime!

All this started with one pastor and five intercessors who refused to give up. Recently, we received an update on the transformation of this community of 20,000. This is what Almolonga looks like as of this writing:

30 Years Ago	Today
92 percent adult alcoholic rate	Less than 5 percent alcoholic rate
36 bars	3 bars
6 jails; very high crime rate	0 jails; no crime
1 truckload of vegetables per week	40 truckloads of vegetables per week
Extreme poverty	No poverty
Idol worship	No idol worship
Divided church	United church
Church buildings empty	20 church buildings full
Less than 5 percent born again	More than 90 percent born again

God didn't just transform the people, but, true to His Word, *He healed their land*—an economy dependent upon agriculture. Prior to transformation, the farmers exported one truckload of vegetables four times a month. Today, those same farmers export 40 truckloads a week! Most of them paid cash for Mercedes trucks. The size of the produce is reminiscent of that which the Israelites found in the Promised Land. The streets have been renamed with biblical names.

In his video documentary, Otis shows between 15,000 to 20,000 people—virtually the entire population of the city—jammed into the streets to worship the Lord. This is in stark contrast to the drunken celebrations of Maximón that still continue in nearby poverty-stricken towns.

KIAMBU, KENYA

Kiambu, Kenya was a place where no one wanted to live. People moved out of Kiambu; they rarely moved there willingly. Neither pastors nor police chiefs wanted to take positions there. But one pastor purposely followed the Lord to Kiambu. He, too, organized a group of intercessors to pray and ask the age-old question, "Why, God?"

The root of iniquity in Kiambu was identified as witchcraft, which we now know is under the authority of Baal. God revealed that one woman in town, who called herself a Christian, was actually a practicing witch who pronounced curses, incantations, and spells on the city and its inhabitants. The prayer process took 10 years from beginning to transformation, but eventually the witch left town and the curse lifted from the city. The transformation of both the people and the land was as staggering a change as it had been in Almolonga.

THE LEGACY OF CHARLES FINNEY

Looking back over the history of revivals here in America, I believe that Charles Finney came closer than any other man to bringing about transformation. Finney taught that true revival comes only on the heels of true repentance. He taught that jealousy and competition among churches and ministers would stop revival in its tracks. In his *Lectures on Revivals and Religion*, Finney wrote:

> All these must repent. God will never forgive them, nor will they ever enjoy His blessings on their preaching...till they repent. There doubtless have been now, as there were then, faults on both sides. And there must be deep repentance. and mutual confessions of faults on both sides.
>
> ...Those who have been engaged in promoting the work must also repent. ...Whenever a wrong spirit had been manifested, or they have gotten irritated and provoked at the opposition, and lost their temper, or mistaken Christian faithfulness for hard words and a wrong spirit, they must repent. Those who are opposed could never stop a revival alone, unless those who promote it get wrong. So we must repent if we have said things that were censorious, or proud, or arrogant or severe.[6]

Finney became famous for a series of meetings he held in Rochester, New York in 1831, which resulted in one tenth of the population of the city coming to Christ. More impressive than the number of conversions was the fact that the entire moral atmosphere of the city changed. Taverns were closed, crime decreased, and for years afterward the jail was nearly empty.[7] That sounds a lot like transformation to me, although no one maintained the victory.

GOING TO THE NEXT LEVEL

The next level of change beyond revival is called *reformation*. Cindy Jacobs defines reformation as "an amendment or repair of what is corrupt, to build the institutions of our government and society according to their God-ordained order and organization." She explains further, "If we are to see nations transformed, we must go beyond a mandate that only sees souls saved to seeing Christians grow in the Lord and seeing the kingdom of God invade every sector of society. God wants His kingdom will to be done on earth through us! If a nation is transformed without being *reformed*, it will soon fall back into its original state of decay."[8]

That's the kind of change we want to see in our states and in our nation—the kind that changes not only the earth, but the very fabric of our culture.

To be honest, when I began this journey I didn't know that such transformation and reformation was possible. I discovered that Billy Graham's statistics showed that after two crusades in Oklahoma City, with hundreds of people responding to the Lord, less than a year later only 2 percent of those people were in church and serving God. This is no reflection on or criticism of Billy Graham, who I consider to be one of the greatest evangelists of our generation. What it said to me was that our American model for revival wasn't working. When I sought the Lord about it, He said, "*You're going to have to come together with purpose, unity, and perseverance.*"

BELIEVING GOD FOR A CITY

My motivation for everything I've done in my life has been to win souls to the Lord Jesus. Because the Bible gives an example in Acts 9:32–35 of everyone in one city, Lydda, and the surrounding region, Sharon, turning to the Lord, I saw no reason why all of Oklahoma City shouldn't be saved.

I'll never forget the first time I heard Reinhard Bonnke say, "All of Africa shall be saved!" Bonnke has been instrumental in changing the course of that continent. I prayed, "Dear Lord, if that man can believe You for a continent, surely I can believe You for a city."

The voice of the Lord challenged me: "Can you believe Me for a state?" It's impossible to pray with great faith for anything without first going to the Bible to search out the will of God about the matter. It's fair to ask, "What *is* God's will for Oklahoma? What is God's will for your city and state?"

In Matthew 6:9-10, Jesus told us how to pray for our territory. We call this the Lord's Prayer, but it's more accurate to call it a model prayer. Jesus said, "Pray, then, in this way: 'Our Father who is in heaven, hallowed be Your name. Your kingdom come. *Your will be done, on earth as it is in heaven.*'"

The will of the Lord is also made clear in 1 Timothy 2:1–4:

> *Therefore I exhort first of all that supplications, prayers, inter-cessions, and giving of thanks be made for all men, for kings and all who are in authority, that we may lead a quiet and peaceable life in all godliness and reverence. For this is good and acceptable in the sight of God our Savior, who desires all men to be saved and to come to the knowledge of the truth* (NKJV).

In 2 Peter 3:9, we are told, "The Lord is not slack concerning *His* promise, as some count slackness, but is longsuffering toward us, *not willing that any should perish* but that *all* should come to repentance" (NKJV).

I suspected that when God said He desired *all* people to be saved, that included all of Oklahoma. Can you imagine God desiring all of Oklahoma City to be saved, but only half of Tulsa? Or all of Anadarko, but none of Elk City? No, the Bible makes it clear that God's will is for *all* people to be saved. So, that's how we must pray for our cities and states if we are to pray God's will.

Is Anything Too Hard for God?

The Apostle John had something to say on the subject as well. John 3:17 tells us, "For God did not send His Son into the world to condemn the world, but that the *world* through Him might be saved" (NKJV).

God, speaking through Ezekiel, says, "Do I have any pleasure in the death of the wicked?" (Ezek. 18:23). In verse 32, He goes on to say that He takes no pleasure in the death of anyone.

We are told in Titus 2:11, "For the grace of God has appeared, bringing salvation to *all* men." There are a multitude of scriptures that make it clear that God's will is for all to be saved and that none should perish. To our finite minds, saving and transforming whole cities and states seems impossible. But Jesus said, "With men it is impossible, but not with God; for with God all things are possible" (see Matt. 19:26).

Genesis 18:14 asks, "Is anything too difficult for the Lord?" And Jeremiah 32:17 echoes this thought: "Ah, Lord God! Behold, You have made the heavens and the earth by Your great power and outstretched arm. There is nothing too hard for You" (NKJV). The Word of the Lord also came to Jeremiah, saying, "Behold, I am the Lord, the God of all flesh; is anything too difficult for Me?" (Jer. 32:27).

The Bible has established that it is God's will for everyone to be saved. It has also established that there is nothing too hard for God. So what's the problem? Why aren't we seeing whole cities and states come to Jesus?

Mark 9:22-23 records that a man speaking to Jesus said, "But if You can do anything, take pity on us and help us!" Jesus replied, "*If You can? All things are possible to him who believes.*"

We need to get that. The question isn't whether or not God desires all of Oklahoma, or any other state, to be saved. Nor is it a question of God's ability. The real question you and I must ask ourselves is, "Can *we* believe?"

"Apostle John," you might say, "I don't think you've read the back of the Book."

Yes, I've read Revelation, and I know that everyone in the world will not be saved. But I find nothing there that relieves me of my responsibility to pray in faith for God's will to be done on earth. There is nothing in Revelation to suggest that an entire state cannot be saved.

I don't want to stand before the Judgment Seat of Christ someday and hear Him ask, "Why didn't you pray for everyone in your state?"

"Well, I prayed for a lot of folks."

"Why didn't you pray for all of them?"

"I prayed for half the state."

"I made it clear that My will is for all to be saved."

"The truth is, Jesus, I didn't believe."

LIMITED BY UNBELIEF

In Psalm 78:41, we are told that Israel limited God: "Yea, they turned back and tempted God, and limited the Holy One of Israel" (KJV). Likewise, God has been limited by our unbelief and our lack of prayer. The Word of the Lord through Isaiah still echoes throughout the ages:

> *Behold, the Lord's hand is not shortened, that it cannot save; nor His ear heavy, that it cannot hear. But your iniquities have separated you from your God; and your sins have hidden His face from you, so that He will not hear. For your hands are defiled with blood, and your fingers with iniquity; your lips have spoken lies, your tongue has muttered perversity. No one calls for*

justice, nor does any plead for truth. ...Then the Lord saw it, and it displeased Him that there was no justice. He saw that there was no man, and wondered that there was no intercessor (Isaiah 59:1–4, 15–16 NKJV).

In Ezekiel 22:30, God says, "So I sought for a man among them who would make a wall, and stand in the gap before Me on behalf of the land, that I should not destroy it; but I found no one" (NKJV).

Today, I believe God is looking for a remnant that will stand in the gap on behalf of each of our states and our nation. May He never record of us in His book, "I found no one."

BELIEVING GOD FOR A STATE

In the early part of the 1990s, with a heart to stand in the gap for the lost, I began praying with a number of pastors. Over the next few years, we held three statewide prayer breakthroughs where we brought congregations together to pray. Then in 1995, the Associated Press voted the Oklahoma City bombing the leading news event of the year. I am told that Oklahoma City had more people praying for it than any city in the world other than Jerusalem. That same year, I started what is now called the Oklahoma Apostolic Prayer Network (OAPN), a network of over 700 churches and ministries, 4,000 intercessors, and key ministry, civic, and business leaders from across denominational and racial lines.

It was the goal of this network to see not just one city, but the whole state of Oklahoma transformed by the power of God. We wanted to see America delivered from all the hand of the enemy.

Can you picture such a thing? Try imagining living in a city where agricultural productivity reaches biblical proportions. Imagine living in a place where the jails shut down due to a lack of crime. Imagine entire families coming to faith in Christ. Imagine football stadiums filled with praise and worship to our God.

I'm not talking science fiction here; I'm talking about a little bit of heaven on earth.

IF OKLAHOMA IS OK, THE NATION WILL BE OK

Many of the Christian leaders in this nation have said that we in Oklahoma are further along than any other state in the process of transformation and that we are a model for the nation. We would never have progressed this far had we not repented and established covenant relationships with key Native American leaders. It has taken our combined covenant and spiritual strength to pull down the strongholds that have held spiritual darkness in place for thousands of years. Although this entire book documents our journey, here I will attempt to distill into two key principles what the Lord has led us to do these past 25 years.

First and foremost, God instructed us to heal the divisions in the body of Christ and allow Him to establish the government of the Church in our cities and state. This involved repentance and reconciliation with groups that had been made to feel inferior, like dishonored and unwanted members of the body of Christ. God expected us to cross denominational and racial barriers, especially with African American and Native American believers.

The Lord let us know in no uncertain terms that we could not move forward without them, and that He required from us more than a simple, "I'm sorry." He expected the kind of covenant relationship that meant we would be willing to lay our lives down for one another.

The second key principle we learned was that there is no statute of limitations for sin and iniquity. This meant that spiritual darkness lingered here because of the unrepented sins of our ancestors. Those iniquities defiled the land and allowed demonic strongholds to blind the eyes of unbelievers to the gospel. It created a mountain of spiritual darkness that resisted real change in every area of our culture—churches, families, education, government, arts and entertainment, media and communications, and the marketplace.

One of the prophetic words spoken over Oklahoma by Cindy Jacobs was, "If Oklahoma is OK, the nation will be OK." Another of many similar words was, "As Oklahoma goes, so goes the nation."

OKLAHOMA WASN'T OK

All you had to do was look at the history of this state to know that if those words were true then this nation was in deep trouble. A series of disasters had long plagued Oklahoma. Long before we became a state, in 1868, the U.S. Cavalry carried out a mass murder known as the Washita Massacre, which caused the innocent blood of the band of peaceful Cheyenne to cry to God from the soil.

In the 1930s, the Dust Bowl wiped out crops and fields with a severity reminiscent of the plagues in Egypt. Like Egypt, a mass of people fled the land. In the 1980s, one bank in Oklahoma, Penn Square Bank, collapsed, triggering a ripple effect across the nation. An escalation of crime culminated with the Edmond Post Office Massacre in 1986, which at that time had the distinction of being the third-largest mass murder in the nation's history. In addition to the Dust Bowl, natural disasters in the form of some of the worst tornadoes in history swept through Oklahoma, leaving untold destruction in their paths.

This series of events came to a crashing crescendo on April 19, 1995, with the bombing of the Murrah Building in downtown Oklahoma City. It was the worst terrorist attack in the history of the nation at that time.

What *was* it about Oklahoma that allowed spiritual darkness to linger?

The answer is broken covenants and unrepented iniquity. According to the Bible, King David was a righteous king, yet for three years during his reign Israel suffered a famine, which the Bible describes as a curse. No doubt, David and all the priests and people were crying out to God for relief, but none came. After three years, an exasperated King David finally asked God why the famine had occurred.

The answer is recorded in 2 Samuel 21:1: "And there was a famine in the days of David three years, year after year; and David sought the face of Jehovah. And Jehovah said, It is for Saul, and for his bloody house, because he put to death the Gibeonites" (ASV).

ONE BROKEN COVENANT

Their prayers hadn't been answered because *hundreds of years earlier* Joshua had been deceived into making a covenant with the Gibeonites. Then, *long before David became king,* Saul had killed some Gibeonites, thereby breaking the covenant Joshua had made with them.

King David didn't create the mess, but he understood that if there was going to be relief from the famine, he would have to deal with it. David went to the Gibeonites and asked what amends he could make so that they would bless Israel. They asked that seven male members of Saul's family be killed.

David carried out their request, and the Bible records one of the most interesting verses in all of Scripture: "After that, God answered prayer in behalf of the land" (2 Sam. 21:14 NIV). *Their prayers hadn't been answered—because the covenant Israel made with the Gibeonites had been broken.*

You may wonder what that has to do with this nation. To understand, it's important to note that the New International Version of the Bible translates the word covenant as "treaty." With that in mind, consider this: During the period from 1778 until 1883, the United States government ratified more than 370 treaties with the Native Americans. At least another 45 were negotiated but never ratified, although some took legal effect.[9] All of them were broken.

Oklahoma is a Choctaw word that means "Home of the Red Man." This land, Oklahoma Territory, became a type of concentration camp for the 66 native tribes that were driven here from different parts of the nation. Today, 39 of those tribes still exist, and all have their tribal headquarters in Oklahoma.

EXTERMINATION NAZI STYLE

You might think it's an exaggeration to refer to Oklahoma as a concentration camp for Native Americans. So, let me explain that Adolph Hitler based his extermination of the Jews on what happened here with the Native Americans.

We get a glimpse into Hitler's childhood obsession with Native Americans through the book *The Biography of Adolph Hitler* by Norsk Skoleforum. In it, Skoleforum explains that Adolph's favorite game to play was *cowboys and Indians* and that he enjoyed reading novels about the West by James Fennimore Cooper and Karl May. Hitler read more than 70 of May's novels about a fictional character called *Old Shatterhand* who always defeated the

Indians. Throughout his years as Fuehrer, he continued reading and rereading them. Hitler often referred to Russians as "Redskins," and ordered his troops to carry May's books with them into battle.

Those fantasies about fighting Indians might be irrelevant if not for Hitler's own words. Author James W. Loewen puts it in perspective in his book *Lies My Teacher Told Me: Everything Your American History Textbook Got Wrong:*

> Ironically, Adolph Hitler displayed more knowledge of how we treated Native Americans than American high schoolers today who rely on their textbooks. Hitler admired our concentration camps for American Indians in the west, and according to John Toland, his biographer, "often praised to his inner circle the efficiency of America's extermination—by starvation and uneven combat" as the model for his extermination of Jews and Gypsies.[10]

SUFFERING THE CONSEQUENCES

What happened to the Native Americans was nothing short of genocide. When Christopher Columbus arrived here in the New World, there were around 14 million Native Americans. By the 1890 census, there were little more than 200,000 remaining. If that wasn't bad enough, most of the land that had been given to the Native Americans by treaties with the U.S. government was stolen from them and offered free to settlers in the Oklahoma Land Run of 1889.

If Israel suffered a famine because of one broken covenant, what might the consequences be to America for more than 370 broken covenants and genocide against the indigenous people of the land? As there is no statute of limitations for sin, might there be natural disasters, an economic collapse, and even terrorist attacks? Like Israel, America has been in a famine for the past 150 years. I'm not talking about a drought—although we've suffered that as well, as you'll read about later in this book. I'm talking about a famine of the presence and power of God.

THE LINK TO TERRORISM

It was no coincidence that the worst terrorist attack on American soil up until 1995 occurred in Oklahoma. With hundreds of broken treaties with the Native Americans, we knew that the United States was ripe for judgment, and that until the sin was fully dealt with more attacks on this nation would likely occur. Although we couldn't stop all of it, we could do our part—which was to begin the process of dealing with all the broken covenants and innocent blood that cried out to God from our soil.

God revealed to us that the Church in Oklahoma must use her spiritual authority to repent for the sins of the past. We realized we must echo King David's words to the people who are linked by covenant to this land: *"What shall we do for you?"*

We had an idea of what needed to be done, but we had no idea how to do it. Pastors, ministry leaders, and intercessors from across the city met weekly to pray. The leaders from across the state met monthly to pray, and we held corporate meetings quarterly. In those meetings, the Lord began to reveal "gates" to the city. Like Jerusalem, when the gates to the city were in ruins, the enemy could sack it. Nothing pointed out our need for an organized Church government in Oklahoma more than the Oklahoma City bombing. To heal, we had to identify and repair the spiritual gates of our city.

We asked God to help us form relationships with Native Americans so we could begin the healing process. On several occasions we attempted to form those relationships, but the hurt and bitterness were too deep, and our overtures were rejected. Meanwhile, the Lord led us to repent of the injustices done to the African Americans in our city. No sooner had we done so than on July 13, 1997, God brought long-time ministers Jay Swallow and Negiel Bigpond into our midst. On that fateful night, we spent two hours on our knees repenting to them. Later in the book they will describe, in their own words, our journey together.

Today, by God's grace we have identified and set in place the primary apostles in Oklahoma City and across the state. We have county and regional leaders, along with hundreds of intercessors, praying throughout the state. In other words, the Church in Oklahoma has a functioning government.

In addition to the Oklahoma Apostolic Prayer Network, God led us to start the Heartland Apostolic Prayer Network (HAPN). To date, HAPN has grown to include leaders and networks in all 50 states and over 110 foreign nations, which are in various stages of the transformation process.

DOCUMENTING THE CHANGE

George Otis Jr. was so convinced that Oklahoma would be transformed that a few years ago he came to Oklahoma with cameras to document life before transformation. Although we have a ways to go, there are definite signs of transformation in almost every segment of our society, which will be discussed in depth later. For now, suffice it to say that during the current time of great economic shaking in the nation, *Forbes* magazine recently rated Oklahoma City the most recession-proof city in America.

There has been a major shift for righteousness in the government. Government leaders now come to us for prayer. After years of devastation, downtown Oklahoma City has become vibrant, alive, and a model for other cities. In other words, Oklahoma is becoming more OK by the day.

C. Peter Wagner, president of Global Harvest Ministries and chancellor of Wagner Leadership Institute, said once:

> In the position that I have, I am in contact with a lot of people who are doing things actually around the world as well as in the United States primarily. I can tell you now that as of the last three years or so, the reports that I get from the Heartland Apostolic Prayer Network are the most tangible, measurable results of high-level prayer and spiritual warfare that I've heard yet in my life. So I want to congratulate you, John, and the rest of the Heartland Apostolic Prayer Network for what you have been doing because actually the way I see it, this is only the beginning. Tremendous, tremendous things are ahead.

The transformation we've seen in Oklahoma and in numerous states across the nation has been tangible and measurable. How did we get there? That's the purpose of this book—to give you a roadmap for transformation in your city, state, and nation.

We had no idea our journey would take us up against a principality named Baal. One of the first things George Otis Jr. told me was that there were ancient caves in western Oklahoma dedicated to the worship of Baal. Who was Baal? What did he have to do with Oklahoma or the nation?

All I knew about Baal was that Israel had worshiped him and Elijah had defeated his priests in a power encounter. I had no way of knowing God was calling the Church in America to confront and defeat him again.

CHAPTER 3

ANCIENT THRONES OF INIQUITY

For your gods are as many as your cities, O Judah; and as many as the streets of Jerusalem are the altars you have set up to the shameful thing, altars to burn incense to Baal.
—Jeremiah 11:13

THE summer sun was warm on my back in 1999 as I climbed the rocky terrain and stepped into an ancient cave in western Oklahoma, near the base of Black Mesa. Inside, the sandstone walls had been carved with pictures and symbols that, for centuries, had been attributed to early Native American art. As afternoon light streamed into the cave, it didn't take long to ascertain that no Native American had carved the drawings. There were pictures of elephants, hippopotami, and crocodiles—animals Native Americans would never have seen as they roamed the plains.

Gloria Farley, a native Oklahoman, had done extensive research and published the results in her book *In Plain Sight*. She compared the carvings in these caves, and similar drawings found in surrounding states, to the artwork in ancient Egypt, Phoenicia, Carthage, and in Celtic regions, and found them to be the same. Harvard professor Dr. Barry Fell, author of *America B.C.*, confirmed her findings after visiting Oklahoma and examining the cave markings.

"They're Egyptian," he confirmed. "One of the caves is clearly a place of worship to Baal (also Bel, Bul), another name for the Egyptian sun god."

Translating the Ogam language into English, Fell read, "We claim this land for Baal." The translation of some of the script reads, "Enact at sunset the rites of Bel assembling at that time of worship." Another is translated, "The sun belongs to Bel—this cavern on the day of the equinox is for the chanting of prayers to Bel."

Dating as far back as 1500 BC, the markings in the cave appeared to be those of ancient mariners who traveled from the Middle East across the Atlantic, up the Mississippi River, into the Arkansas River and then the Cimarron River. Who would have imagined that ancient Egyptians had migrated to Oklahoma?

This was one of five caves that were close together and appeared to have been formed by ancient rivers that once meandered through the area. On the wall of the cave, I saw a drawing of Baal standing on a cube, along with hundreds of other etchings. The symbols formed a primitive calendar of worship. Sunlight strikes a knob on the outside of the cave, casting a beam of light onto various symbols on different days and seasons. It appeared that the beam highlighted for the priest the proper form of worship at any given time. For instance, Gloria Farley discovered that *Epona*, the horse goddess, is lit at sunset on Halloween. In the middle of the cave are two symbols of Baal with what looks like a cedar tree in the middle. In the Ogam language it says, "Baal's cave at Beltane."

All the caves were covered with symbols of deities, but one cave was dedicated to *Anubis*, the Egyptian jackal god of the dead. The jackal god looked something like a coyote with a flail and a headpiece. It was the sketching of Anubis that had most excited the scientists because it helped date the site. As mentioned, these drawings depicted Anubis in animal form with a flail coming out the back. However, sometime between 1480 and 1450 BC, the pharaohs in Egypt had declared themselves gods. Afterward, Anubis was depicted as a pharaoh with a flail. That meant that the Anubis drawn in these caves had to be around 3,500 years old!

The following are drawings of three petroglyphs found in the Baal caves in western Oklahoma.

Petroglyph of Baal, the Egyptian sun god[1]

Petroglyph of Anubis[2]

Petroglyph of elephant and hippopotamus[3]

MORE MYSTERIES UNCOVERED

In 1976, Weldon W. Stout, a man from Oklahoma, read an article by Gloria Farley about Dr. Fell's translation of ancient scripts uncovered in Oklahoma. Stout contacted Dr. Fell about an ancient stone with unusual markings, owned by his friend Paul Ellis. Fell instructed Stout to contact Gloria Farley and make a latex mold of the stone. Farley and Stout then had professional photographs taken and sent them along with the mold to Dr. Fell.[4] The stone carvings depicted a crescent moon and the rays of the sun descending to earth. Called the Pontotoc stele, the Iberian Punic letters on the stone are an abstract from the "Hymn to the Alton," by Pharaoh Akhnaton. It reads, "When Baal-Ra rises in the east, the beasts are content, and when he hides his face they are displeased."[5]

These are not isolated discoveries. In 1838, an engraved Phoenician tablet was excavated from a burial chamber at the base of Mammoth Mound in Moundsville, West Virginia. At the site of Mystery Hill in New Hampshire, one of the chambers unearthed was dedicated to the Phoenician god, Baal. The inscription found on a tablet read, "To Baal of the Canaanites

(Phoenicians), this in dedication." A small metal urn unearthed in 1973 has an image depicting the Carthaginian goddess *Tanit*, considered to be the wife of Baal, the sun god.[6]

In 1975, Dr. Fell translated a carved inscription on the face of a rock near a hilltop on Monhegan Island off the coast of Maine, which said, "Ships from Phoenicia, Cargo Platform."[7] Dr. Fell explains further:

> These inscriptions, therefore, suggest that organized international maritime commerce was well established in the late Bronze Age, that North American ports were listed on the sailing timetables of the overseas vessels of the principle Phoenician shipping companies, and that the same information was circulated to customers in America. As Monhegan Island lies some ten miles offshore it seems likely that the whole island was a trading station used by the Phoenician captains, with some organized ferry system for the transfer of goods to and from the mainland.[8]

THE STRONGMAN OVER AMERICA

What does all this have to do with the Church's cry for revival, awakening, transformation, and reformation? What does it have to do with changing our cities, states, and nation? A great deal, it would seem. Books have been written about the evidence of these ancient mariners, but only recently have Christians begun to awaken to the role these idolatrous roots play in holding spiritual darkness in place.

The Canaanites celebrated Baal's death and resurrection each year with ceremonies that often included human sacrifice and temple prostitution.

Priests taught devotees that Baal was responsible for both good and bad—the rain that nourished good crops as well as droughts, plagues, and every kind of calamity. Terrified of displeasing him, they sacrificed their first-born children to him by burning them alive in a fire.

Other rites included both self-torture and self-mutilation.

Canaanite and Phoenician people settled where the soil was rich, believing it had been fertilized by Baal, who was "owner of the soil." Although *Baal* is often translated as "lord," the term "possessor" or "owner" is a more accurate definition. He was believed to be not only the god of the earth, but its owner.

MULTIPLIED EVIL

Although Baal worship predates Israel's presence in Canaan, once Israel arrived, rather than drive out the inhabitants as they'd been instructed, Israel intermingled with them and attended their festivals of worship. The religious and moral decline of Israel started the moment they began mixing the rites of the false gods with the worship of the one true God. This evil was multiplied when the children of Israel began regarding *Yahweh* not only as one of the Baals, but as the chief of them. Hosea 2:16 says, "'It will come about in that day,' declares the Lord, 'that you...will no longer call Me Baali [Baal].'"

Much later, the Scribes and Pharisees accused Jesus of performing miracles through Beelzebub, a derivative of the name *Ba'al-Zibbul*. Matthew 12:24 records, "But when the Pharisees heard *this*, they said, 'This man casts out demons only by Beelzebul [*Ba'al-Zibbul*, CJB] *the ruler of the demons*.'" Verse 29 says, "Or how can anyone enter the strong man's house and carry off his property, unless he *first binds the strong man*? And then he will plunder his house."

These verses not only identify Beelzebub (Ba'al-Zibbul) as the prince of demons, but also reveals the disturbing fact that long after Hosea's indictment against Israel the people were still attributing the miracles of God to Baal. According to Mark 3:22, "The scribes who came down from Jerusalem were saying, 'He is possessed by Beelzebul,' and 'He casts out the demons by *the ruler of the demons.*'"

The widespread idolatry and Baal worship in the Promised Land may have been why God made the first commandment, "You shall have no other gods before Me," very clear in Deuteronomy 5:7. Nonetheless, Baal worship eventually became so accepted that God spoke through the prophet Jeremiah, saying, "For your gods are as many as your cities, O Judah; and as many as the streets of Jerusalem are the altars you have set up to the shameful thing, altars to burn incense to Baal" (Jer. 11:13).

Jeremiah 32:29 describes not only the altars on the streets, but the altars to Baal that people built on their rooftops: "The Chaldeans who are fighting against this city will enter and set this city on fire and burn it, with the houses where people have offered incense to Baal on their roofs and poured out drink offerings to other gods to provoke Me to anger."

In addition, 2 Kings 16:4 reveals that Ahaz, king of Judah, "sacrificed and burned incense on the high places and on the hills and under every green tree." He also sacrificed his son on the altar to Baal.

Second Kings 21:6 depicts King Manasseh, who "made his son pass through the fire, practiced witchcraft and used divination, and dealt with mediums and spiritists."

AHAB AND JEZEBEL

King Ahab married *Jezebel (Jeze-Baal),* a Baal worshiper and the daughter of the king of the Sidonians. The name *Jezebel* means, "Where is his Highness (Baal)?" Baal worship was associated with obsessive sensuality, and the sex acts involved were a path to power and influence. Jeze-Baal is a personification of that demonic drive for sex, power, and influence.

During that time in history, particularly in the Middle East, it was rare for women to have the kind of authority that goes with a royal seal. Yet a recent archeological discovery identified a seal believed to have been used by Queen Jezebel. Carvings on the seal reveal both her commitment to Baal and her claim to power. One of the dominant carvings on the seal is a winged sphinx with a woman's face and a female crown linked to *Isis*, the Egyptian goddess. Other symbols on Jezebel's seal are those of two cobras, used to denote her power in religion and politics; the ankh, used to denote life; a serpent-like lotus, used to claim regenerative power; and a horned sun disk. The seal attests to Jezebel's aspiration for divine status.[9]

Jezebel wasn't content with her own worship of Baal. She also incited both King Ahab and the nation of Israel to sin. Scripture addresses her influence in 1 Kings 21:25-26: "Surely there was no one like Ahab who sold himself to do evil in the sight of the Lord, because Jezebel his wife incited him. He acted very abominably in following idols, according to all that the Amorites had done, whom the Lord cast out before the sons of Israel."

First Kings 21:8–16 describes Jezebel's plot to have Naboth murdered so that Ahab could steal his vineyard, and 2 Kings 9:7 reveals that she gave the order to murder God's prophets. Jezebel also brought *Ashtoroth* to Israel. Ashtoroth is sometimes used as the plural of *Ashtoreth*, or *Asherah*. Both Asherah and Baal, because they were recognized as having broad powers, were addressed in the plural, such as *Baals, Baalim*, and *Ashtoreh*. Asherah was a demonic force who manifested as a power-hungry goddess of love and sensuality. The men of Israel could not resist the lure of the priestess prostitutes, who filled her shrines and serviced her worshipers.

ONE NATIONAL GOD

Together, Ahab and Jezebel attempted to merge God's chosen people with the Phoenicians under a single national god—Baal. During the reign of Ahab, there were 450 priests to Baal in Israel, and it was during this same time that God called Elijah to demand a power encounter with Baal.

Although this is a familiar passage of Scripture, it took on new significance in January of 2007 at the "Starting the Year Off Right" conference when Dutch Sheets released a word from the Lord: *"Through a season of tremendous warfare in November and December, as well as confirmation from many key leaders, God has exposed the spirit of Baal as one of the strongmen—perhaps the strongman—over America. We need to divorce Baal and remarry the Lord."*

In light of Baal's strongman status over America, it's helpful to see how God has dealt with him in the past. God's purpose in this encounter was to prove to Israel that He alone is God. The events unfold in 1 Kings 18:21: "Elijah came near to all the people and said, 'How long will you hesitate between two opinions? If the Lord is God, follow Him; but if Baal, follow him.'"

You can read for yourself how God humiliated Baal and his prophets and rained down fire to consume Elijah's sacrifice. But it's interesting to note what happened afterward in 1 Kings 18:44-45:

> *"Behold, a cloud as small as a man's hand is coming up from the sea." And he said, "Go up, say to Ahab, 'Prepare your chariot and go down, so that the heavy shower does not stop you.'" In a little while the sky grew black with clouds and wind, and there was a heavy shower.*

Notice that the first and immediate response to Baal's defeat was that the heavens opened and rain once again brought life to the soil. In an article titled, "Ba'al Worship in the Old Testament," author Dennis Bratcher makes the following observation:

> When crops were abundant, Ba'al was praised and thanked for his abundant rain. It is in this context that drought had such impact throughout the biblical traditions. Not only was lack of rain a threat to survival, it was also a sign that the gods of the Ba'al myth were unhappy. It is in this context that the "contest" between Elijah and the prophets of Ba'al carries such significance. The issue is really who controls the rain, Ba'al or Yahweh.[10]

DROUGHT IN THE LAND

Baal is still attempting to control the rain to this very day. For instance, in early summer of 1999, when we drove to the Baal caves in western Oklahoma, the closer we got to our destination the more dismal the countryside became. The area surrounding the caves had been in such severe drought for so long that it took 38 acres to produce enough grass to feed one cow for a year.

Our group, a coalition of apostles from Oklahoma, did spiritual warfare against that principality and broke his hold over the area. Afterward, the heavens opened and rain broke the drought. The owners of the land sent us pictures that showed grass growing as high as a horse's bridle. They had to rent equipment and harvest the grass like wheat, cutting and rolling it into huge bales for winter.

In October 2006, the Heartland, particularly Oklahoma, Kansas, and Texas, were in the midst of a five-year drought. It was almost as bad as the Dust Bowl, and grassfires licked up the moisture and vegetation that the drought had not killed. Lakes in Oklahoma were so low that we were in danger of losing our water supply. Lake Hefner was about 30 feet below normal, and many sailboats sat on dry ground. Lake Altus, in the southwest part of the state, was 90 feet below normal, and Lake Eufaula was somewhere between 20 to 30 feet below normal. A small portion of the panhandle of Oklahoma and Texas was worse than it had been during the Dust Bowl. Meteorologists calculated it would take eight years of normal rainfall for the state to recover.

On October 14, 2006, internationally recognized prophet Chuck Pierce released the following word from God:

> Plant your feet! Ready yourself for change! You are entering a year of shaking and quaking! This year will be known as the Year of Holy Spirit! This will be the year rivers will rise! Watch where the heavens open and floods reach the earth, and document those places! Those are places targeted for a Holy Spirit invasion. Rising flood waters will cause you to move to higher ground. As the River of Holy Spirit rises, you will find yourself moving to the high places. I will position My people on the high places this year. As you worship, I will cause the thrones of iniquity to topple.

DIVORCING BAAL

The drought continued for the remainder of 2006. Then, in January 2007, at the "Starting the Year Off Right" conference in Denton, Texas, Dutch Sheets released a word from God that named Baal as, "one of the strongmen—perhaps *the* strongman—over America." Dutch declared that we needed to divorce Baal and remarry the Lord. Later in private, Dutch told me and a few other people that Baal was the strongman over America; Chuck Pierce agreed with him.

I called Apostle Jerry Mash, who is also an attorney, and asked him to draw up a "decree of divorce" against Baal. He'd heard the word from Dutch and said, "I'm already on it!" I assumed that everyone within the sound of Dutch's voice rushed home, created a divorce decree, divorced Baal, and "remarried" the Lord. I was stunned to learn later that we were the only ones who had done so.

In February and March of 2007, in corporate meetings of leaders and intercessors from across the state, we took our petition for divorce before the Highest Court in the kingdom of God. There, we officially divorced Baal and renounced all the fruit of that union. Afterward, we officially remarried the Lord Jesus, thus renewing our covenant with Him.

Second Chronicles 7:14 states that, "If My people who are called by My name will humble themselves, and pray and seek My face, and turn from their wicked ways, then I will hear from heaven, and will forgive their sin and heal their land" (NKJV). The divorce decree involves God's people repenting from our wicked ways. It is an act of corporate repentance. God then promises to hear from heaven, forgive our sin, and heal our land.

That act of divorcing Baal and remarrying the Lord caused the throne of iniquity that Baal had established over Oklahoma to topple. Just like in the days of Elijah—it began to rain. Not only did it *not* take eight years to recover from the drought, it didn't take even eight months. That year ended up being a record-breaking year for rainfall in Oklahoma, and at one point every river, stream, and lake in the state was at or above flood stage. We had more rain in the first nine months of the year than we'd had during any year in the history of the state.

When I was invited to help divorce Baal and remarry the Lord in Kansas, Texas, Arkansas, Missouri, Nebraska, Illinois, Iowa, and Georgia, each resulted in drought-breaking rain. The drought had gotten so severe in Georgia that Lake Lanier, Atlanta's major water source, had only a three-month supply of water left. One month after we divorced Baal, even with a heavy demand on the water supply, the lake had risen three feet.

After traveling from state to state and witnessing dramatic results, we realized the best way to describe what God was having us do was a *class action lawsuit*. The lawsuit represented Christians across the nation against Baal in the Highest Court of the kingdom of God. (You'll find a copy of the Baal divorce decree in the Appendix. You can also download the document from our website: www.hapn.us. More details about the miracles can be found on the *Transfer of Wealth* teaching on the website.)

THE RESULTING RAIN

As you will see throughout this book, rain is often a sign that Baal's power has been broken, but that is only the beginning of the transformation that occurs when we pull down iniquitous thrones and reestablish the altar of God.

"Well, Apostle John," you might say, "that seems kind of weird to divorce a spirit." I agree that to the natural mind it doesn't make a lot of sense. But one thing we've learned is that when it comes to pulling down principalities and powers, we don't know enough to try to figure it out for ourselves. So when God speaks, we must *listen* and *obey*.

We divorced Baal and remarried the Lord out of sheer obedience, and the results have been miraculous. It wasn't until almost two years later that the Lord showed us that what we had done was scriptural. In the Old Testament, God told Hosea to marry a prostitute who was unfaithful to him numerous times and bore children by other lovers. The Bible makes it clear that Hosea and his wife were symbolic of the Lord God and His wife, Israel. In light of what we know of Baal, the prophet's words in Hosea 2:13, 16-17, and 21–23 take on a fresh new meaning:

> *And I will visit [punishment] upon her for the feast days of the Baals, when she burned incense to them and decked herself with her earrings and nose rings and her jewelry and went after her lovers and forgot Me, says the Lord.*
>
> **And it shall be in that day, says the Lord, that you will call Me Ishi [my Husband], and you shall no more call Me Baali [my Baal].** *For I will take away the names of Baalim [the Baals] out of her mouth, and they shall no more be mentioned or seriously remembered by their name.*
>
> **And in that day I will respond, says the Lord; I will respond to the heavens [which ask for rain to pour on the earth], and they shall respond to the earth [which begs for the rain it needs],** *and the earth shall respond to the grain and the wine and the oil [which beseech it to bring them forth], and these shall respond to Jezreel [restored Israel, who prays for a supply of them]. And I will sow her for Myself anew in the land, and I will have love, pity, and mercy for her who had not obtained love, pity, and mercy; and I will say to those who were not My people, You are My people, and they shall say, You are my God!* (AMPC)

This message spoken by Hosea so long ago is alive with meaning for the Church in America today. To see lasting change in this nation, we must uproot and overturn ancient thrones of iniquity. We must divorce Baal and remarry the Lord. Then, as the Lord promised through Hosea, heaven will respond with rain to replenish the earth, and the earth will respond by producing grain, wine, and oil. As you'll see later in the book, Baal is known as the god of a thousand faces and, as such, impacts every area of society.

I visited all 50 states to divorce Baal. So the entire nation has now divorced Baal. In many cases, droughts have been broken. In fact, in 2010 the Drought Monitor reported fewer droughts in America as a whole than at any time since they began keeping records. God has literally been healing the land, as He promised in 2 Chronicles 7:14. As a result, the U.S. produced record crops of wheat, corn, and soybeans in 2009. We're on track now to produce even bigger harvests. Those are tangible, measurable results!

I could never list all the faithful pastors and ministry leaders who have helped us get to this point in our journey. However, there are five of us who have linked our arms, our hearts, and our shields in order to war over the Lord's inheritance. We are men who got so desperate for God that we gave up our own agendas and anything we thought we knew about doing church and asked Him to teach us. We believe what we're doing in Oklahoma is not only worth living for, it's worth dying for.

The four who have stood with me, without whom none of this would have been possible, are Apostle John Ward, Apostle of the Church at Edmond; Apostle Jerry Mash, Apostle of Church at the North Gate; Apostle Jay Swallow, a Native American from the Cheyenne tribe who has spent 50 years ministering to Native tribes throughout North America; and Apostle Negiel Bigpond, a Native American from the Euchee tribe, an apostle of God who has been in ministry for more than 30 years.

The next four chapters were written by these four mighty men of God.

They are my brothers, and this is our story.

CHAPTER 4

THE GOVERNMENT OF THE CITY

John Ward, Apostle of the Church of Edmond

Everything God builds, He builds on a relational foundation.
—Dennis Peacocke

FOR the people in Oklahoma City, the bombing of the Murrah Building was a lot like when President Kennedy was assassinated by sniper fire on a balmy November day in Texas. April 19, 1995, dawned like that infamous day in Dallas—normal. Normal people woke to a normal day. They packed normal lunches, and had the normal *"Hurry up!"* discussions with their children while rushing them off to school. They drove their normal routes to work.

Those of us who were alive the day JFK died remember with vivid clarity where we were the moment we heard the news. Those of us in Oklahoma City the morning of the bombing remember where we were the moment it happened. Our senses were sharpened so that the images around us were crisp and clear, the scents and smells forever linger, and we still feel the earth quake beneath us from the power of the blast.

It was the worst imaginable wakeup call.

Those of us in spiritual leadership in the city understood in a chilling way that, from a spiritual standpoint, there was something very, very wrong. It was our responsibility to find out what it was and how to deal with it.

The bombing stirred us and brought a new level of unity. People who wouldn't speak to one another before now began working together.

Our journey had not been a short one. Mine began in the 1980s when two revelations changed my life forever. To me, these were epiphanies. The first revelation was this: *The real government in the city is the spiritual government—the Church.* I had read and quoted Isaiah 9:6-7 many times.

> *For a child will be born to us, a son will be given to us; and the government will rest on His shoulders; and His name will be called Wonderful Counselor, Mighty God, Eternal Father, Prince of Peace. There will be no end to the increase of His government or of peace, on the throne of David and over his kingdom, to establish it and to uphold it with justice and righteousness from then on and forevermore.*

Isaiah wrote that the government was upon Jesus' shoulders and that it would never end. Obviously, the Church is Jesus' body on the earth, but the hard, cold fact was that, for the most part, we'd never governed anything. We didn't know how to govern. The whole concept was foreign to most of us.

BUILDING RELATIONSHIPS

The second epiphany came from my friend Dennis Peacocke, whose words were full of life when he spoke them: "Everything God builds, He builds on a relational foundation." Most pastors in Oklahoma City didn't have relationships outside their denomination, camp, church, and inner circle of friends. I didn't know how we were supposed to govern, but if God builds everything on a relational foundation, it seemed that building relationships was the place to start.

In 1980, Dr. Jim Burkett, then a pastor in Stillwater, Oklahoma, started holding meetings in Oklahoma City designed for pastors to fellowship. Later, I picked up the baton and gathered pastors for Saturday morning breakfast at my house. When the group grew larger, about 30 pastors met once a month at the Petroleum Club. This was an important time because pastors across denominational lines began to build relationships and trust. However, when we left those meetings we were still locked into our own church buildings, our programs, and our agendas. Each went his own way.

When I read the Bible, I noticed that it didn't talk about the "First Baptist Church of Corinth" or the "Fifth Avenue Corinthian Church of God." It talked about the church of each city. For instance, in Acts 11:22, the Bible talks about the *church at Jerusalem.* Acts 20:17 mentions *the church at Ephesus.* Acts 13:1 refers to the *church at Antioch.* Colossians 2:1 mentions the *church at Laodicea,* and Thessalonians is written to the *church at Thessalonica* (TLB). Each city had a church, and each church was the spiritual government of the city.

I couldn't help wondering, *If the Lord were to write a letter to the church in Oklahoma City, who would receive it? Would they keep it for themselves? If not, how would they get the message to all of the believers?* Those questions troubled me.

THEOLOGY OF ESCAPISM

When Dennis Peacocke told me that everything God builds, He builds on a relational foundation, he also said we needed to start gathering *gatekeepers.* This was a new term to us, and we just assumed that spiritual gatekeepers were pastors. So, when we gathered pastors, we thought we had gathered the gatekeepers of the city. Today we understand that, while gatekeepers include pastors, they also include key leaders from all the seven mountains of our society over which God desires to be King—religion, family, government, arts and entertainment, media and communications, education, and business.

We didn't understand what God was trying to do back then, because we had no revelation of God's kingdom. We didn't grasp that what God wanted to build, He would build in *us* first. We had no idea that each of us was about to encounter a huge paradigm shift. Our mindset was what I call a "hyper-Rapture mentality." In other words, we believed that Jesus' return was imminent and that left us thinking there was no time to do anything long term for God. We just wanted to get as many people saved as possible so that they could go with us.

Although it was more unspoken than spoken, we had a theology of escapism. We thought the kingdom of God started with the thousand-year reign of Christ instead of when He came to earth in the flesh. Meanwhile, we were like kids dressed in their Sunday best, trying to keep from getting dirty. *Business is dirty, so we'll stay out of that. Education teaches evolution, so we'll keep our hands out of that. The media is run by liberals, so we won't mess with them. The world is a dirty place, and God is going to rescue us out of it.*

We looked so small in our own eyes.

PRAYER AND PROPHECY

Our saving grace was that we stayed in relationship with one another and built a foundation of prayer. We knew that God would move through prayer and intercession. Therefore, long before the bombing we were mobilizing Christians to pray. In addition to our pastors' meetings at the Petroleum

Club, in the early 1990s George Curry started the Statewide Prayer Coalition and had minister Larry Lea in for three statewide prayer meetings. The third prayer breakthrough had already been planned when George announced that he believed John Benefiel should take over the Statewide Prayer Coalition. John agreed to do so.

Immediately after the bombing, we started crying out to God for answers. Why does spiritual darkness linger where it does? Why was there an open door to the enemy? Once we began asking those questions, God sent an outpouring of answers and help. The first and most important help came from Chuck Pierce. John Benefiel had started what is now called the Oklahoma Apostolic Prayer Network, and Chuck came to speak at one of our corporate meetings. We were in the middle of a serious drought, suffering from a record heat wave, and there was no rain in the forecast. Forecasters offered no good news for our shriveling crops and sizzling sidewalks.

"Just to show you that the Holy Spirit is getting ready to rain on you, it's going to be raining when you walk out the door tonight," Chuck prophesied.

A collective gasp rippled through the audience. Talk about putting yourself on the spot! When the service was over, I stepped outside into a misting rain. Stunned, I stood and let the cool rain splatter against my face in wonder.

Who has come to town?

God had our undivided attention.

HYPER-RAPTURE MENTALITY

In another of those corporate meetings, you could almost hear the snap of our hyper-Rapture mentality breaking when Chuck, a prophet whose every prophetic word came to pass, said God had shown him his life through the year 2026. *Was it possible that we weren't going Home any minute? The world had gone to hell in a handbasket and God was leaving us here? Why? What do we do now?*

In addition to sending Chuck Pierce, God also began sending some of the top Christian leaders in the nation to help us. Among them were C. Peter Wagner, Cindy Jacobs, Dutch Sheets, Ed Silvoso, John Eckhart, Jackson Senyonga, Jim Goll, George Otis Jr., and others. Line upon line and precept upon precept, God changed our ideas, beliefs, and theology.

All of us were challenged and stretched, but I felt like I was stretched far past my comfort zone. None of us knew what an apostle was back then, so that was one of our first stretches. My background was Baptist, and I tried to act cool as though the whole idea of apostles hadn't sent an aftershock through me following the doctrinal earthquake I suffered when I learned we may not be leaving by Rapture anytime soon.

Then, when I didn't think I could be stretched any further, Cindy Jacobs arrived to preach. A *woman*. But she wasn't just a woman—she was a *woman apostle*.

AVOIDING DOCTRINAL DIVISION

John Benefiel kept telling us we had to get past the woman issue. I acted calm, not letting my emotions show, while all the time thinking, *You get past it, John, because I'm staying right here.* The doctrinal belief that opposed women in the pulpit was so ingrained in me that I didn't think I could get past it. To my credit, I didn't get up and walk out. I stayed and listened to every word she spoke. Following the service, I had to admit that she spoke the truth and she spoke the heart of God. I recognized the anointing; I couldn't deny it. Over time, we had other women minister truth to us, women like Barbara Wentroble, Barbara Yoder, and Doris Wagner.

apostle in the faith. Negiel, a Euchee (Yuchi), came from a rich family heritage of pastors and had himself spent the past 18 years in ministry.

Together, Jay and Negiel had started the Two Rivers Native American Training Center, which was the first of its kind—Native Americans training Native Americans to minister the gospel to their people. One of the sad realities of the Native people is that the European missionaries, even after winning some to Christ, told them that no Native American could ever have a place of leadership in the body of Christ. That was neither God's plan nor His heart.

On July 13, 1997, the first night Jay and Negiel came to one of our corporate meetings, we spent more than two hours publicly confessing our sins and the sins of our fathers and repenting. They were gracious and forgave us. Perhaps one thing that has hindered repentance and reconciliation with the Native Americans is that when repentance is done as we did it that night, we have assumed that that was the end of the process. We learned that it wasn't even close to the end; it was no more than the first tentative step.

That night, after we repented, Chuck prophesied that when the Board of Reference for the Oklahoma Concert of Prayer (now the Oklahoma Apostolic Prayer Network) reached 300 churches, a Gideon anointing would come upon us, and God would deliver the enemy fully into our hands. At the time, we assumed that the Gideon anointing represented winning a battle for the Lord with a small remnant of people, like Gideon did with his three hundred. It would be years before we got the full revelation of what God was saying to us, and later we would look back on that night and that prophetic word in awe of what God had spoken.

THE WASHITA MASSACRE

As the Lord continued to unveil the iniquities in the land, He required that we take a hard look at a site that was still a throbbing pain and terrible grief to the Native people—the site of the Washita Massacre near Cheyenne, Oklahoma. While the Native men were hunting for food on November 27, 1868, Colonel George Armstrong Custer led his 7th U.S. Calvary into the camp of women, children, and elderly. The Natives raised a flag of surrender when they saw the soldiers approaching, but Custer and his men massacred hundreds of them.

We were so naïve that we thought we could just go deal with the Washita Massacre situation, and it would be done. We asked Jay to take us to the site, and although he resisted because it's a very painful place for him, he finally agreed. Nothing anyone could tell us about that massacre could have broken us like we were broken standing there listening to the moan of the land that literally seemed to be crying out in agony after all those years.

This wasn't a massacre of just Jay's *tribe*; it had been his *family*. Chief Black Kettle was his great-great-grandfather. His grandmother, one of the survivors, had been a child at the time. Someone picked her up and shoved her into a dog hollow where she was covered and hidden. As an adult, she still remembered the screams from her family and friends as they were murdered. There were only eight of us there. But we wept with a brokenness that came not from "head knowledge" but from the depths of our heart, and we begged Jay's forgiveness.

"No, no," he said, "you had nothing to do with it."

"It was men just like us. It was *our government,* Jay!"

Something broke in him, and for the first time in his life, Jay was able to release all the hurt and pain. We said, "Jay, what can we do? We don't have the money to buy back all the land and give it back to you." His answer only broke us more.

"Will you help me get the gospel to my people?"

We knew that reconciliation wasn't enough. We had to do whatever we could to make restitution. We began giving to his ministry both through our churches and OAPN. We began to help pay his expenses to go minister. We gave money to help Two Rivers Native American Training Center with their work. Then Jerry Mash started Mission Native America, which is a ministry designed to give aide to Native Americans in need.

We're still doing all of those things today, almost 15 years later. When we left the site of the Washita Massacre that day, we understood that true repentance and reconciliation would be a long process—and we were in it for the long haul.

VISION FOR A TRANSFORMED COMMUNITY

We had begun the process of repentance and reconciliation, and we were beginning to believe that God wanted more than revival—He wanted transformation. But we'd never seen an example of it in our lifetime. Unbelief tried to hammer us with thoughts of, *Can God really do this?*

I'll never forget the night I sat in the auditorium and watched the first of the transformation videos produced by George Otis Jr. I wept at what I saw God do in places like Almolonga, Guatemala, and Cali, Columbia. *God, You changed the soil! You changed the atmosphere! You changed the government! You stopped the crime! You changed everything, and You want to do it here! You want to transform our cities! You want to transform this whole planet!*

That was what we were after, and now we had a precedent for it. That was George's piece: God sent him here to impart vision for a transformed community and to teach us what he'd learned. He told us about four major iniquities that had to be dealt with, and this state had committed them all. They were immorality, idolatry, broken covenants, and innocent bloodshed.

George also had studied the common ingredients to transformed communities. One of the most important ingredients was persevering leadership.

We were fortunate to have that in John Benefiel. If it had been me in leadership, we would have been stuck on high center. When I first got to know John back in the early 1990s, he made me uneasy. I'm a real laid-back guy. On John's personal side he's as soft as a teddy bear, but if you get in the way of the vision God has given him and his administrative side, it's like, *Just get out of my way—we're going!* He's very focused and has a drive to keep going, which is an apostolic trait.

AVOIDING THE DITCH IN UNITY

Back when I was leading the pastors' fellowship, I just wanted unity among the brethren. But John understood that to get anything accomplished we had to move past simple unity. He understood that there was a ditch in unity that would allow us to be so nice to one another that we'd never get anything accomplished. When that happens, you're reduced to the lowest common denominator.

John wouldn't stand for that. He had the guts and courage to stay focused without the fear of hurting someone's feelings. He just kept pushing and pushing to the extent that I know without him we wouldn't be where we are today. That's what we needed—persevering leadership—and we were fortunate to have him. I'm a more relational person, and part of my role is to follow the wake of John's leadership, calming the waters and always supporting him.

MAKING JESUS KING—OVER EVERYTHING

Another thing the transformation videos did was help us understand the kingdom. One day I said, "God, what is kingdom?"

He said, *"It's the simplest thing—Jesus being King of everything!"*

That was one of those *ah-ha!* moments in my life. God didn't want the Church to hide away in our buildings and wait for Jesus' return. He wanted us to take the gospel to the world—that whole dirty world that Jesus died to save. He wanted us out in the marketplaces. He wanted to be King in our education systems. He wanted to be King over our agriculture. He wanted to be King over the media and over business.

We'd been sitting around waiting for Jesus to return, and He'd been waiting for us to make disciples of all nations and deal with the iniquities in the land so it would become like heaven on earth. He wanted all of our cities to be like Almolonga, whose residents were born again and serving God; whose jails were empty and bars closed down; whose soil had been so transformed by the glory of God that it grew carrots the size of a man's arm; and whose people were prosperous, happy, and at peace.

God's Original Intention

The Lord showed us that His intention for mankind has never changed. His original plan was found in Genesis 1:26–28:

> *And God said, Let us make man in our image, after our likeness: and let them have dominion over the fish of the sea, and over the birds of the heavens, and over the cattle, and **over all the earth**, and over every creeping thing that creepeth upon the earth. And God created man in his own image, in the image of God created he him; male and female created he them. And God blessed them: and God said unto them, Be fruitful, and multiply, and replenish the earth, and subdue it; and have dominion over the*

fish of the sea, and over the birds of the heavens, and over every living thing that moveth upon the earth (ASV).

God's first instructions to man were to rule over the whole earth, to be fruitful and multiply, and to subdue and take dominion. For years we thought, *What does that have to do with us today?* The answer is simple—everything! God desired to be King over the whole earth through submitted men; that's the kingdom of God being established on earth. The first Adam failed to follow those instructions, so God sent His own Son. Then Jesus gave us the authority and the responsibility to establish His kingdom on earth. Even the Great Commission was God reiterating what He said in Genesis: "Go make disciples of all nations. I'm going to be King."

God doesn't want unity just for unity's sake. He wants unity so we can advance His kingdom on earth. One is passive, and the other is active.

MEXICAN GOLD MINE

There comes a time when each of us must ask ourselves tough questions like, "What motivates me?" It's wonderful to build a successful business and meet our career goals. There's joy in making money and having success and accomplishments. Those are worthy endeavors. But when it's all been done, then what? True fulfillment comes only when you build something in God's kingdom that will last forever.

This was brought home to me in a vivid way during a trip to Mexico where I prayed for a Christian man who owns a gold mine. The man is a wonderful person who loves the Lord, loves his family, and has great integrity. But he has no concept of why God raised him up to own a gold mine in Mexico. While we were there we also visited a ministry for orphaned children that was run by a couple who love God, love the children and, like my friend, have noble values. What neither the couple nor the man who owns the gold mine understood was that God's plan for their lives was much higher than their noble values.

There in Mexico, the area surrounding them is an open display of evil, corruption, bondage, and poverty. Drug lords don't even try to hide the fact that they own the police and the federal soldiers. In a system controlled by satan, local police escort the drug lords to their destinations. In other words, satan's kingdom is flourishing in the same atmosphere in which legitimate Christian businesses and ministries are clawing to survive. The culture itself is an untapped gold mine.

Please don't think that I'm critical of these people, because I'm not. They are fulfilling what the Church has taught them about their lives, their purposes, and their destinies. Their situation is a microcosm of Christianity today—good, well-meaning people who love the Lord and are plagued by their failure to see that we must be salt and light, culture changers, opening the way for God's kingdom to rule and reign.

For the most part, satan is going unchallenged because we have no vision for stewarding the territory where God has placed us. Letting God rule in our hearts is crucial, but we must not stop there. We must go further and release Him through worship, strategic warfare, and intercession by exercising the authority we've been given through Jesus' mighty name.

Most people in the body of Christ have been taught that it's enough to win a few people to Christ and maybe train them to live in personal victory without ever equipping them to affect the planet by making disciples of nations and teaching them what it means to pray, "Thy kingdom come on earth!"

Most ministries can't flourish because the powers resisting them are never recognized and dealt with. Those powers so cloud the vision of the lost that we experience very little success. Most of what's done is done out of drudgery and in poverty.

While I applaud our efforts, they bear witness against us that we have not grasped what Jesus meant when He said that the kingdom of God had come to us. Those in ministry must change from an old Church mindset to one of advancing the kingdom of God. Those in business must come to understand that their ultimate purpose is to advance God's kingdom. Our purpose is to encourage, teach, and move the body of Christ into God's kingdom agenda. Becoming kingdom-minded must become the purpose and motivation for everything we do.

JOURNEY TO THE PROMISED LAND

When you understand kingdom, you realize that God's plan is for the Church to have a definite influence on government, media, business, schools, and every part of society. Jesus said it best in John 17:20-21: "I do not ask on behalf of these alone, but for those also who believe in Me through their word; that they may all be one; even as You, Father, are in Me and I in You, that they also may be [one] in Us, so that the world may believe that You sent Me."

We have a long way to go, and from God's point of view we've probably just started. But today, men and women from the civil government are coming to us and asking for our prayers and our blessing so those relationships are being built. When you're taking baby steps, they don't seem major. But when you look back at where you were, you realize there has been dynamic movement.

Our city is being transformed before our very eyes. The revelation of God's kingdom on earth has stirred in us until we're not the same men we were.

Today, we finally have a vision for the kingdom. Pursuing the things of the kingdom of God is the most exciting way to spend your life. It will get you out of bed every morning—if you realize you have a role in that kingdom. We went from a mindset of, "Jesus is coming back tomorrow, and we don't have time to do anything!" to one of, "We've been called by God to establish His kingdom on earth, and we're going to do it!"

Then, because apostles always look to the future, the concept of generational transfer came into the mix. We realized that this was going to be a long process, and wondered, *What if I'm dead and gone before the transformation occurs?* We settled it in our own hearts that if we never see transformation in our lifetime, because of our efforts our grandchildren will get to experience it. We're in it for the long haul.

We feel a lot like Joseph, who said, "When God delivers you out of Egypt, take my bones with you!" He was going to experience his Promised Land one way or another, and so are we. We will see it with our own eyes, or our bones will be buried in a land transformed by the glory of God.

DOING KINGDOM BUSINESS

As wonderful as God's kingdom is, I don't want to mislead anyone. It's hard being a member of a kingdom church. It's the difference between being on a cruise ship and a warship. A kingdom church isn't a little churchy thing. It's a hard road because the kingdom church has demands and responsibilities that other churches do not.

One of those demands is that the pastor/apostle is called by God not just to take care of the flock, but to help take care of the needs of the other pastors and apostles in the city or state. For instance, in addition to leading his own church, John Benefiel meets regularly with pastors in the city to pray and handle issues. He meets with the regional leaders/apostles across the state to do the same. He also meets with county leaders and with other state leaders.

We must build relationships far outside the boundaries of our church or denomination. We must be the spiritual government of the city, praying, interceding, and dealing with iniquities as the Lord reveals them.

John, Jay, and Negiel travel extensively throughout the state and nation, carrying out the mandate of God and spreading the message of the kingdom. We are all confronting the strongman over this nation. Jay and Negiel work tirelessly, taking the kingdom message to Native tribes. They are trying to convince them to work with us and to trust us. Without the Lord, their task would be insurmountable.

Many American Christians have a mindset that they're paying their pastor to take care of them. And while we love our members and want them cared for, there is kingdom business we're required by God to do, and we're going through uncharted territory to learn to do it. In this process, the pastor/apostle isn't around as much as other pastors to take care of the needs of their members. We can't take all their calls. We can't meet with them every time they have a problem. For the apostle, the big picture is always advancing the kingdom.

In addition, most Americans want seeker-friendly churches, and kingdom churches are not that—they have a much larger vision and mandate. The people are sometimes overworked and may feel under-appreciated. They are helping to do the work of the local church while the pastor/apostle helps carry the city, state, or beyond. Being in a kingdom church is not a spectator sport. The result of these things is that many people move out of our churches to a more comfortable environment.

That may improve over time. There are legitimate five-fold ministry pastors whose primary call from God is to take care of the needs of the people. Speaking for myself, I've been so busy being a pastor to my church and learning to fulfill my kingdom mandate that I've been slow to recognize and raise up those pastors to help. In addition, as more believers get a revelation of the kingdom of God, I believe many of them will be willing to carry more responsibility and not be offended over the lack of personal attention from the pastor/apostle.

There is no point in having an attitude that says, "But we've always done it this way!" in a kingdom church because the Lord is radically changing our model.

THE GOVERNMENT AND THE GLORY

We finally understand that apostles carry the government of God. If you're going to have a King and a kingdom, you have to have apostles who represent that government. We were hesitant to take the title of "apostle."

It sounds prideful, and in some cases it has been abused. But as God continues to restore the role of apostle in the Church, we must learn how He wants His Church government to function.

One day as I struggled with the transformation God was doing in *me*, I asked the Lord, "Will you just bottom line it for me? What am I doing here?" His answer was swift and sure. He gave me Psalm 72:19: "May the whole earth be filled with His glory."

That's it, bottom line. That's the kingdom concept.

Revival is wonderful, but God's stated desire is that the whole world would be filled with His glory. *That's* the reason God desires to establish His kingdom on the earth. To that end, may our motives and our prayer be, "Kingdom of God, come! Will of God, be done on earth as it is in heaven! May the entire earth be filled with the glory of God as the waters cover the sea!"

CHAPTER 5

SLAVES IN A FREE SOCIETY

Dr. Jerry L. Mash, Pastor of the Church at the North Gate

*Christopher Columbus introduced two phenomena that
revolutionized race relations and transformed the modern
world: the taking of land, wealth, and labor from indigenous
peoples, leading to their near extermination, and the
transatlantic slave trade, which created a racial underclass.*
—James W. Loewen

IN 1966, the nation quaked with suppressed violence that threatened to
erupt over the issue of racial discrimination. In California, buildings had
been burned down. In Oklahoma City, 800 black sanitation workers and
other black leaders decided to march in peaceful protest against gross discrimination. The workers were expected to pick up trash all over the city,
yet no provision had been made for their personal care. There was no allow-
ance for bathroom breaks—not even any toilet paper—and when it came to
lunch, the workers had to lower the garbage bucket and sit on the back of

the truck to eat lunch. All they wanted were restroom facilities and a decent place to eat their lunch.

One of my friends from the black community asked if I'd be willing to march with them. That wasn't something I had to deliberate about for long. I did question that decision as we walked down Main Street and saw police sharpshooters positioned atop buildings with their rifles trained on us. The tension in the air sizzled like electricity on a steamy summer day.

This is the prelude to death. I didn't want to be there. I knew that if the bullets started flying, it was doubtful I would get out alive. There were itchy fingers up there. You could just feel it. One false move would give them all the reason they needed to start shooting.

What am I doing here?

The truth was that, as a child growing up on the east side of the city, I'd seen too much to be complacent. Back then, blacks were not allowed past Tenth Street, but they usually didn't venture past Sixth Street. My grandfather owned a gas station at Fourth and Walnut, and from there I witnessed firsthand the atrocities of racism.

In addition to the daily demeaning they suffered, blacks were not allowed to walk downtown. They could *work* downtown, but once they passed the Santa Fe Railroad tracks, they had to use the alleys and go through back doors to get to their jobs. In addition, there was not a single restaurant in Oklahoma City that would serve them. The only place they were allowed to eat was in what was called "Colored Town" or "Nigger Town." The least I could do now, I reasoned, was to stand by them in their quest for fair treatment.

Up ahead, we saw that the white police chief had positioned barriers in the street. He had no intention of allowing us to pass through, although ours was a peaceful march. We were unarmed, sitting ducks for their high-powered rifles.

When I reached the barriers, I struggled with myself but knew I had to attempt to intervene. Maybe I could walk up there and say something. Perhaps a white face would make them hesitant to fire. Perspiration dotted my forehead, my mouth was dry, and my palms were clammy as I walked toward the front of the march to speak to the chief.

I stopped behind Pastor W.K. Jackson, a leader of the Civil Rights Movement in Oklahoma City and a leading spokesman in the march. Years later, I learned that standing behind Pastor Jackson was a young man named John Reid, a man who would later play an instrumental role in these events. I listened in amazement as Pastor Jackson spoke with incredible grace and wisdom to diffuse that volatile situation. Because he was very soft-spoken, only those standing close by could hear what Jackson was saying. I had no way of knowing that 40 years later, God would use both that man and that situation to start the healing process in Oklahoma.

STEPPING INTO GOVERNMENT

Of course, back then I couldn't know that my unusual career—having graduated from both Bible college and law school, and attending graduate seminary—was preparation for working in the government of God's kingdom. I'd been a graduate seminary student serving a church in Billings, Oklahoma, when Henry Bellmon, who was a non-horse in the horse race for governor, asked me to help with his campaign.

When Henry won the election as Republican governor in Oklahoma, I stayed on as part of his staff. I didn't know what transformation was back then, but I got to see it in action because Henry was an honest man. The corruption in Oklahoma was notorious at the time. Virtually every county had a commissioner who would ultimately be indicted and put in prison. Some of our Supreme Court justices had been indicted, and we even had a

Speaker of the House go to prison. The corruption was deeply ingrained, but one man stood against an entire corrupt system that had been in place since statehood, and incredible things happened.

While attending law school, I also helped set up Dewey Bartlett's campaign for governor. The Governor's team consisted of only four staff members, and every other elected state official was of the opposing party. I served as legal staff officer and administrative assistant to the governor. Later, I went into private practice, dealing primarily with securities law, and during those years traveled all over the nation. I spent very little time in Oklahoma.

Then the Lord told me to close my law office and He would show me what He wanted me to do next. I spent two years seeking the Lord before He told my wife, Cuba, and me to start a church. In 1992, we started the Church at the North Gate. The Lord dictated the name to me, and I had no idea what it meant. I knew nothing about spiritual gates, and I had very little spiritual understanding. I'd spent 36 years in a denomination that didn't believe in the Trinity. We had a Holy Duo, the Father and the Son. We knew the Holy Spirit was in the Bible somewhere, but He certainly wasn't a part of anything we did. I was totally unprepared for deep spiritual things, but I had a passion for the Lord.

KNITTING THE CHURCH TOGETHER

A pivotal point in my life came the day I heard an announcement on the radio by Pastor John Ward.

"Who are the elders of the city?" he asked. "If God were to write a letter to the Church in Oklahoma City as He did to Ephesus, as He did to Philippi, as He did to Galatia, who would He send it to?"

We were so divided that I wondered, *If He sent it to any church or denomination, who might listen?* That resonated in my heart. I thought, *That's right! He wrote to the Church at Galatia! He wrote to the Church at Philippi. There's supposed to be the Church of a city where God can address the Christians.*

God began to weave John Ward and me together in prayer. I started meeting with the other pastors at the Petroleum Club, and later John invited several of us to get away for a more intense time of concentrated prayer. Each time, we would start on Wednesday and pray for three days. We began on our faces before the Lord, asking, "God, what would it look like if You were the Lord of our city? How would we get there?"

We prayed, sought the Lord, and waited on Him all day. The next morning we'd do it again. This was a small group of eight to ten pastors, but the significant thing was that we all came from different streams. Some were Baptist, some Presbyterian, some Christian Church, some other denominations, and others non-denominational.

God began answering our prayers, not in radical revival, but by bringing together key leaders in the government of His Church. One of them was John Benefiel. John had been in securities with a major firm, and I knew who he was. At that time, none of us knew whom God had called to be among us.

STEPPING INTO A NEW DIMENSION

Up to that time, we'd spent a lot of time praying together as pastors, but we had never joined our congregations. On September 10, 1993, as we pastors prayed together, we felt we were to bring our congregations to pray, worship, and war together against a day of high demonic activity.

On October 31, 1993, ten congregations from different denominations and races came together to worship and pray at the Church at the North

Gate. God showed up in such a tangible way that people kept saying afterward, "We feel the presence of the Lord in our congregations, but this is entirely different." We'd stepped into a dimension that surpassed where we could go in our individual locations.

Shortly afterward, we were led by the Lord to join with another congregation for a fifth Sunday evening. That Sunday we met at Greater Mount Carmel Baptist Church, a black church under the leadership of Pastor K. Gerone Free. In preparation for our arrival, the choir was in a dilemma over what songs to sing. Some people wanted to sing a song we had sung at the Church at the North Gate about tearing the devil's kingdom down. Others said, "No, that's a white pastor! We shouldn't sing that song."

Because the choir was split, they discussed the matter with Pastor Free. Gerone laughed and said, "Do you have any idea who wrote that song? It was Ron Kenoly!" When they still looked blank, he added, "He's a *brother!*"

I told that story because it's a great example of what God was doing with all of us. He embarrassed us out of our own divisive attitudes. So, when we got to Mount Carmel Baptist Church, they sang the same song we'd sung, but they sang it in their own style, and it was thrilling.

HEALING DEEP WOUNDS

When we met that night at Mount Carmel, one of the white pastors, Richard McAfee, who has since gone to be with the Lord, felt the Holy Spirit telling him to speak to a man who was on the front row in the choir. God specifically told Richard to repent and ask forgiveness to the man for the hurt he'd suffered at the hands of white men. Richard had no idea who the man was, but in obedience to God he knelt before him and repented. The man broke down in tears.

Members of that congregation knew what none of the rest of us could have known: that man's father had been killed by a white man. The bitterness he carried against white men was renowned, but God swept in and healed his pain. We were watching God do amazing things that would not have happened had we stayed in our own corners of town.

Gerone later told me that afterward, the entire community around the church kept asking, "What were all those white folks doing down here at night?" Gerone got a chance to tell them what the Lord had done.

For the rest of that year, we went to a different church every fifth Sunday. Then the Lord instructed me to disband our regular evening services at the Church at the North Gate. Instead, we loaded everyone on buses each week and attended services with another church. For 52 weeks we visited another church each Sunday. While we were the only church who did this weekly, other congregations joined as the Lord led them. Over time, the Lord showed me that we were depositing unity all over the city.

As pastors, we continued to pray once a month, usually at different churches, and every few months eight or ten of us would spend three days in a prayer summit. However, we realized that our people knew little about prayer. So we sought for a way to bring people together to equip them to pray. We decided to ask Larry Lea, a man renowned for teaching on prayer, to come to Oklahoma City for what we called "Statewide Prayer Breakthrough."

THE COUNTERFEIT

On Tuesday, April 19, 1995, the Murrah Federal Building was bombed. On Thursday morning, two days after the blast, the pastors were to meet for our regular time of prayer together. I was brushing my teeth when the Lord said, *This is the counterfeit. The greater explosion will be what I am going to do in this city.* We didn't have any reason to think that Oklahoma City was significant enough to be the center of anything God was doing, but I knew the Lord's voice and I heard what He had said.

That day, the pastors met for our scheduled prayer time at Loving St. James Baptist Church, a black church in Spencer, Oklahoma. When we arrived to pray, the pastors were just devastated. The bombing had impacted the entire city, but it had impacted the black community in a devastating way. They had lost so many people in the bombing, so many children in the daycare, and so many lives affected by that terrorist event. At the time, America had never experienced anything like what happened here that day.

The atmosphere that morning was one of defeat, so I told them what the Lord had said to me that morning: *This is the counterfeit.* The greater explosion would be what He was going to do. Pastor W.B. Parker of St. James Baptist spoke what each of those weary pastors felt. "We hope so, Jerry. We hope so," he said.

Later, Rick Haug, a Pentecostal holiness pastor, told us that the morning of the bombing, Chuck Pierce (whom we had never met) had called Dean Garnet Pike of Southwest Christian University to tell him that he saw a dark, ominous cloud hanging over Oklahoma City. While they were on the telephone, there was an enormous explosion. The force rocked Dean Pike's office at the university, which was several miles away from the explosion site, but no one knew what had happened.

At the time of the bombing, pastors in this city had been praying together for years. We'd had the "Statewide Prayer Breakthrough" to mobilize prayer in the state. We'd brought our congregations together to pray. We'd worked to bring unity among the churches. Now, God had warned someone in Denton, Texas, about what was happening? We wanted to meet this man from Texas and find out what God was saying to him about the city for which we'd been praying.

There is an interesting thing about connections. We can make our own, or they can be fabricated. But the significant connections are the ones made by God, and it was clear that Chuck's connection to Oklahoma was from the Lord. From that beginning, God's plan grew from our little vision for Oklahoma City to include the state and now has expanded to all of the United States. It was beyond human machination.

HISTORY REPEATS ITSELF

One Tuesday in June 1996, I was in a deep sleep when the Lord gave me a dream that was like a replay of certain events in my life—events that had happened over a period of 50 years, most of which I had forgotten. I saw myself as a ten-year-old boy riding in the front of an Oklahoma City bus when a black woman got on and had to sit in the very back under a sign that read, "For Coloreds Only." Determined to sit by her, I got out of my seat and followed her to the back. There was a little seat right next to the back door, and I took it. Mine was the silent protest of a child.

The dream then fast-forwarded to 1955. That year, as a high school senior, I was elected to represent Oklahoma at the National Student Senate. I presented a bill to eliminate separate seating, separate waiting areas, and separate water fountains for African Americans connected with interstate transportation facilities. There were congressmen and senators there as advisors, and they ruled that my bill was unconstitutional and would not allow it on the floor.

The event was part of the National Forensic League's national competition in debate and speech. Each student had a maximum potential of 100 points. Twenty-five of the points were for your own bill. Because my bill was ruled unconstitutional, I had a potential to win only 75 points, a virtual impossibility. However, the hand of the Lord was on me. Because I had no bill to argue, I argued everyone else's bill. And for only the third time in the history of the league, I won all 75 points.

The dream fast-forwarded through my participation in the civil rights movement and my involvement in the black community. Then, I was shown the year I'd been elected president of my class at the university. A black male and female were brought to the university to break the racial barrier there. I appointed the black male to represent our class in the Student Senate, and I crowned the black female queen of our class. Of course, I paid for it. I wasn't elected to anything else after that.

The dream fast-forwarded to my work in the governor's office in creating the first Human Rights Commission in the history of the state, and then it moved on to other similar events. I woke the next morning curious about why the Lord had dredged up all that ancient history. I told my wife about the dream and said, "What was *that* about?" I was puzzled.

A HEALING STREAM

A week later, the Lord showed me a vision so clear it was like watching television. I saw thousands of people, both black and white, congregated at Fourth Street in northeast Oklahoma City. The group marched up Fourth Street to Walnut, down Walnut to Second Street, under the railroad track and underpass, to downtown. Then they marched to the site of the old Katz Drugstore, where I saw white pastors washing black pastors' feet and then black pastors washing the feet of the white pastors. While this happened, thousands of people passed by, watching. Then the Lord said to me, "You can do this because of the legitimacy of your life."

That happened in June, but I didn't tell anyone about it. I thought, *Who am I to make that happen?* I held the vision in my heart and waited on the Lord to tell me what to do with it. Three months later, in September, Chuck

Pierce was here preaching to our Oklahoma Concert of Prayer when he stopped in the middle of his sermon and said, "I see a healing stream coming from the east, and it will come into the central part of downtown Oklahoma City. It will be a healing stream. And when the heart of Oklahoma City is healed, the entire city will be healed. But it will have to happen this way—at the heart of the city. And the Lord says, 'I'll give you the details.'" I realized what that healing stream represented, and I knew I was sitting there with the details. I approached John Benefiel, John Ward, Chuck Pierce, and Rick Drapeau, who headed the March for Jesus, and told them about the vision. God bore witness to Himself that it was His plan, and things started falling in place. We determined to carry out the March for Jesus in 1997 exactly as I'd seen it through the vision.

You have to understand that downtown Oklahoma City had spent 40 years in devastation. Most people blamed the condition on an urban renewal plan that had gone awry. But plan after plan to rebuild the area had been implemented to no avail. In the vision, the Lord had said, "Urban renewal didn't destroy downtown Oklahoma City, I did. I took My hand off the city over the reproach at Katz Drugstore. The city will not be restored until the reproach is removed." It was clear to me that the dream was the way to remove the reproach.

KATZ DRUGSTORE

I couldn't help but wonder about the significance of Katz Drugstore. To find out, I called my friend Clara Luper, and invited her to lunch. Clara had long been an important figure in the civil rights movement in Oklahoma. She'd been an advisor to the Oklahoma City NAACP Youth Council during its campaign to end segregation in public facilities. She was known as a pioneer in education, racial equality, women's rights, and social justice. And she had led the sit-ins at Katz Drugstore. When the NAACP Freedom

Center had been firebombed, the mayor had appointed me to lead the city in rebuilding it. So, my friendship with Clara went back 40 years.

When we met for lunch, it was critical to me that I say nothing that might manipulate the situation, so I didn't mention my vision or the planned march. In a casual manner I asked, "Clara, what was the significance of Katz Drugstore? You couldn't eat at the Boulevard Café. You couldn't eat at John A. Brown. There wasn't a single place in the city where blacks were allowed to eat. Is there some special significance to Katz Drugstore?"

"Jerry," she said shaking her head, "there's never been anything like Katz Drugstore. They spit on us. They dragged us off the stools at the counter. They dragged us out of the building and had us arrested. They put us in jail. It's been 40 years, and to this day I still can't walk past the spot where that drugstore stood. Katz Drugstore is long gone. It's not there, but I still can't walk past that place. It's just too painful."

Blacks were spit on and arrested because they asked to be served at the counter. They weren't allowed a meal, a soda, a cup of coffee, or a drink of water. The spirit behind what happened there was, "I will not serve you." No wonder God wanted the repentance to take place at Main and Robinson, where Katz had once stood.

It's interesting that today it is the site of the IRS office. A few years ago, there was a crackdown in the IRS, and it was the Oklahoma City office that they cracked down on the hardest—for not being servants. The Katz building and people who worked there were gone, but that spirit had lingered.

PLANNING THE MARCH

In May of 1997, while making plans for the march, we learned that the black leaders were so resentful toward the city for the way they'd been treated that they wanted no part of the process. We were told they wouldn't meet with us. One of the pastors who refused to meet with us was Dr. John Reid.

Part of the reason the black community resented us was that we hadn't stood up for them. Their feelings about the white community were, *You never come. You don't even care.*

Prior to the march, I was asked to speak at a meeting for the "Concerned Clergy for Spiritual Renewal," which is an interdenominational group of black pastors in the community. I was surprised to see W.K. Jackson at the meeting. Jackson was the man who'd diffused that explosive march back in 1966.

"I owe you my life," I told him. "I don't say that figuratively. I mean I literally owe you my life." Then I explained my presence in that march and repeated what I'd heard him say that day. When the meeting was over, John Reid came up to me and said, "Nobody would know what happened that day in 1966 unless they were there." At that moment, John Reid knew I *had* been there. He knew I'd cared enough to be there. It's one thing to talk and preach; it's something else to stand under a gun.

The leadership of the black community agreed to participate in the March for Jesus. I described what God had shown me, and everything went well until it came time to tell them that I had seen not only the white pastors washing the black pastors' feet, but the black pastors washing the feet of white pastors. I didn't want to say it. I didn't want them to have to do it. I would rather have shriveled up and disappeared than tell them what I'd seen. Yet I knew we had to carry it out the way God said, not the way we felt.

"And then...I saw the black pastors washing the white pastors' feet."

A deafening silence followed. All I could hear was the sound of my heart pounding in my chest. I couldn't even look up. I knew my good friend, James Tucker, who was pastor of Greater New Zion Baptist Church and John

Reid's second in command, was just across the table. A "no" from this group would be devastating to what the Lord had shown me.

Finally Reid, who happened to be the long-time president of the Baptist Ministerial Alliance, looked over at me and said, "Jerry, is that what God told you?"

"Yes, sir, it is."

"Then we'll do it."

A TOUCH FROM GOD

The day of the March for Jesus dawned bright and beautiful. For the first time in the history of the state, black and white Christians joined together in massive numbers. Police estimate that 20,000 people joined the march. As we marched, I turned and looked behind me. What I saw was incredible. It was exactly what I'd seen in that vision. We later learned that the route the Lord gave us took us along the path of every civil rights march in the city.

We had prepared a paper barrier that appeared to be made of stone over the underpass at the railroad tracks. It marked the barrier of prejudice that had held the black community in a form of slavery. When we reached that barrier, the white pastors came forward with the black pastors, and we tore it down. Together, we marched underneath it. I've never experienced anything like it in my life, and neither had anyone else, for who knew how many decades that barrier had existed.

From there we marched to the site of the old Katz Drugstore. There we had placed a flatbed trailer, and on top of it sat a counter with stools like the ones where blacks had been treated with such hatred. A huge banner read, WE WILL SERVE YOU.

Black pastors sat on stools where they had been refused service, and we washed their feet—while thousands of people marched by as witnesses. Then, the black pastors washed our feet. Afterward, I stood beside two black pastors of large and powerful churches. One pastor looked at the other and said, "I've hated white people all my life. I never thought I'd experience anything like this."

Then Dr. John Reid walked over and put his arm around me. "Jerry," he said, "now we can do something."

Immediately following that march, the heart of this city sprang to life. It's continued to prosper from that day to this one. Today, one of America's most vibrant cities is built over the rubble of 40 years of destruction.

HIDDEN INIQUITY

After taking a step to deal with that iniquity, God was ready to deal with another. One of the worst episodes in Oklahoma history occurred in June of 1921 and was kept quiet. I knew it was a cover-up because I'd served on the governor's staff for years. I not only wrote the governor's speeches, but I handled the research on state issues. But I'd never once heard about the "Tulsa Race Riot" because those records had been obliterated.

This was not only the worst race riot in Oklahoma, it was the worst race riot in American history. I later learned that articles about the riot had been cut out of newspapers and microfilm had been destroyed. No child in Oklahoma learned about this dark time in our history.

In 1921, oil had made some people rich and had boosted Tulsa's economy—on both sides of the railroad tracks. On one side of the tracks, in the black community of Greenwood, there were 191 prosperous businesses, including 15 doctors, a chiropractor, two dentists, and three lawyers. The area was nicknamed *Black Wall Street*. Even though residents of Greenwood endured segregation and couldn't shop at businesses owned by whites, jealousy took root over their humble success working as shoe shiners or maids.

On May 30, 1921, witnesses claimed to have heard the screams of 17-year-old Sarah Page, a white elevator operator. The next day a newspaper article claimed Page had been raped by 19-year-old Dick Rowland, a young black man. Rowland was taken into court custody pending a trial. By 8:30 that evening, three white men demanded that Rowland be turned over to them. They were turned away. An hour later, 25 armed men offered to guard the courthouse. They, too, were turned away. By 9:30 that night, a mob of nearly 2,000 armed men encircled the courthouse.

During a scuffle, one shot was fired that lit the fuse to an explosive situation. Otis Clark, a 105-year-old survivor, later described the mass murder of hundreds of the residents of Greenwood before it was set to flame.

"I was standing next to my friend when he was shot," Clark recalled. "Our home was burned down with my dogs inside, and my stepfather's body was never found. I was 18 at the time, and I knew I had to run to get away. Like most of the other survivors, I ran from Tulsa and didn't go back."

The governor was asked to send the National Guard to stop the violence. At first, he refused. Later, survivors reported that National Guard airplanes flew overhead but refused to help. Angry mobs of white men prevented the fire department from putting out the fires. All the funeral homes were given orders to not bury any of the dead. Red Cross records reveal that they were instructed to do nothing to help, so they dumped bodies into the Arkansas River. To this day, no one knows the actual number of people who were killed in that riot.

In an article published in the *New York Times* on December 19, 1999, reporter Brent Staples described the scene:

Corpses stacked like cordwood on street corners, photographed for keepsakes. Corpses piled in the backs of wagons, dump trucks, and along railroad sidings. Corpses buried in an underground tunnel downtown, where one caller said 123 blacks had been clubbed to death. Corpses left to rot for days in a park under the blistering Oklahoma sun. Corpses dumped in the Arkansas River and allowed to float away.[1]

Kinney Booker was eight years old at the time of the riot. Decades later, he still recalled his father pleading with the white men as they took him from his home at gunpoint, begging them not to burn down his house.

Soon as he left, they set our house on fire and we were up in the attic.... Five kids.... [We] were able to get out without injury but bullets were zinging around there.... But when we got down, the telephone poles were burned and falling and my poor sister who was two years younger than I am [said], "Kinney, is the world on fire?" I said, "I don't think so, but we are in deep trouble."[2]

From the night it happened, there was a massive cover-up of the crimes. By morning, the once prosperous Black Wall Street was nothing more than smoke and ash. Page refused to press charges against Rowland, who was exonerated. To this day, no one knows the exact count of the dead, but authorities expect that at least 300 were murdered.

No citizens came forward to help. No Christians raised a cry of outrage. There were 34 churches in Greenwood at the time. No more than 12 or 13 of them were rebuilt and survived.

FIRST THINGS FIRST

Glen Shaffer, a pastor from Claremore, Oklahoma, had worked long and hard to organize churches in Tulsa to repent for the Tulsa Race Riot, but he could find no interest. We learned that God has an order that we'd missed. Oklahoma City is the capital of the state, and apparently God wanted us to deal with our own issues before we reached out to help Tulsa deal with theirs.

However, within days of our march of repentance, God swung open the doors to deal with the Tulsa Race Riot. Greenwood had been leveled and Black Wall Street was a distant memory. Several thousand of us gathered at the site not only to repent, but to bring a measure of restitution. Churches from across the state donated almost $100,000, which was given to the churches that survived as an expression of repentance by the body of Christ. Following the repentance, ABC did a complete exposé on the riot. For the first time in history, the whole nation heard the story. But they didn't hear it until the body of Christ did what God told us to do.

Afterward, we began praying and working for a national apology for slavery. On July 29, 2008, the House of Representatives voted to officially apologize for slavery in the United States.

All I can say is if we had not moved the way God wanted us to regarding these racial issues, I don't believe God would have ever entrusted us with the problems that go deep into the history of this nation. If the land is going to be healed, there must be some kind of legitimate covenant relationship involving the body of Christ. You can't skim over it.

A leading black pastor in North Carolina told me, "We haven't had anything legitimate here at all. There's been nothing valid. A white pastor from a large congregation asked me to bring my congregation over one Sunday so that we could have a time of reconciliation. I was thrilled and honored. At the appropriate time in the service, he called me up and put his arm around me and said he was sorry for the atrocities that had happened to the black community. That was more than three years ago, and I've never heard from him again. I had never heard from him before he called for the service, and I've never heard from him since. That's not valid. It's not legitimate."

That failed attempt at reconciliation actually caused resentment because it was all for show. Reconciliation and restoration are about covenant. It's more than a photo opportunity. If you just kneel down and cry a little bit and say you're sorry, it won't make up for years of atrocities. You have to walk this out together.

NATIVE AMERICAN ISSUES

Prior to dealing with the racial atrocities in Oklahoma City and Tulsa, we'd attempted to make relationships with Native American leaders to no avail. However, within two months of the repentance and reconciliation for the Katz Drugstore, God brought Jay Swallow and Negiel Bigpond to our door. I don't believe God would have entrusted Jay and Negiel into our hands had we not proven ourselves trustworthy regarding the atrocities done to the African Americans.

It is amazing the way God weaves people into our lives. On a snowy day years ago, I'd gotten a phone call asking if I would meet with a Native American pastor who needed legal advice but had no money. I drove to Kingfisher, Oklahoma, where I met Jay Swallow for the first time. I answered his questions and gave him advice, and then I didn't see him again until 1997 when he walked through the door at Church on the Rock in Oklahoma City, where we were holding a corporate meeting of leaders from across the state.

The sanctuary was packed with about 500 people, and I stood at the back of the room. Jay walked inside, recognized me, and said, "I'm just scared."

"What?"

"I've never seen so many white faces," he said. "There are no brown faces out there. My stomach is just flipping."

I put my arm around Jay and prayed. "You'll do great," I assured him.

I was grateful that I'd driven to Kingfisher that day so long ago. I'd made the tiniest investment in Jay's life, but it was legitimate. He trusted me.

Within five minutes, he had 500 people eating out of his hand, and every one of them loves him to this day. That night we repented to Jay and Negiel, but that was just a baby step that started us on a road toward relationship. Healing started when we stood on the site of the Washita Massacre. I was outraged when I read the monument our government had set up at the site. The monument quoted Colonel George Custer, the man who had massacred innocent people. He talked about killing 800 horses, but admitted to killing only 34 people. He killed closer to 300 innocent people—mowed them down with Gatling guns.

At our request, Jay Swallow had allowed seven of us to take him to the massacre site. All eight of us broke down and wept out there on that wind-swept field. There were no choirs singing, no one to see or hear us. There were no cameras, no crowd. It was legitimate, and that legitimacy is what finally set Jay free.

The body of Christ has got to get beyond its programs and designs and listen to the voice of God, because only something legitimate will have any impact in the spirit realm. If you carry out a program, the devil isn't going to say, "Gee, I'm really defeated here."

MISSION NATIVE AMERICA

That's why when my wife, Cuba, said the Lord had told her we were to go to the Native people, I didn't rush out to the nearest reservation. At the time, I didn't know any Native Americans.

"I don't have any problem ministering to Native people," I told Cuba, "but I'm not going to run out to some group on a reservation and say, 'My pale face is here to help.' I'm willing to do it, but we need to pray for God to open the right doors."

After several years of walking out our relationship with Jay Swallow and Negiel Bigpond, Cuba said it was time to sit down with Jay and see if there was anything that needed to be done. During one of our state leaders' meetings, we sat down with Jay during a break and said, "Jay, if there is some kind of need that Native people have which we could meet, we'd like to know about it."

I looked across the table at Jay and saw tears flowing down his face. "I've waited 40 years to be able to do something for my people," he said. "The people I minister to are in need, but I haven't been able to help them. I can't draw from *them* to help people in need because *they* are the people in need. I have no resources to help them, and it has been such a burden for me."

Jay had scheduled a camp meeting on the *Cheyenne Yellow Hair Campgrounds* where Native people would come from reservations around the nation and Canada with only the clothes on their backs and cars with tires so worn they would blow out on the way to Geary.

We contacted a clothing manufacturer that was moving from Enid, Oklahoma to Texas and didn't want to move all their merchandise. "If you'll come get it," we were told, "you can have it." We rented a 28-foot U-Haul truck and filled it with clothes. There was also a man in our church with a connection to tire dealers. I asked him to round up some used tires for me, which he did.

Cuba and I drove the truck to the Cheyenne campgrounds and arrived late at night. There were no hotels or motels available, and most of the people who came slept in tents or tipis, so we slept in the cab of the truck. The next morning, when Jay and his wife, Joan, found out where we'd slept, they set up a tipi for us and put a mattress inside.

The clothing went like crazy, but the most amazing thing was watching what God did with those tires. We had a menagerie of tires of every size. One tiny car didn't have safe tires, but I had a whole set of them. Somebody else had an old monster of a car and I had tires to fit it. Every single one of those tires fit someone's car.

Later, Jay told us about the needs of the people living in Hammond, Oklahoma. They were the descendants of the survivors of the Washita Massacre. They had nothing, so we loaded up three semis with clothing, furniture, tires, refrigerators, and food. One elderly lady in her 80s said, "I can't remember the last time I could open my cupboard and find anything in it."

Cuba and I formed a ministry called Mission Native America. Since then, we've taken semis loaded with goods across Oklahoma to North Dakota, South Dakota, Louisiana, New Mexico, and Arizona. We've delivered over 80 semis filled with goods all over the country.

RIVERSIDE INDIAN SCHOOL

The deputy superintendent of the Riverside Indian School contacted Jay and said, "We've got all these kids here who need so much, but I don't know how to get them what they need. Most of them have never had a gift, yet they see what happens to other kids at Christmas. I'd like to find a way to give something to them."

We'd just finished a big meeting at Church on the Rock when Jay came over to John and me and asked if we could get gifts for the children at Riverside. My mouth opened before my brain kicked in and I heard myself say, "Oh, sure."

Then I discovered that there were 485 kids! It was October, and we needed to do something by December. All I could think was, *How in the world?* Then I justified a plan to buy 100 basketballs and a few things in large quantities. But the Lord had different plans. He told me that each child was to have an individual gift.

The people in the Oklahoma Apostolic Prayer Network responded, but we had no system. We had to find out what 485 kids wanted for Christmas and try to track who was buying what for whom. It seemed impossible. Nobody in their right mind would have said "yes."

Later, the superintendent's wife told me that her husband, whose Native heritage was Wichita, had only met three Christians in his life, and two of them had cussed him out. He kept telling her, "I hope they'll keep their promise, but I just don't think they will."

On the appointed night, we arrived at the south side of the school gymnasium with several hundred believers who had helped us set up all the gifts. The superintendent and his wife came to the north door. All the while he was saying, "Oh, I hope they do something." When he opened the door to the gymnasium he saw hundreds of gifts and just wept. He kept saying, "I didn't think they would!"

THE CHURCH'S PART

The school had been started by a church around 170 years ago, but somewhere along the line the church had abandoned the project. The school had fallen into the hands of the Bureau of Indian Affairs and now was ancient and rundown. The gymnasium had been built in 1935 and had only one or two electrical outlets. Whenever the school tried to use the gym for anything, the power went out. The students came from over 80 tribes from reservations in 20 states, and their families were the poorest of the poor. The superintendent had tried for years to get $135,000 to build a small gym, but no money had come his way.

After the marvelous night of reaching out to all those children, I wanted to go back to the school to see how they felt. Before I could get back to Riverside for our meeting, I read an article in the newspaper that $5.1 million had been released to Riverside Indian School. Later, another $15 million was released.

"We now have $20 million to refurbish the school," the superintendent said. "The money's been allocated to us for years but we couldn't get it released. What happened?"

"A church started the school and then abandoned it," I explained. "When the Church came back to help take responsibility for these kids, God released the funds."

He wasn't a believer, but he said, "There is no doubt that that is exactly what happened."

On one of our trips to Pine Ridge, South Dakota, one of the poorest counties in America, a girl started jumping up and down, smiling and waving. "I'm from Riverside!" she yelled.

We were there with seven semis to meet all kinds of needs and to deliver $250,000 worth of medical equipment and other things. One day Chief Oliver Redcloud, who was in his 80s and was the principle chief of the *Nine Council Fires of the Sioux Nation*, asked to speak to Jay and me.

"I've been watching you for two days," he said. "Many people come to this reservation and they speak words with no power. For words to have power they must come from here," he said, pointing to his heart. "Your words have power." On August 26 of the following year, he gave his heart to the Lord. He is the first Sioux chief in history to become a believer.

It's those kinds of milestones that melt my heart and make me doubly grateful that God has allowed me to be part of this process. It has been through these experiences and others like them that I've learned my most valuable lessons. In the light of awakening, transformation, and reformation, the single greatest pearl of wisdom I can offer is this: God requires a validity of heart before He will release His power. And in His power, there is no word called *impossible*.

CHAPTER 6

PEACE CHIEF AND WARRIOR

Dr. Jay Swallow, Southern Cheyenne

*Few biographical details are known about the Southern
Cheyenne Chief Black Kettle, but his repeated efforts to secure
a place of honor for his people, despite broken promises and
attacks on his own life, speak of him as a great leader with an
almost unique vision of the possibility of co-existence between
white society and the culture of the plains.*
—**PBS, The West**

MY great-great-grandfather on my father's side was *Black Kettle*, a Cheyenne peace chief. On my mother's side I am descended from *Little Bear*, a warrior chief. The legacy of my heritage is that I can make war and I can make peace. Peace chief and warrior chief may seem like a contradiction, but it's not. Jesus is the Prince of Peace, but He is also the One who leads the armies of God into war.

Chief Little Bear was killed by the U.S. cavalry while flying a flag of truce in the massacre at Sand Creek, Colorado, on November 29, 1864. Our people had lived in that area of Colorado for centuries, but gold had been discovered there, and greed is a grim motivator. Although Little Bear died in the attack, during the massacre Black Kettle rescued his injured wife and somehow survived.

Afterward, the U.S. government signed a series of three treaties, known collectively as the *Medicine Lodge Treaty*. The first treaty was with the Kiowa and Comanche tribes, the second with the Kiowa-Apache tribes, and the third with the Cheyenne and Arapahoe. In spite of the Sand Creek massacre, Black Kettle signed the Medicine Lodge Treaty. The treaty was a brilliant move to rid the country of Native people. It reduced the size of the reservations and brought warring tribes like the Sioux, Kiowa, and Comanche into close proximity with the expectation that the tribes would annihilate one another, which did not happen.

Following the Medicine Lodge Treaty, Black Kettle moved his encampment to the land he was assigned near the Washita River, in what is now Oklahoma. Four years after the massacre at Sand Creek, Colonel George Custer led his cavalry in an attack against Black Kettle's peaceful band. In September 1996, *The West,* an eight-part documentary series that aired on PBS stations, described what happened:

> It was Black Kettle's village, well within the boundaries of the Cheyenne reservation and with a white flag flying above the chief's own tipi. Nonetheless, on November 27, 1868, nearly four years to the day after Sand Creek, Custer's troops charged, and this time Black Kettle could not escape: "Both the chief and his wife fell at the river bank riddled with bullets," one witness reported. "The soldiers rode right over Black Kettle and his wife and their horse as they lay dead on

the ground, and their bodies were all splashed with mud by the charging soldiers."

My grandmother was a child at the time of the Washita Massacre. I still remember her sitting near the campfire with the extended family surrounding her, telling stories depicting the history of our people. She was the last of Black Kettle's living descendants, and when she recounted the events of that fateful day alongside the Washita River, I could smell the gunpowder, hear the screams, and feel the fear pounding in my own heart.

I felt as though war and peace battled for my soul, and war had the upper hand. My life was anything but peaceful until January 7, 1960, when I gave my heart to the Lord Jesus. At that time, a prophet said that God had called me as an apostle to the Native Americans. I had no idea what an apostle was, but I knew I was called to make peace by reconciling Native people to God through the blood of Jesus. That call expanded as the Lord worked through me to bring peace between the tribes. I never imagined that He would one day call me to bring peace between Native people and the white man.

Had I known, I might have run like Jonah.

RETRACING OUR ROOTS

The first time I set foot inside Church on the Rock in Oklahoma City, I wanted to run. For 37 years I'd ministered to the poorest of the poor, crossing cultures in almost 300 tribes in North America. But I'd never succeeded at crossing the cultural barrier with the white race. I didn't know if I would fit in. I didn't know if I was adequate. I was used to preaching in outdoor tent meetings or very humble places, not to white people sitting in an air-conditioned building with plush chairs and a fancy pulpit. What could I say to them?

Negiel Bigpond and I looked around and didn't see any other Native faces. When John started talking about reconciliation, he explained that they hadn't been able to find a Native minister willing to participate. All of a sudden, I felt like I'd been put on the spot. A few minutes later, Negiel and I were invited to the platform where key leaders knelt down and repented to us. Of course, I was willing to forgive. But I kept thinking, *Is this real?* Native people have been exploited so much over the years that I had my doubts. When the meeting was over, I wondered if that would be the last time I would ever see any of them.

To understand my concern, it would help to have insight into the history of my people. The Cheyenne are an indigenous nation, which means we are a nation within this nation. In our language we call ourselves *Tsitsistas*, which could be translated "Those Like Us." The Cheyenne Nation was once composed of 10 bands spread throughout the Great Plains. Today, we consist of Northern Cheyenne, who live in Montana, and Southern Cheyenne, who live in central Oklahoma.

Many of the Native ancestors had visitations from Jesus long before any Europeans appeared on the continent. It usually happened when the tribe was camped near a river or lake. A cloud would form, and when it dissipated, they saw a man walking on the water toward them. In addition, one of our ancient ancestors was a prophet whom God called to meet with Him on a mountain. There, the Lord taught him many things, and a good deal of our government is based in His words. His instructions included topics such as cleanliness, hygiene, respect, honor, how to treat others, and how to pray.

God told the prophet that a people with a different color would come from far away with a message that we must receive. He said that the words they gave us would be from the Great Spirit. My people looked forward to the message, which they called "sweet medicine."

God had prepared them to receive the gospel from the white man.

MAKING WAR, NOT PEACE

In the 1400s, when my tribe heard that a people with a different color had arrived on the East Coast, they were excited because they believed the people would bring sweet medicine from the Great Spirit. That was indeed God's plan, but somehow it got perverted.

The white man didn't arrive in the plains until the 1700s, and by then the relationship between the two groups of people had soured. The Europeans, whom God had sent here with the gospel, had fallen prey to a belief that they called "Manifest Destiny." They believed it was their destiny to destroy anyone who did not convert to Christianity. It is the same demonic belief that drives Islam today.

When the bloodshed began, messengers came with news: "Be ready to defend yourself because these people will try to destroy you."

That's when our excitement turned to dread, and we built barriers against Christianity. The missionaries came, but they never got anywhere. They built little missions, some so small that the whole church would hold only a single family. Those few whom they did convert were sent back East as a form of show-and-tell. "This is our Indian." That's what we were called: "Our Indian." The missionaries also told the converts they would never be called to minister. On the Sundays they were absent, they left a sermon for us to read. They said God would never entrust the gospel to our hands.

Today, there is a still a high wall of resistance against Christianity, and less than 8 percent of Native Americans are born again. We have the highest poverty rate, the highest suicide rate, and the highest unemployment rate of any people in America. These are the realities I've dealt with for 37 years in ministry.

MANY DIVERSE TRIBES

The federal government recognizes 586 different Native tribes in the U.S. today. For instance, across the Rocky Mountains you have the Southwest Desert tribes. The Plateau tribes are found primarily across Nevada, Utah, parts of California, and Oregon. The Northwest tribes along the coast of Washington and British Columbia may have their origins in the Orient. Their early migrations didn't come across the land barrier but from an ice bridge. In Oklahoma alone we have 39 tribes. Just imagine 586 tribes in various locations across the United States.

Although all tribes have different cultures, they are grouped linguistically, depending on the language they speak. The Cheyenne are part of the Algonquin language group. Negiel belongs to the Iroquoian group. The Choctaws and Chickasaws are Muskogean.

With 586 different tribes and various linguistic groups, it would be difficult to find anyone to represent all the Native people in this nation. However, all Native American tribes east of the Rocky Mountains can be divided into two large and distinct groups: the Plains tribes and the Woodland tribes. What John Benefiel had no way of knowing was that, as a Cheyenne, I represented the Plains tribes, and Negiel Bigpond, a Euchee, is from the Woodland tribes. When they repented to Negiel and me together, in a sense, we represented all the tribes in the eastern continental United States.

Part of my dilemma about that initial repentance was that, although it was sweet and well-intentioned, none of those people knew me. We had no real relationship, and I didn't just want to be "their Indian." I didn't know if I would ever hear from any of them again after that first night. However, my suspicion was ungrounded. Not only did John contact me again, it seemed as though he asked me to go with him everywhere he went.

THE SCENE OF THE CRIME

A few months later, in September of 1997, John asked me to go with him and a group of other ministers to meet with pastors in Elk City. Elk City is located in the area of our reservation, so I agreed to go. Over lunch that day, John said, "Jay, how far are we from the site of the Washita battle?"

"It's only about a half an hour from here."

"I've never seen it. Would you take us there?"

Right then I had a bad feeling come over me. I felt offended. That place is an atrocity for us, and it's very hard for me to go there. I felt resentful that they wanted an Indian to give them a private tour.

I didn't like the way I felt. I'd been a minister for years, and I knew I shouldn't feel so resentful, so I swallowed my resentment and agreed to take them. We arrived at the site, and John asked me to tell them what had happened there.

I pointed to the monument and explained that there were plaques that told the story. "No," John said, "if you don't mind, we'd like to hear it in your own words."

"I don't think you want to hear it from me, because our story isn't like what's written on the plaques," I said.

"Please, Jay, tell us what really happened."

I started recounting the story, and it seemed as though my grandmother was telling it, much like she'd done around the campfire for so many years. When I finished, we stood there in silence for a moment, and then one of the men put his arms around me and began sobbing uncontrollably. The next thing I knew the whole group put their arms around me and wept.

"How can you ever forgive us?" they said.

"You had nothing to do with it," I said. "It was other people."

At that moment the Lord spoke to me. "Son, it's time to let go. You've been hurting for too long. Those memories have embittered you, and that's why you haven't been able to cross cultures with the white men."

I'd been in ministry for 37 years, but until that moment I never knew that I carried that unforgiveness. I'd carried the pain of that massacre around with me my whole life. I made up my mind that I was going to deal with it once and for all. Standing at the site where my ancestors' innocent blood had been shed, I forgave the men who killed them. I forgave the white race. It wasn't just mental assent—I forgave from the depths of my heart. I felt a great weight lift off of me, and joy replaced it.

MEETING THE ARROW KEEPER

From that point on, I was so busy with the Oklahoma Apostolic Prayer Network that I felt guilty because I spent more time with them than with my people. At first, I thought it would be short-lived, but the momentum has continued to grow. I didn't realize at the time that God was going to use me to help break down barriers of resentment and bitterness that had been passed down through the generations.

Each time I ministered to a tribe, I shared what was happening here in Oklahoma. News began to spread, and soon tribal leaders were asking questions. A lot of tribal grudges were being resolved through true Christian love. It wasn't affecting the traditional people much at the time, but it did affect the Christian communities.

We realized God was using what we were doing here to pull down barriers between Indians and Christians, and between Indians and white people in general. It began to spread through the Cherokees. Then, barriers began falling among the Choctaws. Here in Oklahoma, we saw changes in the Kiowas and the Comanches.

In an effort to make inroads into the Cheyenne tribe, John urged me to develop a relationship with William Red Hat Jr., Cheyenne Keeper of the Arrows. Known as the "Arrow Keeper," Bill Red Hat is less a chief than the spiritual leader of the Cheyenne tribe. We've had an Arrow Keeper for thousands of years, and one of his primary functions has been to keep four sacred, ancient arrows. In the Cheyenne Nation, when the 44 Cheyenne chiefs come to a decision regarding the tribe, they take it to the Arrow Keeper. The Arrow Keeper then goes into the sacred tipi and, through the sacred peace pipe, allows his prayers to ascend to heaven on the swirling smoke.

The Arrow Keeper is on duty 24 hours a day, offering prayers to God and interceding for the tribe. Much like the Levites, he isn't allowed to work a job or take money from the government. His needs must be met through gifts from those who come to him.

There is a certain protocol one must go through to see the Arrow Keeper. You approach only so far, and then you stop. Then, the Arrow Keeper will approach and stop. You must tell him, in our language, why you're there. Only then will he invite you inside. I wasn't in the council, so I was a bit intimidated to develop a relationship with the spiritual head of our tribe. However, the Arrow Keeper received me and our first meetings lasted eight hours each as I explained my connection with the white pastors.

BLOOD BROTHERS

My feelings for John Benefiel, John Ward, Jerry Mash, and the others who were with me at the site of the Washita massacre had not lessened, but rather had grown stronger. I wanted to honor them, so I went to the elders and asked if I could adopt these men. They said if I adopted them into my own family, no one else had a say in the matter. But if I wanted to adopt them into the tribe, I needed the Arrow Keeper's blessing.

When I approached the Arrow Keeper with this idea, he said, "About these men you want to adopt: I'm going to ask you a question, which I want you to answer from your heart. Do you trust them?"

"I would die for them."

His face brightened. "That's what my ears wanted to hear."

In December of 1997, I adopted eight men into the Cheyenne tribe. We held the ceremony at Church on the Rock before a full audience, with the words spoken both in English and in Cheyenne.

Adopting someone into the tribe is a lot like cutting a covenant. Each adoptee is given a Cheyenne name. I was also required to give each of them a gift that was worthy of them. In the old days, a chief might give a buffalo robe that had been cured by a master craftsman tanner in the tribe. I gave each of the men a turquoise ring I had made for them, a pair of beautiful, beaded warrior moccasins, and a Pendleton robe.

Much later, the Arrow Keeper met my brothers and prayed a blessing over them. Afterward he said, "No longer will we distinguish one another by our skin color or even by our mind. We are brothers."

And so we are.

DEATH AT STANDING ROCK

For several years, I'd followed the problems that plagued the Lakota people who lived on the Standing Rock Reservation, which was located in both North and South Dakota. During those years, there were six suicide attempts a month among the young people, and two of each six were successful. I knew it was a spiritual problem, but out of a population of nearly 10,000, only about 80 were Christian.

The tribal leaders didn't understand that the suicides were a spiritual problem that only God could solve. Therefore, leaders rallied health care professionals and some of the best suicide prevention officers in the nation. Leaders spent hundreds of thousands of dollars on every kind of counselor you can imagine. As the suicides continued with unrelenting regularity, eventually the tribal leaders became so desperate they were willing to try anything. That's when they called me.

In 1989, the tribe had voted to have *Sun Dance*, a religious ceremony practiced by a number of Native American and First Nations peoples, as part of their official religion. It wasn't surprising that the suicides started soon afterward. I arrived at Standing Rock in December of 2001. It took about three days to teach on spiritual warfare and organize a group of intercessors. With the cooperation of the tribal leaders, I rebuked and bound the spirits of Baal and Anubis, the Egyptian jackal god of the dead.

From then until 2005, there wasn't a single suicide attempt on the reservation. In 2005, there was one suicide attempt because the intercessors failed to maintain their victory. I went back and gathered the intercessors to make sure the spirit of death could not return, and at the time of this writing, there has not been a single suicide attempt since.

However, that spirit didn't give up altogether. When the suicides stopped on the reservation, the nearby ranchers' children began committing suicide. There has always been bitterness between the Native people and ranchers because the ranchers encroached on tribal property. I knew that bitterness was an open door to the enemy, so we had to go in and bring reconciliation between the ranchers and the Native people. Once that was done, we were able to stop the suicides altogether. Today, there is great camaraderie between the ranchers and the tribe.

JOURNEY TO PLYMOUTH ROCK

In 2002, the Lord showed me a vision of myself leading a delegation of 32 people to Plymouth Rock. In the vision, each of us wore our robes of authority representing our tribe. Everyone spoke in his Native tongue, and I understood them all. When we approached the place where the Pilgrims had landed on our shore with the message of Christ, I saw a deep, dark tornado cloud touching the ocean. We took off our robes and put them on the ground and knelt on them.

Then I saw myself repenting to the Lord Jesus on behalf of the Native people for rejecting His salvation and for using Manifest Destiny to justify that rejection. After I repented, the wind changed and the cloud began to lift. The thunder came, and I heard the words, *"I WILL!"* Then a warm wind blew on us, and the Lord said, "Now you'll tell everyone what happened here." In the vision, I turned around and saw a sea of people watching.

I knew that I was supposed to take a 32-member delegation and that we were to do exactly what I'd seen in that vision. I traveled to Plymouth Rock to make arrangements. When I met with the mayor and told him what we were going to do, he didn't want us to come. "Every time Indians come here, they're angry and they destroy things," he said.

I understood why that had happened. Each year in this country, children reenact the fictionalized version of the arrival of the pilgrims, but they rarely show the Natives' perspective. In the fictionalized story, the Indians were poor, starving people who were saved by all the bountiful food brought and shared by the pilgrims.

The truth is that Native people had been thriving here for centuries. The only thing the Europeans brought that wasn't already here was the fowl, the domesticated cow, and pigs. It was the Europeans who didn't know how to survive here, and none of those early settlers would have survived without the kindness, care, and provisions of the Native people. That part of the story is almost never depicted.

The mayor finally agreed, and I set a date for our trip. Back home, I chose the delegation that would travel with me and began making plans for the trip. I had a Shell credit card for gas, and we were duct taping our old cars and vans together for the journey. We had no money for motels or restaurants, so we planned to eat and sleep at rest stops along the way. Then, at one of our corporate prayer meetings, Chuck Pierce asked how we were going to get there.

"We're fixing up our cars and trying to get tires that will get us there and back," I explained. The next thing I knew, Chuck had taken up an offering of $20,000 for the trip. In addition to our original 32 delegates, a lot of other people wanted to go, too. I asked Jerry Mash to organize the trip.

A DREAM COME TRUE

In September 2002, we traveled to Plymouth Rock in large and comfortable rented buses and we slept in motels. Back when we'd set the date, none of us knew we would be in Plymouth Rock during the Feast of Tabernacles. John's son, Rhett Benefiel, had suggested we find some way of setting up a little booth or tabernacle there, but what we found when we arrived was that there was already a big stone tabernacle canopy over the site. The Lord had everything planned out to the smallest detail, and all we had to do was obey.

In the history of this nation, I don't know of any other time that a representation of Native tribes had publicly repented for rejecting the gospel. But that's exactly what we did that day. It was a sacred and holy time, and everything happened exactly as it had in my vision. After the repentance—just like in my vision—I turned around and saw a sea of people. It appeared that there were tourists from every people group on earth bearing witness to what we'd done. Some were worshiping the Lord.

One man and a young girl were smiling at me, and I remembered them from my vision. They were from England, and their ancestors were among those who had arrived on the Mayflower. Somehow they had heard about our plans for repentance, and the Lord had directed them to come. They presented me with a beautiful old English dish worth thousands of dollars, which had come here by way of the Mayflower.

The mayor had secured a lodge and invited us there for a meal. "We believe that today is going to be our first real Thanksgiving dinner," he said.

After that, news of revival began sparking in tribes across America. Some tribes had laws forbidding Christian activity, but one by one they were overturned. Finally, the gospel was free to move among the Native people.

DARKNESS IN THE CAVES

The Baal caves were another way that spiritual darkness had been held in Oklahoma. They created what George Otis Jr. calls spiritual pathways—openings in the spirit realm that allow spiritual darkness to lay claim over an area. When the Lord instructed us to go to those sites, we didn't do so in haste or presumption. They had remained unexposed for thousands of years, so we prayed and sought direction.

In the summer of 1999, we made a courtesy visit to the Arrow Keeper on our way to pray over the caves. He prayed a blessing over us, and as we were leaving he called me back, using my Cheyenne name.

"Roaming Buffalo, I want to talk to you," he said, drawing me aside so that we could talk in private. "Watch over your brothers when you go there. There are a lot of spiritual things going on there, and all the tribes know this."

TAKING BACK THE LAND

Red Hat's words played over and over in my mind as we drove, and I took that warning to heart. I would be watchful and prayerful, but I wouldn't assert my authority unless invited, which was the custom of our people. The closer we got to our destination, the more dismal the countryside became.

The area surrounding the caves had been in such severe drought for so long that it was clear that there wasn't enough grass to feed a single cow.

We knew the caves were near the base of Black Mesa, but we didn't have an exact location. The people who owned the land didn't want folks wandering around the caves. However, the Lord led us to the owners, who gave us permission to visit.

There are actually five caves right next to one another, probably formed by ancient rivers that once meandered through the area. Stepping inside, we immediately saw evidence that Native Americans hadn't carved on those sandstone walls. There were pictures of animals that had never been seen in Native drawings.

On the most prominent wall were carvings of Baal—the sun god—standing on a cube. The people who carved the hieroglyphics were very smart, because on the wall of the cave was a calendar of worship. At sunset, the shadow inside the cave hit the marks that showed Baal worshipers what ceremonies to perform on certain dates. There were also drawings of Anubis, the Egyptian jackal god of the dead.

Our primary purpose for being there was to take back our land from Baal and declare that it belonged to the Lord Jesus. Larry Brown, who plays the shofar with beauty and clarity, put it to his lips and blew, but it sounded like an old, sick bull. As different ones in the group began to pray, it became clear to me that the prayers weren't getting anywhere. Then, John Ward fell in a hole.

"A blind man could have seen that hole!" he said, disgusted that he'd fallen.

I knew right then what we were dealing with. There was a vortex of power there that left us all feeling disoriented and confused. Still, I wouldn't take the lead—that's not the Native way. We are taught to guard our authority until invited to use it.

Finally, John Benefiel stopped and said, "We don't have the authority to do this. Jay, you do it."

PURSUE, OVERTAKE, AND RECOVER ALL

The anointing of God hit me with such power that I went after that thing. I still didn't know what all the inscriptions meant, but the Spirit of the Lord knew, and by the time we'd finished praying, a cool breeze had blown through. We laughed and praised the Lord, then stopped to eat lunch before finishing what God had sent us there to do. When we had broken the power of Baal worship, as ambassadors of the Lord Jesus Christ, we claimed the land for Him.

Afterward, Larry blew the shofar again. This time, out came a clear and holy sound from heaven that echoed off the canyon walls and clear up the river. When we finished, the whole atmosphere changed. Rains came like they hadn't seen in generations.

The owners of the land later sent us pictures that showed grass growing as high as a horse's bridle.

We knew that, alone, none of us could have destroyed that altar to Baal. And we knew that the rain was a sign from God that we'd accomplished what He'd sent us to do. But it would be years before all the pieces of the puzzle would fit together and we could see what God had been doing all along.

THE ROOTS OF ABORTION

In November 2003, Lou Engle had scheduled "The Call," which was a call to fasting and prayer, to be held at the Cotton Bowl in Dallas, Texas. Lou asked me to join them and use my authority against abortion. Abortion was a non-issue among Native Americans. As a people, we see babies as a blessing and we abhor anything that causes the death of a child. That is evidenced by the almost nonexistent rate of abortions among tribal women. That's not to say that some Native women don't have abortions. They do, but generally they're women who have been raised in the city, not according to our culture or traditions.

To understand our concern about abortion in America, you have to go back to the Sand Creek Massacre, which happened in Colorado in 1864. When members of a nearby tribe reached the site of the massacre, they were horrified by what they saw. Soldiers had cut fetuses out of their mother's bodies and put them on bayonets and sticks to display as trophies. The medicine man walked around and wept, "How could anyone do that? How could they kill babies in the womb?" Then he pronounced a curse. "Whatever happened this day is going to come back on them. The circle will go around and be complete!"

When Roe v. Wade passed in Texas, Native people became concerned because we believed that the curse had come full circle. American babies were being cut out of their mothers' bodies by the millions. Regardless of Native prejudices against white men, babies are precious to us, and our elders felt stricken with guilt.

That's why, when Lou called and asked me to participate in The Call, I discussed it with the Arrow Keeper. He told me the whole story about the curse and then said, "You've got authority. Go and break the curse. That will ease the conscience of our people. While you're praying, I will be in the sacred tipi praying with you. My daughter has a cell phone. Call us before you pray so that I can hear what you say, and we will pray as well."

While I was walking to the microphone at the Cotton Bowl, my wife called the Arrow Keeper's daughter who said that everyone had gathered to pray with us. The speaker was turned up on the phone so that they could hear everything I prayed.

I made declarations in my language and asked God to intervene on behalf of all the babies who were being aborted. I forgave what had been done to our babies and declared the curse broken and that spiritual door closed. Later, the Arrow Keeper told me that while I prayed, they heard a huge flock of birds squawking. When I broke the curse, the squawking stopped.

BEYOND THE BORDERS

I never imagined that I might one day be called to bring down barriers in Argentina, but one day I got a call to do so. The Lord had given Brother Ed Silvoso this word: "Argentina will not be healed until you deal with the First Nations."

When Ed heard that word from God, most city preachers in Buenos Aires and other such places didn't know they had First Nation people living in Argentina. When they investigated, they discovered 32 tribes stuck on land that wouldn't produce and in self-destructive behavior such as suicide, drug addiction, and alcoholism because they had no hope.

In 2005, I found myself flying to Argentina, once again feeling out of my element. I discovered that the chiefs of the tribes in Argentina each had protocols similar to those among tribal leaders here in the U.S. My wife, a team of intercessors, and I walked to a certain place and stopped while the chief of the local tribe waited.

Protocol required that I speak in my Native tongue, even though they didn't understand it. Once I finished speaking in Cheyenne, I switched to English. My interpreter then repeated what I had said in Spanish. In response, the chief, who was in his 80s, said, "I haven't heard anyone say the words he's saying since I was a little child. He is from another Native tribe and requests to visit us in a good way and bring us good news."

He said that it was an honor to accept our visit, and he invited us in. The first thing we did was present gifts to each of them. Then, he made a speech and welcomed us to dinner. They had a meal prepared for us, and we sat and ate with them. Afterward, I discovered that Ed had advertised that I was going to preach. *I didn't know!*

There was a multitude of people waiting outside to hear what I had to say. There were no walls—only a little platform with one light above it. The generator kept kicking off, killing the light and the music. I ministered that night.

Afterward, before the security guards could react, a sea of people converged on me. They grabbed my hands and put them on their heads, and when I prayed they wept. Some of them grabbed my clothes, and it felt like they were going to rip them off. Finally, security surrounded me and got me into a van. Even there, people leaned inside to touch me. It was frightening, but I completed my mission with the tribes. Afterward, revival broke out there.

Brother Ed also called me to work with the Polynesian community on Maui. All their land had been taken except for one little plot of property. Those Natives had been pushed and pushed and pushed, and now they were willing to die for that last piece of land. A developer had already crossed the lines onto their reservation and was going to build on it, and the government wouldn't do a thing about it.

I was called in to help. But before I could bring peace, I had to learn their very elaborate protocol. Finally, we sat down to eat and they uncovered a roasted pig. Once the barriers fell, the Lord proved Himself faithful to them. They finally agreed to meet with the new lieutenant governor, and he gave them back 4,800 acres of land! Those relationships are improving day by day.

I never know what new adventure the Lord will have for me next, but by God's grace, I make war and bring peace. I like to think that both Little Bear and Black Kettle would be pleased.

CHAPTER 7

STRONG COVENANT, STRONG COVERING

Dr. Negiel Bigpond, Euchee Tribe

You're like a river that gives me life,
and without you I can't exist.
—Lillie Bigpond

I stepped into the room where my mother lay dying, her soul still strong but her body wasted as only death can do. "*Auwauday*," she whispered, her voice faint as she called me by my Euchee name, which means "Sky Hunter." "Son, I need to tell you something before I go."

"You're not going anywhere," I said. I loved her. I needed her.

"No!" she said with an edge of authority. "It's time for me to go, but before I leave, there is a word you're going to need."

"What is it, Mom?"

"*Ninzodetouyute.*"

"I've never heard that word in our language."

"It's an old word," she explained, her voice fading.

"What does it mean?"

"White men say, 'I love you.' But we say, '*Ninzodetouyute.*' It means, you're like a river that gives me life, and without you I can't exist." She gazed up at me, willing me to understand.

"You're like a river that gives me life, and without you I can't exist." Then she was gone, leaving me with questions left unanswered.

What did she mean? What was so important about that word that it was the last thing she spoke to me?

"You're like a river that gives me life, and without you I can't exist."

As I rolled the words over in my mind, I finally understood them. It was as though she'd said, "Son, I hear a voice calling me home. Your dad and I did our best by you. We taught you about the Lord. We prayed for you. We taught you how to pray. We taught you how to be healed. You watched your dad preach the gospel. Son, if you don't complete what God called you to do, it will be as though Roy and Lillie Bigpond never existed."

I could almost hear Jesus speaking those last precious words to His disciples before He ascended into heaven. I suspect He said something like, "Ninzodetouyute. You've seen Me do miracles. You listened to Me teach. You watched Me heal the sick and give sight to the blind. You saw the dumb speak and the lame walk, and you witnessed those I raised from the dead. If you don't do what I taught you to do on earth, it will be as though Yahweh had never walked with you."

MY RIVER

Ninzodetouyute. That word puts a drive in me to do all I can for the Lord Jesus. It reminds me of what my pastor spoke over my brother and me. "You have a rich heritage, a royal heritage," he said. "Your great-grandfather, your grandfather, your father, your mother, your uncles, and all your family were great men and women of God." He meant that I am part of their river.

To understand my story, it will help to know something about my river. I am a Euchee, one of the woodland tribes. The woodland tribes include the Choctaw, Chickasaw, Seminole, Creek, and Cherokee. One of the biggest misconceptions about these tribes is that we had chiefs. We never had chiefs until the Europeans gave us that name. We had kings. We lived in a kingdom, so we understand God's kingdom. We understand the kingdom message. A kingdom is a culture, and our kingdom knew no lack.

The Euchee once lived in the eastern Tennessee River valley, the western Carolinas, northern Georgia, and northern Alabama. My people were trilingual, speaking Euchee, Creek, and English, and therefore we worked as translators. Originally mound dwellers, the Euchee are believed to be among the oldest recognizable residents of the southeast portion of the United States.

Spanish explorer Hernando de Soto described the Euchee as a large and powerful tribe. Euchee warriors fought alongside de Soto in the Florida Keys, and, according to the oral history of our people, some Euchee made their way to Cuba. When John Benefiel, Jay Swallow, and I, along with a delegation of people from Oklahoma, went to Cuba a few years ago, I asked the Cubans if they'd ever heard the story. They confirmed that long ago, Native Americans had arrived in Cuba from Florida.

Euchee, as well as other Native tribes, were among the first conservationists in America. They taught the early European settlers how to use controlled burns to increase the crops of wild berries to feed wild animals. They taught farmers how to grow their crops in such a way as to conserve soil and water. They refused to kill a deer out of season and would never kill a nursing doe or her young. They believed in taking care of the environment and avoiding waste.

Euchee fought alongside Andrew Jackson in the Creek War of 1814. Against overwhelming odds and twice wounded, a Euchee king by the name of *Timpoochee* continued fighting until the Creeks were repelled and government troops saved. To Timpoochee's son, Andrew Jackson said, "A braver man than your father never lived."

That bravery and loyalty counted for nothing when President Andrew Jackson forced the Euchee to relocate to Oklahoma Territory by way of the *Trail of Tears.* Thousands died during that cruel march, and those who survived sang to fight their fear.

HONORING THE CALL

Georgia, where my family originated, is called the "Land of Many Waters." Our family name was Many Waters, which was a very honorable name in the tribe. For some reason it changed to Bigpond when we came to Oklahoma, but here Bigpond is considered an honorable name.

However, although my dad was a pastor, I dishonored him at times. As a young man, I got into trouble with the law and was thrown in jail. I drove a truck across country more times than I care to count. When I became strong in the Lord, there were some things I never wanted to do again. I wanted nothing to do with prisons, travel, or counseling. However, God sent me where I didn't want to go.

First, He directed me to start a prison ministry, and for 18 years I ministered in prisons all over Oklahoma and in other states. It seemed as though each thing God has done with me, He's done for seven years at a time. I was a drug and alcohol counselor for seven years, a lineman for seven years, and a truck driver for seven years. For some reason, each assignment ended in the middle of June.

The Lord gave me an evangelistic call to the Native tribes, and I spent years traveling from reservation to reservation. There wasn't any money in that kind of ministry. You might get fry bread and something to eat, but that was about the extent of it. I traveled and preached the gospel on more than 200 reservations in the United States and Canada. Altogether, I've been in ministry for 37 years.

TWO RIVERS

Every year, it seemed as though while everyone else was headed south for winter, Jay and I were always going to the tribes in northern Canada when the temperature was hovering at around 50 below zero. That's how we started working together and sharing our concern about the need for more qualified Native ministers to serve the reservations.

At the time, there wasn't a Bible training center specifically for Native Americans. In response to that need, in 1998 we cofounded Two Rivers Native American Training Center. We built the center on my grandfather's allotted land alongside the church that I pastor, Morning Star Evangelistic Center, located 15 miles south of Tulsa, Oklahoma. We named it "Two Rivers" to represent Jay and me, two men from different tribes but with one vision.

Even though I'd been in ministry for years, there was a sense in which I didn't know my call. I loved the land and felt a connection to it, but I didn't know I had authority over it. The first time that Jay and I walked into Church on the Rock in Oklahoma City, I had no idea God was about to launch us into a new level of authority.

I didn't know what to expect that night. I was afraid of the unknown, of not knowing what these people expected of me. I was a Native American preaching the gospel, and I didn't want to be molded into anything else.

When the repentance began, I didn't know what to think. It was hard for me to receive at first because I'd never had anyone apologize for the past and all those years of destruction.

What's going on here? I wondered. *Are they sincere? Was this really of God?* In spite of my questions, tears began to flow, and I realized that it was giving me a release that let me know I, too, needed to be delivered from the past. What I saw on John's face was sincerity, and I sensed the whole thing was being orchestrated by God. Then I looked at Jay—my elder—and I saw him receive the men and their repentance. That's when I knew, without a doubt, this was an act of God.

A few minutes later, something happened to me that was unheard of among Native people. A beautiful young Creek girl knelt at my feet, weeping almost uncontrollably. "Until tonight, I've spent my entire life ashamed of being an Indian," she admitted. "I was ashamed of our people because of their lack of control over their lives and their lack of leadership. Then tonight I saw you stand up representing Native Americans. I saw people kneel at your feet, weeping in repentance, and it broke my heart. I'm ashamed that I have not been proud of what God created."

I took her by the hand and wept with her. Finally, I said, "From this day you will go as a Native to the Natives with the gospel." Everything else that happened that night was wonderful, but I knew that young girl's life was changed forever, and that sealed it for me.

LEARNING TO LISTEN

The old people in our tribe taught us to look away when people spoke to us. My dad said that the Europeans called us heathens because we wouldn't look at them while they talked. We looked at the ground, because in our culture we were taught that people can lie while they reassure you with their facial expression. They might have a wide smile on their face and a kind, welcoming look, but their intention might be just the opposite. My father said, "Son, don't watch people. Just listen with your ears, and you'll hear the truth."

That's the way I listened to John Benefiel. One of the first things I noticed about him was that he was a good listener. He really listened. Some people ask you something about Native life and then interrupt you so often that you can't answer. I understand people do that because of their culture. But John didn't interrupt. He listened with his ears and with his heart.

In 1975, addressing Native American Christian leaders, Billy Graham prophesied, "You are a sleeping giant, the original American. You are now awakening. Just around the corner, you may become a spiritual super power in this country that could change not only America but the world." What John Benefiel did was the beginning of the fulfillment of that prophecy, and it was huge. It was groundbreaking and new.

But John didn't stop with just forming our relationships. He opened doors for us to meet other people, different ministries, and different streams. Those experiences have been life-changing.

JOURNEY TO NEW STREAMS

One of those people was Jean Steffenson, leader of the Colorado USSPN/Colorado Concert of Prayer and head of the Native American Resource Network. In 1998, about a year after I met John, Jean invited Jay and me to attend a Light the Nations conference in Dallas, Texas. Chuck Pierce, Cindy Jacobs, Dutch Sheets, C. Peter Wagner, and Ed Silvoso were among the speakers.

The trip had a dual purpose for us. Apart from the Light the Nations meeting, Jay and I were working hard to kick off Two Rivers Native

American Training Center, and things were looking up for us. First, a big ministry in Texas had a grant they were going to use to help us. Second, we were honored to be meeting with a Japanese delegation. If that weren't enough, we were going to be interviewed on a television program that would get the message out about our school. It was a packed weekend, and we took a group of intercessors and some little pieces of paper with our vision scribbled across the front.

The first day of the Light the Nations meeting was a duplication of what had happened in Oklahoma City—it started with foot washing, repentance, and establishing the needs of the Native people. The day was just tremendous, and we were excited to be a part of what God was doing. Then, just when everything seemed to be lining up in our favor, our hopes were dashed.

HOPE DEFERRED

First, we got a message that the big ministry with the grant wasn't going to help us after all. It was a disappointment, but we were excited about meeting with the Japanese and doing the television interview. Then, we got a message that the Japanese delegation couldn't meet with us. Still, we were going to be allowed to cast our vision over television. We arrived at the studio at the appointed time and waited because the show they were taping before ours was taking longer than expected. When that show finally finished, we were told that, due to the lateness of the hour, our interview had been cancelled.

We'd been shot out of the saddle from every direction. Jay and I both felt devastated. Jay had to get back to Oklahoma for a meeting, so he left on Friday along with the intercessors. It seemed like the whole trip had been for nothing. I decided to spend the night and leave on Saturday.

I was staying at a cheap motel, and there was so much ruckus next door that I didn't get any sleep. On Saturday morning, I debated about going to the Light the Nations meeting, because all I really wanted to do was go home. I finally decided that on my way out of town I would stop by long enough to say goodbye to Jean.

When I arrived, Jean said, "Peter wants you take part in communion with the clergy."

I looked down at my jeans. "I'm not dressed to go in there."

"Just go anyway," she urged.

I went inside and took communion, and then Ed Silvoso walked onto the stage and motioned for me to come up there. I hated to go because I was dressed in traveling clothes, but I went. Ed put his arm around me and said, "This brother has a vision for a school, and we're flying over the greatest mission field ever." The mission field he referred to was the reservations. "If they don't have, we don't have," he continued. "We need to sow into this."

LORD OF THE BREAKTHROUGH

The only way to describe what happened next is to say that an anointing to give swept the place. People began walking to the front and laying cash, checks, and even jewelry on the platform, and many wanted me to pray for them. The anointing was incredibly strong. It was real and passionate, yet violent. People grabbed my hands, putting them on their heads. For more than an hour, I was on my knees bent over the platform praying for people.

Things had just settled down a bit when an usher whispered something in Ed's ear. Ed grabbed the microphone and announced, "There's a man here who wrote a check for $100,000!" The power of God struck me, and I literally fell over backward.

Later they sent me the film of the meeting, and I realized that it was a miracle I didn't fall off the stage. I wouldn't have felt a thing if I had. All heaven had come down at that point, and people just broke loose. When I finally got to my feet, I walked to a chair to pick up my Bible, and a new wave of anointing hit me. The anointing was so strong that people wept and rejoiced, but they wanted a touch. So many people tried to pull at my clothes that I could hardly breathe. I was engulfed by a sea of people.

There was a black brother there who stood close to six foot, five inches tall. Years before, he'd been a policeman in California who had tried to stop the attack against Rodney King. Finally, he reached in and snatched me out of the mob and began dragging me behind the stage. I don't know what would have happened if he hadn't intervened. People weren't being unkind—they just wanted to touch the anointing. It reminded me of the way the crowds tried to touch Christ while His disciples tried to keep them away.

The leaders wanted me to spend the night, so they put me in a nice hotel room. I seldom even stayed in a motel, much less a hotel. Most of the time when I was traveling, I stayed in my Dodge van. So this was an honor, but it was all new to me.

THE LORD FUNDED THE WORK

The total amount given in that offering came to $151,000. A holy fear came over me about being a good steward of every penny of the money. I called Jay and said, "You're not going to believe what happened."

I told him the story, and he just wept and cried and rejoiced. "I sensed something was happening," he said through his tears, "but I didn't know what it was."

Back then, my church was meeting in a burned-out trailer that we'd fixed up. I'd poured an 80 by 50 slab foundation, and Jay and I decided to use that slab and put a multipurpose building on it for both the school and the church. We're still using it that way today.

Since then, we've added some dormitories and other buildings.

The experience was a far cry from traveling around in broken-down cars or vans to evangelize. I believe the Lord had to separate Jay and me from our normal routines so that He could teach us how to walk in covenant with white men, how to use our authority, and how to work with other ministries. At the time, Native ministers didn't know how to do those things.

Part of our job has been to learn to use our own authority and teach them to do the same. Now we can say, "This is what God wants you to do. This is where your authority lies in the land. There's a reason suicides and accidents are happening on your reservation, and you have authority to deal with it." At first, we had to go everywhere ourselves because we carried the authority, but now we're teaching other Natives how to walk in the authority God has given them.

OVER THE AIRWAYS

Since that day when our television interview was cancelled, Jay and I have been on television many times. Most interviews last five or ten minutes, but God moved on our behalf and it's been amazing to watch what He has done. There is a television station in Midland, Texas, whose owners, Al and Tommie Cooper, host a show called "Light of the Southwest." This program is on the God's Learning Channel and is aired worldwide. They donated 300 satellite dishes, which they're sending to reservations to allow Native people to watch the show.

They give Jay and me two hours on the air. And every two months we tape 12 programs that are aired every day and sometimes twice a day. Without a doubt, God wants this message to get out.

SWAT TEAMS

Early on, God let us know that His plan for Two Rivers was different from our plan. First, people from every race and color wanted to attend, not just Native Americans, so we opened Two Rivers to all people. In addition to the fact that Oklahoma was overpopulated with Bible colleges, the needs on the reservations were too urgent to wait four years until we graduated a class.

One of the most pressing needs on reservations was for spiritual warfare. So, we put the Bible training curriculum on hold and started "Two Rivers SWAT," which stands for "Strategic Warriors at Training." These are military-type settings where students are trained in spiritual warfare. Many of our Native students have come from different reservations, but we've also trained people who are black, white, Hispanic, African, Brazilian, Spanish, and others. We've taken our students to minister on many reservations, as well as in Ireland, Israel, Africa, and Cuba.

GOD'S FIRST-FRUIT PEOPLE

One of the places God sent our covenant group was to Israel, because God is getting the First Nations people to work with the First-Fruit people, the Jews. The Jewish culture and the culture of Native Americans are similar. They both have a kingdom understanding, and each has suffered horrible atrocities. Adolph Hitler admired American concentration camps for Indians and used them as a model in his efforts to exterminate the Jews.

When I pray, I usually pray in my own language because it offers me such full expression. It's interesting that some of our Native languages are very similar to Hebrew. For instance, Cheyenne is so similar to Hebrew that my Jewish friend, Dr. Joseph Ginat, can understand the language. The Euchee language is classified as a "language isolate" because it's not related to any other known language. However, there is some evidence that there could be Jewish roots among the Euchee people. That's a debate someone else will have to settle because I don't have an answer for it. But I do know that I have a specific call to Israel and the First-Fruit people.

"Do you know what your name means?" Dr. Ginat asked during a visit to Two Rivers, the words rolling from the back of his throat.

"Do you mean Negiel?" I asked.

"Yes," he said. "In Hebrew, it means 'Redemption.'" That blessed me, and I tucked it away like a treasure.

On another occasion, a prophet by the name of Danny Strang reached behind his pulpit and pulled out a beautiful shofar with a kind of silver lace around it and the word *Yahweh* written across it. "The Lord told me to give this to you to take to Israel," he said. "When you blow it in Israel, you will heal not only the Jewish people but the First Nations people as well."

From that point forward, the Jewish people and the First Nations people in my life began to unite. I began building a covenant relationship with Rabbi Curt Landry and his church, the House of David, and I see the Lord bringing His people together in a new unity. In addition to Israel, God has opened doors for us to minister in Ireland and Cuba. But I've got a mandate from God to go back to Israel.

THE WEAK AND THE STRONG

Every race has its weak points, and that's true of Native Americans. When we first joined this group, we were weak in covenant. We were weak in covenant with one another, and we were weak in covenant among the tribes. Although Jay and I were in covenant, we were very weak in covenant with the white man. Without that covenant, we had gone as far as we could go alone. The same is true for John Benefiel, John Ward, Jerry Mash, and others.

They had their strengths, but they also had their weaknesses. They had gone as far as they could go without us and our authority. I believe God let John and the others know they couldn't go any further in this weakness. So He pulled us together to establish a strong covenant in order to do what needed to be done here in Oklahoma, in the Heartland, and in the nation. You can't do these things with a weak covenant.

In the early days, when Jay and I were in covenant, we went everywhere together. The same thing happened in the covenant relationships with John Benefiel, John Ward, and Jerry Mash. At first, we went everywhere together because we knew we were pulling one another along. Now, however, our covenant is so strong that we can be commissioned and released separately. The power and authority of the covenant goes with us wherever we go.

THE POWER OF COVENANT

I understand that if I have a strong covenant, then I will have a strong covering. If I have a strong covering, I'm going to have a strong calling. If I have a strong calling, then I will have strong authority. It was through that covenant that I learned our Native place among God's people. We carry an authority as the Host People to recognize spiritual things on the land. Sometimes they're good and sometimes they're bad, but we can discern when something isn't right, and eventually we'll find out what it is. I've grown to know my authority in God through this covenant, and I know that if my authority is recognized it's because that's God's plan.

From the Native standpoint, one of the key words in covenant is *relationship*. We don't cut animals in half; we don't have that type of covenant. We have established ourselves together as one in Christ, and from that oneness we have been granted a strong covenant, a strong covering, a strong calling, and a strong authority.

We're like our own little tribe here. We work together and we cry together. We walk the land together. We try to understand one another. Sometimes we argue with one another. We give one another the right to disagree. But we never walk away. We disagree and are truthful with one another until we reach agreement. We never leave it up in the air and walk away mad. We don't stop until we hit agreement.

The reason this works is that we have a kingdom mindset. In the kingdom, there is a culture. As we began to grow strong in the kingdom culture, I realized that God has a culture just like the Euchee had a kingdom and a culture.

God's culture is tremendously strong, so I sensed that as we began to develop this covenant, the culture would be strong. That's when I began to investigate the word *glory*. The culture of God means the glory of God. We are changed from glory to glory and from culture to culture, because in the kingdom of God you can say nothing except, "I am rich." You can say nothing except, "I am strong." Those are covenant terms.

In this country we vote every four years for a president, and we have a Congress and a Senate that have the right to overrule the President. That's man's kingdom. But God's kingdom is not a democracy. In God's kingdom, we depend on what I call *Gohanthene*. In our language, that means "the Great Overcomer."

BLOOD BROTHERS

I walked in covenant with John Benefiel long before I adopted him into our tribe. Although Jay had already adopted him, I didn't rush into it. Not because I didn't trust John—I did. But I wanted to know his limits, his gifts, and his calling before I took that step. In addition, I live in Oklahoma, but for the Euchee, Georgia is home.

So in early 2008, Jay, John, and I were in Georgia dealing with some land issues when the Lord dropped John's Euchee name into my heart. The name was *Gohaunaunee*, which means "One Who Keeps Peace" or "One Who Carries Strong Authority" or "One Who Lays Down for Peace." It's the word that Native people use for a policeman: "One Who Carries a Big Stick." That was the perfect name for John, because when I look at him, I see a man who carries a huge amount of authority. He is a peaceful man who is very forceful and would give his life for peace.

THE BEAR CLAW

I held the adoption in a church in Atlanta, where I gave him the name *Gohaunaunee* and a ring with the symbol of our clan, a bear claw. Like our clan, a bear is very strong and very peaceful. It doesn't walk around growling all the time. You can look at a bear and see the authority he carries. He doesn't look mean, and most of the time he won't even growl if he sees you. The bear is a very peaceful animal unless he's hungry or you try to disturb him or take his life—or he senses fear in you.

If a bear senses fear, it will take root in him and disturb his peace. That's when trouble begins. The bear doesn't hate you—he hates what you brought to him, which is fear. The Euchee people believe that if you disturb the bear's spirit, especially with fear, you will create problems.

In our language, fear is described as a disease, like cancer. If a warrior went to battle and something put fear in him, he wasn't allowed back in the camp until the fear was gone. When the elders saw fear in someone, they sent the person away to deal with it. They believed that if fear came into the camp, people would get sick and die. Today, modern science has linked fear with all kinds of diseases.

What John brought to us through this covenant is peace that drives out fear. I'm not afraid of anything or anybody—and certainly not the enemy. I no longer have those old fears about dealing with people. I love people. I'm a pastor, and I travel to a lot of places and meet a lot of people.

But there's a difference when you're in covenant with someone. These relationships cause joy to bubble up out of me, and every leader needs that kind of happiness. Leaders get so beat up, so worn out on the trail on their journeys, that we need to be around people with whom we can just relax.

Now I feel almost lonesome when I'm away from my covenant relationships for very long. When I get around these men, it's so peaceful and joyous. Some people get happy about going to the lake or playing a round of golf. I get happy being with my covenant brothers. I laugh a lot when I'm with them. I can laugh with them, and I can cry with them. I can even argue with them because I have that freedom, too.

Even though John Benefiel is the leader, he also looks to us for leadership. He does something that I've never experienced before—he pulls leadership out of us, and I enjoy that. John is a proven warrior. While he is a great leader, that doesn't mean he's always right. What it means is that he's always human. If he makes a mistake, we stand by him. If we make mistakes, he stands by us. Where one of us is weak, the other is strong. It's like a positive and a negative magnet—we are spiritually and forcefully drawn together, and together we are stronger than any of us could be apart.

As I look back over our journey together, one thing is clear: My mother was right. She said there was a word that I would need, and that word was *Ninzodetouyute*. There is richness, fullness, a joy, and an authority in my life that could only have grown out of the deep soil of these covenant relationships. To my brothers I say, you are like a river that gives me life, and without you I couldn't exist.

Ninzodetouyute.

CHAPTER 8

FOLLOWING THE LEADING

Our Father who is in heaven, hallowed be Your name. Your kingdom come. Your will be done, on earth as it is in heaven.
—Matthew 6:9-10

THE goal of modern Christianity in America has been to build a strong local church. We need strong local churches, there's no question about that. However, for too long we've allowed that to be our primary goal. In doing so, we've drifted off the course Jesus set for the Church. Jesus' primary message was about advancing the kingdom of God and bringing heaven to earth.

How would we go about a task like that? How would we change and transform the atmosphere of a whole region? To say that we didn't know what we were doing would be a massive understatement. We had no idea.

Therefore, we determined to follow the admonition found in 2 Chronicles 20:20: "Hear me, O Judah and you inhabitants of Jerusalem: Believe in the Lord your God, and you shall be established; believe His prophets, and you shall prosper" (NKJV).

First, we would pray together and do whatever the Lord told us to do. One of the blessings God had given us following years of united prayer had been to set over Oklahoma a prophet of the caliber of Chuck Pierce, and also to bring other prophetic voices to us. Therefore, we set ourselves to believe the prophets of God, as long as the Word they brought lined up with Scripture, and to do whatever He instructed us to do through them. We discovered that the Word of God through a prophet is usually just a broad outline of what needs to be done with little detail. Our response to each prophetic word was to seek the Lord and pray over how to carry out His instructions.

In 1996, Chuck prophesied that we needed to divide the state into 12 regions and set a leader over each region. George Otis Jr. has identified several common characteristics in transformed communities, and one of them is persevering leadership. I would amend that to say persevering *apostolic* leadership. In Ephesians 4:11–13 we're told:

> *And He gave some as apostles, and some as prophets, and some as evangelists, and some as pastors and teachers, for the equipping of the saints for the work of service, to the building up of the body of Christ; until we all attain to the unity of the faith, and of the knowledge of the Son of God, to a mature man, to the measure of the stature which belongs to the fullness of Christ.*

APOSTOLIC COUNCIL

The apostle is the first line of defense in God's government. Therefore, we were actually setting up an apostolic council over the state. After a great deal of prayer, we began setting those 12 regional leaders in place. This was not a quick process; it took us a long time to get them identified and functioning in their territories. We have another goal of establishing county leaders in each of the 77 counties, which we've not reached as yet.

Setting proper apostolic authority over a region helps to change the land. When it comes to spiritual warfare, the Bible says that one will put a thousand to flight and two will put ten thousand to flight (see Lev. 26:8). Therefore, we established "State Days," which were held every month. On these days, we go to a different part of the state to pray over the spiritual issues for that county and region. The Bible says God will give us every place that the soles of our feet tread upon (see Josh. 1:3), so although it's not always necessary to pray onsite, if you're going to see change take place in a city, state, or region, you will have to go there on a regular basis to pray and make prophetic decrees.

In addition to State Days, every month we hold a meeting at Church on the Rock for regional and county leaders. During these meetings, each leader reports on what's taking place in his or her territory and we pray together. If you don't pray together on a regular basis and seek the Lord over the issues, you won't advance. About once a quarter, we have held statewide corporate meetings.

Pulling down thrones of iniquity over an area isn't something you should try on your own. The warfare is real, and there can be real casualties if you aren't positioned under the right spiritual cover, following the leadings of the Holy Spirit, and operating through an apostolic council chosen by God. Although we've been doing this for years and have a great deal of authority, when Jay and I are asked to go into another region of the country and confront a demonic structure, unless the Lord gives us both clear direction to do so, we won't go. To be successful, you have to be both in God's will and in His timing.

We've been told that our apostolic council here in Oklahoma is more effective than others elsewhere in the country, probably because no one else has had an apostolic council functioning together as a team as long as we have. In addition, God has graced us with the ability to recognize and respect the giftings in each other and to activate them. For instance, Jerry Mash, John Ward, Jay Swallow, and Negiel Bigpond have insights and abilities that I don't have. The same is true of our regional and county leaders.

STAKING THE STATE

In 1998, Chuck prophesied that we needed to "stake" our state. In July of that year, we pulled together 10 teams to go to different parts of the state and pray. Each team took stakes on which we'd written the Scriptures we were praying.

One team went to the far northwest corner of the Panhandle at Black Mesa, which is the highest point in the state. Another team went to the northeast corner, which borders Kansas and Missouri. One team met at the southeast corner, which borders Texas and Arkansas, and another met at the southwest corner near Hollis. In addition, we sent teams to the borders of the state at the places where Interstate 35 enters the state from Kansas and Texas. We also had teams at the border where Interstate 40 enters the state from Arkansas and Texas.

People from neighboring states met us at the border locations. There was also a team on Mount Scott, which is the second highest point in Oklahoma. The last team met at Church on the Rock in Oklahoma City.

All the teams were connected by cell phones so that we could simultaneously pray between noon and one o'clock. Each team drove their stakes into the ground and prayed. Together, we claimed the state for Jesus Christ.

Later, the Lord directed us to have representatives from all 77 counties meet at the state capital. In relay teams, we prayed at the capital for 77 straight hours.

PRAYING THE RIVERS

Because thrones of iniquity don't honor state lines, over the years the Lord broadened the scope of our warfare. For instance, in December 2003, Cindy Jacobs prophesied that Jay Swallow and I were to deal with the political spirit of America that hides in Arkansas. Later, Dutch Sheets said God was going to dislodge the serpent that hides in Arkansas.

After praying, the Lord showed us we were dealing with the spirit of Leviathan that hides in waterways. Leviathan is the father of pride, and many believe it is part of an unholy trinity—Baal, Leviathan, and the Queen of Heaven—which attempts to exalt itself above the Holy Trinity. Chuck Pierce prophesied that after the spirit was dealt with, there would be heavy rainfall.

In response to these prophecies, we went to the headwaters of the Arkansas River, just above Leadville, Colorado. We also had teams stationed along the Arkansas River all the way through Kansas, Oklahoma, and Arkansas to the place it empties into the Mississippi River. After using our authority to dislodge the serpent, there was record rainfall that day in Denver, Dallas, and all across the plains.

These are a sampling of some of the ways the Lord has directed us to take back our land. We also set someone in place to represent us at the state capitol. This person meets with senators and representatives on a regular basis. We have someone praying at the capitol every day that the House and Senate are in session.

THE PROBLEM OF GIVING UP

Getting discouraged and quitting is the major reason people fail in completing the call of God on their lives. God said that He will never leave us or forsake us, so the only possible way we can lose is by allowing discouragement to stop us so that we don't finish our course.

God won't quit on us, but too often we quit on ourselves. When you're on the cutting edge of a movement, it's mandatory that you have a lot of patience and perseverance in order to avoid getting discouraged.

One of the lessons God has taught me is to work with the people He brings and to refuse to worry about those who don't show up. God always uses a remnant of people to do His will. Although He loves everyone, God can't use everyone because one of the requirements is to accept what He says about you, believe it, and act on it.

Most of us are so aware of our inabilities that we struggle to believe what God said about. Inside we think, *Who am I? I'm nobody*. When we focus on our inabilities, we're not focusing on God's ability, and this locks us in unbelief. Too often we look at ourselves in order to judge whether or not we can do what God says we can do. Instead, we should be looking at God and saying, "I can do all things through Christ who strengthens me" (Phil. 4:13 NKJV).

It's God's ability that puts us over. He just wants someone to cooperate with Him.

Throughout the Bible God asks, "When will you believe Me? When will you trust Me?" If you're afraid of what people will think about you, you'll never do much with God. That's why Jesus wasn't able to do mighty miracles in His own hometown—people refused to believe Him. The sad truth is, most people don't want to go all the way with God. We can have all of God we want—He doesn't put a limit on us. We're the ones who set limits.

If God says it's His will that all should be saved, then that must be my goal. It doesn't mean I can compromise when the going gets tough. All means... *all*. So I can be thankful for the progress that has been made, but I can't quit until full salvation occurs and earth is like heaven. I think we should fight this spiritual battle with the same bulldog tenacity that Winston Churchill had when he fought the Nazis. His motto was, "Never, never, never give up!"

It took a lot of prayer and seeking God about who should be a leader over each county or region, but the Lord gave me the greatest team of apostolic leaders anyone could hope for. While I've given you an overview of the big picture, I've selected a few of our county and regional leaders to give you an idea of the issues they've dealt with in their individual territories.

SOUTHEASTERN OKLAHOMA

Former Regional Leader: Pastor Oscar Aguero
Petra Church on the Rock, Howe, OK

As regional leader over the southeastern part of Oklahoma, it wasn't hard to recognize that spiritual darkness existed. But finding the root was a long, arduous process. One of the first things I did was talk to older people who'd lived in the area since statehood had begun.

Most of them said there were places in the region that were just creepy and made the hair on the back of their necks stand up. I took note of those general locations, but did not share the information with the intercessors. For spiritual mapping, we studied the history of the area for hints as to what might have happened to open doors to the spirits of darkness. We also talked to police about where they saw recurring problems. Again, I chose not to share this information with our intercessors because I wanted to know what they picked up in their spirits and not what they might have anticipated, had I told them what I learned.

Briefly, we began identifying spiritual darkness in the area. For instance, one of the counties in my region was reputed to grow the "best" marijuana in the world, and a strong drug culture was in place. The high school in the small town of Arkoma had problems that no other high school in the region experienced. The kids there were in bondage. The school was like a war zone and sported six-foot-tall chain link fences. There was also an old pump station in a canyon where generation after generation of kids went to party and use drugs.

On Saturdays, I gathered teams of 20 to 30 intercessors and we walked all the county roads and prayed. We walked up and down steep mountain passes in places where no real roads existed. We walked all the county lines, praying and setting a blood line. After each walk, I took notes of what the intercessors picked up in the Spirit. They identified every problem area that had been brought to my attention, and they flagged other hot spots as well.

Arkoma led our county in child abuse cases. Its high school had massive problems, and the spiritual darkness affected the churches in town. One pastor said he'd been there for 15 years but couldn't reach the people. When the intercessors walked and prayed over Arkoma, 99 percent of them indicated that there was a stronghold on the site of the school. Every one of them returned physically exhausted.

I mapped the entire region and marked every hot spot that had been identified, giving each of them a color to designate the degree of darkness that lingered there. My research into the history of this area went deeper and deeper until I found the taproot.

ANCIENT THRONES OF INIQUITY

Two to three hundred years before the birth of Christ, this stunning mountainous area was inhabited by what's known as the *Spiro Mound People*, the second largest gathering of people in North America at the time.

If you drove through the scenic countryside today, enjoying the foliage colors and beautiful rivers, you would have no idea that some of the rolling hills aren't hills at all, but mounds. Mounds can be up to 60 feet tall and the length of one or two football fields. They were built with layers of rich soil from the bottomland interspaced with layers of rock.

The largest mounds were for the priests who worshiped Baal and offered human sacrifices. They buried people in stacks, creating higher and higher mounds. The Spiro Mounds region, found in southeastern Oklahoma, is located on the south bank of the Arkansas River. This ancient civilization built 11 platform mounds and one burial mound on 80 acres.

When you know the history of this area, it isn't hard to discern what is holding spiritual darkness in place, but we didn't know that when we began praying over the area and asking the Lord to guide us. Although there is a museum in Spiro that tells about this ancient civilization, nature has reclaimed the mounds, and as far as we know, no one living there had ever associated any of the problems of modern life with those long-forgotten people.

THE TRUTH WILL SET YOU FREE

Still without telling the intercessors what I'd discovered, I wondered if any of the hot spots they'd identified had to do with those mounds. Looking at maps, that didn't seem to be the case, but I talked to an archeologist who told me that the U.S. government marked the mounds anywhere from two to five miles from their actual location because they didn't want people on the sites. In the 1930s, kids addicted to drugs had looted the burial grounds and had stolen artifacts to support their habit.

When we tracked down the actual sites of the mounds, and noted the correlation between their locations, the information gleaned through intercession and spiritual mapping was nothing short of miraculous. Over time, I learned to tell the difference between walking on a hill or a mound. The mounds feel spongy, like a plush carpet, and while the dirt in surrounding areas is red, the dirt on the mounds is almost black because it was brought from the bottomland.

One of the most stunning discoveries was that the high school in Arkoma had been built on top of a mound. We had a prayer rally in Arkoma and one of the pastors said, "I want to win my city for Christ!" After we did a prayer walk through town, pulling down the spiritual darkness and reclaiming it for Jesus, the pastor baptized 20 people.

When we investigated the old pump station where the kids partied and used drugs, we found two sweat lodges in the area, and at one point our compass crisscrossed and went haywire. The area was a portal, or what Jay Swallow calls a vortex. Genesis 33 talks about heavenly portals, but in this case someone had opened an earthly portal to darkness, and that had drawn the kids.

It was in a canyon about a mile wide and between seven and eight miles long—a beautiful spot with rocks and pools of water. It took us months to find the beginning and the ending and to finally shut it down. Interestingly enough, on the map that area is called Devil's Kitchen. The Spirit of God is really moving there now, and we've seen a great deal of spiritual breakthrough.

PRAYING OVER THE ISLANDS

However, as we moved through the region pulling down those strongholds, I knew by the Spirit of God that there was still a site we hadn't uncovered that was very defiled. We had the intercessors do a prayer walk around the lake, and all of them discerned something, but we couldn't find the location. The Arkansas and Poteau Rivers run along the edge of Arkoma, and the mounds were built east and west along the rivers.

Where was it? I wondered, gazing at the beautiful vista. The water of the lake was deep blue and still, interrupted only by the islands that pushed their way up through the waves. *What if they aren't islands?*

The more we thought about that possibility, the more it seemed as though a piece of the puzzle fell into place. What if the lake was once bottomland and the island was really the top of a mound? We took a boat to the first island, and I knew by the Spirit and also by the feel of the earth beneath my feet that it was just an island, nothing more.

The second island had been restricted as a game reserve, and there were undisturbed flints and arrowheads. The moment we stepped on the soil, we noticed a significant difference in the atmosphere—it was intense. We'd walked about 10 to 15 feet when the Lord said, "This is where the God of Abraham, Isaac, and Jacob was defiled by the Spiro Mound people and by the Native Americas." We'd found the priest mound.

At the time, we'd been in a long drought and John had just started divorcing Baal. There were seven of us on that mound, and everything on it felt… *dead*. It was so quiet that we didn't hear a bird sing, the buzz of insects, or the lap of the waves on the shore. Nothing!

I fell to the ground in the deepest travail I'd ever experienced. I saw some things that I still don't have words to describe. I saw levels of darkness I can't explain. At one point the travail was so deep I cried out to another man in the group, "Mike, I'm dying!" But we persevered and prayed through. Afterward, we divorced Baal, and when that was done, the men picked me up off the ground.

RESURRECTION LIFE

At that moment, we felt the island go from dead to quivering with life. It came to life in an instant, and we could hear animals, birds, insects, and waves. After divorcing Baal, the skies opened up, and it rained and rained and rained.

It had taken us two years to find that mound, but it took another three months for me to recover physically from the warfare. Much later, I went to the Baal caves with 30 other people. There was an unholy power present, and I saw Jay Swallow fall into that same kind of travail. It's the kind that takes a physical toll.

There have been many changes in this region since we began identifying and pulling down thrones of iniquity. We started a healing and deliverance ministry, and many of the young people who were in bondage to drugs have come out of that lifestyle and been radically set free. The gospel is being met with far less resistance. The recession hasn't affected us here. Perhaps the biggest change occurred in Arkoma. Things are much better at the high school, and in the two years since we prayed and reclaimed the land for Christ, there hasn't been a single report of child abuse.

NORTHEASTERN OKLAHOMA

Regional Leader: Pastor Garland Thomas
New Life Worship Center, Tahlequah, Oklahoma

Tahlequah was the last stop on the Trail of Tears. This area is marked by beautiful rolling hills, the Illinois River, Lake Tenkiller, and Lake Fort Gibson. Thick, dense trees stand like sentinels guarding the ground where so many Cherokee tears soaked the soil. Those who survived the death march must have looked around and realized that they could carve a good life for themselves here.

Tahlequah is the capital of both the Cherokee Nation and the United Keetoowah Band of Cherokee Indians, and it has the distinction of being the oldest town in Oklahoma. When the Lord called my wife and me from Ohio to Tahlequah, He told me that He'd brought us here to help bring the glory of God to the Cherokee Nation. He directed us to pray over the rivers, anoint the entry points into the region, and pray over all the roads. It's as though He had us setting a boundary around the Cherokees, and I felt as though we were helping set the territory for an outpouring of God's glory.

The Lord told me, "You'll live in Tahlequah the rest of your life." At one point, He said that we needed to make that a public decree. Strange as it may seem, He instructed us to go to the cemetery to pray. I took the whole church with me to the cemetery, which happens to be the highest point in Tahlequah. My godly Grandmother and Grandfather Thomas, who were elders in their church, are also buried in that cemetery. My aunt and uncle, who were pastors of a Nazarene Church in Tahlequah, are buried there. We stood on that high point and gazed out over the territory—the garden which God had given us to govern—and looking out over the horizon, I could almost see in the distance where my father was buried. For a moment, I felt like Moses must have felt looking from a high point over into the Promised Land.

Unlike Moses, I was given an opportunity to possess my promised land. The Lord told me exactly what He wanted me to say. Standing at the cemetery where my righteous forefathers and mothers were buried, I decreed that I would be there to oversee what God had set me over until death or the Rapture took me away.

We had marked our territory—staked its boundaries for God. Now, we had announced to the heavens that we would not quit. We would never run. We would not back down.

AN OLD MISSION

Seven years ago, we started the Cherokee National Day of Prayer, which is held on Cherokee land each April. We used the gymnasium at the Sequoyah High School every year until 2008, when the Lord directed us to hold the event at Oaks Mission. That year, James Goll, cofounder of Encounters Network and director of PrayerStorm, had traveled here to join us, and during that time God had instructed him to study the Moravian Prayer Movement.

He had no way of knowing that Oaks Mission was originally Moravian.

In 1722, a small group of Christians who had been living as an underground remnant in Moravia for 100 years established a new village called Herrnhut in what is now Germany. Like the Church today, major religious disagreements emerged within their number, and by 1727 they had split into factions. The town was brought to unity through the Brotherly Agreement, which they adopted on May 12, 1727. On August 13, 1727, the village experienced a type of Pentecost through a visitation of the Holy Spirit, which resulted in the people learning to love one another. The revival caused Herrnhut to become a center for Christian renewal during the 18th century.

They established a prayer watch, 24 hours a day, that lasted for the next 100 years and emphasized a lifestyle of prayer and worship. In 1801, a missionary team of Moravians went to work among the Cherokee in north Georgia. When the United States government ordered the Cherokee to leave their homes, the Moravian missionaries took a stand against the injustice. When it became clear that the government wouldn't change its decision, the Moravians went ahead of the Cherokee to await them. The Moravians settled in Indian Territory, forming Oaks Mission, where they opened a school and an orphanage. That old Moravian church is still standing in Oaks Mission, although in later years, it was turned over to the Lutheran Church. A Lutheran pastor showed us the original walls and the old wooden ceiling.

If you were to visit Tahlequah today, you would see a lot of Cherokee, but you'd also see other tribes. On a recent Sunday in my church, there were 22 tribes represented. However, the Oaks Mission area has the densest population of Cherokee, estimated at 85 percent. We believe God is restoring His original plan—to release the Moravian prayer anointing on the Cherokee and the entire territory.

NORTHWEST OKLAHOMA

Regional Leader: Pastor Eric W. Cox
Living Word Fellowship, Woodward, OK

The rich, rolling grasslands of this region were once home to the Kiowa, Comanche, Apache, Cheyenne, Arapahoe, and Plains tribes. It was also the place where military expeditions were later led against these tribes. The city of Woodward is situated on the North Canadian River, which was a shipping point for cattle and a place to receive provisions for Fort Supply, originally called Camp Supply.

Camp Supply, which was located right outside Woodward, was the staging point for the Washita Massacre, where Chief Black Kettle and his band of Cheyenne were camped. Those who weren't killed in the raid were brought as hostages back to Camp Supply. The survivors, mostly women and children, were given blankets to keep warm, but the blankets had been quarantined by the U.S. government. Their plan had been for those who survived the massacre to die from disease.

That atrocity allowed a demonic structure to take root, and on that site today stands a psychiatric hospital. I believe that until the Washita Massacre is dealt with in full, great iniquity will continue to hold the psychiatric hospital captive. There is also a minimum-security prison located at Fort Supply.

In spiritually mapping the iniquities of the area, we also discovered that at one time there was a sign outside of town which read, "If you're black, don't let the sun go down on your back." Needless to say, we've been repenting to the Native Americans and African Americans in the area to bring reconciliation.

PUTTING THE OFFENSE ON THE FIELD

There is a Mexican mafia component here that's involved in drug distribution and other crimes. Woodward was also so entrenched with a religious spirit that churches of different denominations refused to work together in any way. There were times when we held a community Thanksgiving service at one church, and others refused to participate. The deepest root of iniquity, however, is the Baal caves, which are located in this region of the state.

Let me say from the outset that I was the new kid on the block when it came to spiritual warfare. Not only was I younger than many others in OAPN, but having come out of a background in business, I was new to the ministry. If I had known going in how hot the battle would become, I would have had an even greater excuse not to get involved. I'm grateful to God that I didn't know.

However, a time came when I was tired of getting beat up and I was tired of watching other people get hurt, so I petitioned the Lord, asking what we should do. I heard the Lord say, "Put the offense on the field." I liked sports, so that answer made sense to me. I understood that the Lord was saying we might not lose with the defense on the field, but we weren't going to win. It was time to go on the offensive.

Although I understood the strategic point of the message, I still wasn't sure how to switch things so that we were on the offense. Once again, I sought God, who gave me a two-part answer.

First, He began talking to us about gates. In biblical days, gates were where the elders gathered. Even in Jerusalem, the gates were where business and commerce were carried out. Deeds and titles were changed at the gates. As we studied and taught on the gates, we began identifying the gates to the seven mountains in our area. By that, I mean the mountains of business, art and entertainment, religion, education, government, family, and media.

LEAVENING

The second part of the Lord's answer concerned leavening. He just wouldn't let me get away from that subject, so I began to teach on it from Matthew 13:33. That's where Jesus said, "The kingdom of heaven is like leaven, which a woman took and hid in three pecks of flour until it was all leavened." The principle of leavening is that it spreads. We were ready to see the kingdom of God spread in our region of the state, so when God gave one of our intercessors a recipe for leaven, we decided to bury leaven at key spiritual gates as a prophetic act.

At the Lord's leading, we started leavening on the 100th Meridian. This is the only place in the United States that the 100th Meridian falls on a state line separating two states—Texas and Oklahoma. We felt as though the 100th Meridian was a spiritual gate dealing with Native American issues, so we asked Apostle Jay Swallow to join us.

One intercessor brought a starter mix, and we also had a loaf of baked leaven. We dug a hole about six to eight inches deep, and put the leaven mix in the bottom and the baked leaven on top. Then, we covered it with soil and declared that the kingdom of God would advance to the north, south, east, west, northwest, southwest, southeast, and northeast. Apostle Jay declared some things from the heavenlies, and I knew we'd made a shift to the offensive. God gave us another sign: It rained that afternoon.

The next day several ladies from our church went back to the site and were stunned to see the starter mix bubbling up out of the ground! They took pictures of it with their cell phones and brought them back for all to see.

MODERN MIRACLES

On July 8, 2008, I taught on leavening during our evening service, and afterward we sent people home to leaven their property. That's when things began to shift. The reports that came back to us were amazing. One man owned 520 acres that he had been trying to lease for oil or gas since 1978. Three days after he leavened his property, the entire 520 acres was leased.

Another couple from our congregation have a wheat farm about 35 miles from Woodward. At that time, farmers were getting anywhere from 19 to 22 bushels of wheat per acre. After leavening his property, he got 41 bushels per acre! The man was at a coffee shop telling other farmers about his bountiful crop, but they didn't believe him. They said it was nothing more than a big fish story. So he went home and brought back the receipts to prove it.

Another of our intercessors owned an interior design business, which is a luxury item. To complicate matters, her business was underneath the Masonic Lodge. We leavened her business, and she had the biggest year in sales she had ever experienced.

Apostle Jay Swallow called one day that November and said, "I wish you could see what I'm seeing outside my window." He and his wife had leavened their property, and after all the rest of the grass had died and the trees had lost their leaves, on the plot of ground where they'd leavened, the grass was green. Apostle Jay also had multiple elm trees in the yard, all of which had lost their leaves except the one tree near the leaven. It still bore green leaves. "It's a phenomenon," Jay said.

Over the next year, we leavened 90 percent of Woodward County. We leavened the courthouse. We leavened the police station. We leavened the city offices. We leavened the hospitals. We leavened all forms of transportation in and out of town—the airport, the railway station, and the highways. This was before the economic slump and before AIG collapsed. We contacted our banks and talked to each president asking for permission to come and pray. Each of them allowed us to pray, and we leavened each property. We leavened different financial institutions and asked God to stabilize them. This was in the fall of 2008, and we had no way of knowing what was ahead for the United States economy, but if the kingdom of God is like leaven, then we were going to call forth that kingdom to expand from that point forward.

GOD'S GOVERNMENT

Isaiah 9:7 says there shall be no end to the increase of His government. If that's the principle of the kingdom of God, which is God's government, then it should be continually advancing on our watch.

I talked to the dean of the new university and asked if we could pray over it before it opened. She not only agreed, but she allowed our intercessory team to pray over every room in the university. The next week, Senator Inhoffe arrived with a check for a million dollars for a new civic center for the university. Is that a coincidence? You decide for yourself.

Not long after we leavened the courthouse, the sheriff was voted out of office for misappropriation of funds. We leavened the recreation department, and soon after the director of our theater was found guilty of embezzlement.

There were also times when we leavened certain things and the rains fell. One winter we were in a drought, so we prayed for precipitation and ended up getting 22 inches of snow here in Woodward and 32 inches in Buffalo. That's unheard of in this part of the country—we usually get one or two inches.

I don't claim that there is anything magical about the leaven, but that's what the Lord instructed us to do here, and we've seen remarkable results. I'm not satisfied with our progress in Woodward, but when I look back at where we were, I am amazed at how far we've come.

For example, in July 2008, the population of Woodward was 12,299, which is a 3.8 percent increase since 2000. In addition, 101 new homes were built between 2000 and 2009. Eighteen percent of those were built between January and October 2009. There are new subdivisions being built both inside and outside the city limits. Forty commercial and non-residential buildings have been built, sales tax revenues are up $225,000, the USDA Field Station expanded by building new labs and offices, and a $10 million gypsum plant has been established in nearby Mooreland.

In one day, five new restaurants opened. We have two new hotels. Walgreens came to Woodward. We passed a $30 million project to rebuild the infrastructure of our parks program, which includes new ball fields, updating the rodeo arena, and a new aquatic park. In July 2009, former President George Bush came for the dedication. Our vo-tech program is one of the top technological centers in the state, and they have a federally funded oil and gas program, which is one of the first of its kind because they teach students how to work on oil rigs. Woodward now has its own wind farm, and the property values have gone up instead of down.

Am I saying we did this all on our own? No. There are other people and other churches praying in Woodward. What I am saying, though, is that the kingdom of God is advancing and while much of the rest of the nation is shaking, our economy is stable. May God receive all the glory.

KINGDOM LIGHT BREAD

3/4 c. warm Welch's grape juice (there's no added sugar or color)

3/4 c. virgin olive oil

1 4-oz. jar yeast

3/4 c. bread flour

The starter is kept at room temperature and fed 1/3 cup of each ingredient twice a week. As the quantity grows, the measure of ingredients must increase as well. Depending on the need, one can keep feeding the starter to share or bake. Or bake it all and be done with it. The oil will rise to the top, so stir before using. The bread will achieve the best rise if starter is used within a day after being fed.

To make bread: To 1 cup warm grape juice, add 1 cup starter that has been stirred. Stir together and add to 4 cups bread flour. Mix, then knead lightly until smooth. Put on a baking sheet that is greased with olive oil. Let rise in a warm place until double. Bake at 350° for 20–25 minutes. There are only four ingredients in this recipe. A simple, free-form loaf is the goal.

This Kingdom Light Bread is a tool—the real power is the Word of God. Because matter has memory, if you declare Scripture over this as you're working with it, it will be saturated with the Word. Then, coupled with the declarations that are made while leavening at the gates, it will certainly advance the kingdom of light—because the Word of God will not return empty, but will accomplish that which it is purposed and sent to do (see Isa. 55:11).

Because this bread has a lot of life in it, after baking, cut in pieces and air dry for several days before storing.

OKLAHOMA STATE GOVERNMENT

Government Specialist Pastor: Yolanda McCune
Dimensions Center
Stillwater, OK

In addition to being pastor of a church in Stillwater, Oklahoma, I am the government specialist for OAPN, which means I represent the interests of OAPN on a state legislative level. I was chosen for this role in part because I had been a campaign director for several campaigns and had been involved in politics since 1988.

In this state, the broken covenants and crimes against the Native Americans are our primary issues. Child abuse, poverty, and divorce rates have been major problems in Oklahoma, and we believe all these stem from 372 broken covenants. Those problems are not going to just disappear; we've got to deal with them.

I believe God wants to say to the legislature, "You're responsible for the laws of the land." However, most of our government leaders don't understand these issues, so it's our responsibility to not only educate them, but to put watchmen on their walls who will stand in the gap and do warfare over them. Most of them don't understand the role of spiritual curses in the land, so we have to appropriate that forgiveness.

RESOLUTION OF APOLOGY

The Resolution of Apology is a necessary first step, which we've been working toward both on a state and national level for several years. While none of us are naïve enough to think that a single apology will solve all the problems, I don't think the anger and bitterness will break until an official apology is made. I've been a Christian counselor for years, and I've discovered that, no matter what the problem is, things break when someone says, "I'm sorry."

Here in Oklahoma, some tribes oppose our efforts because they want land or money, not an apology. Among legislators, the Democrats have been supportive of the Resolution of Apology, but most Republicans have opposed it. Their opposition reminds me of the stand-off that members of the American Medical Association are dealing with. In the past, their stand has been that if a surgeon says, "I'm sorry for your loss," those words make him liable for the death. That's an issue they're trying to resolve.

Likewise, even though the words of our apology do not mention reparation, just the acknowledgment that what was done was wrong and deserves an apology has caused most Republicans to fear that the bill would result in lawsuits and require financial restitution. Without an understanding of what allows darkness to linger, most people—legislators or not—have no concept that the tentacles of these ancient iniquities can hold terrorist cells in place in our country.

For some time, every day that the House or the Senate was in session, either I or another member of OAPN was present at the capitol to pray, intercede, and talk to our legislators. In 2008, we had a campaign to get the resolution onto the floor. At our request, OAPN members bombarded their legislators, asking them to support the bill. That same year, Senator Owen Laughlin was the Floor Leader in the Senate, and he got the bill passed in the Senate without any opposition.

However, the speaker of the House blocked the resolution and never let it reach the floor. The speaker of the House of Representatives is very powerful because he controls what is allowed on the floor. Because it had not passed both House and Senate by the end of 2008, we had to start over in both branches of the legislature in 2009. Since then, we have arranged for an OAPN intercessor in each district to pray for every Oklahoma

Representative and Senator daily. With that in place, we go to the capitol periodically to pray.

We're doing everything we can in the natural, but it's important for people to pray because this is a spiritual battle. In addition to praying, there are a few things that will help. First, emailing mass copies of petitions does no good. A personal hand-written note is equivalent to 1,000 votes. That is increased astronomically by personal phone calls or personal visits to your legislators.

Please join us in praying that the Resolution of Apology will be passed by both the House and Senate in Oklahoma. Then pray that our apology will be accepted.

CHAPTER 9

THE STATE TAKES A SHIFT

All these [gifts, achievements, abilities] are inspired and
brought to pass by one and the same [Holy] Spirit, Who
apportions to each person individually [exactly] as He chooses.
1 Corinthians 12:11, AMPC

I'M sure you noticed from reading the last chapter that although all of Oklahoma has to deal with the issues of covenant breaking and innocent bloodshed, each region has spiritual darkness specific to that area. That's why it's imperative that there be strong spiritual leadership present in those regions. As you read the testimonies from different regional leaders, you likely saw why it would be impossible for our apostolic council in Oklahoma City to single-handedly set the entire state free.

If there is one thing you remember from these chapters, let it be this: The victory you attain, you must maintain. Spiritual warfare is a war. The enemy may be defeated, but that doesn't mean he won't regroup and try again. That's why it's very important that we have to have a warfare mentality.

I also want you to notice that, although these men and women come from different denominational backgrounds and operate in different gifts, together we are a spiritual force to be reckoned with.

This chapter begins with the perspective of John Chambers, the administrative director of OAPN and HAPN, and then goes to the leaders in the southwestern, southeastern, and Tulsa areas.

NORTHERN OKLAHOMA

OAPN Regional Leader: John Chambers
Salvation Springs, Enid, OK

Enid, located on the edge of the plains, was founded in 1893 during the opening of the Cherokee Outlet. I've been a pastor for 20 years, and have spent 15 years in Enid, Oklahoma. I have loved my church and enjoyed the call of God on my life, but in many ways I felt like a round peg trying to fit into a church structure that was, in effect, a square hole. Although our church was serving, praying, and doing good things inside its four walls, as well as in the city, we weren't making an impact on our society, and that bothered me.

In 1990, I read John Dawson's book *Taking Your Cities for God*. The message wasn't new to me; I'd seen that the Israelites were required to take their cities for God and I was already focused on taking "my" city for God. Dawson's message served to refresh and confirm what the Lord had been speaking to me.

My determination was quickened! Passion for my community and the desire to see God's presence in every part of our city and county government and all areas of society continued to grow.

In addition to my role as pastor, I served our local ministerial alliance, coordinated prayer for city council meetings, organized National Day of Prayer activities, and created a prayer calendar for our judges, police, fire department, highway patrol, mayor, and city council members.

These were all good things that I enjoyed, but nothing was changing in Enid. I was too much of a realist to expect that I could continue doing the same things and expect a different result. Even worse, I sensed the Lord's dissatisfaction with the limited progress.

FOCUSING ON DIFFERENCES

Not sure where to turn for help, I contacted the office of Dr. C. Peter Wagner and was encouraged to contact Pastor John Benefiel in Oklahoma City. I drove 70 miles to Church on the Rock in Oklahoma City. Approaching the building, I thought, *That's one of those name-it-and-claim-it churches.* Without stopping, I drove the 70 miles back home. I had focused on perceived error instead of listening to the mature counsel I had sought.

A couple of weeks later, a pastor friend called to say he had someone he wanted me to meet. It was John Benefiel. I instantly knew I had missed God by judging the man and his church. The Lord was graciously giving me a second chance.

John shared his vision over lunch, and when he mentioned an obscure passage (2 Sam. 21:1–3), I felt the hairs rise on the back of my neck. Ten years earlier, the Lord had spent a good deal of time teaching me about His faithfulness to covenant through this very same passage of Scripture. A message titled *Remember the Gibeonites!* was a word I had passionately preached for a decade.

When John used that passage to describe our violation of covenant with Native Americans, I knew he had tapped into the heart of God. God doesn't just sweep things under the rug. Time does not heal all wounds. Although I didn't understand the process John described, I recognized God's hand in it. During that conversation, John asked me what my vision was for Enid. I flashed back to the late 1980s when I'd been fasting and praying over Enid for a week. Afterward, I took a team from my church to the four corners of the city to pray. At the last corner God spoke prophetically and said, "The Light of My Son will shine unhindered over Enid."

Looking John in the eye and without hesitation I responded, "My vision is that the Light of God's Son will shine unhindered over Enid."

"Say that again," John urged, and I repeated my statement. John then asked, "Do you understand the significance of the word *unhindered*?"

I did indeed, and I explained that unhindered meant all of Enid would be impacted by the light of Christ.

When John then told me that they were praying for all of Oklahoma to be saved, I became a committed participant in the Oklahoma Concert of Prayer, which later became the Oklahoma Apostolic Prayer Network (OAPN).

THE POWER OF CORPORATE UNITY

Without a doubt, our efforts to evangelize our state, and the efforts of those who had labored before us, had been hindered. John and the members of OAPN were approaching God in corporate unity as the Church in Oklahoma to hear the Lord's strategy to remove the hindrances. When John told me they were praying for all of Oklahoma to be saved, I felt my heart sigh with relief; I'd found my place.

Over the next 10 years, this confirmation in ministry relationship served as an anchor as we blazed new paths in spiritual warfare. Often, we didn't know what our next move would be. When people believe they fully understand God's plan, someone might well question whether they are embracing God's plan or their own. Are not His ways higher than ours?

I have little confidence in my ability to hear God. However, I have great faith in God's ability to speak in such a way that I can hear. To many people, all the things we've done—staking the state, praying over the rivers, praying for 77 hours on the steps of the state capitol, and most recently "divorcing Baal"—seem foolish. We don't just dream these things up. God is directing the Church in Oklahoma to deal with issues of the land that have, for far too long, hindered the advancement of His kingdom.

We recognize God's anointing, authority, and gifts in each one of us. There is an apostolic imprint and a prophetic imprint on what God is doing. Early on, and still today, some would view the title of *apostle* as arrogant error. Knowing we are not called to be secret apostles, we reject the anxiety associated with the stigma some attach to the office of apostle or prophet in the Church today.

RELEASING RESOURCES

During an OAPN corporate meeting a few years ago, Chuck Pierce prophesied that God was going to start releasing natural resources. I immediately thought of a friend in Kansas who owned a small company that produced oil. Unbeknownst to me, he drilled an average of only one well per year, and for the past 10 years had drilled only dry holes or wells that never recovered the cost of production. He had also just decided to get out of the business of oil production.

At a lunch meeting with him and his wife, I told them God was about to bless their drilling for oil. After their initial shock, it bore witness with him not to get out of the business. Acting on the word of the prophet, they began drilling approximately one well per month. Over the next year, eight out of the twelve wells went into production. God did indeed release the resources! This was clearly in direct relation and timing with the redemption of the land that Apostle Benefiel and the whole OAPN network were accomplishing through exposing, unraveling, and removing spiritual strongholds of darkness.

In 2005, God challenged me to give up my position as senior pastor, along with my steady income, and to become a missionary in my city. Unfortunately, there was no paradigm for that in the body of Christ. If you're going to be a missionary, you have to go to China or Africa. Who ever heard of a missionary to Enid? Furthermore, moving from senior pastor to a missionary promoting prayer in the community appeared to many as a step down on the ladder of success. Some believed a rumor that I had left my wife. Had I fallen into secret sin? Had there been a power struggle in my church that I'd lost? Some felt that doing community service was secular work and not worthy of support as a ministry.

God not only kept us through the transition, He prospered us.

I believe the lines delineating what is spiritual and what is secular are man's invention. The two cannot—and should not—be separated.

On Fire Without Burning Out

One reason pastors burn out is that they're allowed such a limited identity in the community and such a limited sphere in which to use their gifts. When gifting and calling are quenched, they no longer fuel the fire of ministry. Pastors may be hesitant to reveal their extended passions for fear of losing their jobs. It's a sad testament, but I now have more spiritual influence as a regular citizen than I had as a pastor.

In the past 12 years, Enid has seen $30 million of private funds reinvested in its downtown business district. Experiencing a change from abandonment and neglect to economic revitalization of the heart of this town of 50,000 is a testimony of God's blessing and provision.

An alliance of eight churches serving corporately as the community of believers has gained significant recognition in meeting needs within the city and through regularly worshiping together. There are still hindrances to the transformation of Enid, but each passing day reveals continued progress. As the executive coordinator for HAPN and OAPN, I communicate with state and regional leaders on Apostle Benefiel's behalf. John once told me that he couldn't fulfill the call of God on his life without me. The reverse is also true: I can't fulfill my call without him. There is one Church and many apostles, prophets, evangelists, pastors, and teachers.

I'm still not certain whether I'm a square or round peg, but I do know that I fit. And the conjoined gifts and ministries of all sizes and shapes in the Heartland and Oklahoma Apostolic Prayer Networks, along with the rest of the Lord's Body (His Church), are fitting together to bring life, health, and kingdom purpose to the land and the people of it.

SOUTHWESTERN OKLAHOMA

Regional Leaders: Pastors Lonnie and Diana Hanson
The New Rock Church, Lawton, OK

Located in southwestern Oklahoma, Lawton is south of the Wichita Mountain Wildlife Refuge, Mount Scott, and Lake Lawtonka. Fort Sill, which is still an active military base located here today, was established in

1869 while this land was Indian territory. Lawton is the current headquarters of the Comanche Nation.

This land had originally been granted to the Comanche, Kiowa, and Apache tribes by the Medicine Lodge Treaty of 1867. Quanah Parker, the last chief of the Quohada Comanche Indians, along with other Native American tribal leaders, agreed to give the government control of the land for $1.25 per acre, allotting 160 acres to each tribal member and reserving 400,000 acres as grazing land for cattle ranchers. However, President William McKinley gave the government control over two million acres for less than a dollar an acre.

The primary iniquity woven into the fabric of this land is bloodshed, which includes massacres between different Native tribes who'd been forced onto the same land. In addition, Fort Sill was built by Buffalo Soldiers, the first regiment in the U.S. Army who were all African American. Thus, the Native American and African American were in oppositional situations that formed a root of racism.

Currently, the greatest source of opposition is between two factions of Apaches. In 1886, the Chiricahua Apaches were the last Native American tribe to be relocated into Indian territory. They had been promised the land surrounding Fort Sill to settle, but other non-Native people had settled on the land and pressured them to leave. A third of the group stayed while the rest moved onto another Apache reservation in New Mexico. Those who stayed are called Fort Sill Apaches. The dispute between the two tribes centers on the final resting place of Geronimo, the famous Apache warrior who was buried at Fort Sill.

SKULL AND BONES

In 2005, Yale historian Marc Wortman discovered a letter written in 1918 from a member of a secret society called the Skull and Bones. The letter said, "The skull of the worthy Geronimo the Terrible, exhumed from its tomb at Fort Sill by your club and Knight Haffuer, is now safe inside the T—together with his well-worn femurs, bit, and saddle horn." In this situation, it is difficult to separate truth from fiction. One rumor says that members of Skull and Bones, including George W. Bush's grandfather, Prescott Bush, dug up Geronimo's grave while stationed at Fort Sill during World War I.

In February of 2009, Geronimo's descendants from the New Mexico band sued the Skull and Bones, naming President Barak Obama, as well as the defense secretary and Army secretary, as defendants. The Fort Sill band of the Apache Nation doesn't believe the story is true, because at the time of the alleged grave robbing, Geronimo's grave was unmarked. One group wants the grave exhumed and the other wants it undisturbed. We've been praying over this, along with other issues such as the witchcraft that has been brought into the area by servicemen from Europe and other parts of the world.

A few years ago, with the help of Apostle Jay Swallow, we met with the leader of each tribe in order to build relationships with them. Apostle Jay facilitated a traditional presentation with gifts, and we offered them prayer support in working through any problems. As leaders change over the years, we must work on reestablishing those relationships. In addition to the things we've done locally, we've also participated in all the corporate efforts such as praying over and staking all the courthouses and praying the rivers.

One of the biggest changes we've seen in our area has been in the Church culture. When we started this journey, we found that a lot of Christians weren't interested in praying. In fact, we discovered that when most Christians pray, they don't expect an answer. Over the years, we continued working on unity among believers and spreading the word about how God has answered our prayers. Today, we find people much more willing to pray and work together.

A MIXED HERITAGE

Being part of a reconciliation process has been particularly interesting for us because of our own racial heritage. My wife, Diana, is Cherokee, Pottawatomie, and Blackfoot. My family is from Dresden, Ontario, which is where the Reverend Josiah Henson, himself a former slave, built a school for escaped slaves.

The work of Reverend Henson was the inspiration for Harriet Beecher Stowe's novel *Uncle Tom's Cabin*. The best-selling novel of the 19th century, *Uncle Tom's Cabin* had such a profound effect on the nation that when Abraham Lincoln met the author, he is reported to have said, "So, this is the little lady who made this big war."

My bloodline is mixed; there is African American blood flowing in my veins. My maternal grandfather was Mohawk. My grandfather's mother was Dutch. In every branch of our family line there are relatives who are multiracial, so I am a representation of Everyman.

I was raised "colored," but thought I was white. When I was 10, I discovered I was part black, but I wasn't cool enough to be accepted by the African American kids. Then I found out I was Indian, but the Native Americans on the reservation didn't want me. Racially, I never found a place where I fit.

I was at one of our OAPN corporate meetings, and from the pulpit I joked that when I participated in the repentance for the Tulsa Race Riot, I almost felt as though I should apologize to myself. Instead of laughing and going on, the leaders in that meeting said, "We accept you just as you are. You're one of us."

My heart melted at those words. For the first time in my life, I know who I am, and I know where I belong. I realize that what we're doing here in Oklahoma isn't the only thing God is doing, but it's what we are called to do. I never imagined that God would take me on a journey from southwest Ontario to Lawton, Oklahoma, but He did, and it feels good to be home.

TULSA REGION

Regional Leader: Apostle Kathryn Holcomb
Pastor of Breakthrough Church, Tulsa, OK

The Lochapoka clan of Creek Indians was forced out of their home in Alabama in 1834 to begin the long journey to Indian Territory. After two years of travel and the loss of many lives, the band arrived at a drop-off site in what is now Oklahoma. According to their custom, they located a mature oak tree on a hill overlooking the Arkansas River, where they deposited the ashes from their last fires in Alabama. They named their settlement *Tallasi*, which means "Old Town" in the Creek language.

The Council Tree became their gathering point for ceremonies, feasts, and games. Located at the intersection of Cheyenne Avenue and 18th Street, the Council Tree is still alive today. The name *Tallasi* evolved into "Tulsa."

Situated between the Great Plains and the Ozark Mountains, this area is filled with dense trees, rolling hills, and lakes. The city itself is divided by the Arkansas River, which runs through it. According to tradition, the Native American who owned the land on which Tulsa now stands was tricked out of it, which allowed a deep root of covenant-breaking to become established, and this has affected not only this area but the state.

TULSA RACE RIOT

By far, one of the worst ways that the covenant-breaking spirit manifested was through the Tulsa Race Riot in 1921. Another manifestation occurred early in Oklahoma's history when strife broke out between Tulsa and Oklahoma City. Tulsa's city fathers wanted Tulsa to be the capital of the state of Sequoia while Oklahoma City would be in a different state—Oklahoma.

The federal government refused to bow to their wishes, and both cities were located in Oklahoma.

It's my understanding that the break point between the two proposed states was roughly around I-35. When I first came to Oklahoma, you could drive on Turner Turnpike, between the two cities, and feel the warfare. Then another political war broke out because Tulsa wanted to be the capital. We still war against that spirit of pride today. We have bathed the Turner Turnpike in prayer as we've driven that route so many times over the years. At one point, Apostle John Benefiel and I vowed together over communion that we would marry the two cities and see them reside together in unity.

Another way that covenant-breaking manifests here is in a lack of unity. One of the pastors told me that he had been part of every single pastor's group that had risen up in Tulsa for 18 years, and not one of them stayed together. Although Tulsa is blessed with some of the greatest ministries in the world, because of the taproot of pride and covenant-breaking, gaining ground in unity has been very difficult.

That last move of God had strong beginnings in Tulsa. It is often the last move of God that brings the greatest opposition to the new move of the Lord, simply because most of us don't have a revelation of the progressiveness of God. Rather than allowing the last move of God to be the springboard for what He does next, we find ourselves resisting change.

Resistance to Women in Ministry

There is also a strong resistance to women in ministry here. My husband, Dan, was a businessman, and I was an ordained pastor before we moved to Tulsa. Once here, I was stunned at the resistance to women in ministry and found that many women of God here were wounded and felt they had no voice. For a long time, I was the only female regional leader, which speaks to that resistance in this state.

However, from the beginning, I've been accepted 100 percent by John Benefiel and Negiel Bigpond. Those two men gave me the strength and courage to move on as a female leader in the state, and especially in Tulsa. John once told me that I have freedom on any platform he is on. Without John and Negiel's support, I doubt I would have stayed in Oklahoma. Everything that has happened here is a result of our covenant together.

Although I don't think that spirit of pride and covenant-breaking over Tulsa has fallen, there has been enough stability in this prayer network that the majority of pastors and ministry leaders in Tulsa speak well of it, and some of them come to meetings on occasion.

I don't think it's any mistake that God visited economic improvement on Oklahoma City first so He could deal with that pride. As Christians and ministries in Tulsa have begun working together in unity, we've begun to see Tulsa taking the same economic turns toward being viewed as recession-proof. In addition, Tulsa is surrounded by counties that are strong in the Apostolic Prayer Network.

One pastor in Tulsa called me and said, "We don't get over to pray with you, but we never wonder where you are or what you're doing because we've seen your stability. We know who you are, and we know your integrity. We know what you're praying for, and that you will continue to do so."

A PLOT UNRAVELED

Prior to moving to Oklahoma, Dan and I lived in Las Vegas. Six months before we moved, our realtor called and asked Dan to help her ex-husband get a job with his company. Dan could have hired him or taken him to meet the owner since he was a supervisor. Dan took a hard stance and said, "No, I won't hire him, and I won't introduce him."

We were originally from Michigan and so were this woman and her ex-husband. I thought surely Dan could have helped the man, but his stand was so uncharacteristic that I didn't say anything. Dan felt the Lord gave him pause about helping the man or bringing him into the company.

Within a year of refusing to help that man, a couple of significant things had happened. We'd moved to Tulsa and God was drawing me into the work here. The Oklahoma City bombing had also shocked the world. As I watched the coverage of that fateful day and the events that followed, all I could do was thank the Lord for the strong guidance He'd given my husband. I realized that God had used Dan to protect my call here in Oklahoma.

The man he had refused to help was Terry Nichols.

Southeastern Oklahoma

Former Regional Leader/YOAPN Leader:
Pastor Darrin Begley
God's House, Atoka, OK

Atoka is located in southeast Oklahoma, just north of the Texas border. It is named for the Choctaw leader who signed the Treaty of Dancing Rabbit Creek, which relocated the Choctaw here from Mississippi in 1830. In addition to the Choctaw, the Cherokee and Chickasaw also have a strong presence here.

Atoka had the first church in the state and the first Masonic Lodge. The Ku Klux Klan got its start in this area through an unholy alliance with the church and the Masonic Lodge. Back then, the original sign outside the First Baptist Church read, "No Black People Allowed Here."

When the original Masonic Lodge burned, they shared the First Baptist Church building before rebuilding a 15,000 square foot facility. Typical of Masonic Lodges, it is the tallest building in Atoka and had a trap door on the third floor used to hang African Americans.

Because I was a youth pastor for eight years, I know the strongholds in this area, and the drug culture is a huge one. This part of the state has rolling hills, trees, and the rainfall that makes it a perfect place to grow marijuana. The biggest drug bust in U.S. history occurred here and involved a Mexican drug cartel known as the Bandidos. There is also a lot of witchcraft in this part of the state.

In addition, there is a big problem concerning women. The Catholic Church worships them, and the Baptists refuse to let them preach. They're allowed to train our next generation but can't speak to a group of adults. Both extremes are evil in God's sight.

However, the two largest strongholds are Baal and the Queen of Heaven, which I encountered before they were on our radar screen. In 2002, the Lord gave me a prophetic word concerning my wife. He said that the Queen of Heaven was going to try to kill her. Before long, my wife started hemorrhaging. The local doctors were going to fly her to a larger hospital, but before they could, she died. We later learned that she died from hemorrhaging caused by a ruptured tubal pregnancy.

After she died, the enemy immediately said, "What are you going to do now?"

"I'm going to do what God sent me here to do," I replied.

God interrupted and said, "I told you the Queen of Heaven would try to kill her."

At that moment, everything changed. I'd been born and raised in Atoka, the youngest of 13 kids. My dad died when I was four, but my mother was a powerhouse who raised three people from the dead. My brother had been dead for 12 hours, but she brought him back to life. I'd cut my teeth on the supernatural power of God, and I knew God did not intend to let the devil take my wife's life.

So, we raised her from the dead.

The doctor said, "I don't understand...she was dead. Why is she alive?" It was very intense, and that was my introduction to the Queen of Heaven. Afterward, the Lord showed me 1 Kings 18 as a precedent. This was where Elijah confronted the prophets of Baal and God sent fire from heaven to the altar. Then Elijah killed the prophets of Baal, but he didn't kill the prophets that sat at Jezebel's table. Soon after this, we see the great prophet of God running from the spirit of Jezebel, which is the Queen of Heaven. I realized that sometimes we're going after one thing, but there's another underlying spirit that's just as powerful. That's when God showed me how the unholy trinity of Baal, the Queen of Heaven, and Leviathan operated together.

Sometimes I almost feel guilty because of what other state and regional leaders have to go through to search out the strategic things God wants them to know. I stand in the office of a prophet and my church is very prophetic, so God is very precise in showing us what's going on.

I noticed that John Benefiel is the only other person I've met who wars over the prophetic the way we do in our individual lives. When he gets a prophetic word, he writes it down, brings it before everyone, and then fights to win that word.

Paul told Timothy to fight a good fight with the prophecies that had been spoken over him. Yet most Christians say, "Well, we'll just see if God does it or not. If it doesn't happen, that means this was a false prophet." So many people misconstrue prophetic words by thinking that's just the way it's going to be, but that isn't the case because that mentality removes our responsibility from the situation.

We'd like for God to do everything to make that word come to pass, but God doesn't work that way. That's why when John gets a prophetic word, he brings it before us all, and we pray over it and take whatever steps necessary. I believe that's one of the primary reasons John has enjoyed such success, not only in his personal life but in OAPN and HAPN.

SIGNS OF TRANSFORMATION

I was living in Houston when John Benefiel made me a regional leader in OAPN. I said, "John, I live in Houston!"

"I know that," he said, "but I also know you're coming back."

God did call me back to Atoka, and when we arrived Atoka County and Coal County were two of the most poverty-stricken counties in the state. We prayed, and God gave us a word about oil and gas. We started prophesying that God was bringing oil and gas to the area, and people thought we were idiots. We said, "Just wait, you'll read about it in the newspaper."

Of course, God did exactly what He said He would do and the farmers and ranchers in the area, most of whom still owned the mineral rights to their land, became very wealthy. The *Daily Oklahoman* printed the results of a study that showed that for a year, Coal County had more millionaires per capita than any place in the United States. At one point, you could see five gas wells from our church. Since then, a lot of them got pulled when gas prices went down, but it brought a lot of wealth to the area—and it's coming back.

When we arrived in this area, we started prophesying restaurants and new businesses. Since then we have new Chinese, Vietnamese, Mexican, Japanese, and Italian restaurants. They've built three new motels in the past two years, and other new businesses are springing up. There are 24 people from different places who are moving here to be a part of our church.

There has also been a big change in the drug culture, which included some major drug busts. We have more Christians in leadership positions, and more of the favor of God rests on this area. We haven't arrived—there's still more to do, but the changes are compelling people to move here.

Another change has been at the Cottonwood School, in which one of the elders in my church was superintendent. When she took over, the school had 35 kids—now it has more than three hundred. It's a blue-ribbon school, and people from other states come here to tour the school because it's so incredible. Cottonwood only goes through the eighth grade, but students can learn to fly an airplane in this school! Our church has started a school that begins with ninth grade, which is where Cottonwood stops.

In addition to being a pastor and regional leader in OAPN, I also head the YOAPN, which is the youth program for the state. We'd hosted youth camps for years, but I shifted some things because I didn't want us to offer great events but miss the boat on discipleship. We often had four or five hundred kids at a youth camp for two weeks, which was wonderful, but I didn't see the leaders emerge from that group that should have been there. A lot of times kids go to camp and get fired up for God, but when they get back among ungodly influences, their passion doesn't stick. So, we started identifying kids who were sold out to God, and we've established a leadership program so that when we hold camps, there will be strong leaders among the youth to help mentor them.

A Christian hard rock concert is coming to this area, and one of the band members used to be a part of Korn before getting born again. Eleven bands will be there, and they've asked me to preach at the end and give an altar call, which has created no small stir among religious circles. I said, "Listen, if AC/DC asked me to come by and preach at the end, I'm there. You might be upset over their tattoos, but there'll be lost kids there, and I want to win them. I'll let God deal with the tattoos; I want their hearts."

When I was a teenager, I spiraled away from God because the Church took away my hope for a future through the teaching of the Rapture. The unspoken (and sometimes spoken) message was, "You don't have a future. You'll never be married. You'll never have kids. You don't have a destiny. Jesus is coming to take us out of here." I think any young person will rebel when you take away his future, and that's why I won't preach the Rapture to them. If the Lord comes back during our lifetime, let's let Him find us fulfilling the Great Commission and taking the kingdoms of this world and making them the kingdoms of our God and His Christ.

John Benefiel and I were in a penthouse in Cambridge this year, and the Lord brought a lot of students from Harvard and MIT. Young people today are hungry to experience the power of God. They have no interest in a gospel that is only empty words without power. The Lord showed up in a powerful way through the manifestation of the word of knowledge. God spoke His specific will and purpose over their lives and set them on a course.

OKLAHOMA IS A TEMPLATE

I believe Oklahoma is a template for the nation. Let me give you an example. I sat in the pastor's office in a church in Columbus, Ohio, with the pastor and another young man. All of a sudden, a nickel fell out of thin air and hit the ground. I thought it was a neat trick, and I reached over and picked it up.

"How'd you do that?" I asked. They thought I was making a joke, and I added, "If you're going to make money fall out of thin air, how about some Ben Franklins?" We all laughed and went on, but I couldn't get it out of my mind.

A few days later, I called that pastor and asked again. "How'd you do that?"

"You're not going to get me!" he said laughing.

"What do you mean?" I asked.

"I know you did that!"

"Dude," I said, "I didn't do it!"

We both fell silent. If neither of us had done it... "All right, God," I said, "what are You saying?"

God spoke and said, "I told you it was going to fall. Thomas Jefferson is on the nickel."

The Lord reminded me of a word that Chuck Pierce had given prophetically. He said that separation of Church and state in America would cease from Oklahoma. The term "separation of church and state" is believed to have been coined in a letter written by Thomas Jefferson in 1802. The Lord was confirming that word.

God also said that abortion in America would cease from Oklahoma, and we've seen a shift in abortion here. So, I believe that God is making a template for the nation out of this state, and the Apostolic Prayer Network is key to that because we're getting into agreement with God to shift our nation.

I believe that we're further ahead than other states because we've focused on covenant. It's a lot like marriage—you can mess up and make a lot of mistakes, but if you focus on covenant, it will work out. That's why it doesn't matter if my theology is different from John's—the real issue is our covenant walk.

A GREAT AWAKENING

Nationally, I believe we're on the verge of a great awakening. What we do with it is crucial, because if we have an awakening like we've had before, society will not be changed. I'm not interested in starting a move of God. I'm interested in sustaining a move of God.

I've been in one move of God in which we experienced incredible miracles daily. Some people called it the laughing movement in the early 1990s, but they made a mistake to focus on laughter rather than the tangible presence of God. I suspect that every time a move of God stops, it's because we try to merchandize it. We try to put it in a box and sell it. Worse, we try to put it in a place where people have to get it from us instead of from God.

Years later, I visited some places where there was an outpouring of the Spirit of God. The presence of the Lord was there, but it was no greater than we experienced in Atoka. The issue is that we just facilitated it. The problem was that we facilitated it only in the Church. We didn't facilitate it in the business world. We didn't facilitate it in the media. We didn't facilitate it in Hollywood. We kept it in the Church, which wasn't the way Jesus facilitated His presence.

As long as we keep God in the Church, we'll experience another Azusa Street. Don't get me wrong, Azusa Street was phenomenal, but people came to Azusa Street to have a touch from God, and then they left. They didn't take it with them! As wonderful as Azusa Street was, it didn't transform a culture, and unless people know how to function in the anointing in the business world, in Hollywood, and in Washington, it's just a wonderful time of refreshing.

God is teaching us a new paradigm. His paradigm isn't revival—it's reformation.

CHAPTER 10

TOUCHING THE NATION

If my people, who are called by my name, shall humble
themselves, and pray, and seek my face, and turn from their
wicked ways; then will I hear from heaven, and will forgive
their sin, and will heal their land.

2 Chronicles 7:14, ASV

WHEN I started Church on the Rock, my vision was for Oklahoma City.

Later, God expanded the vision to include the state, and before long we found ourselves thrust into national and international situations.

In early 2001, I developed a relationship with Dr. C. Peter Wagner, who formed the International Coalition of Apostles, of which I was a founding member. In 2002, through Jay Swallow, the Lord directed us to travel to Plymouth Rock, where we prayed over the nation during the Feast of Tabernacles. In January 2003, we met with Senator Sam Brownback in

Washington, DC, and asked for his help in a national apology to the Native Americans. In December 2003, Cindy Jacobs prophesied that Jay and I were to go to Arkansas and dislodge the "serpent" that hides there.

More and more, I found myself dealing with national issues that were similar to the ones we had been dealing with in Oklahoma. During the same time, the Lord opened doors for us to minister in Northern Ireland and Cuba. It seemed He was sending us to some of the hot spots on earth. In July 2005, with Peter Wagner and me as part of the Eagles Vision Apostolic Team and the Hamilton Group, God sent us to pray over the Federal Reserve Bank in New York City, as well as Jekyll Island in Georgia, where the Federal Reserve System was conceived. Finally, in late 2006, God directed us to form the Heartland Apostolic Prayer Network.

Again, I would feel as though I'd misled you if you read this book and came away thinking I'd done this myself. What's been accomplished would never have happened without God's blessing, of course, and the enduring work of state, regional, and national leaders. I could write an entire book on their stories alone, but the following is just a glimpse into the lives of some of those people from across the nation.

HAPN FORMER
TEXAS/OAPN REGIONAL LEADER

Pastor Tom Schlueter
Prince of Peace Church and Texas Apostolic Prayer Network
Arlington, Texas

My wife, Kay, and I have pastored Prince of Peace Church in Arlington, Texas, since 1988. We have long known that there were root issues that were causing a halt to Arlington's destiny. For instance, there is a lot of divisiveness between Dallas and Fort Worth, and Arlington is right in the middle of it. In May 2002, we took a prayer walk and circled the city, which is 44 miles around. We had 25 churches involved and about 100 intercessors who prayer-walked the city over a seven-week period. The Lord specifically directed us to bless, not curse, anything in the city.

During one part of the walk, I literally heard the sounds of women and children screaming and crying. The site where I heard the screams was where a Native American (Caddo Nation) massacre took place long before, and I began to research what happened. I knew we needed to deal with the issue, so I invited John Benefiel and Jay Swallow here to help us in 2005.

Although I live in and pastor a church in Texas, in 2006 John Benefiel asked me to become a regional leader for OAPN because he knew that spiritual issues aren't stopped by state boundary lines. In 2006, I was in Belgium with my daughter's high school mission trip when I received an email from Chuck Pierce asking if I would be the Apostolic Prayer Leader over Texas. I was set in as director of the Texas Apostolic Prayer Network in the auditorium of the state capital in Austin.

On April 21, 2007, Texas was the third state after Oklahoma and Kansas to divorce Baal. That day was San Jacinto Day, which represents our freedom from Mexico in 1836, won after the battle of the Alamo. Within the next couple of months, we experienced record rainfalls. All the lakes and rivers had risen to record levels. The aquifers were all refilled, and by midsummer in 2007 the drought monitor showed no drought in Texas.

In July and August, the hottest time of the year here, we were led by the Lord to drive the state. People thought we were crazy, but during our drive around the state, including Brownsville, Big Bend, and El Paso, the temperatures never exceeded 91 degrees, and it rained every afternoon except two. All of Texas was in stunning bloom—the purple sage and the corn crops flourished. Everything was green, even in typically desert areas. It was a tremendous sign that God had established His favor over the land.

At the end of 2007, God gave us our assignment for 2008, which was to visit the four gates of the state. During the prophetic conference at Church on the Rock in early 2008, Chuck had asked John Benefiel to commission me as an apostle, and all the leaders present (including Dutch Sheets, Jay Swallow, and Negiel Bigpond) laid hands on me and prayed.

Afterward, God granted us great favor and opened the way before us. We visited and prayed over the four gates and the rivers of Texas. In October 2008, with over 200 people helping us, we simultaneously staked all 254 counties on the same day. It took three people just to carry the stakes to the car.

The Lord made His will clear concerning Texas when He said, "If you can't work together, you can't have the state." One of our issues was the panhandle of Texas, where people had always been treated like stepchildren by the rest of the state's population. In fact, the people who live in the panhandle don't call their land Texas. They say, "We're from West Texas."

The Lord told us if we didn't help them take their land, we couldn't have our inheritance. So we've been to the panhandle on numerous occasions, including a major reconciliation event when representatives from Texas apologized to leaders of the Comanche Nation. Now the panhandle is connecting and flourishing. God is opening doors that we had no way of opening. God is opening up not just the panhandle of Texas but the panhandle of Oklahoma, along with southwest Kansas, Colorado, and New Mexico. He's causing something to prosper here that has never flourished before.

In April 2009, with leaders from numerous states, we went back to the Baal caves in Northwest Oklahoma and did a multi-state divorcement. Through worship, we established an altar to God.

God is giving us the strategy for the borders, and we'll be working with California, Arizona, New Mexico, and Mexico. Outposts of prayer in the seven major cities along the border between Mexico and the United States are being established.

In 2009, Chuck Pierce went to Tijuana and ministered at a place where there is a border marker between Mexico and the U.S. The visit was followed up by a 2,000-mile journey by other state leaders and myself. Since then, the Lord has literally lifted the "hiding" cover off the enemy, and many of the lords of the drug cartels have been captured.

We have cherished the cooperative nature of the work among those in OAPN and HAPN, and God has allowed us to assist Mississippi, Louisiana, Arkansas, Kansas, and Iowa. In the summer of 2010, we worked closely with the southeast states during the oil spill crisis.

Dutch Sheets made a comment that I've never forgotten. He said, "There are some people you'll eat lunch with, and there are some people you'll go to war with. Now is the time to go to war." When I heard that, I shifted to a war room mentality. Don't get me wrong, we have fun—but then we get serious about how to take this nation for God. It's time for God's kingdom. It's time for reformation and transformation.

As wonderful as it is to work together, we all know that unity itself won't get the job done. If what we're doing doesn't stem from our personal intimacy with God, we'll never be effective. That's the part that's private and personal and no one can do for us. But when we leave the throne room wrapped in an intimacy with God, then together we can do anything.

HAPN Former Kansas/OAPN Regional Leader

Pastors Sandy Newman and DeeAnn Ward
Gateway Prayer House and Destiny Ministries
Arkansas City, Kansas

DeeAnn and I attended a retreat with International Breakthrough Ministries, and while there we talked to an attorney about our dreams for Kansas.

The man stopped us and said, "Nothing will happen in Kansas until you deal with the land issues." We didn't know what he was talking about. We'd been in church our whole lives and had never heard anything about land issues. He continued by saying, "You need to call Jay Swallow."

While I didn't know anything about land issues, I did know that Arkansas City had been the starting point for the Cherokee Strip Land Run. I wondered if that might be a land issue. Jay was in Canada when I reached him on his cell phone, and I blurted something like, "Do you know anything about the Cherokee Strip Land Run?"

There was dead silence for a long time before Jay said, "Yes, I do."

"I'd like to host a Native American reconciliation." *Where did that come from?* I wondered.

"We've been waiting a long time for Kansas to ask for reconciliation," Jay said. "But, in our culture, the offended never approaches the offender."

I scheduled the reconciliation for August 6, 2006, and invited Jay Swallow, John Benefiel, Chuck Pierce, Barbara Wentroble, Alice Patterson, and Will Ford. Then it dawned on me that I didn't know a thing about how to handle reconciliation. We heard that Pampa, Texas, had been in drought for nine years and they were going to have a reconciliation to deal with the Adobe Walls Massacre, so we attended.

ADOBE WALLS MASSACRE

We were at the site of the massacre when Jay began to tell the story of Adobe Walls. It was 109 degrees in a land shrouded in drought—not a lick of moisture in sight. He explained that the buffalo was the Native Americans' source of food, shelter, and clothing. Their whole survival was dependent on the buffalo. Working in conjunction with the U.S. Army, a team of buffalo soldiers hunted down and killed all 200 of the buffalo. What happened next was one of those moments you remember for the rest of your life.

"The buffalo soldiers were from Kansas," Jay explained.

DeeAnn and I both fell to our knees in repentance. Afterward, we knew that repentance wasn't enough; we needed to start the process of restitution. DeeAnn remembered that she had $200 tucked away for my birthday present, so we ran to the car to get it and presented it to Jay—a dollar for each buffalo.

Driving home after that meeting, I said, "Wouldn't it be awesome if Kansas gave Jay a live buffalo?"

"Where are we going to get a buffalo?" DeeAnn asked. "How are we going to pay for it? How would we feed it? How would we transport it? What would he do with it after we gave it to him?"

I didn't have a single answer to any of those questions.

In August, three days before our scheduled reconciliation, I received an email telling me that Richard and Susan Duff, who had done a lot of research about the Native issues, were going to attend our reconciliation. For some reason, I scrolled down to the original email from the Duffs and saw that they were...buffalo ranchers.

I called Richard Duff and said, "I'd like to buy a buffalo from you to present to Jay. I'd like for you to put it in a trailer and bring it here for our reconciliation. Afterward, I'd like you to take it back to your ranch and let it roam free. Is that possible?"

"Yes," he said.

ROAMING BUFFALO

Richard went out to his herd of buffalo and asked the Lord which one to choose. Buffalos aren't anything like cows. Their heads are the biggest things you've ever seen, and they're wild. They don't just walk in and out of a trailer either. So once Richard got the buffalo in the trailer, it was going to have to stay there until it was released back on the ranch.

Once I'd set all this in motion, I realized I should check with someone and make sure I wasn't breaking protocol in some way. So I called John Benefiel and said, "We're buying Jay a buffalo."

John started laughing and said, "Do you realize that Jay's Cheyenne name is Roaming Buffalo? The roaming buffalo was always the lead buffalo. The roaming buffalo went ahead of the other buffalo to find good grassland and water. Therefore, the Native Americans would never kill the roaming buffalo. So Jay—or Roaming Buffalo—is an apostle and leader for the Native people, and that's a perfect gift. I'll tell you what, we'll buy it."

I wasn't going to give a gift that didn't cost me anything, so we compromised and each paid for half. Because Jay's Native name was Roaming Buffalo, that's what we named his buffalo. This happened so fast that no one else knew what we'd done. When I announced the gift at the meeting, John said, "Jay, don't you want to see your buffalo?" He looked around, assuming it was a little statue of a buffalo or something like that. When he understood that it was a real buffalo, Jay went outside and stepped up on the trailer. He looked at the buffalo and said, "I'll never leave you again."

Chuck was just undone over the gift and told us we had no idea of its significance. In biblical days, it was the seventh layer of animal hide that stopped the fiery darts in battle. Chuck then prophesied that because of this gift of restitution, there would soon be a terrorist attack against the United States that would be revealed and averted and that we would hear about it on the news. We gave Jay the buffalo August 6, 2006. Just days later, on

August 9, world news broke the story of a terrorist plot to detonate liquid explosives carried on board at least 10 airliners traveling from the United Kingdom to the United States and Canada. British police foiled the plot, and countless lives were spared.

THE MULTIPLICATION FACTOR

During that reconciliation, Barbara Wentroble turned to John Benefiel and said, "Restitution isn't complete until there's multiplication of the cycle of life, so Texas will buy a female buffalo." They bought the female buffalo from Richard Duff, but before it could be presented to Jay, Richard realized the buffalo was pregnant.

Soon after the calf was born, Richard suspected it might be a white buffalo, but he didn't mention the possibility until he'd tested the calf's DNA. The results were unbelievable—Jay's female buffalo had given birth to a white buffalo. I had no idea the significance of that event.

No female white buffalo had grown to maturity since 1833. The chances of a white buffalo being born were one in 10 million. However, for years, many Native American tribes had watched for the birth of a white female buffalo in the belief that it would be a sign from God of new beginnings, new hope, and prosperity.

Today, many Native Americans stream to Kansas to see the buffalo for themselves. Not only had the cycle of life been reestablished, but with it came the sign of hope that the Native Americans had been expecting for years.

We still have more work to do in Kansas, but the atmosphere over the state has changed. Oklahoma modeled covenant faithfulness and generosity to us, and that spirit of servanthood in Oklahoma has permeated our state and changed the atmosphere.

HAPN FORMER IOWA STATE LEADER

Katherine Watsey
Fire on the Altar Ministries and
Iowa Apostolic Prayer Network
Fairfield, Iowa

My family and I moved to Fairfield, Iowa, in 1995, when my children were young and I was a busy mother home-schooling my children. From the beginning, the Lord told me things that I had no frame of reference to understand at the time.

I have a seer gift, and one of the first things I noticed was that there were a lot of angels coming and going from our house, chariots in my driveway and all up and down and around the street surrounding my house. God told me there was a "gate" there and showed me Genesis 28, where Jacob had seen the angels ascending and descending. God told me that we were dealing with ancient Egyptian structures that were underground. I was visited by four angels who I knew were the "four corner angels" in Revelation 7. They began to give me instructions.

Fairfield, Iowa, is known for being the International Headquarters of Transcendental Meditation (TM). The public face of TM was a man named Maharishi. The Lord told me there is a principle that applies to both people and the land in deliverance. If you don't deal with the root issue, it will keep growing back. He explained that the Maharishi meditation movement wasn't just about the man, but that there was an ancient Egyptian root structure in our state. Back in 1995 no one else was talking about these things. We knew that the Egyptians had indeed been in Iowa because of the Word of the Lord to us. He confirmed it later with archeological evidence, which was the Davenport Steles.

The Lord revealed to me that there were five principalities over Iowa: Leviathan and four others under him. He began teaching me how to deal with them. As I would uncover an iniquitous stronghold through prayer and mapping, a principality would appear; it would come to visit me. I was amazed that they would come into my home late at night while I was praying!

Each of the five appeared in my home, one by one, as the Lord exposed their strongholds. The Lord told me He was training me in my own home! I didn't have to tell a principality to leave. Instead, I repented of ancient iniquities, thereby removing their legal right to stay. They attempted to intimidate and terrify me on each visit, but each time angels appeared and escorted them out of my home.

It's interesting to note that during this time I did not know or have any contact with anyone else dealing with these types of issues. I later learned that while we were getting to know Jezebel, which is another name for the Queen of Heaven, Peter Wagner was dealing with the same spirit and dealing with principalities. When God told me that I needed global unity in order to pull down the strongholds over my city and state and that He would then displace the principalities, I laughed and said, "Where am I supposed to get that?"

"March for Jesus," He answered. At that time, the March for Jesus was being held all over the world, and it did bring a measure of global unity among Christians. God instructed me to plan a seven-week repentance and prayer strategy leading up to the March for Jesus in Iowa, and even our city.

I did what He asked, and we dealt with ancient issues rooted underground for those seven weeks. Because there was an Egyptian root, I kept asking God for an Egyptian to help in repentance.

However, God told me to handle it myself. Years later, I found that my forefathers were Baal worshipers, so I had a legal right to stand in the gap and realized why God told me to handle it myself.

SOLAR ECLIPSE

A couple of months after the March for Jesus and dealing with the five principalities over Iowa, we had a solar eclipse. I was worshiping the Lord at home with my children on that day, and the spiritual portal/gate opened up and angels were coming through the gate that day for about four hours. The Lord greatly touched my children, who also saw the angels. God gave me a giant key that day and said, "This is the continental gateway and here is the key. You are the continental gatekeeper."

On that same day, Maharishi, the international leader for Transcendental Meditation, declared that the earth had shifted on its axis and that Fairfield, Iowa, was no longer the center of the universe. He decided they needed to get out of Fairfield. Many of the TM devotees in our city who had money began to pack up and move out of town!

The eclipse was our sign that the stronghold was falling. If that weren't enough, Earl Kapman, who had given millions of dollars to the TM movement, resigned as their financial supporter.

Another strange thing began to happen. While running around Iowa to pray and minister, I could hear the corn crying out to God in the fields. I saw that each cornfield had two angels on horseback, one riding the length and one riding the width. Later, I was to discover why.

After some of these beachhead breakthroughs, Apostle Barbara Wentroble came to Iowa and directed us to George Otis Jr. When I heard George say there were three continental gateways and that we were on one of them,

I almost passed out. I'd never heard anyone use that term except God, and the only people I'd told were my core group of intercessors and my pastor.

He confirmed that the ancient Egyptians had traveled through this land by way of water and that the Mississippi River was one of the continental gateways. I was indeed the keeper of the gate. Later, God got me apostolically aligned and ordained with Barbara Wentroble and then connected me with others like Chuck Pierce, who was the national leader for USGAPN, and I became the Iowa leader for USGAPN. Later still, I learned that Apostle John Benefiel and Apostle Jay Swallow were dealing with ancient structures in prayer.

SHAKING AND QUAKING

Although God had not released us to deal with Baal as yet, in 2006 I prophesied that when the Lord was ready to deal with Baal, there would be an earthquake in the Midwest and it would be a sign that God was getting ready to deal with Baal. I had also prophesied that Iowa would flood, not knowing the two events were connected and not knowing that the flood was related to dealing with Baal. Then, in 2007 at the Starting the Year Off Right conference in January, Dutch Sheets released a prophetic word that Baal was the strongman over America. I had just heard from the Lord one month before that it was time to start dealing with Baal.

Because we continued to do more mapping in Iowa, we found that there are ancient mounds built by the Mounds People in the northeast corner of the state, right on the Mississippi River. These sites have burial mounds as well as ceremonial mounds.

The Davenport Steles had also been discovered in Iowa. There was a huge controversy about them because they were considered a fake until Dr. Barry Fell deciphered them in 1975 and published his results in his book *America*

B.C. This was our archeological evidence that Egyptians and Phoenicians had been on our land! The (stele) rock is inscribed with three different languages on one side: Libyan, Ogam, and Egyptian Phoenician. The opposite side was written in Algonquin, which is a language of early Native Americans.

I had planned a prayer journey with Apostle Benefiel and our team to go to these sites and then a conference following on April 26, 2008. We were to go to the ancient mound sites to divorce Baal and pray, and then I was hosting a conference for Apostle Benefiel to speak. On April 18, 2008, one week before our prayer journey and conference, an earthquake struck the Midwest at Mount Carmel, Illinois (Mount Carmel is the location where Elijah confronted Baal in 1 Kings 18), close to Baale Park (Baal)—and not far from Fairfield, Illinois.

Apostle Tom Schlueter and his wife, Kay, the Apostolic Prayer Network leaders for Texas, joined us for our prayer journey and Tom was to speak at our conference. Tom had grown up in Iowa playing on the mounds, so he wanted to visit family who still lived near where the mounds were located before he joined us.

On the day of the prayer journey, we were on our way to divorce Baal at the mounds. The rains began to pour so heavily that we could not see to drive. We prayed for a break in the rain while we accomplished our mission. The roads began to flood right behind us so that we could not go back the way we came! Tom had been in the region visiting his family the day before the prayer journey, and he said there wasn't even a hint of any flooding anywhere in sight.

We divorced Baal at the mounds and at the locations where we had prayed. The flooding was so deep in Iowa that we had to cross over into Illinois and drive south to get back into Iowa to the hotel and conference location.

We divorced Baal publicly the next day at our conference as well. On that day the newspapers said "Flooding in the Quad Cities," and the whole Quad city area on the Iowa-Illinois border was flooding. The flooding began there in April, but in June we had 500-year floods in Cedar Rapids, Iowa City, Des Moines, and all around the state. Of the 99 counties in Iowa, 89 of them flooded, but with no loss of life.

Despite the rain or floods, Iowa still had the biggest bumper corn harvest ever recorded. You could see corn piled up on the ground around the grain elevators because they didn't have enough room to hold it. We continued to harvest bumper crops even with that rainfall.

It was at this time that I realized why the corn was crying out to God and the angels were riding on horses over the width and length of the cornfields. First, the corn was crying out as a sign also that God was dealing with the Baals and wanting us to be betrothed to Him. The book of Hosea speaks about God's people following the Baals and tells us that God would have us marry Him again.

Second, the angels riding on horses on the width and length of the cornfields were measuring. He desires to give us wealth (gold and silver), and He wants to provide the corn, the wine, and the oil again. Hosea 2:8 says, "For she did not know that I gave her corn, and wine, and oil, and multiplied her silver and gold, which they prepared for Baal" (KJV). Hosea 2:21-22 says, "And it shall come to pass in that day, I will hear, saith the Lord, I will hear the heavens, and they shall hear the earth; and the earth shall hear the corn, and the wine, and the oil; and they shall hear Jezreel" (KJV).

DEALING WITH ROOT ISSUES

My assignment from God is to deal with Baal on a national and international level. I serve with Apostles Mike and Cindy Jacobs in USRPN. I am the Iowa leader, I serve on the apostolic council for USRPN, and I also serve as the occult specialist nationally, writing prayer initiatives. I also serve with Apostle Benefiel in HAPN in the same capacity. I believe God connected me with Apostle Benefiel and Apostle Jay Swallow because we are all assigned to deal with Baal.

Over the years, I have learned that, to make any significant headway, we have to deal with the ancient structures in the land. Think of the ancient strongholds as a power grid that allows darkness to stay rooted in the earth. You can pray against abortion until Jesus returns, but if you haven't addressed the power grid or the iniquitous ancient Baal root structure, you'll experience no more than a temporary fix.

It doesn't matter what problem you're dealing with—be it a religion, cult, the occult, satanic worship, New Age practices, or the Masonic—they all trace back to Baal. He is the sun god who shows up in every pagan occult structure. He is the "god of a thousand faces." The names change, but the players remain the same.

In ancient times, the ruling nations would name their gods. When another nation came and conquered them, the conquering nation would change the names of the gods to their own names, but the power behind them was always the same—Baal.

The Bible refers to Baal in the plural (Baals or Baalim) because there were so many names and faces of the same entity. The Bible also tells how Daniel stood in the gap because the prince of Persia was resisting the prince of Greece. These are principalities, and we are the ones with the authority to enforce Jesus' victory and make them a footstool under His feet.

CHAPTER 11

GOD'S GOVERNMENT

For to us a Child is born, to us a Son is given; and the
government shall be upon His shoulder, and His name shall be
called Wonderful Counselor, Mighty God, Everlasting Father
[of Eternity], Prince of Peace. Of the increase of His government
and of peace there shall be no end, upon the throne of David
and over his kingdom, to establish it and to uphold it with
justice and with righteousness from the [latter] time forth, even
forevermore. The zeal of the Lord of hosts will perform this.
Isaiah 9:6-7, AMPC

A S you can see, God has convened an amazing group of men and women, and we've seen powerful results. However, as I rejoiced over the way God has ruled in our favor regarding our class action lawsuit as we divorced Baal, I realized that winning a verdict and receiving compensation are two different things.

There has been a great deal of confusion in the Church over the subject of money. Although the Scriptures warn of the love of money and attempts to get rich quick, there is a lot more that the Bible has to say on the subject. The first thing we must determine is who owns the world's wealth.

We are told in Psalm 24:1, "The earth is the Lord's, and all it contains, the world, and those who dwell in it."

Psalm 115:16 tells us, "The heavens are the Lord's heavens, but the earth has He given to the children of men" (AMPC).

The Bible also says, "The Lord has established His throne in the heavens, and His kingdom rules over all" (Ps. 103:19 AMPC).

When God cut a covenant with Abraham, He made it clear that everything on earth was for the purpose of blessing Abraham so that he could be a blessing. In Genesis 12:2-3, God says:

> And I will make of you a great nation, and I will bless you [with abundant increase of favors] and make your name famous and distinguished, and you will be a blessing [dispensing good to others]. And I will bless those who bless you [who confer prosperity or happiness upon you] and curse him who curses or uses insolent language toward you; in you will all the families and kindred of the earth be blessed [and by you they will bless themselves] (AMPC).

The Bible has a great deal to say about wealth. Proverbs 10:22 tells us, "It is the blessing of the Lord that makes rich, and He adds no sorrow to it." I looked up that word *rich* in Hebrew. It means..."rich"!

In Galatians 3:13-14, we see that through Christ, all the blessings of Abraham might come upon the Gentiles.

> Christ redeemed us from the curse of the Law, having become a curse for us—for it is written, "Cursed is everyone who hangs on

a tree"—in order that in Christ Jesus the blessing of Abraham might come to the Gentiles, so that we would receive the promise of the Spirit through faith.

The Bible goes further and makes it clear that the reason Jesus came to earth was to destroy the works of the devil:

[But] he who commits sin [who practices evildoing] is of the devil [takes his character from the evil one], for the devil has sinned (violated the divine law) from the beginning. The reason the Son of God was made manifest (visible) was to undo (destroy, loosen, and dissolve) the works the devil [has done] (1 John 3:8 AMPC).

Satan is a thief who has stolen from God's people for generations, and the Bible is very clear as to what he must do when he is caught: "But if he is found out, he must restore seven times [what he stole]; he must give the whole substance of his house [if necessary—to meet his fine]" (Prov. 6:31 AMPC).

Just in case you still have questions about whether or not God approves of Christians having wealth, read Proverbs 13:22: "A good man leaves an inheritance to his children's children, and the wealth of the sinner is stored up for the righteous." Furthermore, God said this about money: "I will give you the treasures of darkness and hidden wealth of secret places, so that you may know that it is I, the Lord, the God of Israel, who calls you by your name" (Isa. 45:3).

God promises to give believers the power to get wealth: "But you shall remember the Lord your God, for it is He who is giving you power to make wealth, that He may confirm His covenant which He swore to your fathers, as it is this day" (Deut. 8:18). God will give those He is in covenant with the power to get wealth. But He doesn't stop there. The Bible says God will take the wealth of the wicked and give it to those He loves:

> *For to the person who pleases Him God gives wisdom and knowledge and joy; but to the sinner He gives the work of gathering and heaping up, that he may give to one who pleases God. This also is vanity and a striving after the wind and a feeding on it* (Ecclesiastes 2:26 AMPC).
>
> *I will shake all the nations; and they will come with the wealth of all nations, and I will fill this house with glory," says the Lord of hosts. "The silver is Mine and the gold is Mine," declares the Lord of hosts. "The latter glory of this house will be greater than the former," says the Lord of hosts, "and in this place I will give peace," declares the Lord of hosts* (Haggai 2:7–9).
>
> *Though he heaps up silver like dust and piles up clothing like clay, he may prepare it, but the just will wear it, and the innocent will divide the silver* (Job 27:16-17 AMPC).

Based on these Scriptures, there is no question in my mind that God desires the wealth of the world to be in the hands of His Church. As I pondered the concept of winning the war over wealth, I realized we needed supernatural help. I knew it involved another legal document of some sort, but had no idea what it looked like or what it was called.

Once again, I called on Jerry Mash, who had written the Baal divorce decree. I said, "Jerry, we need to petition God, asking Him to plunder the enemy's house and transfer the wealth of the wicked into the hands of the just."

Jerry mulled it over and prayed for direction from the Lord. One night, the Lord woke him from a deep sleep and Jerry heard the words, "Writ of Assistance."

"I've been practicing law for more than 50 years," Jerry said, "and I'd run into a Writ of Assistance, at the most, six times. Most lawyers wouldn't have occasion to use a Writ of Assistance and the majority might not even be familiar with the term."

The Writ of Assistance is a written order issued by a court that instructs a law enforcement official, such as a sheriff, to perform or assist with a certain task. Historically, several types of writs have been called Writs of Assistance. Most often, it is used to enforce an order for the possession of lands and to evict someone from a property. Such a writ is called a *Writ of Restitution* or a *Writ of Possession.*

Writs of Assistance were first authorized by an act of English Parliament in 1660 and were issued by the court to help customs officials search for smuggled goods. In practice, these writs served as general search warrants that didn't expire. They allowed customs officials to search anywhere for smuggled goods without having to obtain a specific warrant.

A writ is used to enforce an order for the possession of lands to be returned to the rightful owner—and that's exactly what the divorce decree from Baal states. Here is an excerpt from the divorce decree:

> The Plaintiff renounces any and all right, claim, or interest in any possession jointly acquired with the Defendant during this Marriage, and that Plaintiff is entitled to have sole right, claim, and interest in and to all the gifts, possessions, and inheritance from Plaintiff's Father, and the Defendant is to be and forever barred from the title, control, or use of any such gifts, possessions, or inheritance.

The Lord ruled in our favor for this, but we needed the Writ of Assistance to enforce the transfer of that property to the righteous. Once again, a Writ of Assistance is a written order issued by a court that instructs a law enforcement official, such as a sheriff, to perform or assist with a certain task. In our use of a Writ of Assistance, think of the law enforcement officials as angels.

In light of this information, think about what the Bible says about angels. "Are not the angels all ministering spirits (servants) sent out in the service [of God for the *assistance*] of those who are to inherit salvation?" (Heb. 1:14 AMPC).

We are petitioning God for angelic assistance to enforce our verdict. The petition requests that God instruct the angels to bind the strongman, plunder his house, and transfer the wealth and lands to us, His people.

You'll find a copy of the Writ of Assistance in the Appendices of this book.

You can also download a copy from our website at www.hapn.us.

In this chapter, you'll hear from Rabbi Curt Landry, a Messianic Jew with a unique perspective of the authority given to the Church when the First Born joins ranks with the First Nations and First Fruits as One New Man.

OTTAWA COUNTY

County Leader: Rabbi Curt Landry
House of David, Grove, OK

Ottawa County is located in the far northeastern corner of Oklahoma, bordering Kansas and Missouri. Typically, Messianic Jews live in large cities, but the Lord sent us to Fairland, Oklahoma, where our church, House of David, sits in a pasture on 55 acres like *Little House on the Prairie*.

Many people wonder why we're here, and I believe the answer lies in an interview Corrie ten Boom gave on TBN. Corrie, a Christian who was sent to a concentration camp for helping rescue Jews during Hitler's reign, is considered among Jews to be *bat Zion*, or "a daughter of Zion." Corrie said that she was flying across the United States when she asked the pilot, "Where are we right now?" The pilot explained that they were flying over this part of Oklahoma near the borders of Kansas and Missouri. Corrie said, "There's going to be a revival that comes from here and affects all the nations of the earth."

I believe that's why we're here and also why we're a part of the Oklahoma Apostolic Prayer Network. Before you can understand our role, it would be helpful if you understood a few things about my life.

My biological father was a Catholic who fell in love with a Jewish girl, who got pregnant out of wedlock in Modesto, California in 1954. They wanted to marry, but there were so many cultural and religious differences that neither the Catholic or Jewish side would agree to the union. There was such a huge disconnect that the couple decided to have an abortion.

However, prior to the abortion, my father said, "Let's go talk to the priest on the Air Force base." The priest suggested that, rather than abort me, they could send my mother to a Catholic hospital in Los Angeles to give birth, and then put me up for adoption. I was born May 11, 1955, and did not get adopted because I was a colicky baby who cried all the time. Six months later, a Catholic man named Ray Landry and his Jewish wife, Rita, came to the orphanage. Rita came from a different culture and had no particular respect for the nun who said, "You don't want this baby because it cries all the time." Ignoring the nun, Rita picked me up and, for the first time, I stopped crying.

"We'll take this one," Rita said.

Once again, I was back in the mixed world of Jew and Gentile, because that's my call. I'm a bridge between the two worlds.

My upbringing was secular, for the most part. I went to a parochial school and to Jewish Boy Scout camp, but there was no Spirit involved in either of them. I didn't know God. I didn't read the *Torah* or the Bible. Those were foreign to me.

SAVED FROM WHAT?

After my wife, Christie, and I married, she was born again. However, the Lord told her not to preach to me, and she didn't. When I was 36, we were living in Seattle, and I was living a Jewish man's dream. I was "Employee of the Year" at my corporation, had just built a custom home, and had two BMWs parked in the garage. I'd accomplished all my goals.

One day, while my wife and daughter were out of town, I thought I was suffering from a nervous breakdown. I felt an overwhelming sense of emptiness in my life. Although I wasn't a man given to tears, I wept and wept, calling out to God and asking for forgiveness. Afterward, I called Christie and told her what had happened.

"You aren't having a nervous breakdown," she said, "you just got saved."

"Saved from what?" I asked.

The following day, I said to a friend of mine, "You've got to have this!" and I led him to the Lord.

Immediately, I began flowing in the gifts of the Spirit. Within a week, I took my daughter to a pond to feed the ducks and saw a young woman who was eight months pregnant jump out of a car in tears. I walked up to her and said, "Don't fear, I have a word from the Lord for you. You and your husband just got into an argument about insurance, and you need $352 to pay the bill." She broke down sobbing and said that was right. "I'm going to take you to my office and cut a check for $352 so that you can go home and reconcile with your husband, because this child needs both of you to raise him."

LIKE DOVES TO THEIR ROOST

Soon afterward, I started praying with a man who said, "The Scripture says that the Jewish people will return from the north like doves to their roost, and we're going to pray for 747s to fly from Seattle to Moscow and transport people back to Israel." It sounded good to me, so we prayed. Soon a man from Alaska arrived and said, "Someone told me that you're praying for airplanes to bring Jewish people out of Russia to Israel, and I want to help." The Lord used an individual to provide the funding for the first plane—it left Seattle, flew to Moscow to pick up Jewish families, and then flew them to Israel.

A few years later, in the early '90s, the man I prayed with said, "The Scripture says that they will return on ships of Tarshish, so we need to get ships." We went to a Jew and a Gentile, filled two suitcases with American money, and went to lease a ship. The ship broker was upset because we were supposed to be there two weeks earlier and now he didn't have a ship. We were in turmoil, but then the man said, "I don't have a ship here, but I do have a ship in Tarshish." The lease of that ship was a fulfillment of prophecy.

Then in 2003, Christie and I became part of a project where ministries united to send a ship, the Spirit of Grace, to Israel. On December 24, 2003, we stood in Israel when the *Spirit of Grace* docked, bringing the first large humanitarian gift from evangelicals and from my church, House of David. Scripture indicates that out of the House of David will come the Spirit of Grace (see Zech. 12:10).

Like I said, to understand the House of David, you have to understand my testimony. House of David is what we call a "One New Man" congregation.

I'm a Messianic Jew, and my co-pastor, Tim Alsbaugh, is a Gentile pastor. We co-pastor as Rabbi and Gentile and operate in what Paul described in Ephesians 2. We're a Christian church, but we celebrate the feasts. We meet on *Shabbat* every Friday night and light the candles, speaking the blessings in Hebrew. My wife and daughter lead worship, and our daughter married a Jewish believer.

My adoptive parents named me Curtis, but prior to that my birth parents named me Joseph, and that's my call. I have a Joseph anointing. God has continued to manifest His call on my life, which is to be a bridge between the Jew and Gentile, and now we're in the process of planting olive trees in the Negev.

THE IVORY COAST

One year, there were hurricanes tearing up the eastern seaboard of the United States and a prophet friend called me and said, "Curt, the path of these hurricanes is the same path the slave ships took from the Ivory Coast in Africa. I believe that if a Jewish prophet will go to the Ivory Coast and repent for the slave trade, the hurricanes will stop. Does that witness to you?"

I told him it did, but I didn't think much more about it. Two weeks later, I got a call from Dr. T.L. Osborn who said, "Curt, why don't you and Christie pray about going with me to Africa?"

"Really, where?" I asked.

"Togo," he said.

"Where's Togo?"

"It's on the Ivory Coast."

We traveled to Togo with him, and our first service was on a huge soccer field with 35,000 people. On the way, I explained to Dr. Osborn about the One New Man described in Ephesians 2:11–16:

Therefore remember that formerly you, the Gentiles in the flesh, who are called "Uncircumcision" by the so-called "Circumcision," which is performed in the flesh by human hands—remember that you were at that time separate from Christ, excluded from the commonwealth of Israel, and strangers to the covenants of promise, having no hope and without God in the world. But now in Christ Jesus you who formerly were far off have been brought near by the blood of Christ. For He Himself is our peace, who made both groups into one and broke down the barrier of the dividing wall, by abolishing in His flesh the enmity, which is the Law of commandments contained in ordinances, so that in Himself He might make the two into one new man, thus establishing peace, and might reconcile them both in one body to God through the cross, by it having put to death the enmity.

When the covenant between Jew and Gentile is restored, as discussed in Ephesians 2, and when both are reconciled to create an abiding place for God, then Ephesians 3:1–12 says it is God's intent to make the manifold wisdom of God manifest through the Church to the powers and principalities so that all the demons and sicknesses have to go:

For this reason I, Paul, the prisoner of Christ Jesus for the sake of you Gentiles—if indeed you have heard of the stewardship of God's grace which was given to me for you; that by revelation there was made known to me the mystery, as I wrote before in brief. By referring to this, when you read you can understand my insight into the mystery of Christ, which in other generations was not made known to the sons of men, as it has now been revealed to His holy apostles and prophets in the Spirit; to be specific, that the Gentiles are fellow heirs and fellow members of the body, and fellow partakers of the promise in Christ Jesus through the gospel, of which I was made a minister, according to the gift of God's grace which was given to me according to the working of His power. To me, the very least of all saints, this grace was given, to preach to the Gentiles the unfathomable riches of Christ, and to bring to light what is the administration of the mystery which for ages has been hidden in God who created all things; so that the manifold wisdom of God might now be made known through the church to the rulers and the authorities in the heavenly places. This was in accordance with the eternal purpose which He carried out in Christ Jesus our Lord, in whom we have boldness and confident access through faith in Him.

Dr. Osborn said, "I like that! Let's see if it works." That first night Dr. Osborn said to his team, "I want to do something different. I'm going to come in late. Let the Rabbi start the service."

THE POWER OF REPENTANCE

I started the service before that huge group with a translator, and when I told them who I was, the crowd began screaming because they associated me as a Jew—as Jesus' brother. The shouting was so loud that it scared me. Finally, I told them that we Jews needed to repent because our money in the U.S. helped fund their slavery. I knelt down and cried out to God to forgive us and the people began to travail.

Afterward, I spoke Jewish blessings over them and I could see waves of the power of God rippling through the crowd.

The whole thing only took 10 minutes, but I was exhausted. It drained everything out of me. As soon as I finished, Dr. Osborn arrived. He had no idea what had just happened. He spoke for five minutes, telling them about God's love.

All of a sudden, to the left of the platform, we heard screaming. Dr. Osborn had them bring the screaming woman onstage. She said she had a spinal injury after the birth of her second child and had gone blind. She had four or five other children, but had never seen them. During the service, she regained her sight. Dr. Osborn asked her son to come forward. A beautiful young man, he looked his mother in the face. She showed no emotion, so the interpreter said, "This is your son." She still showed no emotion. Then she raised her hands and felt his face. That's when she recognized him and began to wail, because she could see him for the first time.

Then people started coming out of wheelchairs.

Dr. Osborn's grandson, Tommy O'Dell, said that it was the first time in 60 years that miracles had hit before Dr. Osborn could pray.

But that wasn't all that happened. The hurricanes stopped. Weather forecasters had said that that was going to be the worst year ever for hurricanes, and that their names would run through the whole alphabet. But they absolutely stopped, and there wasn't another hurricane for a full year.

TWO RIVERS

When Dr. Negiel Bigpond invited me to speak at Two Rivers, I taught on 2 Chronicles 7:13–15:

> *If I shut up the heavens so that there is no rain, or if I command the locust to devour the land, or if I send pestilence among*

My people, and My people who are called by My name humble themselves and pray and seek My face and turn from their wicked ways, then I will hear from heaven, will forgive their sin and will heal their land. Now My eyes will be open and My ears attentive to the prayer offered in this place.

According to covenant, that word was to the Jew first, and I realized that if we repented as a three-strand cord—the Jew first, First Nations second, and Gentile third—in agreement that we've all sinned, the Lord would not only sanctify the land but He would also shake the earth.

That meeting was the first time I ever did Jewish repentance. I repented first, then Dr. Bigpond repented on behalf of the First Nation people, and Tim Alsbaugh repented on behalf of the Gentiles. We fell into incredible travail of spirit and wept for hours, but the travail led to great triumph. That's when I realized that the combination of First Born, First Nations, and First Fruits (Gentiles) was powerful stuff.

Since then, every time we hold a solemn assembly or a feast, we always ask Dr. Bigpond to join us. He adopted us into the Euchee Tribe, and they anointed me as "Golden Eagle" because my anointing is to bring justice, particularly in the area of finance.

FEASTS AND FINANCES

Most Christians have misunderstood Malachi 3:8 because they don't read it from a Jewish mindset. That Scripture says, "Will a man rob God? Yet you are robbing Me! But you say, 'How have we robbed You?' In tithes and offerings."

Most of us have the tithe down, but we've misunderstood offerings. In Torah, your tithe is to the Lord, but it's your offerings that release finances.

The Lord had a specific calendar for offerings. Special offerings were brought to the Lord at the feasts of Passover, Pentecost, and Tabernacles.

The Lord gave me a word that I released at one of our OAPN meetings for something that had never been done before. The Lord said that we should come together as First Born, First Nations, and First Fruits on these three feasts and take up a special offering to the Lord. The Lord also instructed us to not just divorce Baal but to remarry the Lord.

Apostle John Benefiel bore witness to the word and agreed to do that. The next feast was the Feast of Tabernacles, so on October 3, 2009, we held a corporate meeting of OAPN at Church on the Rock in Oklahoma City. The church was decorated for the Feast of Tabernacles and for a Jewish wedding, complete with a *chuppah*. Once again, we divorced Baal, but this time we immediately held a Jewish wedding ceremony to remarry the Lord. I officiated the ceremony, and afterward, as everyone passed through the chuppah, Apostle John, Apostle Jay Swallow, and I served them communion elements. We took communion and took up an offering to be distributed as the Lord directed.

I believe that as we worship together as First Born, First Nations, and First Fruits on God's calendar of feasts at Passover, Pentecost, and Tabernacles, there will be a release of finances and of God's glory. I believe my role has been to bring the Key of David to the Oklahoma Apostolic Prayer Network.

THIRD DAY FINANCES

Part of the reason it's important to have these feasts is that what I call the "Third Day finances" are being released—it's the wealth of the wicked that has been stored up for the righteous. And the reason we have to remarry the Lord is that this money does not come through works but through inheritance.

When my father died, I received my inheritance. His will didn't say, "Curtis has to do 400 push-ups and run around the block." It involved no works; I received the inheritance because of my relationship to my father. The same is true with the Church. As we divorce Baal and remarry the Lord, we are in position to receive what the Lord has stored up for us. But He's looking for those who have been through the process and can be trusted. It's difficult for God to trust financially stressed prophets because of their strong personal need. But there is less temptation where there is no need—and that's what I believe the latter rain prophet will experience.

When you call a sacred assembly, the enemy becomes fighting mad, and the Bible says that trials and tribulations come immediately because of the Word. That's why it's important to look at things in long segments of time—there's no shortcut to this kind of work.

THE SPIRIT OF ELIJAH

Malachi 4 says it is the spirit of Elijah that is the spirit of revelation, and that's what turns the hearts of the fathers to the sons and the hearts of the sons to the fathers. That's a big component of OAPN because Oklahoma is a servant state, and one of the things it serves is revelation. When prophets like Chuck Pierce or Cindy Jacobs come here, they are blessed in return, because the altar in Oklahoma is an altar of revelation to help us see.

It makes sense that God would use Oklahoma to restore covenant, but covenant restoration from First Fruits to First Nations to First Born creates a spiritual covenant with God that goes all the way back to Jerusalem.

I believe that the OAPN is a model for networks not just in this country, but for other countries as well, because when the pattern is right the glory will fall. And, I believe what's coming next is a wave of glory. We've had revelation. We've had anointing. But it will be the glory that ushers in the latter rain that will attract both the Red Man and the Jew, because their spiritual DNA is attracted to the real move of God, and they won't be afraid if it's not "churchy."

The role the United States has played in saying, "Divide Jerusalem for peace," must be broken. And it will be broken by a team of believing Jews, First Nations, and First Fruits. I've known for years that the Jews and Gentiles will stand on the shoulders of the First Nations like Aaron and Hur. The First Nations will be the ones to speak to the land and tell that spirit, "Leave Zion alone!" Dr. Negiel Bigpond knew it was going to happen, and I knew it was going to happen.

In the spring of 2010, the Lord released the two of us to go with Apostle John Benefiel, and my wife, Christie, went representing women.

Flying into Israel in May of 2010, Dr. Negiel Bigpond, Apostle John Benefiel, my wife, Christie, and I knew that we were on a specific assignment from God. At the time, Israel was on high alert and preparing for the possibility of war. Tensions were stretched like a high wire as we asked for government approval to travel to the tops of five key mountains in Israel to release what God desired to be released. This was the furthest thing from a tourist trip. We were restoring the ancient covenant of Abraham, and the rocks of Israel would witness our decrees.

Years ago, when we took our places in OAPN and HAPN, we had no idea that one day God would give us a role in that restoration. Back then, we didn't recognize the power and authority in the rocks. In Joshua 24:27, Joshua told the children of Israel that the stone (rock) would be a witness against them:

Joshua said to all the people, "Behold, this stone shall be for a witness against us, for it has heard all the words of the Lord which He spoke to us; thus it shall be for a witness against you, so that you do not deny your God."

Everything we've decreed at different gates has been recorded in the rocks. For example, while Sandy Newman made decrees in Kansas, Jay Swallow made decrees at Plymouth Rock and Argentina, John Benefiel made decrees in Maine, New York City, and Washington, DC, and I made them in New Zealand and the Ukraine. Gates that had been shut for generations were opened. After completing our assignments, our threefold-cord returned back together into collective unity and with increased authority.

Without having taken those steps, we would never have had the authority to speak to the most important and high gates in the world—the spiritual gates in Israel. Had we never dealt with the Washita Massacre, the Baal caves, and all the strongholds in our own backyard, we wouldn't have had the authority to deal with them in Israel. From each of our completed assignments, we carry all those rewards and the collective anointing from every victory.

The first thing on our agenda was to honor and restore covenant with the wife and daughter of Dr. Joseph Ginat, the man God had used to forge a connection between OAPN, HAPN, and Israel. Next, we met with Tom Hess, the Apostle of Prayer in Israel since 1987, whose ministry sits atop the Mount of Olives. A citizen of Israel, Tom blessed us to walk his land. He also became our HAPN representative in Israel.

Finally, we met one of Israel's great heroes, Rabbi Yisreal Meir Lau. Raised in Poland, Lau was only seven years old when he was sent to a Nazi concentration camp. Most of his family was murdered—including his father, who was the 37th rabbi in the Lau family. Rabbi Lau was the youngest survivor of

Buchenwald and later became the Chief Rabbi of Israel. Rabbi Lau blessed John, Negiel, Christie, and me to release a blessing on the land.

We own an olive grove near the Sea of Galilee. Using anointing oil from those trees, we anointed one another. There among the olive trees, we received the commission of God to restore the anointing of the Ancient of Days.

MOUNT HERMON

The first mountain we approached was Mount Hermon, which is located in the Golan Heights. Whenever Syria or Lebanon enters into peace talks with Israel, they ask to be given the Golan Heights first, even before they talk. Every nation understands the importance of gathering at the high places, and they want whatever the rocks have recorded.

The fact that John, Negiel, Christie, and I were there in unity made Psalm 133:1–3 come alive to us. God said that brothers dwelling in unity are like the dew of Mount Hermon:

> *Behold, how good and how pleasant it is for brothers to dwell together in unity! It is like the precious oil upon the head, coming down upon the beard, even Aaron's beard, coming down upon the edge of his robes. It is like the dew of Hermon coming down upon the mountains of Zion; for there the Lord commanded the blessing—life forever.*

We left 80-degree weather and drove up the mountain to 7,000 feet, where the temperature was below 30 degrees. You must have the highest security clearance to enter this place, especially during preparations for war.

When an American pastor, a Native American, a Messianic Rabbi, and a woman showed up in a minivan asking to go up to the most hostile place on earth, the commander assumed it was a test. He finally called Tel Aviv and learned that we'd been given clearance.

"Why are you here?" the commander asked.

"Just to make a decree, pray, and bless Israel," I explained.

"What's the decree?"

"We want you to agree with us that God will restore all the covenants of Abraham over the land and borders, providing protection and provision according to Torah."

He grabbed my hand in agreement as we prayed.

On top of Mount Hermon, you're so close to Syria that you can be seen from that country without binoculars. What happened was like something out of a Cecil B. DeMille movie. Before we made any decrees, a gray cloud rolled up the mountain and engulfed us. No one could see us from Syria, not even a sniper.

There, hidden and baptized in a cloud and saturated with moisture from the dew of heaven, we divorced Baal. We restored the covenant of Abraham on Mount Hermon and spoke to the rock, restoring everything God had said to Abraham, even those things that might not have been recorded. From that holy mountain, we released life and blew the shofar.

THE GATES OF HELL

After Mount Hermon, we went to Caesarea Philippi to the mountain where Jesus declared that the gates of hell would not prevail against the Church (see Matt. 16:17-18). When Jesus spoke those words, He stood at the largest temple to Baal in the world. I'd been there several times, but until then I'd never felt as though we had the authority to divorce Baal at that location.

"Hundreds of birds live in that cave," I explained. "If this is really the Lord, it will vomit out all the birds."

Halfway through the divorcement of Baal, it looked like a scene from Alfred Hitchcock's movie *The Birds*. John never missed a beat as hundreds of birds swooped out of that cave as though escaping hell. Negiel raised an eyebrow and we continued through the divorce. Afterward, we declared the Writ of Assistance, which I believe is the key to the transfer of wealth.

Our next stop was Beit Hean, which is the city where Saul and his sons were hung upside down. It wasn't God's will for Israel to have a king back in the days of Samuel. Even today, the curse of Saul is on all religious entities operating in dead works. Our primary purpose was to forgive the House of Saul. Bethel is where Jacob's ladder descended from heaven (see Gen. 28:12). It's located in the middle of the West Bank in the heartland of Israel. We went to the top of a water tower where we could see Mount Hermon, Hebron, Judea, Jordan, and all the way to the Mediterranean Sea. This was where God told Abraham that He would give him all the land he could see. We divorced Baal and made our decrees.

DAVID'S MANTLE

When I told my travel agent that I needed a bulletproof vehicle so we could go to Mount Hebron, he refused to get me one. Only when I explained that we would go in a taxi if necessary did he arrange for the bulletproof vehicle. We drove into the most violent area of Israel so that we could go to Abraham's tomb (see Gen. 23:9).

In addition, David reigned as king in Hebron for seven years because the rest of Israel chose Saul's descendant, rather than God's anointed, as king. We had to grab David's mantle, which had been trapped there by that choice.

This was also where David cut the corner, or, in Hebrew, the *tzizit*, from Saul's robe. The knots are tied to represent all the names and attributes of God and His authority. In essence, by cutting that part of the robe David said, "This is the authority that was given to me. If I had been after your authority, I would have killed you."

On Mount Hebron, we forgave the House of Saul, divorced Baal, read the Writ of Assistance, and released the wealth of David.

Back in the car, we headed to Mount Zion, to the literal city of David. Located east of Jerusalem and south of the Jewish quarter, Mount Zion is where David and his men went up the water course to take the city. This is another very dangerous and heated Palestinian and Arab area. We'd met with the Knesset that morning and were still wearing our best suits. There was no way we could blend in. We looked like walking wingtips.

Part of our purpose was to release the mantle of David at the city of David. It was late afternoon, and although you have to buy tickets to get into the area, they were about to close for the day and weren't selling tickets. I jumped out of the car and said, "I have VIPs here. Would you let us in for a little while?"

They waved us through! Standing at the highest point, we divorced Baal and released David's mantle. Then we blew the shofar. It was a powerful moment. The Lord said, "You came here to restore honor. I'm releasing it to kings and priests. I will clothe you with royal robes." We finished our decrees on the top of Mount Zion.

MOUNT SHECHEM

We ran out of time and didn't make it to the fifth mountain, Mount Shechem. However, at breakfast, we saw Jane Hanson Hoyt from Aglow International, and she asked what we were doing in Israel. I explained that we were restoring the ancient covenant of Abraham and shared about the mountains we'd visited. Jane was excited because the purpose of their trip was quite similar, as was evident in the name of their tour: Recalling the Ancient Promises.

We asked Jane if she and her group would go to the fifth mountain and restore it for us and release the blessing of life. They agreed to do so, which meant that all five mountains were covered.

Before leaving Israel, we met with the Deputy of Foreign Ministry, who is responsible for communicating to the world from Israel. I spoke a prophetic word in which God said that situations would erupt shortly where it would not be practical for Israel to defend itself against the media war. The Lord said that their best allies were Christians who would tell the truth through the media. The next day, the Flotilla Debacle erupted and Israel was being crucified in the media.[1] When we returned to the U.S., I was on *Daystar* with Marcus and Joni Lamb, and we communicated the truth, which gave us credibility with Israel.

On September 28, 2010, I stepped into Church on the Rock to speak at the Feast of Tabernacles meeting. I sensed a huge shift in anointing since we'd first begun. Authority flows from honor. Individual honor comes from completed assignments. Therefore, HAPN was experiencing a higher level of authority.

During that service, I stood under the chuppah with a delegation of First Fruits, First Nations, and myself representing the First Born. For years, I'd dreamed of a day when those three groups would come together as one new man and celebrate the feasts of the Lord. I felt overwhelmed by the experience, and I believe that a shift in the earth took place that night. God is pouring down not just physical rain, but spiritual rain on the nations.

CHAPTER 12

UNMASKING IDOLATRY

Lord, they have killed thy prophets, and digged down thine altars; and I am left alone, and they seek my life. But what saith the answer of God unto him? I have reserved to myself seven thousand men, who have not bowed the knee to the image of Baal. Even so then at this present time also there is a remnant according to the election of grace.

Romans 11:3–5, KJV

BAAL is called the "god with a thousand faces," and trying to pull back the veil of deception and discover the truth about this principality is a lot like opening an unending series of nesting boxes. Each time you open one, a new one appears. However, for clarification purposes, the primary thing you need to understand about Baal is that he is assigned to hold back the promises of God.

His strategy can be traced all the way back to the first recorded relationship between God and man in the Garden of Eden. God's promise to man was a life in the lap of luxury in the "Garden of God." God walked and talked with Adam in the cool of the day and met all his needs in an earthly paradise.

He gave Adam dominion over the earth and everything in it. It was a sweet deal, and the only stipulation was that Adam not eat the fruit of one particular tree.

We all know the story of satan's interference. What we haven't realized, though, is that there was a two-pronged attack against man. The first assignment was to stop the promises of God, something that could be accomplished only through sin and disobedience. Satan's second goal was more subtle. While it's true that the devil doesn't want men and women to enter eternity in heaven, the real issue in the Garden of Eden was that he wanted control of the earth and its wealth.

Those two things are still his ultimate goals today—to stop the promises of God and to control the earth and its wealth. Baal is the principality in charge of those assignments.

THE LORD OF WEALTH

Baal-hamon, one of Baal's names, means "the lord of wealth or abundance." Chuck Pierce believes, and I agree, that this is the principality warring against the great transfer of wealth to the Church. You must war against this spirit to see your inheritance released. Claim Jeremiah 51:44. (The word *Bel* in this scripture refers to "Baal.")

> *And I will punish and execute judgment upon Bel [the god] in Babylon and take out of his mouth what he has swallowed up [the sacred vessels and the people of Judah and elsewhere who were taken captive]. The nations will not flow any more to him. Yes, the wall of Babylon has fallen!* (AMPC)

"Yes, Apostle John," you might say, "but I've never worshiped Baal."

While we never meant to worship Baal, you'll see that idolatry is being unmasked in this nation, and we, as Christians, are the hands and feet of Jesus on the earth who are called to deal with it. This is a subject God takes very seriously, as we see in 1 Corinthians 10:19–21:

> *What do I mean then? That a thing sacrificed to idols is anything, or that an idol is anything? No, but I say that the things which the Gentiles sacrifice, they sacrifice to demons and not to God; and I do not want you to become sharers in demons. You cannot drink the cup of the Lord and the cup of demons; you cannot partake of the table of the Lord and the table of demons.*

Further, the words spoken by God and recorded in Exodus 20:3–6 are as true for us today as they were when Moses brought Israel out of Egypt. If we want to deliver our nation out of bondage, we must take a hard look at idolatry in our own backyard:

> *You shall have no other gods before Me. You shall not make for yourself an idol, or any likeness of what is in heaven above or on the earth beneath or in the water under the earth. You shall not worship them or serve them; for I, the Lord your God, am a jealous God, visiting the iniquity of the fathers on the children, on the third and the fourth generations of those who hate Me, but showing lovingkindness to thousands, to those who love Me and keep My commandments.*

THE VIOLENT TAKE IT BY FORCE

It's interesting to note that God instructed Jeremiah to pluck up, break down, destroy, and overthrow the opposing kingdoms. God was fed up with Baal:

> *Then the Lord stretched out His hand and touched my mouth, and the Lord said to me, "Behold, I have put My words in your mouth. See, I have appointed you this day over the nations and over the kingdoms, to pluck up and to break down, to destroy and to overthrow, to build and to plant"* (Jeremiah 1:9-10).

Further, in Matthew 11:12 we read, "And from the days of John the Baptist until now the kingdom of heaven suffereth violence, and the violent take it by force" (KJV).

Jesus came to destroy the works of the devil, and He has never signed a truce with satan. Jesus also said the first sign of a believer is that he or she will cast out demons (see Mark 16:17). So, we can't address the moral and spiritual failing of our nation without first addressing and dealing with false worship.

The kingdom of heaven has been suffering violence, but the Church in recent history has been too weak and divided to take it with violence by force. That just isn't a type of warfare modern Christians identify with, and we've been shadowboxing an enemy who morphed into something else each time we tried to strike a blow. That's why it's important that we unveil the truth about Baal and recognize the ways he manifests in our society.

A FEW OF THE FACES OF BAAL

Baal is a hermaphrodite god. By that, I mean he is as much a male entity as a female one. When we say Baal, we're actually referring to Baal in all his male forms, the Queen of Heaven in all of her female forms, and Leviathan. The purpose of all the faces of Baal is to attempt to confuse us into thinking we have to find and fight them all. That's not the case. We're after the ruler of the demons, which is Baal (see Matt. 12:24). Once we deal with the root, we will have dealt a blow to all of them.

Satan attempts to counterfeit the Trinity with his unholy trio made up of Baal, which represents false authority and government; Jezebel, who represents the Queen of Heaven and false worship; and Leviathan, who represents a false anointing through pride and sorcery. Here is a depiction of the unholy trio.[1]

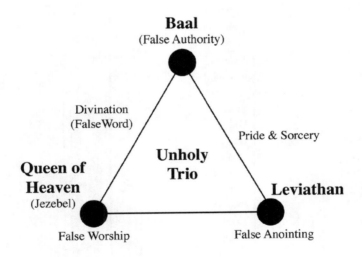

While it would be impossible to name every spirit that masquerades as part of this evil trio, the following chart will give you an idea of some of their identities.

THE BAAL PRINCIPALITY

(god of 1,000 faces)

Baal	Queen of Heaven	Leviathan
Sun god	Moon & Sun goddess	Neptune
Sol Invictus	Mother Earth (Gaia)	Poseidon
Bel	Mother of Harlots	Tiamet
Belial	Mother of God (and	King of children of Pride
HuBaal	child)	Python (Divination)
Hanuman	The Great Mother	Dragon
Nimrod	Asherah	Serpent
Apollo	Ashtaroth	
Zeus	Artemis	
Marduk	Aphrodite	
Ahura-Mazda	Juno	
Osiris	Lilith	
Tammuz	Minerva	
Dagon	Columbia	
Prometheus	Nike	
Jupiter	Astarte	
Mithra	Jezebel	
Ra	Athena	
Lucetius	Beltis	
Dyaus	Diana	
Dionysus	Isis (Horus)	
Hermes	Anahita	
Baphomet	Inanna	
Adonis	Ishtar	
Pan	Mithra	
Hades	Tanat	
Eros	Cybele	
Uranus	Mylitta	
Assur	Hathor	
Merodach	Kali	
Ninus	Semiramis	
Shamas	Andraste	
Zeus-Belus	Amaterasu Omikami	

Notice that the first entity listed under Baal is the sun god. Further down the list you'll see Nimrod. Nimrod was mentioned in the Bible (see Gen. 10:8). An extremely evil man, Nimrod became the first manifestation of Baal in the flesh. Nimrod and his wife are the ones who built the tower of Babel. After Nimrod's death, his wife claimed he ascended to the heavens where he reigned as god in the sun. Thus began the worship of the sun. There have been various forms of sun worship in every society. An example of the worship of the sun god in our society is the Native American Sun Dance.

Statue of Prometheus at Rockefeller Center

You'll also notice *Prometheus* as one of the faces of Baal. The most prominent statue of Prometheus is at the Rockefeller Center in New York City, where it is seen by viewers of NBC's Today show. The Rockefeller Plaza also hosts the Radio City Music Hall and the lighting of the Christmas tree. In addition to Prometheus and Atlas, Rockefeller Plaza features over 100 major sculptures, most of which represent idols. This was no accident; Rockefeller knew what he was doing when he gave them tribute.

Mithra

Another face of Baal is *Mithra*, the Roman sun god. You may be shocked to know that for centuries before Constantine legalized Christianity, the pagan world celebrated December 25, which is around the time of the winter solstice, in honor of Mithra's birth. When Constantine legalized Christianity, he outlawed almost anything Jewish, like Passover. Instead, he attempted to Christianize the pagan holidays. Thus, we celebrate Christmas every year on the day honoring the birth of the Roman sun god.

Do you see how idolatry has been woven into our culture without our being aware of it? Although Constantine's legalization of Christianity stopped the persecution and torture of Christians, it also captured the Church into the Baal structure.

QUEEN OF HEAVEN

The Queen of Heaven is the female counterpart of Baal. She represents all forms of moon or sun goddesses. She is the mother of harlots discussed in Revelation 17 and 18:

And he carried me away in the Spirit into a wilderness; and I saw a woman sitting on a scarlet beast, full of blasphemous names, having seven heads and ten horns. The woman was clothed in purple and scarlet, and adorned with gold and precious stones and pearls, having in her hand a gold cup full of abominations and of the unclean things of her immorality, and on her forehead a name was written, a mystery, "BABYLON THE GREAT, THE MOTHER OF HARLOTS AND OF THE ABOMINATIONS OF THE EARTH" (Revelation 17:3–5).

I heard another voice from heaven, saying, "Come out of her, my people, so that you will not participate in her sins and receive of her plagues; for her sins have piled up as high as heaven, and God has remembered her iniquities. Pay her back even as she has paid, and give back to her double according to her deeds; in the cup which she has mixed, mix twice as much for her. To the degree that she glorified herself and lived sensuously, to the same degree give her torment and mourning; for she says in her heart, 'I sit as a queen and I am not a widow, and will never see mourning'" (Revelation 18:4–7).

One of the faces of the Queen of Heaven is *Minerva*. Minerva is represented on the seal of California, and also on top of the capitol building of Maine. These are just two out of hundreds of examples I could give of idols represented in key locations in this nation.

Ishtar

Another face of the Queen of Heaven is *Ishtar*. Ishtar is the root word from which we get the word "Easter." Have you ever wondered why, when

Jesus was resurrected on Passover, Christians celebrate that event on Sunday with eggs and bunnies? It's another example of mixing Christianity with idolatry.

Ishtar is a demonic entity, one of the manifestations of the Queen of Heaven. The eggs and bunnies are a pagan practice symbolizing the goddess of fertility. How do you think God feels about the Resurrection of Christ being intermingled with worship to Ishtar, the Queen of Heaven? It's idolatry.

God has not changed His mind about what He spoke to Moses when He said, "You shall have no other gods before Me."

In Iraq during the 1930s, an ancient statue of Baal was unearthed. Two stories tall, the idol had the face of a man who wore a crown, the body of a bull (Baal), and wings. This idol wasn't a reproduction. It is an actual idol that was worshiped for countless years. It was shipped to the United States, where it stands in a prominent position in the Oriental Museum at the University of Chicago.

We traveled to Chicago and divorced Baal in front of this idol.

Europa

You just read in Revelation 17 that the Queen of Heaven, called the "harlot," was represented riding the back of a beast, which is Baal. Some of the depictions of the Queen of Heaven on the back of Baal represent her bare-breasted; others do not. It's interesting to note that a woman riding on the back of a bull is the official symbol for Europe. Its symbol, called *Europa*, is where Europe got its name. Below is a photo taken of the statue "Abduction of Europa," located in front of the EU Parliament Building in Strasbourg, France.

Below is a photo of the Euro, the official coin in Europe. Notice that it depicts a bare-breasted woman riding on the back of a bull. We must realize that idolatry is alive and well. The demonic entities that created so much trouble for Israel didn't die. They are still deceiving men into idolatry today.

If there is any question in your mind about how much God hates idolatry, read what He said to the prophet Jeremiah:

> As for you, **do not pray for this people**, and do not lift up cry or prayer for them, and do not intercede with Me; for **I do not hear you**. Do you not see what they are doing in the cities of Judah and in the streets of Jerusalem? The children gather wood, and the fathers kindle the fire, and the women knead dough to make cakes for the queen of heaven; and they pour out drink offerings to other gods in order to spite Me (Jeremiah 7:16–18).

God hated the sin of idolatry so much that he forbade Jeremiah from praying for the people who offered cakes for the Queen of Heaven. He still despises idolatry today.

BAAL TIMELINE

Baal worship began in Babylon with Nimrod and Semiramis, and over time evolved to include Marduk and Astarte, and finally Bel and Ishtar. The Egyptian culture named Baal *Osiris*, and the Queen of Heaven they named *Isis*. The Greeks named Baal *Zeus,* and the Queen of Heaven *Artemis* or *Diana*. Diana was worshiped in Ephesus. The Romans called Baal *Jupiter*, and the Queen of Heaven *Juno*.

Juno is also called *Libertas*, which is also the spirit of liberty. Called the *Freedom Goddess*, she is depicted by the Statue of Liberty. This statue, supposedly representing freedom, was a gift from the Freemasons of France. Today, that idol represents our nation. *Lady Liberty* appeared on our early coins.

Another term for Libertas is *Columbia*. Columbia is also depicted by a woman holding a torch. Columbia Pictures, an American film company, is part of the Columbia TriStar Motion Picture Group, which is owned by Sony Pictures Entertainment.

Dr. Timothy Dwight, president of Yale University, penned the words of this song in 1777: "Columbia, Columbia, to glory arise / The queen of the world and the child of the skies."

Columbia Atop U.S. Capitol

The statue on top of our nation's capital is called the "Statue of Freedom." It is actually a statue of Columbia—the Queen of Heaven. That's why our capital is named the *District of Columbia*. Is it any wonder we elect excellent people into office and they change when they go to Washington, D.C.? Every time we call our capital "the District of Columbia," we are invoking the name of the Queen of Heaven over it.

In December 2009, the Lord directed us to take one leader from each state to the capital to pray and divorce Baal. In March 2010, God directed us to go back with five leaders from each state. On Monday night of that trip, I taught on Baal and we corporately divorced him, remarried the Lord, and pronounced the Writ of Assistance.

The next day, we sent out 12 teams to a total of 38 locations to do the same. A team of 49 people prayed at the Washington National Cathedral, Embassy Row, the Kennedy Center, DuPont Circle, and the Potomac River. A team of 29 prayed at the Supreme Court and the Library of Congress. A team of 39 prayed at the Ronald Regan Building, the International Trade Center, the Internal Revenue Service, and the Department of Commerce. A team of 44 prayed at the National Archives, the Department of Justice, the FBI Building, and the Federal Trade Commission.

A team of 15 prayed at the House Chambers and offices, the Washington, D.C. mayor's office and Council chambers. A team of 16 prayed over the Senate Chambers and their offices. A team of 15 prayed outside the White House, at the Treasury, and at the Old Executive Building. A team of 15 prayed at the Press Club, ACLU, National Educational Association, Center for Democracy and Technology, Government Accountability Office, and the Department of Education. A team of five prayed at the State Department and the Pentagon. The last team prayed at the Federal Reserve, the World Bank, International Monetary Fund, the U.S. Court of Appeals, the Tri-Lateral Commission, and the Council on Foreign Relations.

We had no idea what effect those prayers would have, but I felt certain that as Baal's hold on the government was shaken, it would create a political earthquake that would shift the power.

We took a written petition before the Court of Heaven to get a judgment against Baal and for the saints. It's interesting to note that Daniel 7 is a description of a courtroom:

I beheld till the thrones were cast down and the Ancient of days did sit (Daniel 7:9 KJV).

I saw in the night visions, and, behold, one like the Son of man came with the clouds of heaven, and came to the Ancient of days, and they brought him near before him. And there was given him dominion, and glory, and a kingdom, that all people, nations, and languages, should serve him: his dominion is an everlasting dominion, which shall not pass away, and his kingdom that which shall not be destroyed (Daniel 7:13-14 KJV).

I beheld, and the same horn made war with the saints, and prevailed against them; until the Ancient of days came, **and judgment was given to the saints of the most High** (Daniel 7:21-22 KJV).

And he shall speak great words against the most High, and shall wear out the saints of the most High, and **think to change times and laws** (Daniel 7:25 KJV).

Constantine changed the times and laws when he Christianized the existing pagan holidays. Instead of the Church keeping God's times and laws, we celebrate Christmas and Easter, both of which are occult holidays never celebrated in Scripture. Just as the winter solstice, the summer solstice, the spring and fall equinoxes, Halloween and May Day, Christmas and Easter were pagan holidays.

The good news is that in Daniel 7:22 we are told, "The Ancient of days came, and judgment was given to the saints of the most High; and the time came that the saints possessed the kingdom" (KJV).

That's exactly what the Baal Divorce Decree and the Writ of Assistance are—legal documents presented to the Court of Heaven, asking for a judgment in favor of the saints. One of our leaders pointed out to me that, to our knowledge, this has never been done before. Of course, there have been many written prayers of petition, but none designed to pull down Baal's stronghold and take back God's kingdom.

"I guess you get a lot of attacks, don't you?" a minister once asked me.

"Well, no, not really," I answered, taken aback for a moment. "I've got a lot of wonderful intercessors, but I don't expect attacks. I confess God's protection and practice what I preach."

Why should we feel beat up all the time? Why should we win a few and lose a few? Besides, we're not rushing out on our own to try to deal with Baal. This is a unified, class-action lawsuit before God's court.

A judge cannot unilaterally render a verdict of judgment in your favor unless you bring your case before him. Some activist judges have done it illegally, but it can't happen legally unless you bring your case.

If you're going to bring your case before the court, you have to do it the way the court and the judge say to do it. You have to do it in an orderly manner. You have to approach the bench in the right way. You have to file your case. I don't know anyone who's ever done anything quite like this. Yet we scored judgment against the ruler of the demons, which the Bible says is Baal, and so this is a fulfillment of Daniel 7.

While we were there, we renamed the city *Washington, the District of Christ!*

"How can you do that?" someone asked.

We are God's *ecclesia*, or governmental authority on earth. Until the Church uses her authority to change things, they won't change in the natural. The government of God has to do it first. In the spirit realm, we have changed the name of the nation's capital to *Washington, District of Christ.* Sometime in the future, before or after the return of Christ, the name will be changed in the natural because we used our authority to change it now.

SEXUAL PERVERSION

Baal is the principality behind pornography and every kind of sexual sin. The Bible is explicit in describing Baal's temples: The people offered male shrine prostitutes for Baal and female shrine prostitutes for Baal's female counterpart, *Asherah.*

Sex acts were performed out in the open for all of Israel to see, and the pornography did its trick in luring the men and women of Israel away from worshiping God.[2] In their rituals they danced lewdly around the temple—much like is done in strip bars and clubs today. Not much has changed. From that day until now, Baal has continued to drive the pornography market, sex slaves, homosexuality, and every kind of sexual sin, including adultery and fornication.

While sexual sin and perversion is rampant in our society, even more concerning is that it is rampant in the Church. One study indicated that between 60 and 70 percent of all pastors have problems with pornography. If that many pastors have fallen under Baal's influence, can you imagine how many members of their congregations have fallen into the same sin?

Dutch Sheets said, "I believe that all of the sexual sin and perversion in America is, to one degree or another, under Baal's orchestration. You will continue to see God expose leaders in the Church who align themselves with this spirit. Pray for the Church to be cleansed and for Baal's hold on America in this area to be broken."

ABORTION

Baal is a violent spirit that requires human sacrifice. No one goes to an abortion clinic thinking, "I'm going to worship Baal today." However, Baal is the principality behind all human sacrifice, whether in the form of satanic worship or by abortion.

"I thought they sacrificed them to Molech," someone might say. Molech is under Baal's umbrella of authority.

In ancient Israel, child sacrifice was performed by placing children in the fire, throwing them in rivers, or sacrificing them on an altar.[3] The average number of babies aborted in the United States in a single day was 3,750 in 2010. Back then, an average of 22 percent of all pregnancies in the U.S. (excluding miscarriages) ended in abortion.[4] The U.S. had the third highest abortion rate in the world, after Red China and the former Soviet Union. According to "Abortion Rates Per Country 2020" published in *The World Population Review,* the U.S. has dropped to 15th place with Russia taking the lead and Vietnam in second place.

Cutting, Piercing, and Tattoos

Tattoos began as an ancient practice of cutting one's skin and placing the ashes of a dead person in the cut so that when it healed it would leave a mark. They kept the dead "alive" by praying to them. Tattoos were designed to provoke the spirits.

In ancient times, cutting and body piercing were believed to invoke the spirits as well. The most common places to pierce were the mouth, ears, nose, and body. We see an example of this in 1 Kings 18:28, when Elijah challenged the prophets of Baal to a power encounter: "And they cried aloud, and cut themselves after their manner with knives and lancets, till the blood gushed out upon them" (KJV).

Am I saying those with tattoos or body piercings are worshiping the devil? Absolutely not. What I'm saying, though, is this practice is an expression of Baal's influence on our society.

Baal is behind the death cultures of *Goth*, the vampire culture, witchcraft, and the occult—including *Wicca*. One way that it manifests is through the *Twilight* sagas. Many people justify the *Twilight* movies and books as just a "good romance." A good romance is not about sucking blood. This is a satanic trap. If you've watched these movies or read the books, repent!

A lot of people think Wicca is just witchcraft-lite, but there is no such thing. Anything, including the *Harry Potter* books and movies, that glamorizes witchcraft is under the authority of Baal. If you've participated in it, repent.

Baal is leading the fight against the great awakening among our young people, and he is using the concept of "good witchcraft," or "witchcraft-lite," as a way to do it.

FREEMASONRY

Another manifestation of Baal is Freemasonry. I want to be clear from the outset that we are not against Freemasons. My father and grandfather were Masons, and my mother was a member of the Eastern Star. Most Masons, like those in my own family, are good people who don't understand that when they go through the initiation into Freemasonry, they're being told to swear an oath to Baal.

There are two forms of Freemasonry: the *York Rite* and the *Scottish Rite*. The York Rite swears to a secret name of god: *Jahbulon*. It takes three Masons to say the three syllables of the name. *Jah* is a derivative of the name *Yahweh*. The middle part of the word, *bul*, stands for *Baal*. The last part of the word, *on*, is the city of the sun god—another term for Baal.

The Scottish Rite swears to the secret name of god: *Abaddon*. Abaddon is mentioned in Revelation 9:11 as the angel of the Abyss, and his name means "destruction." It isn't until an initiate reaches the 33rd degree that Lucifer is declared to be their god.

> *Over them as king they have the angel of the Abyss (of the bottomless pit). In Hebrew his name is Abaddon [destruction], but in Greek he is called Apollyon [destroyer]* (AMPC).

Albert Pike

The Words of Albert Pike

It isn't until they reach the 33rd degree that members are told what was written by Albert Pike. For those who doubt that Freemasonry is a religion, Pike's words settle the question:

The Masonic Religion should be, by all of us initiates of the high degree, maintained in the purity of the Luciferian doctrine. Yes, Lucifer is God, and unfortunately Adonay is also god...the true and pure philosophical religion is the belief in Lucifer, the equal of Adonay; but Lucifer, God of Light and Goodness, is struggling for humanity against Adonay, the God of Darkness and Evil.[5]

Some Masons deny that Albert Pike is prominent in the movement today. However, in 1944, Freemasons petitioned Congress for the right to remove Pike's bones from their burial place in Little Rock, Arkansas, to the Scottish Rite House of the Temple in Washington, DC. Located 13 blocks north of the White House, the first thing you see when you enter the temple is a bust of Albert Pike and the resting place of his remains.

A shocking number of our presidents and governmental and military leaders have been and are Freemasons. There are numerous good books documenting the truth about Freemasonry. However, the best book I've read on the subject is *Masonry: Beyond the Light* by William Schnoebelen.

A former Roman Catholic priest and member of Wicca, Schnoebelen, hungry for power, joined the Masons. He reached the 90th degree and was invited to join the *Illuminati*. Faithful to send his tithe check to the church of satan each week, a young bank teller sent him a note that said, "I'm praying for you, in the name of Jesus." Within a matter of weeks, he lost his powers and soon after gave his life to the Lord Jesus.

I've met Mr. Schnoebelen, and I feel that his knowledge and insights into Freemasonry are unparalleled. It would be worth your time to read the book and repent if you or members of your family have been duped into becoming a Freemason, thereby swearing an oath to Baal. You'll find the prayer of repentance in Appendix G.

In 2010, I sent teams from all 50 states to all the Masonic Lodges in the nation—somewhere around 10,000 sites in the United States—to divorce Baal. All 50 of our state leaders took teams to divorce Baal at the Masonic Lodges in their state. In Oklahoma there were about 250 lodges, while Georgia had about 600.

As I point out, some of the churches have been duped by the Freemasons—let me say, we've all been duped by Baal in one way or another. My own grandfather was a 32nd degree Mason and a member of the Ku Klux Klan, which was started by Albert Pike. Pike planned the financing for both sides of the Civil War. Also documented is the fact that he and his friend, Mazzini, conspired together. Mazzini formed the *Mafia* in Italy, and Pike formed the Ku Klux Klan in the United States. The Mafia, the Klan, and Freemasonry were all pawns of the Illuminati, of which both Mazzini and Pike were a part.

Many Southern Baptists were duped as well. More than any other entity, they were responsible for spreading Freemasonry in the United States and justifying slavery. The Southern Baptists split from the rest of the Baptists over slavery, and they have never reunited. Many Southern Baptists preached that God was for slavery. Many justified slavery for their own economic benefit and twisted the Scriptures to try and make their point. I'm not saying that Baptists today believe in slavery. I'm just pointing out how these Baal influences have crept into the Church.

We all must admit that we've been duped and deal with those past iniquities so that God won't say of us what He said to the Church of Thyatira:

> *And to the angel of the church in Thyatira write: The Son of God, who has eyes like a flame of fire, and His feet are like burnished bronze, says this: "I know your deeds, and your love and faith and service and perseverance, and that your deeds of late are greater than at first. But I have this against you, that you tolerate the woman*

Jezebel, who calls herself a prophetess, and she teaches and leads My bond-servants astray so that they commit acts of immorality and eat things sacrificed to idols. I gave her time to repent, and she does not want to repent of her immorality" (Revelation 2:18–21).

We must repent. Yes, I know it wasn't our generation that created the problem. But let it be recorded in heaven that it was our generation that took responsibility to deal with it.

ISLAM AND FREEMASONRY

In Oklahoma City, the Shrine Temple shares a parking lot with the mosque. I don't believe that's an accident. If you look at the symbols of the Shriners and Islam, you'll see similarities in the crescent moon and the fez the Shriners wear. At one time, *Allah* was known as *Baal-Allah* and *Hubaal*. Allah is just another of the thousand faces of Baal.

Without going into detail, let me say that some other ways that Baal influences our society are through divorce, business and partnership failures due to greed, corporate espionage and corporate crime, illness that steals financial well-being, legal and illegal drugs, and betting, casinos, and lotteries.

FEDERAL RESERVE BANK

The Constitution of the United States, Article 1, Section 8, says: "Congress shall have the power...to coin money, regulate the price thereof, and fix the standards of weights and measures." Congress has the right to issue money and set the value of it.

America was on the gold standard until April 1933. Prior to that, in November of 1910, Senator Nelson W. Aldrich and A.P. Andrews, Assistant Secretary of the Treasury Department, gathered on Jekyll Island, Georgia with five other men who together held an estimated fourth of the world's wealth. In a secret meeting, these men planned the Federal Reserve System.

Congress passed the Federal Reserve Act in 1913. In the simplest terms, it is neither federal nor a reserve. Prior to forming the Federal Reserve, we didn't have a federal income tax. However, the Federal Reserve began printing money and loaning it to the government, and that's when the federal debt began climbing, and it has not stopped.

The debt continues mounting because it is *fiat money*—paper money that isn't based on gold and has no promise of redemption. The Federal Reserve Bank is privately owned. Although secretive, the major controlling stock owners are the Rothschild family of Europe, the Rockefellers, and the central banks of Europe and Japan.

Baal is the principality behind this system, as you'll see.

I said above that America's economy was based on the gold standard until April of 1933. That's when President Franklin Roosevelt ordered all Americans to turn in their gold. In return, they were given fiat money, or irredeemable paper currency not backed by gold. The gold was turned over to the Federal Reserve—not the government—but to private individuals behind one of the worst schemes ever perpetrated against the American people.

ILLUMINATI

If you look on the dollar bill, one of the first things you'll notice is an Egyptian pyramid. You may wonder what a pyramid is doing on our dollar bill. It's a truncated pyramid with an eye suspended above it. The "all-seeing eye" is from the *Illuminati*. You'll also see the Roman numerals for 1776 on the foundation of the pyramid. If you're like me, you assumed that represents our country's independence in 1776. However, that's not what it represents.

May 1, 1776, is the day the Illuminati was formed. May Day (May 1) is one of the highest holy days in the occult. October 31 and November 1 are called *Samhain*, and are the highest holy days. The second highest holy days in the occult are April 30 and May 1. May Day is known as *Beltane*. Both Beltane and Samhain are inscribed on the walls of the Baal caves in Oklahoma, where they directed the priests of Baal how to worship.

A REMNANT CHOSEN BY GRACE

In Romans 11:3, Elijah's words echo from the Old Covenant into the New Covenant when he cried, "Lord, they have killed your prophets and torn down your altars. I am the only one left, and they are trying to kill me" (NIV).

In Romans 11:4-5, the Bible records God saying, "'I have reserved for myself seven thousand who have not bowed the knee to Baal.' So too, at the present time there is a remnant chosen by grace" (NIV).

You and I are covenanted to be a remnant chosen by grace. I've read the back of the Book, so I know that Baal will be thrown into the lake of fire. And today, as always, God has a plan of redemption.

When my friend, Dr. C. Peter Wagner, asked me to be part of the Eagle's Vision Apostolic Team (EVAT) and the Hamilton Group, I was honored to do so, but I had no idea what God had in mind through the association. Dr. Wagner is a convening apostle to thousands of Christian leaders worldwide, but that wasn't the only thing God had in mind when He spoke prophetically that we should go to Jekyll Island and to key places in New York City, like the Federal Reserve Bank, in order to pray and repent.

A key leader in forming our government, and the founder of the banking system in America was a Christian by the name of Alexander Hamilton. Some credit Hamilton for being the man most responsible for forming the U.S. government. He was George Washington's adviser, and his picture is on our $10 bill.

Peter Wagner is a double descendant of Alexander Hamilton. One side of Peter's family is descended from Hamilton's wife, the other side from Hamilton himself.

Chuck Pierce prophesied that the anointing God had placed on Alexander Hamilton for wealth, government, and finances had been passed down to Peter Wagner. Cindy Jacobs prophesied that Peter needed to go to the graveside of his ancestor, Alexander Hamilton, and do some prophetic acts. Eventually, Peter tracked down the site in the graveyard of Trinity Church in New York City. Curiously, the church is at the foot of Wall Street, one block from the New York Stock Exchange and two and a half blocks from the Federal Reserve Bank.

BACK TO THE FUTURE

At Peter's invitation, in June 2005 those of us involved in EVAT, along with Jay Swallow, traveled to New York City. Trinity Church is probably the most famous church in America. It's the church where parts of the movie *National Treasure* were filmed. Alexander Hamilton's grave was prominent and well-marked.

Wall Street got its name because the settlers in New York built a wall to keep Indians out. Part of the repentance and prophetic acts the Lord instructed Peter to do was to repent to Jay on behalf of our founding fathers who tried to build a wall to keep out the Indians.

After repentance at the gravesite at Trinity Church, we decided to cross Broadway and go to Wall Street. About that time, they closed off Broadway and a parade of between 300 and 400 economical school graduates passed by right in front of Peter. It was as though the Lord was saying, "I'm going to parade the economics of the world in front of you, Peter, and you'll have authority over it."

We walked about a block and a half to the Federal Reserve Bank, which you now know is neither federal nor reserve. A private tour had been arranged for us ahead of time. We were taken down five stories into the vault, which is in bedrock. We were told that one quarter of the world's refined gold is stored in that vault. It's the largest concentration of gold bullion anyplace in the world. U.S. gold, however, is stored in Fort Knox and has less than half of the gold in the Federal Reserve Bank. The gold in the Federal Reserve is owned by 48 different governments and entities. It's held there because the vault is considered the safest place in the world. At the time of our visit, gold prices were around $400 an ounce, and there was $92 billion worth of gold in the vault. Today, it would be worth more than $360 billion.

Standing in front of that vault, I spoke the words of God recorded in Haggai 2:8: "The silver is mine, and the gold is mine, saith the Lord of hosts" (KJV). The Lord doesn't care who thinks they own it; according to the Bible, it belongs to God.

The next stop on our journey was Jekyll Island. We met in the same room where Rockefeller and other international bankers had conspired to form the Federal Reserve in 1910. We prayed, repented, and performed prophetic acts as directed by the Lord. Chuck Pierce prophesied that a new system would be in place in the future.

THE GOLDEN RULE

In the fall of 2008, the stock market was in a freefall. God spoke to Cindy Jacobs and said that the strongman over America presides over New York City rather than Washington, DC. Don't take that to mean Baal doesn't operate in our nation's Capital, because he does. Baal is a governmental entity, but his primary goal is to control the wealth of this nation. New York City is the seat of wealth in America. The world's golden rule says that he who controls the gold, rules. The gold is in New York City.

The Lord told Cindy to go to New York City with the U.S. Reformation Prayer Network before the anniversary of the Stock Market crash of 1929. Thus, a select group of us traveled once again to New York City in October of 2008. We began our prayer journey back at Trinity Church, and from there we visited the Stock Exchange, where we saw that the five huge rooms used for daily trading had been reduced to two, with a fraction of their previous number of employees.

Afterward, we walked back out onto Broadway and down a block, where we found ourselves standing in front of a huge statue of a bull right in the middle of the road. Interestingly, the city never commissioned the statue. Someone made it and placed it in the middle of the street where it stands today. The bull symbolizes Baal. When we talk about being "bullish" in America, what are we saying? Remember, in Elijah's power encounter with Baal, God told him to sacrifice a bull, and He rained fire down from heaven to consume it. The bull on God's altar represented Baal. Afterward, Elijah killed 450 prophets of Baal.

It's a sad commentary, but people come from all over the world to rub the bull statue for luck. Standing by the bull, Cindy asked me to lead the group in a divorcement of Baal, which I did. We divorced Baal, with the God TV network filming the whole event.

Voting Stock

Our next stop was back at the Federal Reserve Bank. You must understand that those who control the Federal Reserve and the central banks of the world control the money supply. Because they control the money, they control the country. It matters very little who the President is because, to a large extent, they control both political parties. They have financed both sides of our wars since the early 1800s. They financed both sides of the Civil War. They financed both sides of World War I and World War II.

In addition to the Federal Reserve, they also control through such entities as the Council on Foreign Relations, the Trilateral Commission, the Club of Rome, and Bildeburgers. Currently, our government is in debt to the Federal Reserve for about $15 trillion.

In addition, the money the government used to bail out businesses didn't belong to us—it was money borrowed from the Federal Reserve. When we gave the money to commercial banks to keep them from going under, the U.S. government took *preferred stock* in exchange. This wasn't *common stock*, or "voting stock." It was preferred stock, which gets dividends. Recently, the President converted the preferred stock to common stock. What's the advantage? Much of the voting stock for the largest banks in America is now in the hands of the President.

In the natural, there is no hope for this situation, but I want you to understand that God isn't worried over it.

Statue of Liberty

During our second day in New York City, we went to Ellis Island and the Statue of Liberty. It is a great relief to me to know that our liberty doesn't come from a statue. It comes from God alone. We prayed at all the locations, but divorced Baal only at the bull on Wall Street, Rockefeller Plaza, and during the conference in Brooklyn that Cindy had scheduled one evening. Since then, we've gone back and divorced Baal at the locations we missed.

INCREDIBLE RESULTS

Once we divorced Baal in New York City, things began to happen. First, the plunging stock market stopped going down, and afterward there was a rebound. That doesn't necessarily mean it will stay up. I don't know what's going to happen, but the freefall stopped as soon as we divorced Baal. But that was only the beginning.

Immediately after our second trip to New York City, huge corruption was exposed on Wall Street. Like the rest of the world, we watched the events unfold on national television within a couple of weeks after our trip to New York City. The largest prostitution ring ever busted was huge news, but the real story was that almost all the clients were Wall Street executives, bankers, lawyers, and investment bankers.[6]

They were using their corporate credit cards to pay for the prostitution, taking it as a tax deduction, and some of the same companies had just been bailed out with our bailout money. So, literally, our taxpayer dollars, if you follow the trail of money, were funding prostitution on Wall Street. The company was set up as a consulting firm, but it was only a shell company, and that's how they were paying for the prostitutes.

Think about that. As we all know by now, Baal worship was tied to temple prostitution, which was one of their central forms of worship. Here, you have New York City, the economic center of the nation, intertwined with prostitution. You can't pinpoint a clearer example of the stronghold of Baal than Wall Street executives up to their eyeballs in prostitution.

I believe it was the judgment of God. We divorced Baal and took his control out of that realm, and within weeks the homes of some of the top money brokers on Wall Street were in foreclosure. If you look back in history, you'll never find any kind of scandal that met this proportion. To make matters worse, when the scandal broke and the list was taken to the New York City district attorney, they wanted nothing to do with it. They refused to take the list and wouldn't press charges—except against the madam who took the evidence to the authorities.

These weren't just guys who worked in the mail room. These were very wealthy men who were not only sexually immoral, but financially immoral as well. In order to get bonuses, they drove phantom profits that were unsustainable. Basically, they were betting with their stockholder's money. When you smell greed and prostitution, you've just picked up the scent of Baal.

DISMANTLING THE POWER GRID

Although it was aired on television's *20/20*, the story didn't go far, simply because the district attorney refused to prosecute the money men. It's the kind of thing that anyone else would have gone to jail for and never gotten a get-out-of-jail-free card.

However, although the district attorney refused to prosecute, when we, as the body of Christ, used our authority to dismantle the power grid, there was swift judgment from God.

ABC News reported the following about the scandal:

> Manhattan madam says clients had payments disguised. Some of the men contacted by ABC News denied using their corporate credit cards and ABC News could not independently confirm if the credit card numbers listed were company accounts. Davis says one CEO ordered her to send him invoices for roof repair on a warehouse to disguise the payment for prostitution from corporate funds.

On the heels of news of the Wall Street prostitution ring, Bernard Lawrence "Bernie" Madoff, founder of the Wall Street firm of Bernard L. Investment Securities LLC, was exposed. Rather than an investment account, it has been described as the largest Ponzi scheme in history. Madoff stole an estimated $65 billion that went missing from his client accounts.

I've shared only the tip of the iceberg regarding blatant idolatry in our society. The warning that tugs at my heart, when I see these altars to Baal, is the warning that Jesus gave to the Church at Thyatira:

> *But I have this against you, that you tolerate the woman Jezebel, who calls herself a prophetess, and she teaches and leads My bond-servants astray so that they commit acts of immorality and eat things sacrificed to idols* (Revelation 2:20).

God hates complacency. Jesus rebuked the Church at Thyatira because they tolerated the sin of Jezebel, which was idolatry. In essence He said, "You knew this was there, and you did nothing about it."

Likewise, we tolerate evil in our cities, states, and nation.

"Well, there's nothing we can do about it," someone might argue. That's almost blasphemy. Prior to ascending to the right hand of the Father, Jesus delegated authority to the Church. The first enemy we must overthrow is our own complacency. Then we must use that authority to overthrow principalities, powers, and every spirit that opposes the kingdom of God.

The Basilica of the National Shrine of the Immaculate Conception is the largest Roman Catholic Basilica in North America. Also known as Mary's Shrine, it has more than 80 chapels dedicated to the Virgin Mary under her title of Immaculate Conception. They teach that Mary was born without the stain of sin, that she was sinless. Many believe and are taught that she is the co-redeemer along with Jesus. That means that she is considered a savior along with Jesus.

When you walk through the doors it reads, "Blessed Art Thou, O Virgin Mother, Queen of Heaven." The Queen of Heaven is the female manifestation of Baal. Notice that she holds a scepter and stands on a crescent

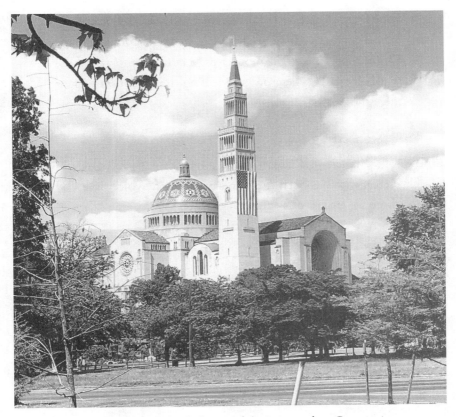

Basilica of the National Shrine of the Immaculate Conception

moon, a sign of Islam. That's because she is the goddess of the sun, moon, and stars.

Jesus is personified as a baby. He has a crown, but it and He are much smaller than Mary. His importance is diminished while hers is exalted. Christians should esteem Mary as a virgin who gave birth to our Savior, but she is not to be worshiped or considered on equal status with Jesus.

We divorced Baal at the Basilica in December of 2009. In December of 2019, Pope Francis took this stand:

Pope Francis appeared to flatly reject proposals in some theological circles to add "co-redemptrix" to the list of titles of the Virgin Mary, saying the mother of Jesus never took anything that belonged to her son, and calling the invention of new titles and dogmas "foolishness."[7]

What a wonderful answer to prayer!

The following chapter is written by internationally recognized prophet Chuck Pierce, who has been the primary prophetic voice over Oklahoma, and to whom we are eternally grateful.

CHAPTER 13

CONTENDING FOR THE LAND

Chuck D. Pierce

GOD desires to heal, transform, and reform America. He wants to make us one nation under God. In 2 Chronicles 7:14, God says, "If my people, who are called by my name, will humble themselves and pray and seek my face and turn from their wicked ways, then I will hear from heaven, and I will forgive their sin and will heal *their land*" (NIV).

Notice that it doesn't say He will heal our nation. It doesn't say He will heal our churches. Of course, God wants to heal our nation and transform His Church. However, the result of all that humbling, turning, and repenting is that God said He would heal our *land*.

The connection between God, His people, and the land has been lost for the most part by the modern Church. When I first began teaching on this topic, people said, "Our walk with the Lord has nothing to do with the land!"

Nothing could be further from the truth.

Second Chronicles 7:14 says if we do our part—including turning from our wicked ways—God will heal our land. You might ask what land He wants to heal. Obviously, He desires to heal all the land in the United States. But, where to start?

God put His finger on the deepest root of iniquity in America—that throbbing time bomb we know as Oklahoma. What does Oklahoma have to do with transforming America? Everything.

If a patient were rushed from the scene of a car wreck to the emergency room, the attending physician would treat the deadliest, most life-threatening injuries first. That's how the Great Physician is dealing with this nation. The deadliest issue in the nation was the land where 372 treaties had been made and broken with the Native Americans. Have other treaties been broken? Are there other iniquities in the land? The answer is a resounding "yes!" But a good physician doesn't work on a broken bone when there is a hemorrhaging artery.

Although I'm from Texas, my history with Oklahoma is a long one. I taught a master's course at Southwestern Christian University in Oklahoma City, so I'd been in and out of the city for years. However, things were different when I returned to Oklahoma in April 1995 to help one of my students plant a church. I drove into downtown and felt a tremendous burden. I had an overwhelming sense that something was wrong, but I had no one to tell. Oklahoma was very "churchy." By that I mean everyone was building a church, but no one was building unity in the body of Christ.

I was so burdened about the evil that had been amassed against the city that I stood in the parking lot of my hotel, looking and feeling like a fool, and shouted toward Tinker Air Force Base, "Somebody please hear me! Something is wrong in the center of your city! Go down there and find out what it is!" I shouted into the atmosphere because there was no *ecclesia*—no governing leaders—aligned in the city.

The Lord gave me a word for Oklahoma City. He said, "Prophesy that what they see this week they won't see next week. Tell them that whether they're ready or not, the city will come to the door of the Church."

I met with a small group of leaders and began by saying, "There's something wrong here, and I don't know where to start to tell you prophetically that your city is in trouble." Then, I prophesied what the Lord had given me.

The following Wednesday, Dr. Garnett Pike, who'd been out of town the week before, called and said, "I hear that you have a problem with our city."

"There's something very wrong in Oklahoma City," I said. "Something is going to happen there that will shake things greatly. I don't know if a tornado is coming, but I sense evil abounding. A door has been opened to the city, and there isn't anyone to close it."

A BLAST LINKED TO THE PAST

While we were on the phone, a bomb was detonated from a Ryder truck in downtown Oklahoma City, killing 168 people. It affected my life greatly. I never wanted to be anywhere again where I had no one to tell the message that God had given me.

That bombing touched the whole nation; we were all affected. It was the first act of terrorism on U.S. soil, and it posed the question, "Why Oklahoma City?" It was a valid question, because once you have broken covenants in your midst, your land is set for a great blow.

It was after that terrible time that I met Apostle John Benefiel, who said, "I'll start gathering leaders so we can meet and hear what God is saying." We knew God was developing a prophetic blessing over the state, because without the prophetic utterance, a people perish. Since that time, we've met in Oklahoma City approximately once a quarter, and the Church government has risen to take its place.

It's interesting that since then, God has chosen to release prophetic warnings and strategies for the entire nation from Oklahoma. For instance, in

2000, we were in worship in Oklahoma City when the Lord showed me that the nation was going to war and that things would shift by September 18, 2001. Afterward, I released the word prophetically. You may wonder why, considering all the places in the nation that I travel, God released the prophetic word about the nation going to war from Oklahoma.

God made Oklahoma a model to show us how to save the nation. In order to understand, you must understand our connection to the land.

GOD, MAN, AND THE LAND

God gave mankind land. He planted a garden for him and set up boundaries around it. The land was both God's gift to man and where satan intervened to take it. Man is the only creature with the authority to give up the glory of the land. Man's sin resulted in a cosmic fall.

After the Fall, Abel was a husbandman of the land who brought the kind of sacrifice that was pleasing to God. Cain chose to bring whatever he wanted. His sin allowed an iniquity to touch the land, which resulted in cities. If you read Genesis 4, you'll see that entire cities were created outside of God's presence because one man refused to give God his best.

In other words, man is a divine connector between heaven and earth. Imagine the power of God coming like lightning, flowing from heaven through you to the earth where you stand. It's that power and glory that breaks up the ground and allows God's plan and the pattern of heaven to come down.

The earth is the Lord's and the fullness thereof. The land belongs to God, and it had its God-given purpose from the beginning. We're not here to change the purpose of the land; we're here to develop God's plan. We're here to cooperate with God and to bring about His purposes, but too often, we work against His plan.

You're not disassociated from the land. One day the Lord might say, "You're going to pray for Kansas, and I'll show you the spiritual forces embedded there." He might say, "Peru is yours!" Then all of a sudden you're going to see the ruling spirits and understand how they connect. You'll see how they're holding back the harvest. You'll understand how they're covering things over.

LAND IS LINKED TO YOUR FUTURE

"I'm nothing but a little housewife."

You're the best candidate I know. I don't care if you're a housewife, a mechanic, a grandparent, a lawyer, or anyone else. Open a geography book at home and watch God illuminate one of the pages to you. God cares about restoring the land to its original purpose, but He needs your cooperation.

Biblically, land is linked with a vision of a coming age. Whenever you start praying, prophesying, and dealing with the land, you're dealing with the future. You're not dealing with the past. In Oklahoma, we've spent years dealing with past iniquities, but it was because God wanted to unlock our future.

Land is the place where our relationship with God is lived out. It was in the Garden of Eden that God asked, "Adam, where are you?"

God hasn't changed. If you're not in communion and connection with God, He asks, "Where are you? I've got to have a relationship with you to change the earth. When you're in a relationship with Me, change happens wherever you step."

The land is where man's obedience or disobedience to God is measured. When you understand the Bible, you'll realize that your disobedience touches the land wherever you walk. If you're obedient before God, the glory of God touches the land wherever you step.

LAND IS LINKED TO GLORY

You can't disconnect man's obedience from the glory of God resting on the land. If there's no glory resting on the land, it's because we've become a stiff-necked, disobedient people. There's no other way to look at it.

There isn't a homeless soul out there drinking every day who can't stop, put down the bottle, and experience the glory of God. The moment he sets that bottle down and cries out to God, His glory will come and begin to change the land.

The next principle you need to understand is that God always appointed a First People in a land. He appointed Adam in the Garden of Eden. He appointed the nation of Israel over that small strip of land in the Middle East. God called a nation out of obscurity and gave them land and a boundary, which was similar to what He did in the Garden of Eden.

God had a plan and purpose for Oklahoma, but it got perverted and the land became a concentration camp instead of a Garden. The Church in Oklahoma has made great strides in reversing the curse and cooperating with God in returning the land to its original purpose.

In Oklahoma, as well as in this nation, God appointed the Native Americans as the First People, and it was to them that He gave authority to rule. You don't get to choose to rule a land simply because you're white. There is a redemptive quality built into the First People that will release victory and triumph in the days ahead.

One of the historic things that advanced the purposes of God in the nation was when the Lord directed us to ask Apostle Jay Swallow to gather leaders from as many tribes as possible. The Lord said, "You're going to have to do this to move forward. Those who are willing to hear Me will show up."

That's how simple it gets in some of these meetings. You can't try to rationalize and understand what you're doing. You just have to show up and do it. Then, all of a sudden, the Spirit of God backs it and unlocks some things. From that moment on, you can set your plumb line in a new and fresh way over how to advance.

That's what happened the night God directed the Native leaders to commission us. It had never been done, and God let us know that we couldn't advance any further without that commissioning. Native leaders came to restore a foundational structure and release those who were trying to serve in their territory. That's the way commissioning works.

In other words, we needed to be commissioned from and by the First People. Therefore, it was a very significant and historic event. I compare what happened in that commissioning to Jesus returning after the Resurrection, as recorded in John 20. Until then, He'd been training and teaching the 12 as disciples, but now He commissioned them as apostles. The word *disciple* means, "one being taught; a learner." But then Jesus commissioned them to be "one sent."

Likewise, a lot of what's been happening in Oklahoma the past 15 years has been us learning so that we could be sent to do.

A DEFINING PLACE

Oklahoma is a model for this nation, but it's more than that. Oklahoma is one of those defining places—it defines the call of America. That's why when God does something in Oklahoma, it's very important for the nation. In Genesis 1, God chose a land mass in a territory and said, "From this place I will work out the obedience to change a whole nation." He did the same thing in Oklahoma when He made them a model for us. The contending for the land in Oklahoma over the past 15 years has brought us to a place where we're seeing the enemy delivered into our hands. From there, we'll move to deliver the nation.

That doesn't mean every state and territory doesn't have a part to play and a redemptive purpose, but God said there was a mantle and a model in Oklahoma and a people with a particular gifting whom He would use to shift the nation. God didn't say that to Texas. He brought the model and developed it in Oklahoma. Texas, like other states, has an opportunity to connect into the model in Oklahoma and move forward.

You have to understand God's heart for a land. In the fullness of time He says, "Wait a minute! All of those First People who I put here were pushed into boundaries that are called Oklahoma. They have the gifting to understand the land and what it was supposed to be."

God looked at what we did to the Native People in Oklahoma and realized that we'd developed a whole land that was set against His covenant people. He said, "Let me start back with the land where I established My covenant. That covenant plan will touch Israel. It will restore states. It will unlock the bloodlines of people who were captured. I've gathered people and amassed them here, but now I'm going to start sending those gifts out. I will bring those people in and then send them out in order to begin a process to change a nation. I will realign this land."

It's important to understand that we can't rely on the past ways of praying and our past ways of understanding. We can't rely on the wars we won in the last season, because we're being called forth in a new way. I remember when God said to me, "I want you to lay down what you've been doing." What I'd been doing was good, but God was on a mission to save the nation. He gave Dutch Sheets similar instructions and an awakening message. God sent Dutch and me on a prayer journey through every state in the nation, and now He has called John Benefiel to go to all 50 states to stand against the strongman over America.

Oklahoma has been contending for their land for years, and in the process the Lord has taught us some things about what it takes to truly humble ourselves, turn from our wicked ways, and repent so that God can heal our land. Here are a few things we've learned along the way.

LESSONS LEARNED FROM OKLAHOMA

1. You have to know your field. Knowing your field applies to you personally, corporately, territorially, and on a generational level. The Apostle Paul equated our field with not just a physical place, but our apostolic rule.

When I met John Benefiel, he knew his field. He knew he had a promise for Oklahoma. I'd never heard anyone communicate promise for a state the way he did. It seemed as though every time he stood in the pulpit he decreed, "All of Oklahoma shall be saved." I wasn't sure if even he knew what all that included, but I knew this: He kept saying it because he knew his field. He knew his call, and he knew his apostolic authority.

2. You have to hear God's prophetic voice over your field. The Bible says God predetermines your place and your time of living. You have to hear His prophetic voice over the place where you're assigned. God chooses a place where He can develop a people who will respond to Him. And He chooses certain places from which to prophesy. The Church in Oklahoma has been assigned its place and the responsibility of hearing God's voice to set things in order to restore nations. It also means some of us must go to Oklahoma to get the revelation for how to change a nation.

3. You must have apostolic authority to execute God's plan. In September 2007, the Lord told me I was to resign my position of overseeing a prayer movement because it was shifting and becoming an apostolic movement. That shift meant the prophetic needed a new wind. Once you have prophetic revelation, you must have the apostolic authority to execute God's plan. Without apostolic execution, prophetic revelation doesn't take root.

God is amassing His troops to move in a new way. It's called apostolic rule, and there's nothing wrong with that word. The Lord told me I need to be very clear about that. If you aren't willing to use the words *apostolic* or *apostle*, you're not willing to use your Bible. You're saying that you're going to pick and choose what words you'll use from the Bible, but we can't do that. We have to use God's terminology and not the world's. Too often the Church tries to lead us the world's way by saying that we need to be relevant.

Joseph was a type of father figure to Pharaoh. That means he was an apostle over Pharaoh. That's what the word means. As Christians, we have revelation and understanding greater than anyone in the world. For instance, I can tap into and gain financial strategies that no one in the banking industry can gain unless they know the same Holy God who created it all. We must learn to be shrewder than the world.

I'm a well-educated and very capable person, but I learned a long time ago that if I don't know what God thinks about something, I'm as ignorant as a goose flying backward in a hailstorm. Ignorance is allowing the world to rule us and not tapping into the spiritual realm, where we get the Lord's mind on the matter.

I began working with the Soviet bloc countries in the 1980s, doing the same thing we're doing here now. We held ourselves accountable to pray and send people into the Soviet bloc countries that held prisoners, until those prisoners were released. Then I began working with a group in China, with whom I'm still very involved. In both the Soviet bloc countries and China, I watched things shift as we fought spiritual warfare.

The war we're fighting here is about to intensify. However, this isn't the type of war we've known in the past. It's not just individual confrontation—God is amassing His troops in a whole new apostolic way. We're moving from a time of gathering to a time of being established.

You must know what tribe you're with and how to mobilize. *God* created tribes. All you have to do is look back at His covenant with Israel to see that He had tribes. In order to win the war, the tribes had to move together. It's imperative that you know your tribe and how to mobilize it to move forward in the midst of battle. I believe we've come to Oklahoma, in part, to learn how to mobilize our tribes.

4. You have to uncover what is trying to prevent prophetic revelation from taking root. This was my problem in 1995. I could prophesy all day, but there wasn't any amassed leadership to hear me. Everyone was doing his or her own thing, building his or her own church, but no one was building the kingdom of God in Oklahoma. In each state and region, you've got to uncover what is resisting prophetic revelation.

5. What iniquities are contending for your land? When it comes to dealing with iniquities contending for our land, one of the best examples is the number of iniquities my wife and I dealt with in order for her to have children. Pam and I had been trying to have children for years, but it wasn't happening. Yet God told my wife, "You will be pregnant."

You must understand that once God says something to you, you can war with that word. When God told Pam she would be pregnant, she could tell every demon in hell to let go of her. However, Pam didn't understand that. I kept saying, "Pam, it's your covenant right to be healed and for us to have children. It's your heart's desire, and God told you that you can have them. You can decree that it's your covenant right to have those children."

"I have a hard time thinking I can command God," she said.

"It doesn't have anything to do with God." I said. "God has already given you a covenant, and He gave you a personal word. You command every demon in hell to let go of you!"

The day the Spirit of God fell on her, Pam turned to me with wide eyes and said, "There are demons everywhere." She finally understood that it had never been God holding back her heart's desire. Pam got pregnant, and today several of our five children have children of their own as our family continues to multiply.

Likewise, our problem is that we have a covenant right to our land, our territories, our families, and our businesses, but we must see who's trying to stop that covenant blessing.

It's time to uncover what's been holding back your heart's desires. Some who are reading this book are going to have burdens to see entire cities changed. In this next season, you're going to know what demons have been stopping you. You're going to know what's been holding you back from seeing these things come to pass. You're going to know why you've been held in poverty. You're going to know why you couldn't break through. You're going to see what's happening.

6. You need to understand your ruling civil structure. What's the predominant civil structure that's ruling the society where you live? Is it government? Is it education? What's *really* ruling your city? What's really ruling your life? Once you understand what's ruling, you'll see the spirit behind it.

7. Do you see the kingdom of God being built? Take a good look around your city and state. Do you see the kingdom of God being built and established? Or do you see a lot of people building their own churches? I'm not talking about building a church building—I'm talking about vision. Are you part of a group that's on the move and building the kingdom of God?

8. Do you see an apostolic/prophetic alignment that embraces Israel and the First People of the land? There may be a lot of churches executing wonderful programs in your area. However, God is doing a very specific thing in this season. He's working with apostolic and prophetic leadership, the kind of leadership that headed the early Church. He's aligning His Body with covenant relationships, primarily with Israel and the First People.

If you don't see these things—*run*. If you do see them, it means you're in an environment that understands covenant. It means your covenant with God will multiply. It can't help but multiply.

LAWS AND TIMES

We're no longer a nation under God. Don't get me wrong, we still have the right to be based on the Cross, but that's not how we're being ruled. The Bible tells us in Daniel 7:25 that the devil attempts to change the laws and times. Although satan doesn't have the right to rule us spiritually, the moment we align with him legally, he has the right to rule over our territory. That's how he changes our laws and times.

For example, most Christians don't realize that in the fourth century, the Church got captured by the Baal structure under Constantine. The early Church experienced an incredible power that was linked to Passover and an understanding of the blood of Jesus. Christians had suffered through intense persecution, but all of that changed when Constantine legalized Christianity. In other words, the enemy changed the laws and times.

Although Christianity became legal, Constantine made it illegal to participate in Passover. That's when the Church shifted into the Baal system. Instead of the power of Passover, Christians were allowed to participate in *Ishtar*, or "Easter," which is part of the Baal system of worship. The Church was compromised and lost much of its power through losing an actual understanding of the Blood.

The Church has been captured and compromised for centuries. So it's interesting that one of the primary assignments of Oklahoma is to deal with the Baal structure in their state and in the nation.

COVENANT ROOTS

On May 31, 2008, we were at the Statue of Liberty, Ellis Island, and Liberty Park, where we had a meeting in New Jersey. On the last night, God caught me up in a vision and showed me the states that still had a covenant root that was viable and working. Then, He showed me states whose covenant root was so layered and veiled through legal demonic structures that it was no longer viable. Finally, He showed me some states that had never formed a covenant alignment with God.

Every state had a measure of the presence of the Lord, and every state had a remnant of people capable of gathering, but that wasn't gathering. For instance, New Hampshire has been one of the more difficult states spiritually. Iowa is another one of the more difficult states, yet they have some of the strongest people of prayer. You have to understand that it takes more than people crying out day and night in prayer to transform a state. You have to deal with the ruling legal structure.

When the Lord caught me up and showed me this nation, I saw structures circled with glory and fire. "Lord, what are those?" I asked. He said they were *Freedom Outposts*. Not every state had Freedom Outposts, but where they had developed, God would start training them over the next three years to be a vibrant dimension. When people walk in, what they experience will go through their soulish realm and straight into their spirit.

The next thing I noticed was that every state had a movement of glory. It looked like fire moving, and it trickled down like the beginning of a river before it widened and connected to a Freedom Outpost. I asked the Lord what I was seeing, and He said it was His *Triumphant Reserve*.

Triumph means you are called to "obtain a victory." Based on your assignment, you live in the ability to conquer. *Triumph* also means "joy." In other words, God is saying, "I have a people with the ability and the call within them to My kingdom to rule, who are filled with joy." One of the definitions of *triumph* is that you can "succeed only through joy." You can't succeed any other way. You've got to move with joy because joy is linked to prosperity. Joy is linked to strength. Joy is linked with the ability to flourish.

YOU ARE GOD'S TRUMP CARD

I used to play cards, and sometimes I entered spade tournaments. In order to win, I had to learn how to *trump*. Triumph means you will play the right trump card at the right time. It doesn't mean you have the strongest card. It's about when to play that card. That's very important.

I consider that the Host People are our strongest reserve. God is calling up every remnant of His Triumphant Reserve and saying, "This is who you are. Here is your apostolic rule to move forward."

A *reserve* is "that which has been kept for future use." Any military state understands this concept. In other words, you're capable of being used, but you're not being used because God has another plan for you. He's going to trump with you.

You're God's trump card! That's why some of you don't need to strive to come off the shelf. God knows where your card is, and He knows when to play it.

Where you've been restrained in your freedom, all of a sudden a Triumphant Reserve will break out into a new release. That's where we're headed over the next 10 years.

CHAPTER 14

SIGNS OF TRANSFORMATION

*In the position that I have, I am in contact with a lot of people
who are doing things actually around the world as well as in
the United States primarily. I can tell you now, that as of the
last three years or so, the reports that I get from the Heartland
Apostolic Prayer Network are the most tangible, measurable
results of high-level prayer and spiritual warfare that I've
heard yet in my life.*

C. Peter Wagner

Note: While the information in this chapter is accurate,
it is more than 10 years old. In the following chapters you will
read more recent signs of transformation.

I'VE grown weary of well-meaning ministers touting the latest theory
about how to heal our nation when they haven't even changed their
neighborhood, much less a city or state. We can't afford to be naïve any
longer. If the kingdom of God is advancing, there will be tangible results.
However, the Church has gone so long with few results that most of us no

longer expect any. We must throw off that old mindset and realize that, just as King David attempted to move the Ark of the Covenant, when we tap into the power of God for transformation, we must do it His way.

It would require writing another book to document all the signs of change we've experienced over the past 15 years. However, the most dramatic, tangible, and measurable signs of transformation have occurred since God directed us to divorce Baal and remarry the Lord. After witnessing powerful results when we divorced Baal in Oklahoma, Texas, and Kansas, Chuck Pierce asked if I would be willing to travel to all 50 states and lead them in divorcing Baal and remarrying the Lord.

The results have been nothing short of miraculous.

As you know by now, one of the ways Baal manifests his presence is through drought. He still considers himself to be the god who controls rain, and therefore the crops.

On October 14, 2006, during the Feast of Tabernacles gathering at Glory of Zion in Denton, Texas, the Lord spoke the following word of prophecy through Chuck Pierce:

> Plant your feet! Ready yourself for change! You are entering a year of shaking and quaking! This year will be known as the Year of Holy Spirit! This will be the year the rivers will rise! Watch where the heavens open and floods [physical] reach the earth, and document those places! Those are places targeted for a Holy Spirit invasion. Rising flood waters will cause you to move to higher ground. As the River of Holy Spirit rises, you will find yourself moving to the high places.

At the time of that prophecy, much of Oklahoma and Texas were experiencing severe drought. Following is the drought monitor that shows areas of drought in the United States during September 2006. The darker the color, the more severe the drought.

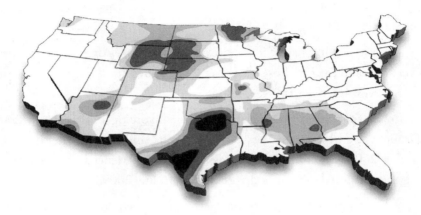

U.S. Drought Monitor September 2006

After divorcing Baal and Mammon in the Heartland in February, March, April, and June of 2007, there was no drought left in the Heartland states.

Drought Monitor Archives

Before: U.S. September 2006   After: U.S. June 2007

RECORD FLOODING

In 2006 and early 2007, after Chuck prophesied that the rivers would rise, the lakes and rivers in Oklahoma were so low that meteorologists predicted it would take eight years of regular rainfall to refill them. After divorcing Baal in February and March 2007, rains came, and soon every lake and river in the state was at or above flood levels. That year turned out to be the wettest since records began in 1889.

The same thing happened in Texas and Kansas. After divorcing Baal, every lake and river in those states were at or above flood stage. Kansas City, Missouri experienced 100-year floods.

Iowa experienced 500-year floods after divorcing Baal in April 2008. Droughts were broken in Mississippi, Alabama, and Georgia after divorcing Baal in 2008. Connecticut and Massachusetts experienced extensive flooding and torrential rains after divorcing Baal in July 2009.

When I was asked to go to Georgia and lead them in divorcing Baal and remarrying the Lord on February 29, 2008, the drought was so severe that Atlanta had only a three-month supply of water left. Below is the drought monitor prior to our divorcing Baal there, followed by successive drought monitors following that event.

Georgia Drought Monitor

December 25, 2007   April 1, 2008   May 20, 2008   December 8, 2009

What you attain in spiritual warfare, you must maintain. After being free of drought in 2007, by 2009 Texas once again experienced areas of severe drought. It was so dry in San Antonio that the trees were dying. Within 30 days of our divorcing Baal again on August 25, 2009, San Antonio had over 13 inches of rain and Austin had over 10 inches of rain and flooding. The drought monitor below tells the story.

Texas Drought Monitor

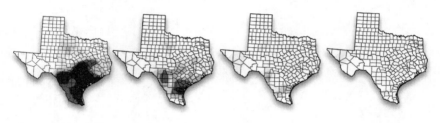

August 25, 2009   October 6, 2009   February 2, 2010   April 6, 2010

California is the breadbasket of the nation, providing a large percentage of our fresh produce. Yet when I was invited to lead in the divorcement of Baal at three different locations in California, the entire state was in drought. Below, you will see the drought monitor prior to divorcing Baal, and three following.

California Drought Monitor

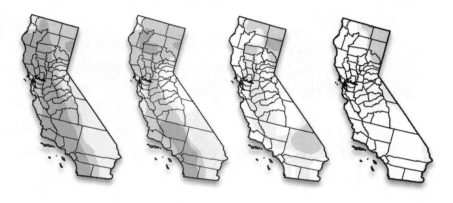

October 13, 2009   October 20, 2009   February 2, 2010   August 17, 2010

Below is the U.S. drought monitor for December 2007 and August 2010. According to meteorologists, at that time there was less drought in the United States than at any time during the past 100 years! Do you think that's a coincidence? I don't. I think it is the finger of God. If you look at the areas where drought still exits, you'll see the states where I had yet to divorce Baal.

U.S. Drought Monitor

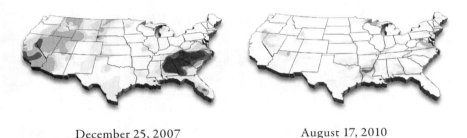

December 25, 2007   August 17, 2010

HEALING THE LAND

So the drought has broken, and we've experienced rain. You might ask what, if any, resulting signs we've seen.

In 2009, Russia was the third largest exporter of wheat. In 2010, due to devastating drought and wildfires, Russia put a ban on wheat exportation. Meanwhile, in the U.S., corn, wheat, and soybean farmers produced more than in any year in history! In 2010, God had healed the land to such a degree that the crops exceeded the previous year's crops, resulting in the highest annual production on record. The crops for 2011 were projected to be even higher. God is literally healing the land, as He promised. In addition to production increasing, our farmers' income increased due to Russia suffering the worst drought in 130 years.

DIVORCING BAAL IN NEW YORK CITY

The stock market was in a freefall in October 2008, when we divorced Baal at the New York Federal Reserve Bank, the New York Stock Exchange on Wall Street, and at the statue of the bull (Baal) on Broadway. Almost immediately, the stock market recovered and stabilized. That's not to say it hasn't or won't go down again. However, it is now clear that Baal is the entity behind the global financial shaking.

A few months after we divorced Baal in New York City, *20/20* released a story about one of the largest prostitution rings ever busted. Only this one was specific to Wall Street executives, bankers, lawyers, and investment bankers who were paying as much as $2,000 an hour for prostitutes with their corporate credit cards.

A month later, Bernie Madoff, a stock broker, investment adviser, and chairman of the NASDAQ stock market, was arrested for operating what may well have been the largest Ponzi scheme in history. Once we divorced Baal, God began uncovering layers of corruption.

DIVORCING BAAL IN WASHINGTON, DC

On Monday, December 7 and Tuesday, December 8 in 2009, at the Lord's direction we gathered at least one leader from all 50 states in Washington, DC. The first evening, I taught on divorcing Baal, and as a group we did so.

For years prior to this event, we had worked with Senator Sam Brownback in pressing legally for a Resolution of Apology to the Native Americans for the atrocities this nation committed against them. Although the resolution had not passed on either the state or federal level, that evening, for the first time in the history of this nation, a spiritual leader from all 50 states repented to the Native Americans gathered there. It was a historical moment.

The next morning, we took two buses to the Lincoln Memorial. Standing on the site where Martin Luther King Jr. gave his famous "I Have a Dream" speech, I led the delegation in divorcing Baal.

Next, we traveled 13 blocks north of the White House to the House of the Scottish Rite Temple, where the 33rd degree of Freemasonry is conferred. The 33rd degree is the level where the men are told that lucifer is god. It's the highest degree of Freemasonry in the U.S. We toured the temple and covertly divorced Baal.

Our third stop was at the largest Roman Catholic Basilica in the U.S.— the Basilica of the Immaculate Conception. The doctrine of the Immaculate Conception says that Mary's mother, Ann, was a virgin when Mary was conceived, and that Mary, like Jesus, lived a sinless life. Therefore, she was proclaimed co-redemptrix with Jesus and could be prayed to. We happened to be there on their national feast day, which is the highest celebration of the Queen of Heaven. It even has the words "Queen of Heaven" over the doorway.

Please, remember that we have no quarrel with Masons or Catholics. We love them all. However, we cannot afford to deny idolatry where it has a foothold in this nation. The Scottish Rite Temple is one of the seats of Baal—the male part of the Baal principality. The Roman Catholic Basilica represents the female part of the Baal principality—the Queen of Heaven.

THE COPENHAGEN TREATY

I've been told that a treaty is the highest law of the land, as high as the Constitution. We orchestrated our trip to Washington, DC, in order to be there when President Obama was leaving for Copenhagen to sign the Copenhagen Treaty, in hopes that we could thwart it. The treaty is unconstitutional and would have given much of the nation's sovereignty to the United Nations, who would have determined our taxation.

The treaty, based on the global warming theory and protecting the environment, would have trampled our Constitution. President Obama flew to Copenhagen, fully intending to sign the treaty. It looked unstoppable. However, after we divorced Baal in Washington, DC, the Copenhagen meeting came to naught. The only thing the leaders agreed on was to meet again in a year to sign the treaty. They met in Mexico City in 2010, and the treaty wasn't signed. To date, it still hasn't been signed.

THE COBELL CLASS ACTION LAWSUIT

Fourteen years ago, Eloise Cobell sued the Department of the Interior and the Bureau of Indian Affairs for the mismanagement of hundreds of thousands of dollars in Native American trust funds over a period of 150 years. The money, lands, mineral rights, and everything else in those trusts could not be accounted for by the government, who admitted to the crime. However, the government was trying to settle the case for $100 million. That may sound like a lot of money, but it's nothing compared to the vast wealth that was stolen from the Native people. The court case had languished for 14 years when we arrived in Washington, DC, to divorce Baal.

However, the day after we divorced Baal, the government announced it would settle the lawsuit for $3.4 billion. That isn't as much as it should have been, but it's a step in the right direction. Apostle Jay Swallow pointed out that the money would go to about 300,000 Native Americans, which is roughly a tithe of the Native Americans in the U.S. today.

RESOLUTION OF APOLOGY

Twelve days after we divorced Baal in the nation's capital, on December 19, 2009, the Resolution of Apology to the Native Americans was passed by the Senate and the House of Representatives and signed by President Obama. This was a joint resolution sponsored by Senator Sam Brownback that formally apologized to the American Indians for centuries of government mistreatment. The resolution acknowledged a long history of government misconduct against Native Americans, including forced relocation from tribal lands, theft of tribal assets, and the breaking of treaties and covenants.

The Cobell lawsuit was a major step toward restitution with the Native Americans, and the Resolution of Apology was a step toward reconciliation. We now have steps toward both reconciliation and restitution, which mirrors what King David did for the Gibeonites in 2 Samuel 21. Although there is still more to do, we've passed some major hurdles.

POLITICAL SHIFT

We held the first Binding the Strongman conference in Massachusetts in July 2009, and we divorced Baal there. The senate seat in Massachusetts was key to the upcoming election, but from a political standpoint, shifting that senate seat appeared impossible. Scott Brown ran for the seat as a Republican in the bluest of the blue states. Only 13 percent of the population of Massachusetts was registered Republican.

In January 2010, in a landslide political shift, Scott Brown won the election. Please note that we do not take anything away from the hard work and campaigning of Scott Brown; nor do we lessen the power of the Massachusetts voters. However, many people believe that divorcing Baal there also made a spiritual difference.

The following is a message I received from Pastor Raffoul Najem, who hosted the Binding the Strongman conference at the Community Christian Fellowship in Lowell, Massachusetts:

> Well, it wasn't until the day after the election that a young man from our congregation called me to say, "Hey Pastor, it happened! We divorced Baal, and God won the election!" It was then that I got it and shouted, "Yes! Yes! Yes! That's exactly right!" It rained that weekend after we divorced Baal. And, oh, did it rain for a whole month after the conference! And now, there's this great shifting in the political arena in Massachusetts that's going to release a great shift in the spiritual arena, that will give birth to a Great Awakening. And yes, I strongly believe that what we did in Boston that day, with all the apostles gathered with us and divorcing Baal in a strategic place, has led to this great victory on January 19, 2010.

Then, I received the following text from Lance Wallnau:

> Hey John, I'm in a board meeting with Rick Joyner, Wellington Boone, Bob Weiner, and others. Just shared the connection between your trip to Massachusetts and the recent election. Well done. Figured you would appreciate hearing how much people appreciate your work.

The spiritual and political climate of Washington, DC, has been drastically changed, as evidenced by the elections of 2010.

WHITE BUFFALO

Since 1833, no female white buffalo born in this country has grown to maturity. For years, the Plains Tribes have looked for the birth of a female white buffalo as a sign of hope for their people. A female white buffalo—not an albino—was born from the female buffalo given to Jay Swallow by the state of Texas as an act of restitution, and has grown to maturity. The odds of a female white buffalo just being born are 10,000,000 to one.

MISSION NATIVE AMERICA

Mission Native America, a ministry founded and led by Apostle Jerry Mash, who is one of the leading apostles in OAPN and HAPN, has delivered over 80 semitrailer loads of food, clothing, furniture, and medical supplies to reservations around the country. Those donations, to date, have a total value of over $22,000,000.

This ministry's faithful work among Native American tribes resulted in the salvation of key Native leaders, such as 87-year-old Chief Oliver Red Cloud of the Sioux Nation. He is the first principal chief of the Sioux to give his heart to the Lord Jesus.

HEARTLAND APOSTOLIC NETWORK

It's amazing what God has done. When I first started Church on the Rock in Oklahoma City, my vision was that our city would be saved and transformed. Over time, God expanded that vision to include the entire state. Then He led us to start the Heartland Apostolic Prayer Network.

Today, HAPN is 50 states strong! Not only do we have spiritual leaders and networks in place in all 50 states, but God has given us a prophetic word about touching not just this nation, but other nations of the world. Today HAPN includes Benin, Blackfeet Nation, Burundi, Cherokee Nation, Cheyenne-Arapaho Tribes, Comanche Nation, Costa Rica, Cree Nation, Denmark, El Salvador, England, Ethiopia, Ghana, Guatemala, Haiti, Honduras, Iceland, Israel, Japan, Kenya, Kurdistan, Lebanon, Liberia, Malaysia, Muscogee (Creek) Nation, Navajo Nation, Nicaragua, Nigeria, Northern Ireland, Norway, Ojibwa, Peru, Puerto Rico, Rwanda, Sudan, Sweden, Tanzania, Thailand, Uganda, and the Virgin Islands.

SIGNS OF TRANSFORMATION IN OKLAHOMA CITY

Fifteen years ago, Oklahoma City was so spiritually disjointed that when God sent a prophet to warn us of impending doom, he could find no cohesive group to tell. The bombing in downtown Oklahoma City left it deserted and looking like a war zone. Our economy had long suffered as Oklahoma stood at the back of the class in most areas of our society. There was nothing here to draw people or businesses.

Today, the Church in Oklahoma City is strong, and Christian leaders have taken their place in Church government. We have leaders in each region and meet together on a regular basis to pray. If that weren't enough, God has established our efforts as a model for the nation.

National Recognition

In addition to national spiritual recognition, the transformation of Oklahoma City is well documented. For instance, while the nation is in the middle of a huge recession and wide-scale unemployment, *Forbes* magazine listed Oklahoma City as the number one most recession-proof city in the nation.

- *USA Today* headlines declare, "OKC Defies Recession."
- *Business Week* lists Oklahoma City as No. 3 among the "40 Strongest Economies" in the nation.
- In 2010, Oklahoma City hosted the World Mayor Project of London. (No other cities in the U.S. even made the list.)
- *The New York Times* describes Oklahoma City as "Booming with Oil and New Exuberance."
- *Forbes* magazine cited Oklahoma City as No. 6 among the "Most Livable Cities."
- The Oklahoma City Thunder, our first major league sports team, now makes their home in Oklahoma City.
- In 2010, Oklahoma City hosts to National Conference of Mayors.
- Oklahoma City Mayor Mick Cornett was recognized as second best mayor in the world by the World Mayor project of London.

- *CNBC* listed Edmond, Oklahoma as No. 1 on its list of "10 Perfect Suburbs." Looking for suburbs with the best mix of affordable housing, good schools, educated neighbors, low crime, employment and reasonable commutes, they found the unemployment rate in the metro of 4.9 percent, the median house value of $201,770 and that Edmond's public schools are ranked higher than 59 percent of all other U.S. public schools.

Infrastructure

The once shelled-out remains of downtown Oklahoma City now draw tourists after more than $5 billion has been invested in the downtown core. An additional $5 billion will be poured into downtown over the next five years.

The Ford Center Arena, completed in 2002, now seats 19,000. A $100 million upgrade to the Ford Center has put it in the top five national arenas.

Also, $777 million has been allocated to create a new 70-acre central park with a new convention center.

Enterprise

Since we formed OAPN, Oklahoma City has gone from having one luxury hotel downtown to thirty. We have the first and second largest independent oil and gas companies in the nation. Both companies, Devon and Chesapeake, have been named among the best 20 companies to work for nationwide.

Devon Energy is currently building a $750 million skyscraper in Oklahoma City, from cash, which will be the fifth tallest building west of the Mississippi.

Oklahoma City has been named the fourth highest city in entrepreneurial activity in the nation, and listed number one among the top five states for construction activity.

Real Estate

While real estate prices have declined 14 percent nationally over the past 12 months, during that same time, real estate prices in Oklahoma have increased 4.1 percent. Moody's Credit Rating Service lists Oklahoma City's business real estate market as second best in the nation.

Personal Income and Family

During the past three years, personal income growth in Oklahoma City has been 50 percent higher than the national average. Personal income rose 6.9 percent in Oklahoma City from 2007 to 2008, which was the highest increase in the nation for that period and the first year of the recession.

Oklahoma City ranks seventh in the nation among U.S. cities with the highest income growth.

In 2009, while the national poverty rate soared to 14.3 percent, the poverty rate in Oklahoma dropped to 12.9 percent. This is the first time in our history that the poverty rate in Oklahoma has dropped below the national average.

Over the past three years, the Oklahoma City metro has had the lowest unemployment rate of the 49 largest metro areas in the nation.

Oklahoma has the lowest tax burden of any state.

The city's total revenue, plus personal income, is expected to grow by 3.7 percent per year over the next five years.

On October 4, 2011, *24/7 Wall St.* ran an article titled "9 Small Towns with Big Opportunities." Small towns across the nation with 10,000 to

50,000 residents were judged on their economy, job opportunities, and unemployment rates below the national average. Nationally, nine small towns met all the criteria. Four out of the nine—Ardmore, Tahlequah, McAlester, and Enid—are in Oklahoma.

It's no wonder Oklahoma City is rated the fifth best midsized metro area to relocate a family.

Laws Passed

In July 2004, we didn't have the divorce decree, but we knew we were dealing with Baal. So we went to all the buildings that had a Freemason cornerstone. The largest of these was our state capital. Then, we met to pray at the rotunda of the state capitol building. While we were there, the Sergeant of Arms of the House of Representatives asked one of our members what we were doing. He was told we were praying and casting out demons. In response, he invited us to pray inside the House of Representatives, where we anointed every seat, prayed, and made our declarations for over an hour.

In November of that year, for the first time since statehood, the House of Representatives was taken over by conservative Christians, and things began to change. In 2006, we did the same thing in the Senate, and there was a major shift in the fall election. In 2008, we witnessed a full shift with both the House and the Senate controlled by conservative Christians. Here are some of the laws that have been passed in Oklahoma since 2004:

- Constitutional amendment defining marriage as between one man and one woman
- A monument of the 10 Commandments is being placed on the state capital grounds.
- Civil justice reform

- Education reform
- Increased penalty for possession of child pornography

Anti-Abortion Laws Passed

Several years ago, Chuck Pierce prophesied that abortion in American would cease from Oklahoma. These are all steps in that direction:

- 2007—No state funds, employees, or facilities may be used for abortions.
- 2008—Protection for healthcare providers refusing to participate in abortion. Regulates the use of dangerous chemical pill RU-486. Ensures mother's consent to abort is truly voluntary. Provides a woman with an ultrasound of her unborn child prior to undergoing the abortion. Bans wrongful-life lawsuits that claim a baby would have been better off aborted.
- 2009—Allows a pregnant woman to use deadly force to protect her unborn child. Bans abortions based on the sex of a child. Requires all physicians to report information about women seeking abortions or medical care after an abortion, makes it a misdemeanor to attempt to clone humans.
- 2011—Requires abortion providers to determine the age of the fetus prior to abortion. Bans abortion after 20 weeks on the basis of fetal pain. Bans insurance coverage for abortions.

Our newly elected governor, lieutenant governor, attorney general, and State Superintendent of Schools have all been here to OAPN to receive prayer, and they're good people. We've learned that there are no Christian failures—only Christians who give up.

STATE OF THE NATION

Today, there are still problems. Things aren't yet like heaven on earth. However, even looking back over the past 50, years I can assure you the world continues to improve. When I was a child, we didn't have central heat and air, color television, world news via satellite, power steering, space travel, or the World Wide Web, which although it has been abused, grants us instant access to people all over the globe.

Back then, the earth was still reeling from the Great Depression, World Wars I and II, and all the atrocities of Hitler. On the heels of those wars were the Korean conflict and the war in Vietnam. Those were not the good old days.

Furthermore, as we—the Church—take responsibility for repentance and reconciliation and learn to use our authority as God's government on earth, we will see whole cities, states, and even nations transformed.

I know that doesn't sound like what we've grown to expect as the world spins toward its final countdown. We've been taught a gloom and doom theology of the world getting worse and the Church going into hiding. Although that teaching is widespread, it isn't scriptural. The Bible says:

> For a child will be born to us, a son will be given to us; and the government will rest on His shoulders; and His name will be called Wonderful Counselor, Mighty God, Eternal Father, Prince of Peace. **There will be no end to the increase of His government or of peace** (Isaiah 9:6-7).

Did you notice that the Bible says there will be no end to the increase of His government or of peace? That's why things keep getting better! God's government continues to expand and grow, changing the world for the better.

In addition, think about the kind of Church Jesus is returning to receive. Here's what the Bible says about that end-time Church:

> *That He might present the church to Himself in glorious splendor, without spot or wrinkle or any such things [that she might be holy and faultless]* (Ephesians 5:27 AMPC).

I don't know about you, but that doesn't sound like a cowering Church to me. In addition, the Bible is filled with incredible promises that if we humble ourselves, pray, and turn from our wicked ways, God will heal our land. Because we were blinded to the idolatry among us, for years we failed to repent and turn to God.

However, God is healing our land! Transformation has begun!

For 150 years, we suffered a famine of God's transforming and reforming power in our nation, but as we tear down the altars to Baal in our own backyard, God has already begun pouring out His presence and His glory. God will do for you what He has done for us. He will transform your cities and reform your society. His heart's desire has never changed. He wants life on earth to be like that in heaven.

"Yes, well, it has taken you fifteen years," someone might say. "How long will it take us?"

I would hope that our journey will make yours shorter. But what if it takes you longer? What were you planning on doing with your life? There's nothing more worth living for than advancing the kingdom of God.

"Wait a minute!" someone might say. "We haven't seen the kind of healings that happened under the ministry of Oral Roberts, Kathryn Kuhlman, or at Azusa."

We will see those kinds of healings because our bodies are made of earth, and God is healing our land. In addition, what we're about to see is far greater than healing. In Deuteronomy 7:15, we are told, "And the Lord will take away from you all sickness, and none of the evil diseases of Egypt which you knew will He put upon you, but will lay them upon all who hate you" (AMPC).

Can you imagine God taking sickness and disease away? That's the promise God made to the children of Israel coming out of Egypt. Remember, Egypt was a country steeped in idolatry. Not only are we going to see miraculous healings; as we obey God in pulling down the altars to Baal in our society, He will take sickness and disease away from us.

Another thing to consider is that while the healing ministry of Oral Roberts, Kathryn Kuhlman, and Azusa Street was miraculous, it didn't affect society as a whole. What we're seeing and documenting now is the power of God touching our cities, our states, and our society. We've allowed God to break out of the walls of the Church.

Be encouraged. God is blessing America, again.

CHAPTER 15

GROWING A HOUSE OF PRAYER

Apostle John Benefiel

Is it not written, "My house shall be called
a house of prayer for all the nations"?
Mark 11:17

A lot has happened in the years since the information in the last chapter occurred. We've had many more prayer initiatives and victories. Everything we did mattered; God built this House of Prayer step by obedient step. That said, I don't think we would be where we are today had Negiel Bigpond, Willie Jock, and All Tribes D.C. not done what they did in October of 2016. We had reached a place of critical mass where the horrific sins of this country against the First Nations people had to be dealt with.

I consider what they did in gathering so many tribes together and forgiving our nation to be as important as the Declaration of Independence. I'm not exaggerating the degree to which that mattered. If they hadn't done what they did, we would never have gotten free until some president made a public apology.

Without that act of unconditional love and forgiveness on the part of the First Nations people, the enemy would still have had a legal case against the nation in the Courts of Heaven. It would have continued to give him a legal right to hold darkness in place.

When Negiel decided to offer forgiveness to the nation, he asked me to go. I declined, not because I didn't want to be there, but because I knew Negiel would defer to me out of honor. The last thing I wanted was for there to be even the appearance that this historic event was led by a white man. It wasn't worth taking the risk.

I don't have words to express the depth of my emotions for Negiel and Willie and All Tribes D.C.

In a very literal sense, they set us free.

Someone might ask why Negiel didn't just forgive years ago. For the same reason that people who posed before a camera and asked forgiveness from a Native American and then walked away from them never did any good. God isn't looking for a Kodak moment.

He was always looking for covenant.

He wanted us to walk out our covenant together, not for days or weeks. For a lifetime.

Likewise, Negiel could no more have grabbed a few people and forgiven the nation than I could have waltzed into all 50 states and divorced Baal without someone with authority in that land. In Negiel's case, he had to grow All Tribes D.C. into a House of Prayer large enough to represent the First Nations people and shift the nation.

In other words, it had to be done right for it to be legal in the Courts of Heaven.

What All Tribes D.C. did was the most important *first* that ever happened through HAPN. However, we've had lots of firsts. One of them occurred in 2009 when the Lord told me to gather someone from each state to convene in Washington DC, As far as I know, that was the first time there had been a gathering of people from every state to our capital for the sole purpose of repenting of our sins of idolatry.

Another first happened in 2007 when God spoke to me through Chuck Pierce and asked me if I would be willing to go to every state and divorce Baal. I guarantee you that no one had ever done that before. On a personal level, my life took a dramatic turn that year.

Dutch Sheets released the word that we needed to divorce Baal and remarry the Lord in January of 2007. Jerry Mash wrote the Baal divorce decree and we began using it. Later that year, Chuck Pierce, who came here to speak into our meetings four times a year, was here to speak. We sat beside one another. Turning to me he said, "Are you willing to divorce Baal in all 50 states?"

I opened my mouth and was about to say, "I don't even know anyone in all 50 states." Thank God, I caught myself before saying that. The prophet of God had asked me a question, and I was about to make a huge mistake by speaking doubt and unbelief.

When God speaks, our response should always be a faith-filled yes.

"Yes," I said to Chuck, "I'll do it. God will have to show me where to go and who He wants me to connect with."

I knew I didn't have the authority to step off a plane in each state and divorce Baal by myself. I had to find the right person in each state who carried authority over the land and was willing to partner with me. It was a huge undertaking that took the better part of four years to complete.

I traveled at least once a month, but most of the time twice a month, to hold meetings and teach on Baal before we divorced ourselves from him.

The upside was that it was through those connections that we got state leaders for all 50 states.

I often have people ask how we did all that. Looking back, I know that Judith and I prayed this through in tongues. Beginning in the fall of 1987 through May of 1991, we both felt compelled to seek God's will for our lives. With fervent hearts, we prayed in tongues. I still worked as a registered financial advisor. In addition to my job, I prayed at least an hour in tongues and up to four hours a day. Judith prayed in tongues anywhere from two hours to twelve hours a day. We were still praying that way when our pastor retired and sold the church building. By then, we knew God's will. The very next Sunday we started Church on the Rock.

We realize now that we spent those years praying out the process of starting a church and a prayer network. Thank God we had the wisdom to do that.

In this chapter, you'll read about the early days of the ministry and the network. My wife, Judith; my son, Rhett; my longtime secretary, Janet; and our HAPN Administrator, Andy Leong will share their experiences along the journey.

Later, you'll also hear from my dear friend, Robert Henderson. We were friends long before he got the revelation about how to operate in the Courts of Heaven. When I heard his teaching, I understood at a new depth why we'd been getting such astounding results. In obeying God by preparing legal documents such as the Baal divorce decree and the Writ of Assistance, we'd shifted things in the Courts of Heaven, which shifted things on earth.

If you haven't already done so, read all of Robert's books on how to operate in the Courts of Heaven. This will help you shift your life and the lives of your family.

You'll also hear from Jon Hamill of Lamplighter Ministries. Jon is one of the founding members of the One Voice Prayer Movement, which has seen wonderful fruit. I first met Jon in 2008. Since getting to know him, I've found in Jon not only a friend, but a like-minded brother in the Lord.

Jon's first role in HAPN was in 2010 when he became our Maryland State Leader. Later, he took on the responsibility of leading the Regional Mid-Atlantic area. In 2016, he shifted to become our leader over government. That same year, Jon and his wife, Jolene, led a prayer and revival journey called the Glory Train, touching all 50 states with God's promise for national turnaround.

Jon and Jolene are very prophetic and have deep insights into what's happening in our government, both in the natural and in the spirit. When we first met, Jon and Jolene lived in the suburbs close to Washington, DC. Knowing that they would have more authority if they lived in DC, they moved. Their home offers a stunning view of the Pentagon and the Potomac.

Jon describes the call on his life as a White House watchman. This is a call he and Jolene fulfill very well. Jon's new book, *White House Watchman,* is a must read. I consider it a companion book to this one.

JUDITH BENEFIEL

Pastor, Church on the Rock, Oklahoma City

It's amazing to see how God has built and orchestrated this international prayer network! I've witnessed my husband's obedience and passion for this God-given assignment. He has always been quick to obey when he's gotten clarity of revelation about God's will. It's obvious that he's called to be a leader of leaders. This network is full of wonderful people who are themselves capable leaders who love God, people, their countries, and the world. They are giving their lives to be a vital part of advancing God's kingdom.

In the beginning, it didn't *look* so impactful as John drove to many towns in Oklahoma and surrounding states with a heart to help ministers pray and work for transformation in their areas of influence. Zechariah 4:10 says, "Do not despise these small beginnings, for the Lord rejoices to see the work begin, to see the plumb line in Zerubbabel's hand" (NLT).

In my opinion, the key to my husband's success is that he doesn't despise small beginnings and, furthermore, doesn't view any assignment from God as small, even though others might.

I see a similarity to this network in nature. While in Hawaii, I went on a whale watch. While watching those huge yet graceful creatures, I heard them sing by way of a microphone in the water. The guide told us that scientists have discovered that whales sing a new, different song every year. Even if they are in waters a thousand miles apart, they are singing the *same* song each year. I wept, just knowing that our God is orchestrating and conducting that miraculous symphony.

How much more amazing and beautiful it is when God-loving people all over the world, who have a free-will choice to obey or not, are singing, working, strategizing, and praying in unison to worship God and do His will on earth!

RHETT BENEFIEL

Executive Pastor at Church on the Rock, Oklahoma City

In February of 1995, my wife, Julie, and I were in college, living in a one-bedroom apartment in Norman, Oklahoma. I had my life mapped out. After college, I would work for a major company as a Certified Public Accountant.

One night I had an experience that was the closest I've ever come to saying I heard the audible voice of God. I went from a deep sleep one second to being wide awake the next. God said, *"Wake up!"*

I went to our little living room and prayed in tongues. I saw a vision of a calendar turned to June 1997. *"That's when you'll be asked to become part of the vision of Church on the Rock on staff."*

"Well, Lord," I said, "You know that's not my plan, but I want Your plan. Thank You for this word. It's so specific, 28 months in the future, that if it comes to pass I'll know it was You."

I didn't tell anyone about that experience, not my parents, John and Judith Benefiel. I didn't even tell my wife, Julie. I didn't want anything to happen through the arm of the flesh.

I was very passionate about Church on the Rock. I was there every time the doors were opened. I tithed, having started when I was twelve. I gave offering messages. I served as an usher. I worked in the nursery. I served in children's ministry. I ran cameras. I ran sound and worked in the food ministry. I ministered to the youth, and I was a small group pastor.

I loved all of that, but I had zero desire to do it as a career.

I never mentioned that visitation from the Lord to anybody. I graduated from college and went to work for an international accounting and consulting firm. It was one of the largest service-providing organizations in the world at the time, with over 85,000 employees.

Church on the Rock has now been in existence for 29 years. In all that time, we've only lost two associate pastors. We lost them both, one to death, in May of 1997. That caught my attention, because it was only one month before the date I'd seen in my vision. I still didn't say anything.

"The day we lost our second associate pastor," Apostle John recalls, "I wondered who I would have as associate pastor. The Lord said, *Who do you want?"* Without even thinking about it I said, 'Rhett.'

"Then my mind took over and I remembered that he'd just gotten a great promotion when a client of his firm hired him to lead a team. It wasn't likely that he would want to give that up. I talked to Judith and she said, 'Well, ask him.'"

It was around late May when Dad called and asked if I would consider going on staff.

"Well, Dad, let me tell you a story."

I told him about how God had prepared me for this 27 months earlier. I accepted the position and turned in my notice. I started my job at Church on the Rock on June 23, 1997.

Even knowing it was God's will for my life, it was still difficult to give up my own dream job. However, God provided the grace I needed for my new career. Looking back, I know how important it was that God showed me in such a powerful way what He wanted me to do. If all I had to stand strong was that my dad wanted to work with his son, it wouldn't have been enough to keep me going in the long run. I lasted because I knew it was God's plan.

We'd started the Oklahoma Concert of Prayer in 1995. I think it's significant that I came on staff in June of 1997. Just a few weeks later, on July 13, we repented and began walking in covenant with Jay Swallow and Negiel Bigpond.

That changed everything.

It set us on a trajectory of growth to what we have now in HAPN and GAPN. I knew in a sense that a big part of God calling me to that position was to free up Dad's time. Over the years, there has been as much as 50 percent of his time, sometimes even more, spent on HAPN and the network. He couldn't have done that if he'd had to run the day-to-day affairs of the church. I believe God put me in place to free up his time.

Although the prayer network had very humble beginnings, I think it has become the most impactful network of its kind in the world. I don't mean a network of any kind, but of its own DNA.

My dad is different from a lot of apostles and apostolic networks in that he is so incredibly relational. He's always been that way. It was a part of his nature that caused him to be so successful as a financial planner.

In the early days of the church, he called every single visitor. I was in college at the time and would sit and listen to the calls. They were such heartwarming conversations. He was interested in the details of their lives because he cared.

For years we were one of the fastest growing churches in Oklahoma City. Part of that was because he's so grounded in the Word, and part of it was because he is so relational.

HEART OF A SHEPHERD

My dad is an apostle, but he has the heart of a shepherd. To some people in certain circles of apostolic theology, the word *pastor* is a bad word. I've never understood that. The way some people talk, the only way to be more apostolic is to be less pastoral.

I disagree with that. Jesus was *the* greatest apostle who ever lived. We're told in 1 Peter 5:4 that He was and is the Chief Shepherd. "Chief Shepherd" is the Greek word *archipoimen*. *Poimen* is the word translated in Ephesians 4:11 as *pastor*, one of the five ascension gifts Jesus gave that caused God's kingdom to expand greatly. Jesus was the perfect apostle *and* the perfect pastor. There is no conflict between those two callings, but divine harmony. David was an Old Testament type of apostle, but he was also a literal shepherd, which is part of what made him a man after God's own heart.

I think something unique about my dad is that he built his shepherd's heart into the DNA of HAPN. I believe that instead of an apostle and pastor being separate, they need to be synergistic, caring and loving people—like Jesus.

One of the ways that shepherd's DNA manifests is how we handle the last evening of our annual conference. Instead of having one last meeting, all the HAPN leaders are invited to my sister and brother-in-law's house for a meal and to socialize. We have a wonderful time getting to know one another better. How many networks do that at their annual conferences?

I also think that the branches that were created to expand HAPN have helped it multiply. It's the Jethro principle found in Exodus 18. Jethro told Moses that he was wearing himself out. Setting other leaders in place distributed the work load.

While Dad traveled to all 50 states to divorce Baal, I was handling the building of our new sanctuary, nursery, and children's area. It was important to us all that the church reflected the fact that it was the center of a worldwide prayer network.

We paid 75 percent of the $5 million in cash, and now we are out of debt. As a church, we've always tithed and given offerings. As of March 6, 2020, Church on the Rock has given away $6,295,215. That doesn't include what was given through HAPN and GAPN. When you add them together, the church and the network have given well over $7 million.

I know God gave us favor and financial strategies. However, I think He also blessed us because of all the years Church on the Rock supported the prayer network. That just proves to me that it's excellent soil.

JANET SIMPKINS

Secretary, Church on the Rock, Oklahoma City

God gave me a dream in 1985 that has defined the last 35 years of my life. I have no idea how many times that exact scene has played out in real time over the years.

In the dream, I sat at the computer. John Benefiel stood looking over my right shoulder. We were both looking at the computer, and I knew it was in a coworker environment.

I woke the next morning and thought, *That will **never** happen. I know nothing about stocks and bonds. My field is banking.* I dismissed the dream.

I met John and Judith when I joined Church of the New Life where they attended. At that time, John was still working as a stockbroker, registered investment advisor, and certified financial planner. I was one of the bank officers at a local bank, supervising one of their departments. One morning at my desk I prayed, "Lord, I want to go back to being a secretary for one person."

I didn't know that John was getting ready to move from his downtown office to a branch at Waterford. His assistant wanted to continue working downtown. John would need someone to work for him.

Judith and her friend, Anna, were praying about it when Anna said, "Have you thought about asking Janet to work for John?" Later, Judith was driving home one day when the Lord spoke to her about it.

Soon afterward, I sat at the Bible study and prayer meeting that John and Judith led on Monday evenings. John walked over and said, "Do you know anything about IRAs?"

"No, not really. I have a guy in my department who handles them."

"Would you be interested in coming to work for me?"

Remembering the dream, I agreed. When John called to talk about it, I told him about the dream. I felt like God had given me a heads-up so that I would have no qualms about making the transition. I went to work for him on May 7, 1986.

We both attended Church of the New Life, which was a pioneer charismatic church at the time. Our pastor, U.L. Harshfield, was the first person to bring Kenneth Copeland to Oklahoma City to speak in 1973. He also brought in other ministers like Kenneth Hagin, Frederick Price, and Charles Capps. We were well fed.

A family gave a donation to the church designated for John and Judith's ministry. At the time they didn't have a name for their ministry, they were just faithfully doing what they felt the Lord was directing them to do—teach a weekly Bible study. The church set up an account for us and called it Benefiel Ministries. Benefiel Ministries grew from John and Judith's Monday evening Bible study and prayer meeting. We went through the process of registering the ministry, getting bylaws in order and making it legal. I was so excited to have our very own post office mailbox! To me it was a tangible stake in the ground that we were moving forward even though we had no idea that it would grow to what we see today.

John and Judith were out of town on business when our pastor announced that he was retiring and selling the building that housed the church. The church would cease to exist. When John called the office on Monday to check in, I gave him the news. Our church would be no more.

John and Judith had been praying for several years asking God, "What's next?"

"We're going to start a church," John and Judith announced. "The first service will be held on May 5, 1991." I was the church's first employee, not John. He continued his career, was the pastor, and for several Sundays played the keyboard for worship.

We started the Oklahoma Concert of Prayer in October of 1995, which has grown into HAPN and GAPN. I think this had been in John's heart for a long time. Even when he led that first Bible study he kept saying, "I know there's more. I know that God wants us to get more people together to learn to pray."

I stepped into John's office one day and found him with a pencil and paper. He was trying to figure out how to get pastors from the north, south, east, and west to gather and pray. Later, we held a regional meeting for Church on the Rock International. Dr. Lawrence Kennedy prophesied to John. While I don't recall the exact words, the gist of the prophecy was, "You're trying to put paper and pencil to this and figure it out, but you're not going to be able to do it. I'm going to lead you by My Spirit, because it's not going to be like you think. You're not going to be able to line it out."

On April 20, 1995, Dr. Lawrence Kennedy gave John this word: "You're going to influence multiple thousands of people. And I also predict this, folks, and I heard it with the other prophetic team here. This is going to be a very large church. It's going to be a very large church. What I'm talking about—it's going to be in the thousands numbers. I'm not going to say how many thousands. I'm just saying in the thousand-plus numbers. A significant ministry is going to be here."

That word was so accurate it made me wonder, *What's this going to look like?*

I was at the church early one morning praying when the Lord gave me a vision. I saw myself standing on the south end zone of the University of Oklahoma football stadium. I watched the players line up, but they weren't straight, they were zig zagged, like a chevron pattern. The Lord said, *"All John can see is the end zone. He doesn't see the defensive lineup trying to inter-fere and stop him."*

I felt like the Lord was saying that John had to keep his eye on where he was going, which was the end zone. My job was to help set the steps and get him to the end zone. A few times over the years I got frustrated and thought, *Doesn't he see these things?* Then I remembered that John doesn't see all the steps. He has to keep his eyes on the end zone.

I can look back over the past 35 years and see how small things made a big impact. For instance, one small prayer sitting at my desk asking the Lord to let me be a secretary again. Another small prayer moved me out of my comfort zone to a Spirit-filled charismatic church, which changed my destiny.

I look back and notice all those key moments that didn't seem big at the time. Before I knew anything about Chuck Pierce, I saw his picture and an article he had written about prayer. I simply prayed, "Lord, we need a man like Chuck Pierce to help us. We need someone who really has a heart for prayer and to see things accomplished." That's all I said, and I probably wasn't the only one praying about that, but to me it was one of those little things that ultimately was a big thing.

None of us knew it was a divine connection and a momentous moment the day that Dennis Latham came to talk to John about meeting a man named Jay Swallow. Or the times that John's life intersected with John Ward, Jerry Mash, or Negiel Bigpond.

John is correct in saying that we didn't know what we were doing. How did we go from a small Monday Bible study to a worldwide prayer network? We did it through thousands of moments of prayer that turned out to be momentous. We did it through hundreds of divine connections. Through millions of small steps of obedience.

Looking back, it is a reminder to me, and hopefully to you, to enjoy and remember the small things in life for one day they could lead to the biggest things—exceedingly, abundantly above all that we ask or think (see Eph. 3:20)! Never under estimate the small things in your life; you never know how big that mustard seed can grow! "Do not despise these small beginnings, for the Lord rejoices to see the work begin, to see the plumb line in Zerubbabel's hand" (Zech. 4:10 NLT).

ANDY LEONG

HAPN Administrator, Pastor,
Church on the Rock, Oklahoma City

I grew up in Penang, Malaysia, in a Christian home where we spoke English, Chinese, and Cantonese. We also spoke Malay, the official language in Malaysia, along with Mandarin and a couple of other Chinese dialects. None of my family had ever been to the U.S., but from the age of seven I'd always planned on going to college there.

As I reached college age, I applied to a number of universities in the U.S. and was accepted to them all. "I heard from God, and I know where you're supposed to go in the U.S.," my mother said one day.

"Well, tell me!"

"No, I'm not going to tell you. You need to hear God for yourself. Then I'll confirm it."

After praying I said, "I believe God is calling me to Oklahoma."

"Yes, that's what I heard too," she replied.

A prophet by the name of Jacob Kurien, who lived in Houston, spoke at my church in Penang. I had no way of knowing at the time, but Jacob had prophesied Church on the Rock into existence.

"I'm going to college at Oklahoma Christian University in Oklahoma City in August," I explained to Jacob in 1995. "Can you recommend a church?" Jacob recommended Church on the Rock and Faith Fellowship.

When I arrived in Oklahoma, I looked up the location of both churches that Jacob had recommended. It was an easy decision. Church on the Rock was located on the same street as my school, just a few miles distance. I called the church, and Hershell and Helen Hughes offered to drive me to and from all the services.

While attending college in the U.S. had always been my dream, I had no idea how much I would miss my family. I arrived in August and went home for Christmas break. Flying back after Christmas was much more difficult than leaving home the first time. The first couple of years were so difficult due to loneliness that I decided to move back home after I graduated.

Chuck Pierce started prophesying into our prayer network in 1995. One of the words he spoke over Church on the Rock was that it would become the greatest revival house in the United States. Each time he came, he talked about a new sound. He said we needed original sound and music to help shift the atmosphere.

I came home from church after a Sunday service in 1998 and took a nap. I had a dream in which I was telling my mother what Chuck said about Church on the Rock becoming a great revival house. During the dream, I looked at all the notes I'd taken from the meetings with Chuck. As I told my mother what God was saying about Oklahoma, I started weeping.

"I know God is calling me to stay even though I don't want to," I said. "I feel like God is changing my heart and telling me that I'm supposed to stay."

I woke from the dream and realized that I was physically weeping. I sat up in bed feeling the presence of God heavy in the room. In my spirit, I heard words and music to a new song. Within 10 minutes, I had written the following song taken from Joshua 8:7:

Rise and Take This City (All of Oklahoma Shall Be Saved)

> Lord we humbly bow before You
> We receive this call on our lives
> Lord we thank You for this honor
> To be called the remnant of this land

Lord we hunger for Your glory

We want to see Your power in this land

Lord together as one people

We declare revival is at hand

And we shall rise

And we shall take this city

And we shall take this state

In the name of the Lord

And we say, "All of Oklahoma shall be saved!"[1]

I couldn't believe that God chose me to write this song, because my heart wasn't here. I was leaving, except after that dream I knew God had called me from Malaysia to Oklahoma—to stay.

A CALL TO WORSHIP

At my home church in Malaysia, I'd become the worship leader at age 17. After graduating with my degree in computer science, there was a time I had to move to St. Paul, Minnesota, for a while in order to keep my green card. I had been visiting a church when the pastor asked me to be their worship leader. I laughed and said, "In that case maybe I should join the church."

I'd always seen myself leading worship at Church on the Rock and HAPN. I didn't see how that could happen so I never mentioned it to anyone. Then one Sunday afternoon in 2006, Pastor Judith called and asked me to take over the worship team. That was the fulfillment of what God had put in my heart. I knew I was supposed to say yes.

In 2008, I wrote a song for Jay and Joan Swallow to honor the Cheyenne tribe. The name of the song is *Maheo*, which is the Cheyenne name for God.

Maheo

From afar You have called us

To inhabit this land

You have given us Your Word

So we could follow Your command

Somehow through the years

We have lost The Way

But we stand this day and say

We are Your people

You are our God

We are Your people

You are our God

Every tribe, every nation

Every tongue in this land

You have poured out Your Spirit

So we could be restored again

We turn and seek Your face

And You have healed our land

So we stand this day and say

Maheo Maheo Maheo Maheo[2]

Jay and Joan Swallow were so moved by the song that they did something I'd never imagined. On April 30, 2010, they presented me with a beautiful pair of handmade moccasins and adopted me into the Cheyenne tribe. They gave me a Cheyenne name, which means Holy Horse.

I had given up living near my family to follow God to Oklahoma. In return, He gave me a tribe. Even more important was the authority I received by being adopted. God had called me here from Malaysia, but I felt like a transplant, never rooted. When Jay and Joan adopted me, I became one of the First Nations people, with the authority to do what God had brought me here to do. This is why I always travel with All Tribes D.C. I am one of them. In addition, our HAPN Germany leader loved the song and translated it into German. They sing it at their church as well.

That same year, in 2010, we moved into our new sanctuary, and I passed another milestone by becoming a U.S. citizen.

I still worked for a computer software company based in New York. It was a very stressful job, and I felt like it was time to move on. I prayed about it, and God impressed me that I should talk to Pastor Rhett. I knew the church couldn't match my salary, but I didn't care about that. I wanted to do work that was more fulfilling. In July 2011, Pastor Rhett hired me full time. They split my time and salary between the church and HAPN.

As HAPN administrator and also as the worship leader, I've traveled to take part in many of our initiatives. For instance, I've been in Washington, DC, for every initiative we've done there. The same goes for many things we've been led to do across the country.

I handle most of the communication for HAPN. I also coordinate things behind the scenes for OAPN, HAPN, First Nations, and GAPN. I plan out the details of our annual conferences each year.

I believe that the Lord has brought HAPN to a level of prominence. I know that a lot of what we do is covert, but that doesn't mean we don't still have prominence. God is placing people who are a part of HAPN in strategic places to have the ear of those in authority.

Although we operate behind the scenes, we speak into situations and change them. We're a lot like Daniel. We may not be the primary person, but we're the ones who have the king's ear.

We may not be the governor, but we govern.

We may not be president, but we're ruling.

I look back over the past 25 years, and I see that God called me from Malaysia to help fulfill the vision of this church and prayer network. It's more fulfilling than anything I've ever done because it's eternal.

God is continuing to refine our vision. He is continuing to show us more. We never feel that we've arrived. After all these years, we're still saying, "Here we are, Lord, send us."

CHAPTER 16

POSITIONED IN THE COURTS OF HEAVEN

Robert Henderson
Apostolic Leader of Global Reformer Prayer Center
A Global House of Prayer for the Nations

But you have come right up into Mount Zion, to the city of the
living God, the heavenly Jerusalem, and to the gathering of
countless happy angels; and to the church, composed of all those
registered in heaven; and to God who is Judge of all; and to the
spirits of the redeemed in heaven, already made perfect.
Hebrews 12:22-23, TLB

PETER WAGNER said that HAPN has the most tangible, measurable results of high-level prayer and spiritual warfare that he'd heard in his lifetime. I agree with him about that, and those results are not an accident. I see several reasons that while many people and organizations pray and see no results, HAPN is shifting things in the spirit world. They're moving and changing spiritual reality. Those changes are being manifest in the natural.

The first reason that's happening is that John Benefiel is recognized in heaven. Not everyone is esteemed the same. Everything that's esteemed on earth is not applauded in heaven. The results all begin with the apostle whom God has called and anointed.

For instance, nobody can just decide one day that they're going to walk into a courthouse on earth and try a case. You have to have studied and graduated with a degree in law. Even that's not enough. You have to pass the bar exam and be approved as being in good standing with the state. Even then, not any lawyer can waltz into the Supreme Court and speak; those things have to be earned. Apostle John has been called, anointed, and appointed for what he does. He has been faithful, endured, and is honored and recognized to operate in the Highest Court of Heaven.

How someone is perceived in the spirit is very, very important. We know this in part because of the men and women who are listed in Hebrews 11. Being mentioned in the Hall of Fame of Faith is a big deal. The Bible says that they all by faith obtained a good report. That means they had status in heaven.

Someone else might pray the exact same words as Apostle John and do the same prophetic acts. However, it doesn't have the same effect because they don't have the same position or status granted to them that he does.

In Ezekiel 14:13-14 we read about Noah, Daniel, and Job:

> *"Son of man, if a country sins against Me by committing unfaithfulness, and I stretch out My hand against it, destroy its supply of bread, send famine against it and cut off from it both man and beast, even though these three men, Noah, Daniel and Job were in its midst, by their own righteousness they could only deliver themselves," declares the Lord God.*

Notice that it says that *by their own righteousness they could only deliver themselves.* It's righteousness that gives us our position before the Lord. We're told in Genesis 15:6, "Abram believed the Lord, and he credited it to him as righteousness" (NIV). Our righteousness grants us a level of authority before the Lord.

This is one of the major reasons that John Benefiel and HAPN gained a place of authority in the spirit world. When you do something from that position, it causes things to move and manifest in the natural. In Isaiah 56:7 we're told:

> *Even those I will bring to My holy mountain and make them joyful in My house of prayer. Their burnt offerings and their sacrifices will be acceptable on My altar; for My house will be called a house of prayer for all the peoples.*

REGISTERED IN HEAVEN

It takes a house of prayer to represent a culture before the Lord in the Court of Heaven. God doesn't need everyone to repent. He needs a house of prayer who will stand before Him and shift a culture.

God works from a governmental mindset. If He has a house that does that, it's as if the whole culture has repented. It gives Him the legal right to show mercy.

Heaven recognized John Benefiel and it recognizes HAPN because it is a house of prayer built by the apostle who was called to do it. I see HAPN in Hebrews 12:22-23:

*But you have come right up into Mount Zion, to the city of the living God, the heavenly Jerusalem, and to the gathering of countless happy angels; and to the church, composed of all **those registered in heaven**; and to God who is Judge of all; and to the spirits of the redeemed in heaven, already made perfect* (TLB).

Notice that He describes the church that is registered in heaven. A church or house of prayer that is registered in heaven has the right to represent something before the Lord. How do I know that HAPN is registered in heaven? By the results. HAPN is shifting cultures so they must be registered in heaven.

We know that not all churches are registered in heaven. Some have been registered in heaven but that right is taken away. For instance, Jesus warned the church at Ephesus that if they didn't repent for having left their first love, He would take their candlestick away.

If Jesus removes His candlestick from a church, it might still be registered on earth. But it won't be registered in heaven. Heaven won't recognize it.

I also see HAPN represented in Isaiah 2:2, "And it shall come to pass in the latter days, that the mountain of Jehovah's house shall be established on the top of the mountains" (ASV).

HAPN is a government entity that has the right to stand at the tops of the mountains. Therefore, it can do things necessary to cause the nations of the earth to come under the atmosphere of God's blessing. God recognizes it as a house of prayer that has a right to stand before Him.

BOC DENIED

In November 2011, I had been teaching about operating in the Courts of Heaven for 10 years when I had a dream. In my dream, Dutch Sheets' wife,

Ceci, sent me Dutch's official response to 9/11. It was several paragraphs written on Dutch's letterhead. At the bottom of the page, Ceci had written that she had seen in the spirit that 9/11 had been allowed to happen.

She had seen four living creatures crying out "Holy! Holy! Holy is the Lord God Almighty!" There were four demonic counterparts also standing before the courts. They declared, "BOC denied! BOC denied! BOC denied!"

When I woke, I had no idea what BOC stood for. Was it Greek? Was it Hebrew? I couldn't find it. Finally, I just Googled it. Here's what popped up: body of Christ.

I knew that was the correct interpretation. I also understood that the enemy had claimed a legal right to deny the prayers of the body of Christ. The lack of prayer had created a vacuum that allowed 9/11 to occur.

All of our individual prayers were not enough to stop it. It would have taken a house of prayer that could represent the culture.

Understand, 9/11 was not the judgment of God.

It was the absence of the Church.

I think we've come a long way since then with HAPN and other prayer networks that have been recognized in heaven.

When I first started teaching on how to operate in the Courts of Heaven, I got a lot of flak from people who opposed. Apostle John Benefiel was probably the first person who heard my teaching and said, "Yes, this is right." He gave it credibility because what I taught showed him why HAPN had had such incredible results.

John had followed the direction of the Lord and created an actual legal Divorce Decree and a Writ of Assistance. These were legal documents, drawn up by an attorney, and presented in the Courts of Heaven. When John heard my teaching, the puzzle pieces fell in place.

They were operating in the Courts of Heaven.

The other thing that I see about HAPN is that it isn't just a network. It operates as a covenantal relationship of family. I know this from all the times I've attended HAPN meetings. That's very important because God is all about covenant and family.

Another thing God looks for is alignment. It matters who you're aligned with in this season. Abraham understood who Melchizedek was and aligned with him. How? He honored Melchizedek with his finances.

I believe our finances allow us to claim that we're a house. For instance, when I'm speaking before the Courts of Heaven, I say that we have the right to be a house and present cases before the Court because we are joined through the honor of finances.

Cornelius is a good example about how our finances speak. The Lord said, "Your prayers and your alms have come up for a memorial before God" (Acts 10:4 NKJV). God counts financial giving as well as prayer as a memorial before Him.

That's why I send Apostle John a check every month. I do it to honor John, knowing that it aligns us in the spirit realm. It gives me drawing rights. Those finances give me the right to say, "I'm part of this house. I'm not just coming on my own. I'm coming as a part of this company. I'm able to stand in their status and ask that you remember my family."

The primary thing that creates a connection is honor. My giving says, "I honor this one. By spiritual discernment I understand who this person is. I understand what this ministry is and I honor it with my finances."

That alignment also provides a covering and offers protection. When God blesses HAPN, He also blesses me.

CHAPTER 17

WINNING GOVERNMENTAL WARS IN HEAVEN'S COURT

Jon Hamill
HAPN Government Mountain Leader
Lamplighter Ministries

For a child will be born to us, a son will be given to us;
and the government will rest on His shoulders; and
His name will be called Wonderful Counselor,
Mighty God, Eternal Father, Prince of Peace.

Isaiah 9:6

THE government is ground zero for spiritual warfare and the conflict of thrones. The enemy always wants to exalt himself over the highest governing body. That's why you can look in the Bible and see that when nations were being shifted, God always had men like Daniel and Joseph in places of authority next to the highest leader in the land. They understood the times and seasons, praying out God's plans.

Daniel's assignment was to bring God's people out of Babylonian captivity. God had shown Daniel that it was time to return the exiles out of Babylonian captivity to Jerusalem. Daniel prayed and set God's plan in motion using his spiritual authority. However, to get the job done, God needed a deliverer.

He chose the most unexpected man—Cyrus, the King of Persia. God compelled him to send the exiles home, send back the sacred vessels taken from the temple, and help pay for rebuilding it.

Daniel couldn't have accomplished his assignment without Cyrus. Cyrus wouldn't have been compelled to act had it not been for Daniel setting things in motion. However, they still needed someone to oversee the project. For that job, God appointed Zerubbabel. An aristocrat born into captivity, Zerubbabel was the grandson of the last king of Judah before the Babylonian conquest.

When God rescues a nation, He always calls a Daniel, a Cyrus, and a Zerubbabel. I had no idea when I met John Benefiel that he had prophetically been given the anointings of those three men.

For instance, on June 13, 1994, Jacob Kurien had prophesied this over Apostle John: "I have called you, just like I have called Zerubbabel, Zerubbabel, saith God. In the midst of oppression, in the midst of depression, in the midst of idolatry, in the midst of apostasy, I have called Zerubbabel to be the Governor of Jerusalem. I have called Zerubbabel to be a great builder, saith God. But I have called you to stand for Me. Stand for Me before the people, before the people in authority, before the people in power, before the people who hold the keys of this city, saith God. So I say unto you, My son, you are not just a pastor of this church, but you have a higher calling. And this church will continue to be built as an international church. I'm going to expand the borders of this church, and I will keep on expanding. I will keep on expanding. I will keep on expanding, saith God."

Barbara Yoder prophesied that Apostle John had the anointing of Cyrus on September 11, 1996: "And the Lord would say, that even as I have called you Cyrus, I'm linking you with Cyrus in the territory, that I'm linking you even with the king in this area. The Lord said that, even in the future, I'm going to cause you to become intertwined with many political, governmental leaders."

Cindy Jacobs prophesied the Daniel anointing over him on January 12, 2000: "And God says to you, I'm giving you an anointing for wealth; I'm giving you an anointing for a war chest. So the Lord says, I'm doing a new thing through you. I have given you the Daniel anointing, and I'm going to give you the anointing to impart the Daniel anointing, says the Lord."

A Long Journey of Nobility

I looked at the work John Benefiel had done, which not many people understood. He had brought together the First Nations people and European descendants. The reconciliation took such a long time because they walked it out in pain and nobility. It took a long time for deep trust to be earned.

That was the foundation that brought such great success to the divorcement of Baal. The First Nations apostolic authority was absolutely essential. What they did wasn't out of obligation. It was from the heart. They modeled this for the rest of the nation.

I met John in 2008 on a prayer journey though Wall Street. I didn't get to know him then. Later, Terry Deckard told me about a man in Oklahoma who was receiving very similar revelation to what we were hearing. Terry said, "You've got to get in touch with these people. It's really important. I feel it's because you're both saying the same thing. They figured out a way to see break through with the divorcement of Baal."

At the time, Terry had a wonderful watchman's perch right between the Capitol and the White House on Pennsylvania Avenue. Jolene and I prayed with her there many times.

A few months earlier, we'd gone to the four points of Washington, DC, dealing with Freemasonry as best we knew how. At the time, we didn't have the language of divorcing Baal. The Lord had given us language about approaching the Courts of Heaven, but it was much more concise with the divorce decree.

"John Benefiel is going to Vermont," Terry said. "You need to go too." That's how I got catapulted to Vermont. It was right around Halloween in 2009, and we divorced Baal at the capitol in Montpelier. Judy Ball prophesied over both of us.

Judy had called Apostle John a month earlier and prophesied that the Lord wanted him to convene at least one person representing each state in Washington, DC, and divorce Baal.

Apostle John said, "Lord, please help us. I don't even know people from each state."

The Lord said through Judy that in December, 2009 President Obama would be out of the country signing away the sovereignty of the United States. The plan was to create a transnational government. Once the contract was signed, if we didn't abide by it the nations could impose discipline on the U.S. government.

In response to that word, we gathered with HAPN at the L'Enfant Plaza Hotel on December 7 and 8, 2009. Pierre L'Enfant was the man who laid out Washington, DC, according to the Masons, which was the occult. Native Americans were very well represented. That was essential because they carried the First Nations apostolic authority. Apostle Jay Swallow was there with a mandate from God who'd shown him a scroll from heaven that said, "Turn these principalities over to the Courts of Heaven."

We boarded buses and traveled to the Lincoln Memorial and to then to the House of the Temple. A Masonic temple, it serves as the headquarters of Freemasonry. It stands 13 blocks north of the White House, which is no coincidence. We got a tour of the temple, including seeing where initiates of the 33rd degree kneel at the altar.

We also went to the Basilica of the National Shrine of the Immaculate Conception, which is the largest Roman Catholic Basilica in North America. Diane Buker, known as God's Battleax, had told Apostle John to make sure we went there. As we walked inside, the sign over the door read, *Blessed Art Thou, Oh Virgin Mother, Queen of Heaven*. The Queen of Heaven is the female representation of Baal. It's a shrine for the worship of Mary. They believed she was sinless and a co-redeemer with Jesus. While all Christians should esteem Mary, she should not be worshiped. The Bible makes this clear in Acts 4:12: "And there is salvation in no one else; for there is *no other name* under heaven that has been given among men by which we must be saved."

We divorced Baal in all three places.

A DEMONIC PLAN UNRAVELED

The *very next day* President Obama was supposed to sign the treaty making a transnational government. However, the conference fell apart. There was nothing for him to sign. That meeting morphed into the Paris Climate Treaty. I'm so thankful that God told us what was about to happen and how to intervene. We could never have figured that out on our own.

The next month, in January 2010, Judy Ball called John again. "The Lord says we're supposed to gather two people from each state in Washington, DC, in March."

On March 16, 2010, we convened again in Washington, DC, this time with at least two people representing each state. There were around 250 of us who divorced Baal at key places all over the city. We divided up into small teams of four or five. Spreading out, we went to dozens of government agencies like the State Department, the Department of Defense, and the Federal Reserve.

Along the way, Apostle John's team was making their way to a site when he stopped to use the restroom. They were in front of the International Monetary Fund. He asked to use their facilities, and they allowed him to pass security and enter the building. Inside, he prayed the prayer of divorcement of Baal. Back outside, he realized that they were across the street from the World Bank. Going into the lobby, they divorced Baal there as well.

I wondered at the time why we were going back to places we'd already been. I thought once we divorced Baal we wouldn't have to do it again. The Lord showed me that everything in the spirit realm works by covenant. We were having to break those evil covenants and reestablish new covenants with Christ. You don't find a throne without a covenant that gives it a legal right to operate. We had to continue until we'd removed all of the enemy's legal rights.

In 2010, Apostle John, Curt Landry, and Negiel Bigpond met with high-level government officials in Jerusalem. They asked the officials what they would like for them to pray. "Please pray that the United States would recognize Jerusalem as the official capital of Israel."

Later during that trip, John, Curt, and Negiel stood on the vacant lot in Jerusalem that the United States had purchased to build a new U.S. Embassy. It stood empty, owned but never used. They divorced Baal there and declared the Writ of Assistance, then asked the Courts of Heaven to rule in their favor to recognize Jerusalem as the capital and move the U.S. Embassy there.

The Lord directed Apostle John to divorce Baal at all Masonic Lodges in the nation. Between 2009 and July of 2011, HAPN divorced Baal at well over 10,000 altars of historic idolatry.

Then from October 3, 2011 to November 11, 2011 we followed the Lord's direction to have prayer and worship for 40 days in Washington, DC. Then the Lord gave us a clear mandate to return to Washington, DC, and ask for God's hand in marriage in order to restore covenant with Him.

My forefathers were among the pilgrims who cut covenant with the Lord for this nation in Massachusetts. So I've been passionate about seeing our covenant with Christ restored. As a watchman, part of my responsibility is to watch over Heaven's Court. That's my pursuit. It's also why I entered this experience with Apostle John and came under his leadership.

In order to restore covenant, we believed the Lord wanted us to return to the place where we'd started—the Lincoln Memorial. Our purpose was to present the finished work of divorcing Baal and ask for God's hand in marriage.

On July 4, 2011, we gathered at the Lincoln Memorial. I was reminded of a prophetic dream that Rick Ridings had back in the late 1990s. He saw a giant nut over Washington, DC. He knew that it represented the hard shell of demonic resistance. The Lord showed him that when enough push came from both the north and the south, it would crack that stronghold.

I had written a document called the Declaration of Covenant that I prayed through and presented before the Court of Heaven that day. We asked that the restoration of covenant be validated by Heaven's Court. We also asked that God crack that hard resistance from Baal over Washington, DC, and grant us a breakthrough.

THE EARTH SHOOK

On August 23, 2011, which was 50 days from that declaration, an unprecedented earthquake rocked Washington, DC. We don't get earthquakes here. Even though it came from Virginia, it cracked the Washington Monument, the gargoyles toppled off the National Cathedral, and the altar was damaged and the roof cracked at the House of the Temple.

I believe that when God brought down His gavel and said, "Covenant with Christ is validated," the earth shook and those idolatrous structures cracked.

On October 27, 2000, Chuck Pierce had released the following prophecy:

> For I say to you, abortion is linked with *false idolatrous worship* and I am about to cause a dethroning by the release of My power through true worship. Gather and worship Me from state to state throughout the land and I will deliver even those who have not yet been born. There is a war over the justice of this land. I will establish justice in the midst of My people; therefore, there will be war over laws that have been established wrongly. Cry out for My shield of faith to be established from state to state. *Abortion in America will cease from Oklahoma* (italics added).

In 2013, the 40th anniversary of Roe v. Wade, the Lord gave us instructions to divorce Baal at every abortion clinic in America. We'd all prayed about abortion. We'd repented for letting it happen and letting it continue.

One element that had never been dealt with was the connection between abortion and idolatry, which God spoke in the prophecy through Chuck Pierce.

Once we divorced Baal at all those abortion clinics, we saw tremendous breakthroughs. It didn't just shift the courts. It didn't just shift Planned Parenthood. It shifted the culture. That year, more abortion clinics closed than during any previous year. The culture turned on a dime from being pro-choice to being pro-life. While abortion hasn't ceased, it has received a death blow through the Courts of Heaven.

In 2014, the Lord directed us to go to every seat of authority in Washington, DC, even those in Congress and the White House. We even went to the intelligence agencies and claimed those seats of authority for Christ. I don't think it's any coincidence that virtually every seat of authority that we prayed for is now held by believers. These results came from repenting for idolatry tied to government and restoring a covenant with Christ.

On October 6, 2016, when Negiel Bigpond, Willie Jock, and all those tribes gathered in Washington, DC, it had an incredible effect. As a group, they forgave a nation and its government that had never even acknowledged that they needed to be forgiven. I think we had reached a place in the history of our nation that if they hadn't done what they did, we would still be held in bondage to all those broken covenants. We'd still be suffering from the effects of those massacred. Their act of unselfish love and forgiveness removed satan's court case against us in the Courts of Heaven.

Regardless of where we each stand politically, it's clear to me that the positive things we're seeing are a result of our repenting of idolatry and restoring covenant with Christ. Although some people represented in this book may not have voted for President Trump, the majority of us would probably agree that he was God's choice for the job. In my lifetime, I've never seen so many prophets from different streams around the world who said the same thing. They prophesied that God was going to put Donald Trump in office. The also said that he'd been called as a modern Cyrus.

Cyrus wasn't a Jew. He was a Persian King and a contemporary with Daniel. Daniel showed King Cyrus what Isaiah had prophesied about him 150 years before the king was born. It's found in Isaiah 44–45. After reading the prophecy, King Cyrus decreed that the Jews could go back to Jerusalem. He sent them back with all the sacred vessels that had been removed from the Temple by Nebuchadnezzar at the time of its destruction. King Cyrus helped pay for the Temple to be rebuilt—the same Temple where Jesus would teach in years to come. Cyrus was known as the forefather of religious freedom.

Like Cyrus, President Trump has taken an unprecedented stand for religious freedom. Not only did he start restoring the freedoms Christians in America were losing, he has also become a voice for the voiceless around the world. In 2019, he hosted the first gathering of the United Nations on religious freedom.

He has taken an unprecedented stand for Israel by moving the U.S. Embassy to Jerusalem and recognizing Jerusalem as the capital of Israel. Why would Israel have been allowed to become a nation on May 14, 1948 with the requirement that Jerusalem remain under the sovereignty of the United Nations? While many former U.S. Presidents made campaign promises about recognizing Jerusalem as the capital of Israel, none had done so until now.

We've also witnessed unprecedented judicial reform, beginning with Neil Gorsuch and Brett Kavanaugh. At one time, the Ninth Circuit Court was known for trying to overthrow the nation's motto, *In God We Trust*. Now that the judicial system has been repopulated with almost 200 judges, that same Ninth Circuit Court upheld President Trump's decision to defund Planned Parenthood.

That's another answered prayer and sign of transformation. Most Americans never imagined that we'd see Planned Parenthood defunded. Yet it has happened.

It's also interesting that within a short time of President Trump getting in office, he got rid of the scourge of ISIS. We no longer see Christians being beheaded by ISIS. We no longer see ISIS perpetrate acts of terror around the world.

Yes, these decisions were made by President Trump. However, no matter who would had gotten into office, none of these things would have happened had we not won our appeals to the Courts of Heaven.

God has ruled in our favor.

CHAPTER 18

EXPANDING AROUND THE GLOBE

Apostle John Benefiel

*Ask of me, and I will give thee the nations for
thine inheritance, and the uttermost parts of the
earth for thy possession.*
Psalm 2:8, ASV

A S HAPN grew, the Lord showed us what we needed to do to secure our future. In response, we added four new divisions: the Global Apostolic Prayer Network (GAPN), HAPN First Nations, HAPN National, and HAPN Kingdom Culture.

Dr. Abby Abildness, who is also our HAPN Pennsylvania State Leader, accepted the position as HAPN International Director. As such, she is the apostle who leads the Global Apostolic Prayer Network (GAPN). Abby is an ordained pastor, former behavioral science professor at Penn State University, and pastoral care and counseling professor at Myerstown Evangelical Theological Seminary.

Abby and her husband, Dr. Jim Abildness, founded Healing Tree International. Their mandate is to heal and restore destinies of people and nations. They have trained leaders in 30 nations on how to implement global healing and apostolic centers. Through the Global Leadership Council, they have spoken to government and business leaders. Abby has operated as the Global Peace Ambassador and as a prayer leader at the United Nations.

Dr. Negiel Bigpond leads the First Nations division of HAPN. Dr. Bigpond has ministered and evangelized to multiple reservations throughout the U.S. and Canada as well as around the world. He founded and leads All Tribes D.C. He also leads Two Rivers Native American Training Center and pastors Morning Star Evangelistic Center.

We seek to restore honor to the First Nations people, whose honor had been in tatters for years. This division includes all indigenous people in the global community.

Apostles Ed and Lynn Alderson are HAPN's U.S. leaders. They have accepted authority and leadership over the HAPN National Division. They lead all 50 state and regional leaders. They are wonderful strategists and a great addition to our team.

Lynn serves on the Board of Directors for Take the City Inc. and also as the COO for the ministry. She is the Co-Founder, Chairman of the Board, and Executive Director of Kingdom Authority Ministries, Inc., a regional apostolic training and equipping hub whose goal is to train, equip, impart, and activate individuals and organizations to fulfill their God-given destiny.

Dr. Yolanda McCune has worn many hats for HAPN. She is the former Government Specialist for OAPN. She is Director of HAPN Kingdom Culture, overseeing leaders of the seven mountains—religion, family, education, government, media/arts and entertainment, protect and serve, and economy. She has also taken oversight of the specialty leaders. She serves as the Coordinating Apostle over the Oklahoma Apostolic Prayer Network.

Yolanda also travels to Washington, DC, and other places representing me when I'm unable to attend meetings.

She has been a principal and teacher in grades K-12, a college professor, and teacher of adult education for the Cherokee Nation. She earned her doctorate degree through Wagner Theological Seminary. Dr. McCune is the pastor of Church on the Rock, an apostolic center in Stillwater, Oklahoma. She is the Director of Shekinah Educational Services, Co-Director for Tree of Life Healing Center, and a member of the International Society of Deliverance Ministers.

HAPN has grown and flourished with the help of all these wonderful leaders at the helm of their divisions. We're grateful to each and every one.

You'll notice in some of the stories ahead that people mention the term *vav*. This is a Hebrew term and a letter of the Hebrew alphabet. It means a hook, spear, or tent peg. A *vav* is what Jael used to drive through Sisera's head. For our purposes, a *vav* was used to strike the earth, connecting it with heaven and God's will. For instance, at one time we *vav'd* every state capitol in the nation.

A beautiful example of this is called The Guardian, a bronze representation of a Native American that stands atop the Oklahoma Capitol Building. He carries a spear attached to his waist by a strap and driven into the earth. He *vav'd* himself to the earth, symbolizing his commitment to stand his ground and fight. I like to think it symbolizes us as well.

LYNN ALDERSON

HAPN U.S. Director

The first prophetic word spoken over my life was, "You know what you are, right? You're a strategist." I thought about that the night I listened to

Kim Johnson lead a HAPN prayer call for her region. My spiritual father, Mark Hawkins, had called asking me to take the leadership role over Georgia. When I hesitated, he suggested that I listen to the call without announcing myself. Partway through, Kim prayed, "Oh Lord, send us a strategist. We need a strategist."

That shook me to the core. My husband, Ed, came to the door of my office and mouthed, "Are you okay?" I shook my head no. Then I sent a text to Mark: "I'll submit to whatever the Lord wants me to do."

That was February 2012. I'd read Cindy Jacobs' book *Possessing the Gates of the Enemy*. I'd read a lot of apostolic books and intercessory prayer books. As far as governmental intercession, I'd been astounded the first time I heard Apostle John Benefiel teach. I'd never heard such revelation.

We came in toward the end of divorcing Baal at the Masonic Lodges. There were still quite a few left to be done in Georgia, so we finished them.

Once I was in, I was all in. In October 2014, Kim stepped down as regional leader. I was asked to take over that position, which I did.

In 2014, we did the restoring the land assignment. We released that verdict from heaven against the political, religious, and mammon spirits. It was a powerful national call, involving the leaders of all 50 states.

We had a huge political spirit operating in Georgia, functioning in high offices. In 2016, we shut down the demonic astrological star portal in Washington, DC. It was a joint assignment with HAPN, RPN, and Becca Greenwood's network. It was exciting to have everyone on the same assignment. The unity helped make it very effective.

Then in 2018, I was asked to be the U.S. Director for HAPN.

Our ministry is called Kingdom Authority Ministries. Our assignment is to serve the destiny of kingdom leaders. When Apostle John called and asked us to serve in national leadership over the U.S., we knew it lined up with our mandate. It was our passion.

It has been a good fit for us. We were called to develop kingdom strategies for bringing restoration, so we were very like-minded. It was like meeting someone you already know.

I saw some things modeled at HAPN that I'd never seen before. Each time Chuck Pierce released the Word of the Lord, HAPN picked it up and developed strategies based on what the prophet spoke. I'd read about that happening, but never seen it modeled.

We saw how the apostle and prophet functioned together. I believe that's part of the reason we see such amazing results. Another powerful thing I've seen is the way HAPN mobilizes intercessors. It provides a high-level spiritual covering. All we have to say is, "Here's what we're doing." We're soon covered in prayer and spiritual warfare. That's a huge component that's often missing in non-apostolic led groups. We have protection without backlash.

This network, which started as prayer over Oklahoma, is now international. The network is like a big puzzle. We each carry our piece. When we come together, everything snaps into place.

In addition to leading HAPN on a national level, Robert Henderson asked us to be the North American leaders for his ministry. We do the same thing for Robert as we do for HAPN. As Apostle John says, "We're not in competition, we're in cahoots."

We have been supernaturally protected through everything we do. We are living out my life Scripture: "If they hearken and serve him, they shall spend their days in prosperity, and their years in pleasures" (Job 36:11 ASV).

DR. YOLANDA McCUNE

HAPN: Kingdom Culture Director
OAPN State Leader
Dimensions Center
Stillwater, Oklahoma

All prayer networks aren't the same. There are three basic functions where they fit. Think about them in terms of the military. HAPN is what I consider Special Ops. We're like the Navy Seals. We send in very small, covert groups to do our assignments. No one knows we were there.

The second group is what I call the Marines. This is usually a large group, very public. They are intercessors who go in and clear the area of demonic snipers and ambushes. Their firepower is impressive. Intercessors for America is a great example of this.

The third group is the one that maintains the victory. They may live in the area. After the enemy has been cleared, someone has to maintain the altar of God. Sometimes these groups set up 24/7 worship.

My desire has always been to link those three groups so that each do their part while honoring the other. Over the years, I've seen these groups learn to function like the military of God. Because of this partnership, we don't have to retake the same hill hundreds of times.

Apostle John began sending me to Washington, DC, and other places to represent HAPN when he couldn't get away. In the early days, I found it very frustrating.

What happened in many of those meetings was what I'd encountered in corporate America. Everyone had their own agenda. They each wanted to be the one with the most influence in order to further their cause. I couldn't understand how Christians could bring that same worldly thinking to spiritual warfare. Many people just wanted to promote their own agenda rather than wait on Holy Spirit to tell us what He wanted to do. I didn't enjoy meetings where you get hit with friendly fire.

In time, I saw an amazing thing happen. The favor and grace of God rested on HAPN in such a way that people knew we weren't there to usurp them. We weren't seeking attention. We wanted to be quiet and do what God had assigned us to do. As our credibility grew, so did our partnerships.

THE POLITICAL SPIRIT

I think one of the most significant things HAPN has done is deal with the political spirit. Faisal Malick wrote a book called *The Political Spirit*. He explained that the political spirit forms an unholy alliance with the spirit of religion and the spirit of mammon. That alliance is what allows terrorism into a nation.

On October 30, 2015, Faisal Malick spoke to HAPN. Here is a part of what he said to us:

> The primary purpose of the political spirit and the Herodian spirit is to stop the apostolic government. So this is your responsibility and your authority. Oklahoma City was the first place where terrorism took place on American soil. And it is the place that is going to reverse that spirit in this nation.
>
> A governmental authority from Oklahoma City is going to reverse the spirit of terrorism in the United States of America. It was the thing that marked the birthing of this movement. And what was birthed in times of crisis will become the landmark of the fruit of God's Spirit in your apostolic mission.

We knew that in order to fulfill this word, we had to bring representatives from all 50 states together on a conference call. I worked with Faisal to create the wording for our document. We needed to not only repent for letting that political spirit be here, but we needed to kick it out and remove its legal right to operate here.

We convened the group in January of 2016, going before the Courts of Heaven. We repented and shut open doors. We asked the Righteous Judge to require the enemy to lay all of his documents regarding this on the altar. Those documents would have dealt with political manipulation, terrorism, and control tactics over our presidents and government.

Holy Spirit instructed us to apply the blood of Jesus to those documents on the altar. We did, and then we asked the Judge to rule in our favor.

The following week, all hell broke out in America. Every candidate for president, regardless of the party, started attacking Donald Trump. Those spirits were furious because he was the only candidate not under their control.

The political spirit had been manipulating people in our government for decades, but no one had ever challenged his right to rule. Even though Donald Trump had an impossible year, he won the election. Everyone was against him, even his own party. I believe that removing that demonic alliance opened the door for God to put His candidate in office. I don't think the outcome would have been the same if we hadn't taken it down.

FORGIVENESS

The latest tactic in our arsenal of spiritual warfare is taking forgiveness to a new level. We know that the weight of sin is so heavy that all of creation groans for the manifestation of the sons of man. That sin weight removed the *kabowd*, which is the glory of God. Creation is now heavy with the sin weight instead of glory. Its purpose is to pervert everything. Imagine the sin weight as layers and layers of invisible slime.

The slime blinds people to God's goodness. It stops them from hearing and understanding the good news of the Gospel. Jesus gave us the key to removing the sin weight from the world when He appeared to His disciples following the resurrection.

> *If you forgive the sins of any, their sins have been forgiven them; if you retain the sins of any, they have been retained* (John 20:23).

Too often, we've accused people of their sins, therefore retaining them. Each time we say, "Your sins are forgiven," a layer of sin weight is removed.

Jesus ministered to the paralytic and said, "Son, your sins are forgiven" (Mark 2:5). That got all the religious spirits stirred up.

On the Cross as He was dying, Jesus said, "Father, forgive them for they do not know what they're doing." Likewise, when Stephen was being stoned to death, he too asked that God forgive them.

We aren't doing the works of Jesus if we're not forgiving sins.

Lest you misunderstand, this forgiveness doesn't mean the person is automatically born again, putting his trust in Christ. Asking God for personal forgiveness is a further choice each person makes for himself in becoming a fully committed follower of Christ. However, removing the sin weight does make a difference in how people hear the Gospel.

How many times have you poured out your heart to share the Gospel with someone, but they look at you like you appeared from another stratosphere? Next time before you go, say, "Your sins are forgiven."

What would the world look like if the weight of sin slime was removed? What if the glory of God was restored?

What if I say to Muslims, "The sin weight on you is forgiven"? What if I said to the abortion industry, "Your sin weight is forgiven"?

We know how to war in a new way. We know how to enter and plead our case in the Courts of Heaven. It's time to forgive at a whole new level.

DR. ABBY ABILDNESS

GAPN Director, HAPN Pennsylvania State Leader and Middle Colonies Regional Leader

I worked as a behavioral science professor at Pennsylvania State University's Hershey Medical Center where I taught healing for the body, mind, and spirit. One day the Lord spoke to me, *There's a wrong altar here. I want you to go establish My right altar.*

I realized that the Lord wanted healing prayer in the chapel of the medical center, which would allow God to have a place there. When God first told me to do that, I thought He meant that there was a wrong altar in Hershey Medical Center. What He meant was that there was a wrong altar from the U.N. on down in healthcare. The wrong altar is humanism. Their god is science. God had not been welcome in the medical centers.

I knew that we not only had to tear down the wrong altar, but also build an altar to God there. In order to do that, I brought Dr. John Benefiel and Dr. Negiel Bigpond to the chapel at Hershey Medical Center. Dr. Benefiel declared the Baal Divorce Decree and we worshiped the Lord. Negiel said, "From a Native perspective, we not only divorced Baal but made a strong covenant that provides a covering. That old altar could not be restored."

I established healing prayer in a meditative worship atmosphere in the chapel at Hershey Medical Center. We prayed that God's healing in the interfaith chapel would draw others to the God who heals (see Exod. 26:15). People, including many international leaders, were drawn to it. They wanted to see what God was doing. That's where I met many of them and how I was invited to establish healing centers in their countries.

Before anyone knew who I was, a word from the Lord had been released on Elijah List. "There's a womb of healing to the nations from Hershey."

We started Healing Tree International based on Revelation 22:2: "the leaves of the tree were for the healing of the nations." Our mandate is healing and restoring God-ordained destinies of people and nations.

I was working in the chapel when an emergency medical doctor from another hospital came to see what I was doing. "I'm going to be training Muslim doctors in Iraq, and I want you to come," he said. "I'll train them in family medicine. I want you to train them in healing for the body, mind, and spirit."

This would have been around 2006, right after Saddam Hussein was ousted from power. We were the first group that went into Iraq that weren't military. When I trained Muslim doctors in Iraq, I told them, "You have to forgive. Even with the best medicine, bodies won't get healed if you collect hate." They didn't even have a word for forgiveness. The head of the department of health put a message on a board to help the doctors understand what I was saying: "An eye for an eye makes the world blind, but forgiveness heals."

I led an Iraqi department of health leader in doing identificational repentance because Saddam Hussein had harmed even the medical people.

After ISIS came to Iraq, I got a call: "We now have a million refugees," they said. "We only have seven psychiatrists. You get the best results, so would you come first?"

Some of the Muslim leaders became Christians. They said, "ISIS comes and kills. You Christians show love and mercy. You help us. Please, we want to become Christians."

I was in Israel speaking with their Rabbis about interfaith healing in hospitals. They didn't know I was a Christian until I brought up the concept of forgiveness. That's a Christian concept and not what they do. They realized that the fruit of forgiveness is healing, and it had a powerful effect in Israel. They invited me back to teach at their chaplains' conference.

I established healing centers and trained people in so many places around the world that I couldn't go to them all. In response to their need, I wrote a book: *Healing Prayer and Medical Care: God's Healthcare Plan.*

Once I connected with HAPN, I learned through Dr. Benefiel the power and authority of corporate prayer, overcoming strongholds, and turning hearts of nations to God. What I've done in other countries is demonstrate God's love. Then they choose God because they see the fruit.

I am also Pennsylvania State leader for the Congressional Prayer Caucus and pray with legislative leaders for religious freedom legislation. Because Pennsylvania is the holy seed of the nation, it was birthed to be the holy example for kingdom governance. Two years ago, I was on the stage with international leaders at HAPN. Chuck Pierce and Rick Ridings spoke prophetic words over us.

"It's pretty simple," Chuck said to me, "you're going to reform nations."

Rick Ridings said, "Yes, you're going to change constitutions of nations, starting in Iraq."

I already have a vision for constitutional reform from William Penn's first frame of government. It was used as a model for the United States Constitution.

One of the most important things I learned from Dr. Benefiel is corporate strategy and authority to overcome the enemy in our state and nation.

I've found it so lifechanging to teach people that they can have God's authority in what appears to be impossible situations.

Years ago, God called me to open a door for Him in the healthcare system. Now, with the worldwide pandemic going on, Jody Wood, our GAPN New York United Nations Leader, called me. "New York City is the epicenter of COVID-19 in the U.S.," she said. "I need you to talk to the leaders in hospitals and help them. They need God's support."

Jody brought me in as a God Care expert, to bring God back into hospitals in New York City. "It's a war zone," they said. "We're so traumatized that we can hardly survive."

I talked to them about not just going clinically from trauma bed to trauma bed, but to bring the presence of God into hospitals through prayer. The hospitals were closed to everyone except staff and patients, so we couldn't take healing teams inside. Instead, I encouraged them to pray in emergency rooms, in surgical suites, and to pray over their patients. They did, and they reported phenomenal results. Instead of reporting their trauma, they began telling me many God stories and sensed a shift in the atmosphere.

I noticed God stories springing up from all around the world in the midst of the pandemic. That's part of the healing of the nations as kingdom healing emerges in the midst of the COVID-19 crisis.

SPIRITUAL AUTHORITY FOR THE NATIONS

Aligned with the United States HAPN network, we began building an influential Global Apostolic Prayer Network. This included country leadership teams and continent leadership teams to turn the heart of nations to God's covenantal purposes. Our apostolic leadership teams have leaders with hearts governed by God. Their ministry hubs are positioned in key locations such as the Jerusalem houses of prayer, The Hague Peace Palace, African Revealing Light Healing Centers, and Indian apostolic hubs impacting ministry, business, and government. The European UN, the New York UN, the EU, UK.

Australia and New Zealand recognize their call to coordinate a WE BOW healing wave of shofars from Oceana back across the nations to Jerusalem. Many of our GAPN country leaders are prayerfully influencing their prime ministers and presidents to choose to move their embassies to Jerusalem. This is indicative of their choosing publicly to honor God and demonstrate publicly their faith to become sheep nations. Presently we have 112 nations in our GAPN. We are adding many of the 44 European nations and 40 of the 54 African nations as networked continents.

On June 3, 2019, nations gathered and aligned with and in Jerusalem for the Knesset-led Jerusalem Prayer Breakfast. Nine of our GAPN international leaders gathered at Rick Ridings' Succat Hallel where I spoke and led a Restoration of Israel Declaration from the Nations (inspired by Romans 11). We declared as a spiritual UN declaration:

> "We the People of God honor the holy seed of the nations from Jerusalem to the world. We recognize the holy roots of the tree of life from our creator who reigns as King over all the earth. His original intent was the covenantal purpose that Abraham and the patriarchs be consecrated and set apart for God. So we also, their descendants, are set apart. If the roots of a tree are holy and set apart for God, so too are the branches. Some branches have been pruned away, but their temporary rejection released the reconciling power of grace into the world. By faith we declare the restoration of Israel and her spiritual inheritance and the realigning of the nations with the Spiritual United Nations in Jerusalem. We stand in

solidarity with Israel and the King of Kings, united for His purposes."

HAPN legal decrees inspire GAPN country leaders to bring authority of heaven as priests influencing kings to impact the healing of nations!

DR. VENESSA BATTLE

GAPN Leader for Bahamas and Liberia
HAPN Multicultural Affairs Leader
Apostle of New Gate International Church in Duluth, Georgia

I knelt before the President pro tempore, members of the legislature, media, and a huge throng of people in Liberia, Africa. "I'm so sorry for what freed slaves from America did to your country. I repent before you for killing and displacing so many people in your nation. I repent for the civil war that tore apart the infrastructure of your nation."

People throughout the crowd wept.

"Who told you to do this?" a senator demanded. "Why are you doing this?"

"God told me to do it," I said, "He told me that I couldn't do what I needed to do in the U.S. until I repented to your people."

Back home, I'd been praying about the situation with African Americans and slavery. The Lord said, *"You've got to first go and take care of the things done by African freed slaves from America in Liberia. Take a look at the indigenous people there."*

I had no idea what He was talking about, but I studied and learned. Back in 1817, a group called the American Colonization Society was formed to send freed African-Americans back to Africa. In 1822, the society established a colony on the west coast of Africa, which became the independent nation of Liberia. By 1867, they had sent more than 13,000 freed slaves there.

They tried to Americanize Liberia. They tricked the ingenious people out of their land, their cities, and their government. They named the capital Monrovia, for the U.S. President Monroe. They did the same terrible things to the indigenous people that had been done to them in the United States. This resulted in a civil war in which over 200,000 Liberians were killed.

As an African American, the Lord wanted me to repent on behalf of freed slaves. When I told them that the Lord sent me, they wept and opened their hearts to me. Their pain was as great as if those events had just happened. I saw a deep measure of healing and deliverance take place. They repented to me of their deep hatred of us.

They asked me to come back to a new stadium that had been built and make it a national time of repentance. That began my many years of working with the people of Liberia.

I learned about identificational repentance through the 17 years that I've been in HAPN. The first time I witnessed it, I was shocked at how powerful and impactful it had been. I was also amazed at the organization, the people, and their leader. I could see that Apostle John was a father who cared for his children.

I needed the right spiritual parents to guide me. I asked to meet with him in the lobby of the hotel where he and Judith were staying. The first thing he said was, "How can I help you?"

Tears streamed down my face. I'd never had a leader say something like that to me. "Will you be my spiritual father and cover me?"

"Yes, I will. Now, what can I do for you?"

"I'm doing some things in Africa."

He pulled out his phone and sent me the contact information for a lady in Tanzania. "Call her," he said. "What else do you need?"

"I'm dealing with some legal issues."

"Here's the contact information for a good attorney. Call him."

Nothing like that had ever happened to me with any other leader. Not only did Apostle John agree to be my spiritual father, Judith agreed to be my spiritual mother.

KETURAH'S CHILDREN

Another life changing revelation the Lord gave me was found in Genesis 25:1–6:

> *And Abraham took another wife, and her name was Keturah. And she bare him Zimran, and Jokshan, and Medan, and Midian, and Ishbak, and Shuah. And Jokshan begat Sheba, and Dedan. And the sons of Dedan were Asshurim, and Letushim, and Leummim. And the sons of Midian: Ephah, and Epher, and Hanoch, and Abida, and Eldaah. All these were the children of Keturah. And Abraham gave all that he had unto Isaac. But unto the sons of the concubines, that Abraham had, Abraham gave gifts; and he sent them away from Isaac his son, while he yet lived, eastward, unto the east country* (ASV).

The first thing you need to know is that Abraham, the Father of Many Nations, married and had children with an African woman, Keturah. The children that Abraham bore with Keturah were African Jews. I studied with some rabbis who taught me a great deal about Keturah and her children. Jews called African people *oxen* because they're big, strong, and resilient.

Abraham sent his children away while he and Keturah were still alive so that they couldn't overtake Isaac after he died.

All of Keturah's children became fatherless.

They became orphans.

If you look at African Americans today, so many of our young men are fatherless. They're incarcerated, abandoned, and angry. There's so much anger, resentment, and hatred among many African Americans. I believe it's hard to penetrate because it's a generational curse passed down from Abraham and Keturah's children.

I believe that's the source of the orphan spirit on African Americans.

We held a major service at HAPN where someone stood on behalf of Abraham and Isaac. Someone else stood on behalf of Ishmael. I stood on behalf of Keturah and her children. We did identificational repentance and a major reconciliation. I believe it shifted our nation regarding racial and cultural issues. It's been used to heal all types of cultures: African American, Caucasian, Asian, Hispanic, Spanish, Africans, French, Germans, and Scandinavians.

Apostle John commissioned me to do a 50-state tour, taking this message of healing to all the HAPN state leaders. I saw the same results. Racial barriers and walls fell down. I wrote a book, *Keturah Revealed*, and a workbook with the same name that is being used in many Bible colleges.

One of the last places I visited was Wyoming. I was taken to a place called Empire. Years ago, there was a group of African American professionals who decided to create their own city to get away from all the racial prejudice. They got 800 acres, founded Empire, and did quite well. They built their own schools and stores. They used dry land farming techniques. It's said that their farms looked like the Garden of Eden. They won all sorts of awards for their crops.

Then the enemy got involved. There was a lynching, and they were run off their land. We took a group of people from Nebraska and Wyoming and stood on the land that had once been Empire and did identificational repentance. I went back in September of 2019. During one of the services, I was given the deed for 20.17 acres of land that had been a part of the original 800 acres.

DR. RON HESSER

GAPN Continental Leader for Africa
CRIO Ministries, Oklahoma City, OK

Africa is a continent of extremes. In South Africa you can shop in one of the nicest malls you've ever seen. Three miles away, a million natives live in a slum with only tin huts. Africans have a deep spiritual hunger for God, but they are very aware of the evil spirit realm. It's easy to get Africans saved. All you have to do is tell them that you know someone more powerful than the devil.

The primary spirit over Africa is deception, which is a manifestation of Baal. That's why you have to be prayed up and operate in spiritual warfare to minister there. Muslim imams and witch doctors try to disrupt meetings. They might cause a cobra to appear. The evangelist has to pray and make it disappear in order to be believed.

We've planted churches in more than 40 countries to date. There is enough need in any one country to stay busy for life. However, our goal is to plant a church in every country in Africa.

Another goal is to reach the many Muslims in Africa. It's still illegal to preach the Gospel in many Muslim nations. We've found Muslims open and willing to convert to Christianity once we get workers in the field. That's why we often use ex-Muslims, sending them to reach Muslim nations.

We've planted a church and school in Mali, which is 99 percent Muslim. In Nigeria, where 50 churches were burned down by Muslims, we have several churches. We have an underground church in Somalia. We have an underground church in Djibouti. We have many other connections to Muslim countries because that's where we see the greatest need.

Africa is a long way from Perry, Oklahoma, where I grew up. I met and became friends with John Benefiel when we were college students at Oklahoma State University. Following college, I attended dental school and became a full-time dentist.

During my time in the Air Force, I moved to Oregon and founded an interdenominational evangelistic group. We held city-wide revivals for youth and adults and saw many people saved. While I was there, I was trained and ordained.

In 1990, I moved to Poteau, Oklahoma, where I continued to work as a dentist. There were no nondenominational, charismatic churches there, so I helped found one, which I also pastored. From the beginning, we supported missionaries in Africa.

I was inspired when those missionaries came to speak at our church. One described his church of 2,500 people in Nairobi. In 2001, I traveled with him to Africa. I found there were many small churches with no support and little money for the simplest building. I started doing what I could to help. I discovered that when a church got its own property, it often doubled in size. I started buying property and planting churches while authoring a Bible college curriculum program to train leaders.

While my daughter was at Christ for the Nations, I met 10 more African pastors. We kept adding pastors because they like our methods and the infrastructure we provided. At the same time, we started supporting orphans and building orphanages.

LAWLESSNESS

There has been great genocide in the Congo. There's no road that connects the east to the west, which allows lawlessness in Eastern Congo. That's where the Lord's Resistance Army has been hiding. Don't let their name fool you. This group has nothing to do with our Lord. Designated as a terrorist group by the United Nations, they have abducted over 67,000 youth and children who they train as child soldiers and sex slaves.

We have a church in that area. We have a pastor in Kindu who held a crusade for years with over 10,000 in attendance. He also raised a child from the dead. We held a pastor's conference in the Congo. People walked 60, 70, 80, and 90 miles to attend. In Africa, if a family can't afford both a car and to put their children in Christian school, they choose the school and go without a car.

When I moved to Oklahoma City in 2018, I joined Church on the Rock. In October, I attended the annual HAPN meeting with Brother James, one of my African pastors. That was my first exposure to HAPN and GAPN. I accepted the role of continental leader for Africa with GAPN.

HAPN and GAPN have been a catalyst for our ministry. Our pastors and the people in Africa are hungry to learn and I send them a lot of great teachings from HAPN. Many of the pastors in Africa are taking what they've learned and have started their own prayer networks.

They are such serious prayer warriors. A lot of them fast and pray for 40 days at the beginning of the year. Many of them pray all night every Friday. They are very faithful to intercessory prayer, and they love the teachings we send.

I see Africa as the greatest source of revival and spiritual energy for the rest of the world. They are so hungry for God. They're so expressive in their worship and sold out to the Gospel.

Now is the time to plant the Gospel in Africa. Population projection studies project that by the end of this century, all the largest cities in the world will be in Africa. Only one of the top 50 largest cities is projected to be in Asia. Please pray for Africa. There's no time to waste.

BARRY AND CAROLINE TIMMS

GAPN New Zealand

On September 27, 2018, we received instructions to carry out the Capitol Turnaround Project through HAPN. A month earlier, in August, the Lord directed my wife, Caroline, and me to move to the far north of New Zealand. He'd shown us that our scroll contained "working with our First Nations people to bring about unity, but not in a colonial way." The following month, when we received the Capitol Turnaround Assignment, our Father had us in the right place at the right time.

A short background on our nation is that somewhere between 600 and 1,000 years ago the Maori, our First Nations people, migrated by way of canoe to New Zealand. In 1769 Captain James Cook discovered New Zealand and claimed it for England. Settlers began arriving and settling in the various parts of the North Island, which caused great friction.

The Treaty of Waitangi was first signed on February 6, 1840 by representatives of the British Crown and the Maori chiefs for the North Island of New Zealand. Today, the Maori own less than 6 percent of the land.

When this assignment came to us from HAPN, we had only one Maori contact, Bradford Haami. Earlier in May, we had given Bradford the first edition of *Binding the Strongman Over America.* Three months later, Brad rang us and said, "I've read the book, and it's exactly what we need!"

Father God led Caroline and me to go to the location of the nation's first capital. Brad arranged for two Maori leaders to join us, and we brought them up to speed with the decrees. Brad and Peter Martin went to Mount Victoria in Wellington, which is the nation's current capital.

Brad felt led to first approach the Court of Heaven to divorce New Zealand from the effects of treachery of the early deals that devastated the Maori people. Then they went to the Lookout, spoke the decrees, *vaved* the spot, poured oil in the hole, and replaced the *vav.* They spoke over the representatives of Parliament and took communion. They sensed the presence of the Lord in an awesome way. Brad then felt led to find five stones, anoint them with oil and take them to specific places in the city, including the parliament grounds.

Our team crossed over on the ferry from Opua and arrived at our chosen location at 7:15 in the morning. We approached the Court of Heaven for our right to represent two nations. The shofar was blown and the presence of God was manifest on us. We spoke the divorce of Baal and proceeded with the Capitol Turnaround Project in both languages.

We rededicated the capital and prophesied that the spiritual capital of the land would return to this place. Then we *vaved* the land and prayed by name over members of the House of Representatives. We shared communion and stretched out our hands toward the seat of the treaty that would be restored. An amazing presence of the Lord fell upon us. Among other things, the Lord told me, *"Don't ever get tired of winning."*

Further joint prayer assignments have followed this one. The Waterways Project was carried out in conjunction with Maori when we learned that Lake Taupo is considered by many Maori to be the Womb of the Nation.

Father directed Caroline and me to undertake that project. We carried out a prophetic act of tipping a small bottle of clean water into the lake to cleanse it. In January of 2020, we went back to find lake weed regressing and the water much clearer already.

CHAPTER 19

TRANSFORMING SOCIETY

Apostle John Benefiel

Any gospel that doesn't work in the marketplace doesn't work.
Lance Wallnau

I F you summarize what we're doing, it's taking a systematic approach to dismantling idolatry in society. That's what God calls turning from our wicked ways (see 2 Chron. 7:14). It is the opposite of pulling the head off a dandelion and thinking you've solved a weed problem. It's uprooting the deepest roots of iniquity, pulling down ancient strongholds to set people free.

One of the reasons I'm having so many people share their experience is to demonstrate that repenting of sin, using the Baal Divorce Decree and the Writ of Assistance, reproduces the same incredible results in a multitude of settings.

You'll read about how two of our cultural mountain leaders are bringing change to education, arts, entertainment, and media. It has brought down strongholds over cities, states, and nations. It is affecting business and economy.

Entire territories are being set free as God continues to heal our land from these idolatrous sins. These same principles that brought such drastic results in our nation have done the same thing in a multitude of countries around the world.

They will change your world too.

ROSIE PHILLIPS

HAPN Kingdom Culture Executive Assistant
HAPN Western States Regional Leader

I first met Apostle John and Apostle Jay Swallow when they came to Washington, DC, in June of 2009. We were at the Washington Monument when Apostle Jay started praying in his native language. I thought the ground was going to tremble. I'd never been around that powerful of prayer and anointing.

While we were there, the subject of the Masonic came up: "There's a ley line that goes from the Jefferson Memorial to where we're standing and up 16th Street. From here it goes through the White House. From there it goes up 16th Street to the Scottish Rite House of the Temple, which is where Masons are accepted into the 33rd degree."

"Can we visit there?" Apostle John asked.

It was getting close to closing but they let us in and gave us a short tour. That's when Apostle John decided to bring leaders there when they came back in December.

"I vaguely knew something like that existed," Apostle John said, "but we didn't know where it was. I realized it was the key to HAPN dealing with the 33rd degree Masons."

We focused on Freemasonry between 2009 and 2012. We partnered with Cindy Jacobs' Reformation Prayer Network (RPN) and divorced Baal at well over 10,000 Masonic Lodges in the nation.

We focused on Islam during 2011 and 2012, again partnering with RPN. We divorced Baal at Islamic Mosques, businesses, and restaurants. My journey of connecting the strongholds of Mormonism, Freemasonry, and Islam began in 2004 when my husband and I moved to Washington, DC. We drove past a large building, and I felt an ominous sense of foreboding. "What is that?" I asked my husband. "Is it a Mormon Temple?"

It was the George Washington Masonic National Memorial.

There were a lot of weird things there. It was a mixture of sacred and profane. For instance, there was the Knights Templar Christian Chapel; in another room was a display of red Shriners' Fez hats from various cities around the United States. Each hat was embroidered with Islamic names.

The Cedars of Lebanon room displayed a small-scale model of the throne and interior of King Solomon's Temple. There was a cedar wood floor, symbols of the 12 tribes of Israel, the Star of David, and a replica of a large bronze animal cleaning basin with 12 bulls at the base. I'd seen a similar basin in a Mormon Temple. I knew in my spirit then that Freemasonry and Mormonism were linked.

Another room displayed a replica of the Ark of the Covenant. The tour guide explained that in Freemasonry, one can worship any God he chooses. That seemed to make a mockery of the Ark of the Covenant on display. The narration on the tour exalted the Christian God and then exalted other gods.

In the basement there was a large wall mural of Arabian Muslims trekking to Mecca. They were all Caucasian Shriners in red robes with spears, scimitars, and camels. The very top of the memorial was capped with a small Egyptian pyramid and flame. It was designed after a lighthouse in Alexandria, Egypt.

In 2011, we moved to Washington state. I saw Apostle John there at a conference held by Jon and Jolene Hamill. Apostle John was one of the speakers. He told me that the HAPN Washington state leader had just resigned. He asked me to take over, and I agreed.

I led Washington state for four years. In 2016, we knew we were going to move to Idaho. That state had a leader, so Apostle John asked, "What kind of duties are you interested in?"

"Does Yolanda need help?" I asked.

John started laughing because she'd been asking for help. That's how I became her assistant in Kingdom Culture, which focuses on the seven mountains. I took that position in April of 2016.

In March 2017, he asked me to be the regional leader for the western states, and I accepted that role as well. To be honest, there were times that I was so busy I thought about giving up some of those responsibilities. Each time that happened, I had a dream.

God gave me one dream before Apostle John asked me to take the leadership role for Washington state. In the dream we were in a gym. Apostle John was moving from one end of the parallel bars to the other, hanging by his hands. His face was red and sweat ran down his face in sheets. He was exhausted. I walked alongside of him saying, "You can do it! You're almost done! You can do it!"

In February of 2019, I dreamed that Apostle John was driving a black sedan. Pastor Judith sat in the front passenger seat, and I sat in back. A faceless person sat beside me. We were driving on a dirt road beside a river. The dirt mounds were golden brown as the sun shone on them. He drove fast over a mound and the car went up high in the air and landed hard, bouncing a bit. It was like a roller coaster ride. Apostle John was having so much fun, he was gleeful. Judith and I didn't know what to think but we smiled, glad that we were safe. The destination was some sort of ministry meeting in a multi-level house. The car landed by the basement door, and I knew the whole house was full of ministry people there for a meeting.

I believe that dream was about Apostle John, Judith, and HAPN going to new heights, new levels, and new adventures. Apostle John was excited, happy, and lighthearted. Basements are symbolic of foundational, ground-level work. I sensed that this new season would be more relational because the meeting was in a house. I've been told that faceless people in dreams represent angels. I believe angels will accompany us on our adventures.

RAY GARCIA

HAPN First Nations Assistant Director
The Impact Center, Lawton, Oklahoma

"This location," the police officer said, motioning to the building where we were starting a church, "is one of the most dangerous areas in Lawton. We're called out here all the time for every kind of crime. Drugs. Sex trafficking. Molestations. Trafficking children. Bank robberies. Gangs. You're right in the middle of it."

God had chosen the location and put our church in the worst part of the city. I believe that if you're going to change your city, you have to love it. I had fallen in love with Lawton. In addition, God knew I'd had a rough start as a child that had prepared me for it.

My parents immigrated to America from Puerto Rico. The Puerto Ricans consist of a mixture of the Taino Indians, Spaniards, and African Americans. The Taino are a calm tribe from the hills of Puerto Rico. They were fishermen and farmers. Both of my parents' families go back to the Taino in the mountains of Puerto Rico.

Born and raised in Brooklyn, New York, I was eight years old when my parents split up. My mother moved to Louisiana with my sisters and left me with my dad. When he brought home another woman, I got in the way. From the ages of 10 to 12, I lived on the streets.

I ate the food thrown out in dumpsters behind restaurants. Sometimes I hid there, sleeping in a dumpster to stay out of the weather. I stole clothes as I grew and took showers at the YMCA. Somehow, I managed to stay in school. Many nights I wept, wondering why I had been born.

When my mother discovered my situation, she sent me a ticket for a Greyhound bus. I slept on a mattress on the floor at her house until I graduated high school. After a stint in the military, I married my wife, Richelle Darby. Her parents led me to the Lord. They were lifelong friends with Jay and Joan Swallow.

Her parents often led worship for Jay's meetings, and he took me under his wing. In time, I led his youth meetings. When Richelle's dad went home to heaven, Jay took me as his son. He connected me with John Benefiel in 2007.

In 2014, we were sitting in the lobby of Church on the Rock when I told Apostle Jay that I was going into full time ministry and starting a church. "I've been waiting on you!" he said. He came to our building and prayed over it.

In addition to the city, we have Fort Sill here. In the late 1800s, the fort was established as a concentration camp to control the indigenous people. In particular, Kiowa, Comanche, and the Apache. As late as 2000, the government was still taking land away from the Comanche.

Fort Sill is the largest field artillery training center in the world. People come to learn about field artillery from everywhere. We've met people from Kuwait, Japan, and Asia. We're located about 100 yards from the main entrance of Fort Sill.

It's been a challenge, but I'm able to discern when things are shifting in the city. We've built relationships with four other churches to cover the four parts of the city. One of the greatest strongholds was the Good Ole' Boy System. It's a system of individuals who controlled everything that came in or went out of the area. It included government officials, police officers, and businessmen.

We traced the deep roots and went to 12 different sites to declare divorce from Baal and proclaim the Writ of Assistance. We took authority over principalities and powers and realigned Lawton with heaven. I've learned to unleash the untamed faith within me.

When the Lord told me, "If you don't love the city you're in, you'll never change it," I fell in love with Lawton and Fort Sill. As a child of God, I have inherited them. They're part of my inheritance. When I fell in love with it, I went to the Courts of Heaven and asked God if He would allow access to His books for Lawton and Fort Sill.

He granted me access. Knowing God's purpose helps us bring transformation and healing, because the land is still crying out. There are still challenges, but faith works by love and love never fails.

Another stronghold here was the spirit of division, disconnection, and distrust. God has allowed us to be a bridge between the different sides and bring unity.

Since we began this process, the chief of police, the gang unit, and the mayor have all told me the same thing. "We don't know what you've done in this area, but God has done something. We don't get calls about crime here anymore."

Apostle John has demonstrated a love for the First Nations people that I've not seen in many places. His embrace has been life-changing because his love is sincere. He has given us a platform to be able to release apostolic and prophetic words. He has opened the door for us to take governmental authority over the land.

In 2012, Apostle Jay brought representatives from the 39 tribes to sign a letter stating that we support Israel. That letter is still in the Knesset in Jerusalem today.

In 2018, Apostle Negiel Bigpond asked me to be his assistant director over First Nations. I help coordinate initiatives with the First Nations people and HAPN. Through that connection, we get wisdom and revelation.

We've been to Washington D.C. many times, but the most powerful was in 2016 when we worshiped God at the Washington Monument and released forgiveness to the nation.

In order to bring healing to a nation, we've got to love it.

MELANIE HEMRY

HAPN Arts, Entertainment, and Media Mountain Leader

My primary role on the mountain of arts and entertainment has been as a Christian author, with over 60 books and hundreds of articles to my credit. While working on the updates of this book, I found myself almost singing with joy. I kept saying, "Thank You, Lord." I paused to ponder what was happening.

The Lord showed me that I'd been created to write this book. That's different than being called. For instance, I've written for Kenneth Copeland Ministries for 30 years. There's no question that I've been called to help them. There is a difference between being created to do something and called to do something. When you're created to do something, your spirit, your soul, and even the organs of your body sing for joy.

I will admit that when we wrote the first edition of this book, the warfare was unlike anything I'd ever experienced. My brain got so foggy I had trouble thinking. Twice I fell out of my chair without knowing why. Each time, I called Jay Swallow and he broke the assignment against me.

When we began the process of updating the book, I wondered how I would handle the warfare since Jay had graduated to heaven. I'm thrilled to report that we've grown in power and authority to such a degree that there has been no spiritual attack—nothing but joy in doing what I'd been created to do.

If you think about the mountain of arts, entertainment, and media, you might assume that the deep iniquitous roots are in Hollywood. That's not the case. Long before Adolph Hitler came on the scene in 1933, anti-Jewish riots, called pogroms, took place off and on for hundreds of years. However, a much bloodier wave broke out from 1903 to 1906. Many of those who survived fled to America, settling in New York City and along the East Coast.

Hoping for a new start in a new land, Jewish scholars, lawyers, and businessmen found themselves shunned and refused participation in any form of legitimate business.

Victorian Christians considered vaudeville and nickelodeons as questionable, cheap, and base, better left to the immigrants. Desperate for even entry-level jobs, the Jewish immigrants bought up the nickelodeons.

The nickelodeon was the first type of indoor exhibition center dedicated to projecting motion pictures. Usually set up in converted storefronts, these small, simple theaters charged five cents for admission.

Under the direction of the Jewish immigrants, the nickelodeons prospered. By 1907, two million Americans had visited a nickelodeon. By 1908, they tallied *80 million admissions a week.*

That's a *lot* of nickels. The same businessmen who refused them entry to business became jealous. In an effort to escape intense persecution, the Jewish filmmakers moved as far from New York as they could get, settling in a small, unknown town named Hollywood, California.

Under the mountains of arts, entertainment, and media, the roots were all combined. Many of the owners of the movie studios often owned—and still own—the news media. For instance, six major corporations control a staggering 90 percent of what we read, watch, and listen to each day. Those six corporations are General Electric, News Corp, Disney, Viacom, Time Warner, and CBS. These six companies control 70 percent of cable television content. They control one out of every five hours of television content. News Corp owns the top newspapers on three continents. In 1995, the FCC forbade any company from owning over 40 radio stations. However, Clear Channel owns 1,200.[1]

> The trend of media conglomeration has been steady. In 1983, 50 corporations controlled most of the American media, including magazines, books, music, news feeds, newspapers, movies, radio and television. By 1992 that number had dropped by half. By 2000, six corporations had ownership of most media, and today five dominate the industry: Time Warner, Disney, Murdoch's News Corporation, Bertelsmann of Germany and Viacom. With markets branching rapidly into international territories, these few companies are increasingly responsible for deciding what information is shared around the world.
>
> There are also major news organizations not owned by the "big five." *The New York Times* is owned by the publicly-held New York Times Corporation, *The Washington Post* is owned by the publicly-held Washington Post Company and *The*

Chicago Tribune and *Los Angeles Times* are both owned by the Tribune Company. Hearst Publications owns 12 newspapers including the *San Francisco Chronicle*, as well as magazines, television stations and cable and interactive media.

But even those publications are subject to the conglomerate machine, and many see the "corporatizing" of media as an alarming trend. Ben Bagdikian, Pulitzer-prize winning journalist, former Dean of the Graduate School of Journalism at UC Berkeley and author of *The New Media Monopoly*, describes the five media giants as a "cartel" that wields enough influence to change U.S. politics and define social values.[2]

When it comes to news, we only have the illusion of choice.

In short, all the deepest roots for these mountains were located in New York City.

On April 20, 2017, Yolanda McCune, Rosie Phillips, and I flew to NYC to ask God to rule against the prince of the power of the air over our communication system. Knowing we couldn't walk around New York City with our *vavs*, the Lord gave Yolanda a witty way to deliver our verdicts. She gathered many very small bags of sand. Prior to going, the sand was prayed over and cleansed. Then Apostle John spoke the decree of divorce from Baal and the Writ of Assistance into the sand. He also spoke many scriptures. Worship was loaded into it as well.

I asked Apostle John, Yolanda, and Rosie if they had any inkling of what kind of changes we might see as a result of our efforts. None of them did, and neither did I.

Our first full day in NYC, we spread out our bags of sand and went before the Courts of Heaven. We stood in the place of those who operated in antisemitism, greed, pride and jealousy, which opened doors to the enemy.

Using identificational repentance, we pled guilty to all the charges and asked for forgiveness based on the Blood of Jesus. We asked that all cases, known or unknown, be put on the altar. Then we asked that the Courts of Heaven rule in our favor. The Judge of the Universe heard our petition and ruled in favor of our petitions.

Afterward, we delivered the verdict via sand to the world headquarters of ABC, CBS, NBC, FOX, Time Warner (who owns CNN), the *New York Times,* Trump Tower, Hearst Tower, Broadway, and Herald Square, a site of the early nickelodeons.

The Pulitzer Building, home of the *New York World,* had been torn down in 1955. However, one of the stained-glass windows hung at Columbia University. It is in Pulitzer Hall in the school of journalism where the Pulitzer Prize is presented. We had prayed asking for Columbia University to be a representation of all journalism and broadcast journalism schools.

"At the site of the stained-glass window in Pulitzer Hall," Rosie Phillips recalls, "I felt an extreme witness that God was cleaning house. It reminded me of another assignment we'd done in March 2014. When we issued a verdict there, Apostle Benefiel said, 'That was Illuminati!'"

We flew home, curious to see what would happen. None of us knew what to expect.

That very month, God started exposing and judging sexual predators on those mountains. We believe that our repentance broke an ungodly covenant with sexual perversion. Sexual perversion is a form of blood sacrifice. Intended as a covenant act, it binds the victim to the predator, keeping the evil covenant in place.

Harvey Weinstein's 23-year sentence sent a message to everyone that the days of unbridled sexual power had come to an end. To date, 262 celebrities, politicians, and CEOs have been accused of sexual misconduct *since April 2017,* the very month we carried out our assignment. Being accused does not mean that the person is guilty, but the sheer volume demonstrates that this may be the tip of a huge iceberg.

FAITH BASED FILMS

We've also seen major advances in movies. While Hollywood ignored Christian audiences for years, God raised up many excellent independent Christian filmmakers. Two of note are Tyler Perry and also Alex and Stephen Kendrick. While independent Christian films have been excellent, they often weren't in as many theaters for as long as Hollywood films. However, that trend seems to be shifting.

The Kendrick brothers' latest release, *Overcomer*, came out in the top 10 movies released at that time. The film in first place was released in 3,300 theaters. *Overcomer* was released in 1,700 theaters and came in at number three. During *Overcomer's* fifth week, it expanded to another 300 theaters. By then, it had already been translated into 71 languages and covered the world.

Pure Flix, an evangelistic Christian company, has released titles such as *God's Not Dead, Do You Believe?, Woodlawn,* and *The Case for Christ.*

Hollywood can no longer ignore such an audience. Christian films are the fastest growing genre in the industry. Sony established Affirm, which is the banner under which the Kendrick brothers' movies are made. Lionsgate established Kingdom Studios for their Christian films.

I was watching national news one day when the announcer highlighted the 10 top places to make movies. Did California hold the number one spot? No, Oklahoma held it.

That's not to say that most movies are made in Oklahoma. It means that God has helped our filmmakers and lawmakers pass great financial incentives for making movies here. Perhaps the most anointed movie made in Oklahoma was *I Can Only Imagine.*

Stillwater, Oklahoma, is a small town, home of Oklahoma State University. It also happens to be where Yolanda McCune lives and prays. More than 30 years ago, churches of different denominations in Stillwater joined a national movement called Life Changed Sunday. The purpose of the movement was to pray against abortion in a peaceful way.

Members of each church spent the year praying against abortion. Each year, on the first Sunday of October, members of between 25 to 30 churches stood on the sidewalks with signs. The message on the signs were, "Abortion Kills Children," "Adoption is an Option," and "Jesus Forgives."

Yolanda first learned that a movie was going to be filmed in Stillwater when the directors contacted churches asking for them to get involved. While it was being filmed, different churches had prayer teams onsite. Yolanda sent in covert groups to handle special ops issues.

If *I Can Only Imagine* was the most anointed movie filmed in Oklahoma, the one filmed in Stillwater was the most apostolic. The name of the movie?

Unplanned.

Released by Pure Flix, the movie followed the memoir of Abby Johnson, a clinic director for Planned Parenthood and her subsequent change to oppose abortion. The film grossed $29 million and made back its $6 million budget the first weekend. Reaction to the movie has been stunning, with many employees walking away from their jobs in Planned Parenthood.

On October 27, 2000, Chuck Pierce prophesied, "Abortion in America will cease from Oklahoma." Abortion in America has not ceased as yet. However, when we heard those words in 2000, none of us imagined that God would use a movie to strike a nail in its coffin.

NANCY HUFF

HAPN Education Mountain Leader

A former teacher in public and private schools, I have a B.S.E. in Mathematics and a Master's degree in English as a Second Language. I also have a heart to see transformation on the cultural mountain of education.

I participated in Dr. C. Peter Wagner's Mapping Your Profession project in the late 1990s. That's when I began spiritually mapping education in America. From my research, I wrote a book, *Taking the Mountain of Education: A Strategic Prayer Guide for American Education.*

I am the Founder and President of Teach the Children International (TCI), a nonprofit organization that reaches out to children at risk in hard to reach places in the United States and abroad. We have worked with refugees in Kosovar, Macedonia, Albania, Algeria, and Egypt, where I helped established a school for Sudanese refugee children.

In 2015, Heartland Apostolic Prayer Network (HAPN) asked me to serve as the lead prayer coordinator for North America, where I coordinate prayer for education in all 50 states.

One of the most important lessons I've learned about prayer through HAPN is the importance of an apostolic leadership in bringing together an effective prayer strike force. When apostolic leaders take an assignment to address a territory or a cultural mountain, God brings in a network of influencers to carry that assignment forward. Next comes the prayer strategy, and then the intercessors come together to complete the assignment. The apostolic leadership brings the cohesiveness to the assignment and will see it through to completion.

ROOT CAUSES OF
HUMANISM IN EDUCATION

During the first week of March 2014, HAPN intercessors visited ten locations in the United States, identified as significant entry points for Baal to enter America's educational system.

1. Harvard University in Cambridge, Massachusetts—the first college established as Christian to be taken over by Unitarians.

2. The Statue of Horace Mann in Boston, Massachusetts— Horace Mann is known as the Father of Public Education. He is the first one to start secular education using taxpayer money.

3. The Kansas State Department of Education in Topeka, KS— the location of the first declaration by parents giving the state authority over their children.

4. The University of Vermont in Burlington, Vermont—the location of John Dewey's grave site—and the University of Chicago, where John Dewey taught when he gathered the major influencers in 1933 to write the Humanist Manifesto. John Dewey was a major socialist educator and promoter of humanism in public schools. He penned the Humanist Manifesto, the blueprint for the religion of our public schools.

5. The United States Supreme Court in Washington, D.C.—on June 17, 1963 the Supreme Court ruled that prayer would no longer be allowed in public schools.

6. The Supreme Court of the United States—the location of the court ruling that removed any display of the Ten Commandments in public school classrooms.

7. The County Courthouse in Dayton, Tennessee—the location of the Scopes Trials that resulted in only evolution being taught in public schools—as well as the office at the ACLU located at 4301 Connecticut Ave. NY, Washington, D.C.

8. The Office of the National Education Association (NEA)—the major influencer for socialism, sex education (K-12), and anti-Christian material in America's public schools.

9. Two State Board of Education locations were targeted—Texas Educational Agency in Austin, Texas as well as the California State Board of Education, Sacramento, California. These two states are the major influencers on which textbooks are used in the United States.

10. National Department of Education located at 400 Maryland Ave. SW, Washington, D.C.—major influencer for student loan debt and enforcement of civil rights in public schools.

PRAYER RESULTS

1. Harvard University is currently under investigation for accepting large sums of foreign money from China and Qatar.

2. There is currently a case before the Supreme Court to be decided early summer 2020, Espinoza vs. Montana, State Board of Revenue. If won, the case will allow school choice. February 2, 2020, President Trump in his State of the Union address called for Congress to pass a school choice option for parents. Passing a school choice bill would also strengthen families.

3. January 27, 2020, President Trump held a press conference where he brought to the forefront the religious liberties that are available to students, teachers, and parents who have children in public schools.

KIM DRIVER

HAPN Regional Leader

April 24, 2010, was the annual day of prayer for the Western band of the Cherokee Nation. The Carter County Resolution of Apology was presented to the Cherokee leaders in Tahlequah, Oklahoma. They accepted the resolution and released the land from the curse Dragging Canoe spoke over Tennessee 235 years before. Dragging Canoe had cursed Tennessee, saying that it would be a dark and bloody land.

That same day, there was a 3.3 magnitude earthquake in East Tennessee. The epicenter was in a Cherokee village called Tenasee, which had served as the government seat of the Cherokee Nation.

We'd gathered in Washington D.C., repented, and divorced Baal. The following week, we prayed on site and also divorced Baal. It started raining in Nashville on May 1 and didn't stop. By May 2, the roads were being closed due to flooding. We were a landlocked state having historic flooding that year.

I'd already agreed to meet Mark Rodgers and a group of people that day at the Observation Tower in downtown Nashville at the courthouse overlooking Fort Nashborough. Inside, the granite in the top two stories had the history of Tennessee etched into it, along with a portion of the original Cumberland Compact of 1780.

We had a copy of the Watauga Compact of 1772, the Transylvania Compact of 1775, and the Cumberland Compact of 1780. We were going to meet on May 2 and release the Baal divorce decree. Mark Rodgers had gone to Tahlequah, Oklahoma, and received the walking staff from the Cherokee village to bring back to Tennessee as a symbol of peace.

It was an unusual coincidence that my husband was home that time of day. He'd been watching as roads closed and said, "You're not going down there."

"Wait," I said, "I have to go. This has to be done and this is the time to release it."

"You're not driving in this rain."

"I've got to do this."

"Then I'll drive you."

We made it to the location, released the Baal divorce decree, and symbolically burned part of the Cumberland Compact. As we were doing that, our state bird, a mockingbird, perched on the railing to observe.

The reason it was important that Mark Rodgers be there was that he was a direct blood descendant of Watauga, the recipient of the first broken treaty. Fast forward two years. My husband was doing an ancestry search because his great-grandmother was Cherokee. Imagine our surprise when he realized that his fifth-great-grandfather was the chief called Old Hope, who was the uncle of Dragging Canoe.

I thought it was a fluke that my husband had been home that day and drove me to the site. We had no idea that he was a direct descendant of Dragging Canoe. That's just one example of the way God has orchestrated everything.

ARTEMIS

In Centennial Park in Nashville, there is a 42-foot statue of Artemis, the Queen of Heaven, overlaid in gold. There had been a lot of prayer over the statue, and a lot of backlash. Mayor Eugene C. Lewis had been the Director General of the Centennial Celebration when it was built in 1896 and 1897. He was also the chief architect, responsible for the conception and construction of this false god. His great-granddaughter was an intercessor on our team.

It was still raining when we gathered at the statue. Mayor Lewis' great-granddaughter repented on behalf of her ancestor and read the Baal divorce decree. She released a generational mantle to build and establish the righteous kingdom of God within our region. There was a notable shift in the atmosphere. There was also a notable shift in her countenance as the weight of that burden lifted off of her.

That same year, we divorced Baal at all 351 Masonic Lodges in 95 counties in Tennessee. We took part in every initiative that HAPN did. Without mentioning them all, I'll just say that there were signs and wonders following.

For instance, before everybody else started booming, the economy of the state changed in 2013. One thousand new jobs came to Nashville. There were 43 fewer murders than the year before. There was a decrease of 2,000 major crimes in the state, and three percent fewer road fatalities.

ANDREW JACKSON

At one point, the Lord told me, "I want you to take my decree and reverse the decrees of Old Hickory." Old Hickory was Andrew Jackson, whose portrait hung in the state Capitol. We carried out the Lord's strategy with seven tribal chiefs involved.

There was a lot of bristling over it, but the end result was that Andrew Jackson's portrait was removed from the Capitol. We had a bust of Tecumseh put in its place. The governor ordered all Tennessee state flags flown at half-mast that day to honor the First Nations people.

Of course, it was pouring rain on June 27, 2010 as I walked up the steps of the Capitol with Negiel Bigpond to the gallery inside the House chamber, which had huge red velvet curtains. As we walked up, someone ran up to me and said, "Kim, there's red water running down the stairs!"

It looked like it was raining indoors as red water poured off those curtains.

"Negiel, oh no!" I couldn't believe this was happening.

"No, Kim," Negiel said in his quiet, unflustered way. "It's just washing it from the inside out."

TERRI BROWN

HAPN Colorado State Leader and Regional Leader

In February 2013, an effort to deal with the massacres that had occurred in Colorado after the Aurora movie theater shooting, several prayer networks, pastors, and government leaders invited Jay Swallow to come to Colorado. It was a time of exchanging gifts and listening to Apostle Swallow. Apostle Jay gave us one assignment: Deal with John Evans.

As the team researched John Evans, we realized Evans had created a regional stronghold of a political spirit allowing darkness to stay in place. Regional strongholds are not to be dealt with lightly. To take them down, we must have strategy, unity, and authority.

John Evans was the territorial governor who ordered the Sand Creek Massacre. He resigned afterward, but still went on to form two prominent universities. He made a great deal of money and had mountains, towns, and schools named after him in Colorado. He was the root that allowed the political spirit to rule in our state.

During the summer of 2013, we had teams go all over the state on the same day. To Evans, Colorado; to the top of Mount Evans; the Sand Creek Massacre site; Evans Avenue in Pueblo; Denver University; Evans Avenue in Denver, the site of his original home; governmental buildings; and a civil war memorial where the Sand Creek Massacre is listed as a civil war battle. We first repented for how the church in the state had operated with the political spirit and then dealt with the root of the political spirit at each of these sites.

Without any communication from us, in June 2014, Bishop Elaine Standovsky, United Methodist Bishop over the Rocky Mountain region, led 650 Methodists to go to Sand Creek and repent to descendants of survivors of Sand Creek for the role of the church. Chivington, who led the massacre, had been a Methodist pastor. Both Chivington and Evans were Masons. Some descendants of Masons privately repented for the massacre.

In November of 2014, Governor Hickenlooper publicly apologized on behalf of state of Colorado for the Sand Creek Massacre. He was the first Colorado governor to do this. Native leaders went to the grave sites of two soldiers who bravely refused to participate in the massacre. For the first time in their histories, Denver University and Northwestern University investigated the role of Evans in the massacre and found him culpable for the massacre. At Northwestern University, they set up a scholarship for native students. Denver University removed a chair that they had named after Evans.

In the fall of 2015, Faisal Malick, author of *The Political Spirit*, spoke at HAPN. He declared that HAPN had authority over this spirit. He explained how it worked and stated the importance of our next president not being under this spirit's control. In the fall and winter of 2015 and 2016, state leaders went to all 50 capitals and repented for operating in the political spirit and decreed it would not affect the next election.

When the candidates came forth for the Republican party, many were impressed by the multitude of strong candidates, excepting Donald Trump. After watching him, we realized that he wasn't under control of the political spirit. Others prayed many important things to see President Trump elected, including Willie Jock and Nigiel Bigpond's releasing of forgiveness to the nation at All Tribes D.C. Dutch Sheets and his team carried out the assignment of re-digging covenant roots. Many other nameless and faceless people did their part, but I think HAPN's role was significant.

LLOYD MILLER

HAPN Montana State Leader

One of the HAPN intercessors gave me a first edition copy of *Binding the Strongman Over America*. It was probably the most impactful book that I have ever read. After reading the book, I had an opportunity to put the concepts in the book to the test.

I'm a home builder, and our company had built a home for a Christian couple. The house was finished and beautiful. The couple we built it for found all kinds of faults with it. They threatened to force us to replace it. They had withheld the money due us for months. The assault against our company and the men who work there was relentless.

I read *Binding the Strongman Over America* on the way home from a meeting. Two hours later, I attended our weekly prayer meeting. One of the owners of our business and the crew boss were there asking for prayer. Having read the book, I understood that the attack was demonic.

Not knowing what else to do, we cried out to the Lord and applied the principles in the book. We took authority over the demonic spirits that were tormenting the men and threatening a lawsuit against the company. That night, we broke through the powers of hell. We decreed and declared the truth of God's Word. When we sent the men on their way, I told them that they would see the situation transformed when they met with the couple the next day.

When they arrived the next day to go over everything with the couple, the situation had changed. The woman turned to the CEO of our construction company and began sobbing and asking for forgiveness. The man handed us a check for the balance due on the spot.

The following Sunday, several members of the church came forth to say that the home was located on land that had been used for a witches' coven in the recent past. It had a history of demonic presence that we used our authority to uproot.

Until that moment, I'd never seen a turnaround happen so fast in a situation that oppressive and difficult. It was dramatic and not unlike what I read in the Bible and *Binding the Strongman Over America*. As general overseer of our church and community, I'd always believed in these kinds of results. How amazing that the day I read the book, the Lord gave me an opportunity to put the principles into practice.

CHAPTER 20

THE WORLD IS GETTING BETTER, THE FUTURE BRIGHTER

Dr. John Benefiel

He did this to present her to himself as a glorious church
without a spot or wrinkle or any other blemish.
Instead, she will be holy and without fault.
Ephesians 5:27, NLT

ONE of the greatest deceptions the enemy ever perpetrated against the body of Christ was to cause us to become so pessimistic about the future that we became apathetic. I don't buy that lie, and I hope you don't either.

That negativity is what prompted decades of Christians to cower before the enemy with a defeatist mentality. *Let's just hold on until Jesus rescues us.* That's not what the Bible teaches. It says that Jesus is returning for a glorious church. There is no mention in the Bible of a cowering, fearful church.

It's impossible to be victorious *and* apathetic. I have such an optimistic worldview that to me the term pessimistic Christian is an oxymoron. Yet many Christians *expect* things to get worse and worse. Let's take a look at what the Bible says about that.

> For a child will be born to us, a son will be given to us; and the government will rest on His shoulders; and His name will be called Wonderful Counselor, Mighty God, Eternal Father, Prince of Peace. There will be **no end to the increase of His government or of peace,** on the throne of David and over his kingdom, to establish it and to uphold it with justice and righteousness from then on and forevermore. The zeal of the Lord of hosts will accomplish this (Isaiah 9:6-7).

God said that His government will never stop increasing. That's a pretty big promise. We're told in Psalm 34:19, "Many are the afflictions of the righteous, but the Lord delivers him out of them all." According to this verse, there will always be problems in this world. We don't get a pass on that. But He also promises to deliver us out of a few of them. No, He promised to deliver us out of *all of them.* I believe He'll do that through His ever-increasing kingdom.

We're told in Matthew 6:10, "Your kingdom come. Your will be done, on earth as it is in heaven." According to this verse, when God's kingdom comes, His will is done on earth as it is in heaven. Again, how can everything get worse? For that to happen, His government would have to *decrease,* not increase.

THE PARABLE OF THE SEED

In the parable of the seed, Jesus compared the kingdom of God to a man who scattered seed and then went to bed. The seed sprouted and grew, although the man didn't know how, except that God made it grow.

And He said, "How shall we picture the kingdom of God, or what parable shall we use to illustrate and explain it? It is like a mustard seed, which, when it is sown on the ground, even though it is smaller than all the [other] seeds that are [sown] on the soil, yet when it is sown, it grows up and becomes larger than all the garden herbs; and it puts out large branches, so that the birds of the sky are able to make nests and live under its shade" (Mark 4:30-32 AMP).

If God's kingdom grows so large that the birds nest in its branches, how does that support the world getting worse?

Romans 14:17 describes the kingdom of God this way, "For the Kingdom of God is not a matter of what we eat or drink, but of living a life of goodness and peace and joy in the Holy Spirit" (NLT). If things were going to get worse, shouldn't it describe the kingdom of God as a life of fear, grief, and sorrow?

In contrast, Proverbs 4:18 says, "But the path of the righteous is like the light of dawn, that shines brighter and brighter until the full day." This describes the kingdom of God as getting brighter and brighter, *not* darker and darker.

Jesus described the Church this way, "I also say to you that you are Peter, and upon this rock I will build My church; and the gates of Hades will not overpower it" (Matt. 16:18). Jesus said that the gates of hell won't overpower the Church, but we've been taught a different theology.

We're *not* going to be defeated unless we quit.

A GLORIOUS CHURCH

We're told in Ephesians 5:27, "He did this to present her to himself as a glorious church without a spot or wrinkle or any other blemish. Instead, she will be holy and without fault" (NLT).

Ephesians 1:22 says, "God has put all things under the authority of Christ and has made him head over all things *for the benefit of the church*" (NLT).

If He did all this for the benefit of the Church, how has the body of Christ been duped into believing God for things to get *worse?*

There are two reasons for this.

The first is that following World War II, Christians began taking what Jesus said in Matthew 24 out of context. His disciples asked how they would know the coming of the end of the age. Jesus described wars and rumors of wars, persecutions, famines, earthquakes, lawlessness, and the destruction of the temple. Instead of relegating them to the past when they happened, some Christians believed it was describing the future.

One of the things they failed to notice was what Jesus said in Matthew 24:34: "Truly I say to you, this generation will not pass away until all these things take place." A generation is about 40 years. Those things did come to pass in that generation. They were never meant for ours.

Since then, Hal Lindsey wrote *The Late Great Planet Earth*, an apocalyptic book suggesting the rapture would likely occur in the 1980s. Later, but along the same lines, were the *Left Behind* series of novels by Tim LaHaye and Jerry Jenkins. I don't throw stones at them, because we were all taught that doctrine.

I taught gloom and doom until I read Harold Eberle's book, *Victorious Eschatology*. In it, Harold, an amazing scholar, sorts out the timeline of what the Bible says and when those events happened. When my spiritual father,

Dr. C. Peter Wagner, read it he said, "I've always known what I didn't believe. Now I know what to believe, and why I believe it."

If you don't believe in a victorious eschatology, you don't believe the kingdom of God is advancing. You don't believe that Jesus is *already* the King of Kings and Lord of Lords. You believe He will be *someday*, but that's not what the Bible says.

The Bible says that Jesus is already seated at the right hand of the Father. He is ruling and reigning as King of kings and Lord of Lords, waiting for us to make His enemies His footstool. How can we do that with a mentality of defeat?

My friend, Dr. Eddie Mitchell, told me that when he was growing up, he was taught that there was no need for him to go to college or save for retirement. Why? Because they believed that Jesus was coming back so soon that there wasn't time. That proved to be a lie, but many young people were taught the same thing. In some cases, it stole their destiny.

Jesus is coming back for a victorious church, not a beat down hag who's sitting around waiting to be rescued.

NEGATIVE NEWS MEDIA

Another strategy of the enemy is to bombard us with negative news. There are only six major corporations that control over 90 percent of the world news. They bombard us each day with hours of negative, pessimistic news. Believing that fear sells, they cram it down our throats. The enemy's agenda seems to be to keep the masses dejected, depressed, and fearful.

That's a lie; don't believe it.

In addition to buying Harold Eberle's book, *Victorious Eschatology*, read *Factfulness: Ten Reasons We're Wrong About the World—and Why Things*

Are Better Than You Think by Hans Rosling. It's not a Christian book, based on a Christian viewpoint. It's a secular book based on facts and statistics.

It addresses issues like—is evil growing around the world? Is humanity descending into greater chaos? Is the media right in claiming that the world is getting worse?

We've already looked at the Truth, which is God's Word. Let's take a look at the facts. By every measurable standard, life is improving around the globe.[1] Darkness is fading and the goodness of God's kingdom is taking root.

WAR AND VIOLENCE

Prior to World War II, the nations of the world seemed to stay in conflict. Many Western European countries initiated war every few years. However, facts reveal that since the peak of the Cold War, civil wars, genocide, and terrorist attacks have decreased by a significant amount around the world.

Dr. Steven Pinker, a Pulitzer Prize-winning author and Harvard psychology professor, wrote:

> The basic problem is that journalism is a systematically misleading way to understand the world. News is about things that happen, not about things that don't happen. You never see a reporter standing on the streets of Angola, Sri Lanka, or Vietnam saying, "I'm here reporting that a war has not broken out today." It's only by looking at data on the world as a whole that you get an accurate picture of the trends.[2]

The media broadcasts negativity. Pinker believes that even in times of very low violent deaths there will always be enough such incidents for the media to exploit—enough to warp our sense of reality. He went on to say:

Today we may be living in the most peaceful era in our species' existence. By any standard, the world is nowhere near as genocidal as it was during the 1940s, when Nazi, Soviet and Japanese mass murders, together with the targeting of civilians by all sides of World War II, resulted in a civilian death rate in the vicinity of 350 per 100,000 per year....

The trend lines for genocide and other civilian killings fortunately point sharply downward. After a stark rise during the Cold War until 1992, the proportion of states perpetuating or enabling mass killings of civilians has plummeted.

England, Canada and most other industrialized countries have also seen the homicide rates fall in the past decade. Among 88 countries with reliable data, 67 have seen a decline in the past 15 years. Rates of rape or sexual assault and violence against intimate partners have been sinking for decades, and are now a quarter or less of their peaks in the past.

Violence has been in decline for thousands of years, and today we may be living in the most peaceable era in the existence of our species.[3]

POVERTY

In 1820, an estimated 84 to 90 percent of the world lived in poverty. In 2010, according to the World Bank, only 21 percent lived at that level of poverty. In an astonishing show of God's expanding kingdom, from 1980 to 2000, over 700 million people around the world moved out of extreme poverty.

Max Roser, who is the research director in economics at the University of Oxford, wrote:

Before modern economic growth, the huge majority lived in extreme poverty, and only a tiny elite enjoyed a better living standard. With the onset of the industrialized world, poverty started its decline and slowly but steadily a larger share of the world population was lifted out of poverty. And since 1980, world poverty declined from 50 percent to 21 percent—at the fastest rate in history.[4]

The Oxford Poverty and Human Development Initiative looked at trends and made the following forecast for the world's poorest nations: If the current pace of poverty reduction continues to the end, then half of the countries would eradicate poverty within 20 years. Eighteen of the 22 countries would eradicate it within 41 years, and the remaining four countries within 95 years.

In June of 2013, economist Jon Berkeley wrote:

> Nearly 1 billion people have been taken out of extreme poverty in 20 years. The world should aim to do the same again.
>
> In his inaugural address in 1949, Harry Truman said that "more than half the people in the world are living in conditions approaching misery. For the first time in history, humanity possesses the knowledge and skill to relieve the suffering of those people." It has taken much longer than Truman hoped, but the world has lately been making extraordinary progress in lifting people out of extreme poverty. Between 1990 and 2010, their number fell by half as a share of the total population in developing countries, from 43% to 21%—a reduction of almost 1 billion people.
>
> [In the future]...if growth is a little faster and income more equal, extreme poverty could fall to just 1.5%—as near to zero as is realistically possible. The number of the destitute would be about

100 million, most of them in intractable countries in Africa. Misery's billions would be consigned to the annals of history.[5]

Regardless of what you hear on the evening news, the world is becoming more prosperous. Poverty's fierce hold on the world is losing its grip.

HEALTH AND LIFE EXPECTANCY

People are living longer and healthier. Child mortality rates have also taken a dive. In the 18th century, 33 percent of the children in the industrialized West died before reaching adulthood. In the 19th century, 25 percent of the children died. At this time, less than one percent of the children in industrialized nations are dying.

While child mortality rates have remained high in third-world countries, even this figure has plummeted. Around the world, infant mortality rates have dropped from 46 per 1,000 in 2004 to 34 per 1,000 in 2013. Worldwide, the rate is now less than four percent.

Without question, the earth is a healthier place in the 21st century. Smallpox, malaria, and other diseases have been eradicated or greatly diminished. Terminal diseases still circle the globe, but health conditions are better than at any other time in history.

THE SPREAD OF CHRISTIANITY

The Church is experiencing explosive growth in difficult environments that have opposed the Gospel. Unprecedented advancement of Christianity is taking place in Africa, Asia, Latin America and the Middle East.

George Weigel documented this about Africa:

Africa has been the most stunning area of Christian growth over the past century. There were 8.7 million African Christians in 1900 (primarily in Egypt, Ethiopia and South Africa); there are 475 million Christians today, and their numbers are projected to reach 670 million by 2025. Another astonishing growth spurt, measured typologically, has been among Pentecostals and charismatics: 981,000 in 1900; 612,472,000 in 2011, with an average of 37,000 new adherents every day—the fastest growth in two millennia of Christian history.[6]

Missionaries Heidi and Roland Baker have planted 2,700 churches in Mozambique. Prior to that, the province was 99 percent Muslim. The area where they minister was once called the graveyard of missionaries. The government, however, has announced that it is no longer a Muslim province; it's a Christian province.

Latin America has also experienced spiritual transformation. Since 1900, the number of Latin American Christians has grown by 877 percent. In Guatemala, over 40 percent of the people identify themselves as Pentecostal Charismatic Christians. The numbers are even more significant in Brazil. Known as a land in revival, miracles and healings take place there on a regular basis. Yet, prior to 1970, less than three percent of the Brazilian population was evangelical.

The growth of Christianity in China is staggering. The People's Republic of China had about one million Protestants in 1949. A conservative estimate is that there are now 58 million Protestants in China today. An article in *The Telegraph* reported this:

> The number of Christians in China is growing so steadily that by 2030 it could have more churchgoers than America. ... On Easter Sunday thousands of worshipers will flock to this

Asian mega-temple to pledge allegiance—not to the Communist Party, but to the Cross.

The 5,000-capacity Liushi church, which boasts more than twice as many seats as Westminster Abbey and a 260 foot crucifix which can be seen for miles around, opened last year with one theologian declaring it a "miracle that such a small town was able to build such a grand church."

The building is one of the most visible symbols of Communist China's breakneck conversion as it evolves into one of the largest Christian congregations on earth.[7]

A leading expert on religion in China, Professor Yang predicts, "By 2030, China's total Christian population will exceed 247 million, placing it above Mexico, Brazil, and the United States as the largest Christian congregation in the world."[8]

THE TRUTH ABOUT ISLAM

If you think that Islam is growing faster than Christianity, you need to get your facts straight. Back in December of 2001, Sheikh Ahmad al Qatanni, president of The Companions Lighthouse for the Science of Islamic Law in Libya, said this:

Islam used to represent Africa's main religion, and there were 30 African languages written in Arabic script. The number of Muslims in Africa has diminished to 316 million, half of whom are Arabs in North Africa. As to how that happened, there are 1.5 million churches whose congregations account for 46 million people. *In every hour, 667 Muslims convert to*

> *Christianity. Every day 16,000 Muslims convert to Christianity. Every year, six million Muslims convert to Christianity.* Every year, a tragedy has happened (emphasis added).[9]

Note that he's just talking about Africa! This phenomenon is happening around the world at unprecedented rates!

Harold Eberle, author of *Victorious Eschatology*, has a ministry goal of seeing 20 million Muslims come to the Lord, and it's coming to pass. In Pakistan alone, he has seen hundreds of thousands give their hearts to Christ at a single meeting. Millions are becoming Christians.

In an article, "The Truth About Islam," the author writes the following:

> Adolph Hitler said, "If a lie is repeated often enough and long enough, it will come to be perceived as truth." One such lie often and long repeated is, "Islam is the fastest growing world religion." Despite the fact that Muslims are much more reproductive than other people groups, Islam as a religion is not growing, but dying fast, very fast. Every day thousands of Muslim intellectuals are leaving Islam. They are finding that Islam is inconsistent with science, logic, human rights and ethics.

> More and more Muslims are discovering that the violence advocated by their religion is not an aberration, but is in fact a quest for dominance inspired by the teachings of the Quran. However, the exodus from Islam is not limited to intellectuals. Average Muslims are finding that Islam is not the way to God, but to ignorance, poverty and wars. They are leaving Islam to embrace other religions, especially Christianity.[10]

TRANSFER OF WEALTH

That's not all of the good news. Not only is the world coming out of poverty, we're getting ready for the greatest transfer of wealth ever seen.

"Well Apostle John," you might say, "you talk about money a lot."

That's true, I do. There are two reasons for that. First and foremost, the Bible talks about money a lot, and I say what God says. The second reason is that I've been given by God an anointing to unlock wealth. I didn't know that until prophets began speaking it over me.

For example, on January 12, 2000, Cindy Jacobs prophesied this over me: "And God says to you, I'm giving you an anointing for wealth. I'm giving you an anointing for a war chest. So the Lord says, I'm doing a new thing through you. I have given you the Daniel anointing, and I'm going to give you the anointing to impart the Daniel anointing, says the Lord."

October 16, 2011, Chuck Pierce spoke this over me: "I believe you're called to unlock the wealth of the world. I believe you're called to unlock the wealth in this nation. And I don't mean just physical, material wealth—I mean the wealth that is stored in the kingdom of God in this land."

On May 17, 2013, Martha Lucia prophesied: "For the Lord would say I have given you nations. I've given you the wealth of the nations. And there is wealth in every nation to do what I've sent you to do to those places. The Lord said wealth, wealth, wealth is your portion. This new apostolic mantle to create prayer teams that know how to see wealth created is something that I'm going to give you the pattern for." So the Lord would say, "Even today it's going to begin to come into your spirit to create these prayer teams that know how to create wealth."

September 13, 2015, Barbara Wentroble spoke over me: "This is our season to multiply, our season to increase. I say this is going to be a place that wealth creators will arise, that entrepreneurs will arise, that people will arise says the Spirit of God...and I say that in the same way that God is unlocking finances and wealth in this place, I say now it's going to flow out and I say every place that HAPN goes, I say the blessings of the Lord are going to break them out of a poverty spirit. I say I'm going to cause wealth to begin to spring up in those other places, says the Lord, for the apostolic line of supply from this place is going to reach out and it is going to deliver even regions and territories from the curse of a poverty spirit."

As you can see, I have a call from God to unlock wealth, to release people to create wealth, and to deliver people and territories from a spirit of poverty. That's already happening to a member in our church. After we prayed with him and sensed from God that the timing was right, David left his previous job and became the CEO and one of the founding principals of a local investment advisory firm. The enemy tried to hinder the launch, but together with David we took authority in the spirit realm and things began to move in a positive direction. Then, a much greater acceleration came when two things happened.

On September 10, 2019, my son, Rhett, and I went to his new office to pray and prophesy over his business. I remember prophesying that he would have a billion dollars of assets under management. Then I saw two billion. The number continued to go up, until I saw five billion under management. "You're going to five billion," I said, "But before you get there, you're going to take a hit. It won't be a hit that takes you down. It will feel like a hard hit, but it will propel you forward."

As I prophesied, David's jaw dropped, but he agreed with it and released his faith. From that time forward every morning David prayed, "Thank You, Lord, that You are making us wildly profitable, and that You're growing us into a firm with assets under management in excess of $5 billion."

In October 2019, at our annual HAPN meeting, I commissioned him as a marketplace apostle. I commissioned him and mantled him with the wealth anointing that had been prophesied over me. David had already prayed the divorcement of Baal and the Writ of Assistance over his business.

When the coronavirus hit hard in late February, 2020, the market started to react to what COVID-19 would do to the American economy. By mid-March David's firm had received $200 million in new business that came mostly in the form of cash. In the same time when the public markets were hit hard, David's firm achieved a billion dollars of assets under management. Without a doubt, this was the hard hit that the Lord prophesied, but God used it to propel him ahead.

That's one of the most solid and dramatic examples of wealth transfer that I've seen. It's interesting to note that David gives his clients a copy of *Factfulness* in order to give them hope for a bright future.

PASSOVER AND PENTECOST

This year, 2020, was the first time since Moses led the children of Israel out of Egypt that the whole world experienced a true Passover. Due to COVID-19, the world sheltered at home as the death angel passed over.

Pentecost, which comes 50 days after Passover, is the time of harvest. We're about to experience a rich harvest of whatever we've sown. Some people need to pray for a crop failure, because they've planted things they don't want to reap.

However, it also works the other way. Those who've sown wealth are about to reap a very rich harvest. Part of unlocking harvest is to go before the Courts of Heaven and divorce Baal, remarry the Lord, and declare the Writ of Assistance. That legal process releases angels to bind the strongman and bring our harvest. Even if you've done so before, gather your family and do it again. This will open the legal pathways for you to receive your harvest.

I've never been this excited about the future. I believe that the kingdom of God will sweep the earth, changing nations, cities, and families. I believe we'll have prayer leaders in every state of every nation—including China. Do I know how that's going to happen? No, but we've never known how any of this was going to happen. All that matters is that we know and obey the One who does know. I believe that the Light of the kingdom of God will grow brighter and brighter. We are winning. Our prayers are working. The kingdom is advancing!

TIMELINE OF RECENT HAPN INITIATIVES

2007–2011

◯ Dr. John Benefiel divorced Baal and remarried the Lord in all 50 states in the U.S.

DEC. 2009–JULY 2011

◯ Released Baal Divorce decree at over 10,000 altars of Masonic Lodges.

2011

◯ Prayer at Lincoln Memorial, Washington, DC (July 4, 2011)— Declaration of Covenant presented before the Courts of Heaven.

- D.C. 40 Initiative (Oct. 3, 2011–Nov. 11, 2011)—Prayer and worship in Washington, DC, for 40 days.

- Philadelphia Eleven Initiative (Nov. 12, 2011–Nov. 22, 2011)— Prayer and worship in Philadelphia for 11 days.

2012

- Chicago 50 (June 5, 2012–July 16, 2020)—Prayer and worship in Chicago for 50 days.

- Bridal Canopy (Oct. 31, 2012)—Raised the Bridal Canopy over all the states.

- HAPN Proclamation of Alignment with Israel (Dec. 12, 2012)—All 50 states signed a Proclamation of Alignment with Israel.

2013

- New Birth of Freedom Project (Jan. 22, 2013–Feb. 12, 2012)—Jan. 22, 2013 was the 40th anniversary of Roe v. Wade. Released Baal Divorce decree at all abortion clinics.

- 50 States on One Conference Call (Mar. 20, 2013)—All 50 State HAPN Leaders joined with Dr. Jay Swallow and Kansas leaders to close a pit of hell where the root of abortion had been in Kansas. It was near the place where we raised the Bridal Canopy in 2012 and was the geodetic center of all surveying lines for North America.

- 50 Hours of Prayer for Marriage (Mar. 25, 2013–Mar. 27, 2013)—A consortium of Prayer Ministries came together in unity to have a

50-hour continuous prayer call to create a Fire Wall of Intercession around the U.S. Supreme Court as they heard the cases for DOMA and Prop 8. HAPN State Leaders passed the prayer torch hour to hour and acted as host to various National Prayer ministries that led that hour.

- 50 Days of Worship (Mar. 25, 2013–May 14, 2013)—From Passover to Pentecost, 50 Days of Releasing the Light to all Mountains of Culture. Each state took a day.

- Worship at the River (Oct. 23, 2013–Nov. 4, 2013)—Worshiped at the river (or any body of water).

2014

- HAPN D.C. Assignments (Mar 7, 2014–Mar 9, 2014)—Three initiatives where we addressed:

  o Mountain of education 10 entry points (6 in D.C.).

  o Around 200 embassies and consulates in D.C. (Securing the Glory Doors for the Nations).

  o Accomplished Cindy Jacobs' prophetic word to Apostle John Benefiel for rebinding the strongman in D.C. at strategic places.

- Worship Down Under (May 5, 2014)—Worshiped in underground places.

- OAPN Staking the Corners of Every County in Oklahoma (July 21, 2014–Aug. 15, 2014).

2015

- Evil Eye Assignment (Mar. 24, 2015)—The assignment to close the "Evil All-Seeing Eye." And the assignment to address same-sex marriage.
- Manifest Destiny (July 13, 2015)—Addressed the Manifest Destiny roots of this nation.

2016

- Strike the Match (Jan. 12, 2016–Jan. 19, 2016)—Praying at colleges and universities.
- Political Spirit (Jan. 14, 2016)—Addressed the political spirit as instructed by Faisal Malick.
- Re-staking the land at the capitol ground in all states/nations (Jan. 15, 2016–June 3, 2016).
- Re-attaching the Head of the Bride (June 3, 2016).

2017

- Media, Arts, and Entertainment Prayer Assignment in New York City (Apr. 20, 2017).
- Official announcement of the new branches of HAPN (July 7, 2017):

  o HAPN U.S. led by Lynn and Ed Alderson.

  o Global Apostolic Prayer Network (GAPN) led by Dr. Abby Abildness.

  o Kingdom Culture led by Dr. Yolanda McCune.

2018

- Official announcement of the new branch of HAPN—HAPN First Nations led by Dr. Negiel Bigpond (Mar. 2, 2018).
- Retracing the Trails (Apr. 12, 2018)—Prayed at ancient trails (or any trails) in the land.
- Capitol Turnaround Project (Sept. 27, 2018)—Re-vaving the Capitol grounds in conjunction with the Rome to Jerusalem Prayer Journey by Jon Hamill, James Nesbit, and Ed Watts.

2019

- Justice in the Waters (June 20, 2019–June 30, 2019)—Praying at bodies of water.

2020

- Unveiling Grace (Feb. 17, 2020–June 28, 2020)—Mormon initiative.

BAAL DIVORCE DECREE

THE HIGHEST COURT OF THE KINGDOM OF GOD

IN RE THE MARRIAGE OF:
THE PEOPLE OF GOD,
Plaintiff

versus

THE PRINCIPALITY OF BAAL
(Including Baal, Queen of Heaven, Leviathan),
Defendant

DECREE OF DIVORCE

THIS matter comes on for hearing before the Supreme Judge of the Highest Court of the Kingdom of God on the petition of the People of God seeking a Decree of Divorce from the Principality of Baal, the Defendant in this matter (see Hos. 2).

The Court finds:

1. The Plaintiff's sins are forgiven. The Court recognizes the Plaintiff's request that this verdict be rendered in favor of the people of God based upon the Court's everlasting precedent granting the remission of all sins through Jesus Christ. The Court recognizes the Plaintiff as an ambassador of Christ, appointed as a steward of His gift of righteousness and ministry of reconciliation, restoring the world to favor with God (see John 20:23, 2 Cor. 5:18-20, etc).

2. The Plaintiff's assertions are fully substantiated:

    a. That this marriage was entered into by the Plaintiff based on lies and deceit by the Defendant, and

    b. That Plaintiff relied on fraudulent inducements and enticements by the Defendant, which Defendant had neither the intention or ability to deliver.

3. The Plaintiff renounces any and all right, claim, or interest in any possession jointly acquired with the Defendant during this Marriage, and that Plaintiff is entitled to have sole right, claim, and interest in and to all the gifts, possessions, and inheritance from Plaintiff's Father, and the Defendant is to be (now) and forever barred from the title, control, or use of any such gifts, possessions, or inheritance.

4. The Plaintiff repudiates any and all joint claims with the Defendant, and requests this Court to sever all relationships with the Defendant of any nature, however and whenever such occurred, and seeks enforcement by this Court of

Plaintiff's desire to be known by no other name than that given by Plaintiff's Father.

5. All offspring of this marriage are hereby released into the sole jurisdiction of this Court, effective immediately. The Defendant's request for either sole or joint custody is denied. As per the Plaintiff's request, all claims by the Defendant to their lives and bloodlines are rescinded.

6. The Plaintiff also seeks an everlasting restraining order against the Defendant so as to keep the Defendant away from all persons or property belonging to the Plaintiff.

7. The Plaintiff seeks perpetual enforcement of this requested judgement in favor of the saints, restraining the enemy and releasing the saints to possess the Kingdom (see Dan. 7:22).

THE JUDGEMENT

WHEREFORE, this Court being fully advised in the evidence does find for the Plaintiff and against the Defendant in all matters material to the Plaintiff's Petition of Divorce, and does by this decree grant the Plaintiff a Divorce and all requests set forth above. That being the Order of this Court, from and after this date, so shall it be.

THE SUPREME JUDGE

Composed by Dr. Jerry Mash with Apostle John Benefiel (OAPN, HAPN.US). Revised by Jon Hamill on April 18, 2018.

WRIT OF ASSISTANCE

THE HIGHEST COURT OF THE KINGDOM OF GOD

THE PEOPLE OF GOD,
Plaintiffs

vs.

THE PRINCIPALITY OF BAAL
(Including Baal, Queen of Heaven, Leviathan),
Defendant

WRIT OF ASSISTANCE

THIS matter comes before this Court seeking enforcement of its prior decisions in favor of The People of God, the Plaintiffs.

The Plaintiffs seek to employ a Writ ancient in its application and consistent in its purpose. In its origins, a Writ to assist the subjects of the King in fulfilling their duties to the King, and in more recent time "a mandatory injunction; (the) effect of which is to bring about a change in the possession of realty—it dispossesses the occupant and gives possession to one adjudged entitled to it by the court" (63 P2d 756,759).[1] The Writ of Assistance is a process issued by a Court of equity to transfer the possession of lands, title, or possession to which the Court has previously adjudicated as a means of enforcing its decree (110 P2d 554,556).[2]

ACCORDINGLY, THE COURT FINDS:

1. The People of God have sought and obtained from the Court a Decree of Divorce wherein the Plaintiff was found to be entitled to have sole right, claim, and interest in and to all gifts, possessions, and inheritance from Plaintiffs' Father and Defendant was forever banned from the title, control, or use of such gifts, possessions, or inheritance (Ps. 24:1; 115:16).

2. The People of God have committed, and do continue to affirm their commitment, to avoid any contact or participation with the Principality of Baal and its vast extensions, and to be trustworthy in the use of the gifts, possessions, and inheritance to which they are entitled.

3. The People of God are entitled to the blessings of Abraham (Gal. 3:13-14) and are entrusted with those blessings to be a blessing in the earth (Gen. 12:2-3). This Court holds that the blessings of the Plaintiffs' Father are to make the People of God truly rich, and He intends no sorrow or toiling to be added to it (Prov. 10:22). Additionally, this Court finds the wealth accumulated by those following the Defendant's

practices lawfully belong to the Plaintiffs remaining in right standing with this Court (Prov. 13:22; 1 John 3:8).

4. In addition to this Court's Decree of Divorce entered against the Principality of Baal in favor of the People of God as Plaintiffs, this Court finds that previous proclamations of this Court support the issuance of this Writ of Assistance, including the following:

    a. The thief must repay sevenfold, and must give all the substance of his house (Prov. 6:30-31). He must restore seven times what he has taken.

    b. The wicked man, though he piles up silver and has plentiful garments, the just will wear them and the innocent will divide the silver (Job 27:13-17).

    c. The Plaintiffs' inheritance is from the Father who purposed only that His House be filled with splendor because the silver is His, and the gold is His, and it is to His House that He grants peace and prosperity (Hag.2:7-9).

    d. It is the Will of the Father of the People of God that the Plaintiffs alone receive the "treasures of darkness and hidden wealth of secret places" (Isa. 45:2-3).

    e. While the Defendant claims as his own vast possessions, this Court has ruled, and does here again rule, that he who by charging excessive interest and who by unjust efforts gets gain and increases his material possessions gathers it for those who are kind and generous to the poor—the Plaintiffs here (Prov. 28:8 AMPC). While the Defendant has gathered it, this Court rules he must give it to the People of God who are "good in God's sight" (Eccles. 2:26).

The Highest Court having fully considered the Plaintiffs' plea for a Writ of Assistance to enforce its prior rulings and proclamations, and finding the request timely made, does this day issue this Writ of Assistance on behalf of the People of God, the Plaintiffs:

1. Giving the People of God this day power to gain wealth to confirm this Court's covenant to their fathers (Deut. 8:18).

2. Ordering that all those empowered by this Court to enforce its rulings and proclamations forthwith grant full assistance in the transfer of all wealth, possessions, properties, and gifts belonging to the Plaintiffs as the People of God, to employ the Power and Might of this Highest Court to perform this Word, calling into obedience all enforcement authorities to continue in this transfer until it is fully completed and the People of God are in unchallenged possession (Ps. 103:19-21). This Writ extends to all the extensions and manifestations of the Principality of Baal, however named or designated, known or hidden, and however related to this Prince of Demons (Matt. 12:24).

It is the unlimited authorization of this Writ to bind this strongman and the entire house over which he has rule, to authorize the carrying off of all property in his possession or delegated under him to any part of his principality or in any way related to him, and to plunder his house (Matt. 12:29).

Therefore, let the Writ issue, and from this order there shall be no appeal.

THE SUPREME JUDGE

1. [178 OKL 592].
2. [57 Ariz 41]
3. Composed by Dr. Jerry L. Mash (Oklahoma Apostolic Prayer Network), Copyright ©2010

PROPHECIES GIVEN TO JOHN BENEFIEL

Seven Anointings:
Cyrus, Zerubbabel, Gideon, Daniel, Mordecai, Joseph, David

DICK MILLS—FIRST PROPHECY RECEIVED (EARLY 1970S)

*I will go before thee, and make the crooked places straight: I will break in pieces the gates of brass, and cut in sunder the bars of iron: And **I will give thee the treasures of darkness, and hidden riches of secret places**, that thou mayest know that I, the Lord, which call thee by thy name, am the God of Israel. For Jacob my servant's sake, and Israel mine elect, **I have even called thee by thy name: I have surnamed thee**, though thou hast not known me* (Isaiah 45:2–4 KJV).

*And so he that had received five talents came and brought other five talents, saying, Lord, thou deliveredst unto me five talents: behold, I have gained beside them five talents more. His lord said unto him, Well done, thou **good and faithful servant**:*

thou hast been faithful over a few things, I will make thee ruler over many things: enter thou into the joy of thy lord (Matthew 25:20-21 KJV).

(In Latin, *Benefiel* means good and faithful.)

JACOB KURIEN—JUNE 13, 1994

The Lord says unto you, "My son, I am the Lord, your God. I have called you, just like I have called *Zerubbabel, Zerubbabel*," saith God. "In the midst of oppression, in the midst of depression, in the midst of idolatry, in the midst of apostasy, I have called *Zerubbabel* to be the governor of Jerusalem. I have called *Zerubbabel* to be a great builder," saith God. "So I say unto you tonight, it is not because there is no church in this area, but this church I have raised up with a specific plan, with a specific mission, with a specific assignment, with a specific revelation, and with a specific vision," saith God. "And I am the Lord your God. I am the builder of this church. Nobody else is the builder. I am the builder," saith God.

"So I say unto you, nobody will get the glory, but I will get the glory because I am the Chief Architect of this church," saith God. "And I am the builder and I am the cornerstone. *I am the Rock of this church*," saith God. "But I have called you to stand for Me." (Adopted into the Cheyenne Nation and named "*Ma'heo Neh'est*," meaning "God Stands" or "Holy Man Standing for God," December 1997.) "Stand for Me before the people, before the people in authority, before the people in power...*this church will continue to be built as an international church. I'm going to expand the borders of this church, and I will keep on expanding. I will keep on expanding. I will keep on expanding,"* saith God. "And I say unto you, I am the Lord, your God. I will give you the right place to expand the borders of this church. I will bring the faithful people. And I will build people with faithfulness, people with integrity. I'm going to build with you shoulder to shoulder," saith God.

BARBARA WENTROBLE—SEPTEMBER 13, 2015

I say this is going to be a place that wealth creators will arise, that entrepreneurs will arise, that people will arise says the Spirit of God. They will break curses out of the generations of their family. I declare a new season over Church on the Rock, and I say that in the same way that God is unlocking finances and wealth in this place, I say now it's going to flow out and I say every place that HAPN goes, I say the blessings of the Lord are going to break them out of poverty spirit. I say I'm going to cause wealth to begin to spring up in those other places, says the Lord, *for the apostolic line of supply from this place is going to reach out and it is going to deliver even regions and territories from the curse of a poverty spirit.* I say this is a new day and I say you are stepping in to that that your heart has longed for but I say now you will see the manifestation of it.

BARBARA YODER—SEPTEMBER 11, 1996

And the Lord would say, "That even as I have called you *Cyrus*, I'm linking you with *Cyrus* in the territory...even in the future that I'm going to cause many political governmental leaders to become for you, to become intertwined with them. ...I will make you a man of strategy. There is great strategy even in those that you join arm in arm in and I shall even link you to key men outside the church in the governmental structures of the city that have keys to unlock the territory." The Lord said, "Even go around the boundaries of your own physical home. Put the Blood around the territories of your home," for the Lord said, "I will not allow the enemy to cross the boundaries of your physical property." For the Lord said, "I'm putting a scepter in your hand and I'm going to teach you how to rule even in this territory as a man of strength and a man of power and a man with the Word of the Lord for the hour."

CHUCK PIERCE—JULY 13, 1997

Because we have gathered together God has started the process for us to double. When the Board of Reference reaches 300 churches we will have a *Gideon Anointing* upon us (Judges 7:15). Chuck declared that when 300 churches network together across the state, "I will deliver the enemy camp fully into your hands. Everything that has been broken there will start a reversal and I say My people will arise; I will shine on this state. I will begin to awaken it, and you will be used to touch this nation in days ahead."

CHUCK PIERCE—OCTOBER 1999

"I say not only will riches be released but I say now keys and methods for healing will now be restored to My church," saith the Lord. "I say I am now going to send *this angel* that guarded this church and to begin to visit you, and it will show you that which would trap you but *it will also guide you into places that will cause you not only to deliver My people but to receive the plunder that has been held.* I say rejoice, for you have set motion in this earth," saith the Lord.

NANCY COEN—OCTOBER 1999

God is really going to put an anointing on you to prophesy into corporate structures. He said you'll not just prophesy and encourage the people but you'll also prophesy the kingdom of God into the structures and systems themselves. ... There will be doors of most prominent people in your whole community are going to be open to you...and even though you have prospered in everything you have laid your hands to the Lord said *that anointing that is on you for prosperity is going to be transferred to those who are in your own congregation. The Lord is going to put a teaching mantle on you and He is going to allow you to gather and convene other pastors together to speak to them concerning God's desire to loose the anointing for prosperity amongst the churches. God is raising you up for in this hour to bring the message that the wealth of the wicked is about to be restored to the bosom of the righteous.* That You'll give to him revelation and prophetic words that will call forth their destiny and purpose the thing they were created for. *Father, we thank You for this anointing that is on him to raise up Josephs and Daniels* that wherever he goes there will be those who speak to governmental rulers and people with high level authority and economy, and I give You praise, Lord, for the open doors into the marketplace and for the professionals that will seek him out. We just ask You to begin this new work and to increase it and increase it.

ADDITIONAL—OCTOBER 1999

I hear the Lord is calling you. He says you're like a pastor's pastor; He's going to use you as a mentor even for other pastors. He's going to begin to network with you and you're going to raise them up and He's even going to move you into an apostolic position where you're going to work with many, many, many, many pastors; you're going to begin an impartation to them. The Lord said you're going to be like a father figure to a lot of young pastors; *I even see that father mantle that is upon you.*

CINDY JACOBS—JANUARY 12, 2000

Father, in the Name of Jesus, we just thank You for the anointing right now. Lord, in the Name of Jesus now give him a double portion of favor. The Lord says, "You better pack your bags, brother, because I am getting ready to do something that will astound the nations. Look among the nations and be astounded," says the Lord. And the Lord says, "I'm putting together teams from Oklahoma. They are going to go forth from Oklahoma, and even this Native coalition," the Lord says, "I'm going to do a new thing with the Native coalition." The Lord says, "I'm going to give you a *war chest*, I'm going to give you money for these things...." And *God says to you, "I'm giving you an anointing for wealth;* I'm giving you an anointing for a *war chest*." And the Lord says, "Even this advisory capacity that I'm putting you in is going to affect Europe." For the Lord says, "I'm doing a new thing through you. I'm giving you the *Daniel anointing* and I'm going to give you the anointing to impart the *Daniel anointing*," says the Lord.

JOHN KELLY—NOVEMBER 18, 2001

My son and daughter...this is the time of the new anointing unto you, for I shall now give unto thee the anointing of courage that will release the finances for the house. I will give thee a new release of the wisdom of God...I am taking you to a place of *wealth,* says the Lord. Hallelujah! For I have not given you the spirit of fear but the Spirit of Power. Signs and wonders are being restored to this house. The power gifts of the Holy Spirit are being restored in even a greater way. ... You're going to have apostolic wisdom and knowledge and understanding to build the house, to increase the house. I see people coming from the north, the south, the east, and the west to receive and that this apostolic anointing is for both of you. ...For a new kingly anointing is on this house, says the Lord.

JIM GOLL—FEBRUARY 15, 2002

Pastor, I know you know that you are one of the modern-day *Mordecais* whom God is raising up. In the job of *Mordecai* he had a spirit of adoption that came upon him, and he adopted Hadassah as his own, raised her, taught her, trained her. Hadassah, who became Esther, was released to her appointment under the Apostolic overflow under the governmental intercessor of *Mordecai*. Then Esther was empowered; she was released to go before the King's throne. And so you have a scepter in your hand and you will stretch out this scepter and you will raise more than 5,000. For this is just the beginning; put a zero behind it and you will find out from God—when you reach 5,000, which will soon occur—God will give you faith for 50,000. They shall fill the stadiums; they shall fill the stadiums. As a *Mordecai* comes on the scenes and blows a trumpet for such a time as this.

BARBARA YODER—FEBRUARY 13, 2004

There is a big anointing on Pastor Benefiel for *wealth*.

CHUCK PIERCE—MAY 2, 2004

The Lord told me last night...I want you to begin to operate as *Joseph* operated. I don't quite know what that means...He said, you will begin to administrate the way *Joseph* administrated—I'm not sure what all that means for us. For God to say that I always feel like the place He says it is linked with what He is going to do. Now that's real important. Now for a word like that to come to me last night the place God speaks to me like that when it's so clear and so sovereign like that, that is the place that that word is linked into not only atmospherically but into the ground. So get ready for the *Joseph* anointing to come on Oklahoma. Now that could mean all sorts of things, but yet it's coming here.

EMANUELE CANNISTRACI—JANUARY 27, 2005

You are audacious. You have audacious faith! Some have seen the audacity of your faith and mocked you. People will say, "The man is a dreamer." Dream on! For I have given you that dream! The same God who gave the dream to *Joseph*; you have a dream! And from the dungeon, and from the pit, and from your business, and from your background in finance, and from your background in the marketplace I have taken you now to a place of preeminence. And you will excel! And you will be superly above and beyond the normal, traditional pastor or apostle. You're moving in the New Testament Apostolic dimensions. You don't even know what you are really getting a hold of; it is beyond your finite mind. For eye has not seen nor ear heard, neither has it entered into your heart what I have in store for you. You're getting little glimpses here and there. But rejoice, I'm a God who keeps My promises to those who are in covenant with Me.

Audacious: 1. having the courage to take risks; bold; daring. Syn: fearless, adventurous. Ex: John Glenn was the audacious pilot of the first U.S. spacecraft.

CHUCK PIERCE—OCTOBER 16, 2011

The one ministry that has defined me, as much as any other ministry in my life, is the ministry of Church on the Rock. Why would I say that? I believe we have through that ministry created a prototype for the future. There's two things I want to say: *I believe you're called to unlock the wealth of the world. I believe you're called to unlock the wealth in this nation, and I don't mean just physical, material wealth—I mean the wealth that is stored in the kingdom of God in this land.* The other thing I want to say to you, I have been so excited how you have taken the helm and actually gotten in and led this nation in this past couple of seasons in the prayer movement.

I want to thank God for everything that Church on the Rock has done. Janet, I want to thank God for you. I want to thank God for Rhett. I want to thank God for all the leaders there. *You have created a model of what a kingdom Church needs to look like.* How you've mobilized your state, and how now you're mobilizing the nation. *All I can say is, may you prosper and may you lead us into a new level of prosperity.* We bless you here from Global Spheres—thank you for being a part of us. We look forward to a day when you will be down here with us. We thank God for all of you, and we bless you there at Church on the Rock. Keep leading us into the future, in Jesus' Name!

BILL HAMON—APRIL 27, 2013

The Lord says, "Son we have entered into a new stage; we've entered into a new order of dimension of life and ministry." The Lord says, "You have broken through, you've broken through." It's just like when they first broke the four-minute mile and then when they broke through the sound barrier and when they broke into a different realm. You broke into a new realm like they do in science and aviation and different places. You've broken into a new realm in the heavenlies; you've broken into a new dimension of God's glory and God's power and God's authority, and the Lord says, "*You're going to start demonstrating the kingdom of God like never before.*" The Lord says, "Son, you're getting ready to move out and to move in to the greater dimension." *You're like David who took Jerusalem and then he started expanding and expanding and expanding the kingdom* of Israel until he fulfilled the Abrahamic promise...and then you are going to expand and extend the promises of God and the kingdom of God and the Lord says you are moving into a whole new realm.

*You're coming up to a four-star general...*and you are going to impart and educate and activate and bring them into spiritual warfare on how to take the kingdom, how to demonstrate the kingdom, how to establish the kingdom, and the Lord says, "This is a new day, this is a new hour, you've been promoted." ...You're moving into another realm that you'll only move like a general and direct the army. You don't get down in the trenches but you do give strategy and wisdom. You've come to a new level so I want you to understand new levels, new devils, but new power and new authority, new anointing. The Lord says, "You are going to teach My people how to win wars, teach My people the strategy how to take and establish." The Lord says, "You've prepared yourself, you've been educated by My Spirit and you've allowed Me to do the work in you; now allow Me to extend you and expand you and to spread you to the people throughout the nations and throughout the world." The Lord says we are going to accomplish more in the next five years than we have in the last thirty. "You are going to see Me do things that are going to have a chain reaction—it's going to go around the world and effect people in many, many places, in many, many ways. So you're in My will, you're walking in My way; step by step we are going to make it, so continue on and be sensitive to what I have to say and do for we are about to launch into a realm beyond anything we have known before."

It's just like when they take space travel to other areas or go to other planets—you are coming to that new realm in the spirit. The Lord says, "...Very few have found it, but you've found it; you've entered into it so you'll teach others and bring others into it. So know this is a new day, this is a new hour; do not look at the past, look at the present and future for you are about to move into realms beyond anything anybody else has known. You're going to reveal it, and instill it, and impart it, and activate it, and bring the church to a new dimension, to a new authority."

MARTHA LUCIA—MAY 17, 2013

For the Lord would say, "I have given you nations, I've given you the wealth of the nations, and there is wealth in every nation to do what I've sent you to do to those places." *The Lord said, "Wealth, wealth, wealth is your portion. This new apostolic mantle to create prayer teams that know how to see wealth created is something that I'm going to give you the pattern for."* So the Lord would say, "Even today it's going to begin to come into your spirit to create these prayer teams that know how to create wealth." In Jesus' Name.

CHUCK PIERCE—FEBRUARY 18, 2016

"I have chosen to *unlock* Oklahoma, and in *unlocking* Oklahoma I will *unlock* this entire nation. For My First People are in that place, and DNA for the nation exists there. So from the east, I will begin to manifest My Spirit in a new way."

DECLARATION OF COVENANT

Jon and Jolene Hamill

WHEN in the course of human events it becomes necessary for one people to dissolve the political and spiritual bands which have connected them with another, and to seek and receive from their Creator both a Pardon and a re-constitution of Covenant with the Lord Jesus Christ, a decent respect to the opinions of mankind requires that they should declare the causes which impel them to this dedication.

We hold these truths to be self-evident: that all men are created equal, that they are endowed by their Creator with certain unalienable Rights, that among these are Life, Liberty, and the pursuit of Happiness. And as an Act of Liberty, our Nation was covenanted to Jesus Christ, in the Presence of Holy Spirit, by women and men sent by Him to establish both community and governance for "the glory of God and the advancement of the Christian faith"—

And as successive generations, motivated by greed, compromised these Godly covenants—endorsing the subjugation of their brothers and sisters, both Host People and Immigrants; and embracing various forms of Baal worship, including Freemasonry and the occult—

Thereby yielding in part the corporate will of the people, in community and governance, to the influence of Baal and the consequential denial of justice, even to the unborn—

And whereas stewards of this Nation, rooted in the Land, appointed by God as repairers of the breach, have wholeheartedly repented of these sins, restored covenant, and have labored for a reprieve from the endless reproach these sins have brought upon this land and people—

Having sought and obtained from their Creator a Verdict of divorce from Baal, including the issuance of an everlasting Restraining Order and a Writ of Assistance for the restoration of all the Highest Court has granted as a covenantal right of Possession—and having throughout the year approached this Court with the same intent in every State of the Union, and in towns and cities therein, receiving the same verdict in favor of the saints—

We now, in the Presence of God, present ourselves before the Highest Court of the kingdom of God, with the intent to re-consecrate this Nation according to the covenants made with Jesus Christ by our forefathers.

And with all solemnity and deference to Your Majesty, we request that this Nation, as spoken by Isaiah and Hosea, might again be Married to the Lord, apart from all idols from which You have granted said divorce. And that Your Glory, the Presence and Power of Holy Spirit, might fully return and reside again in this land, releasing awakening, union, and reformation. And that by this covenant renewal, as Abraham Lincoln articulated, our Nation, under God, might have a *new birth of freedom*.

For consideration in this Petition, we present to You the Covenantal legacy of the Pilgrims, who on November 11, 1620 committed the land and government to "the glory of God and the advancement of the Christian faith," according to the Mayflower Compact.

And we present to You the Covenantal legacy of the Huguenots who came to this land with the same intention—whose blood was spilled and mission aborted—whose founder died chanting Psalm 132, begging Your Majesty that this land would be a "dwelling place for the Mighty God of Jacob."

And we present to You the original intent of many Host people of the Land—who agreed from the beginning that both ownership and stewardship belongs to their Creator and Father. Who sought with reverence to honor the Laws of Nature, and Nature's God. To whom You endowed great wisdom, even to convey and implement principles of democratic governance that framed the United States Constitution.

And finally, we present to You the legacy of the Seed of Abraham, by which Your Covenant with Israel and Mankind has been perpetuated. Our gratitude is immeasurable that You have chosen to graft us into this Covenant—even, as Asher Intrater observed, the Pilgrims "saw themselves as a New Israel, a nation wholly covenanted with God." To this end, we fully commit our covenantal stewardship to resource the dream of Your heart for Israel, the Jewish people, and for the nations.

In the Name of God, Amen. Having undertaken, for the glory of God and the advancement of the Christian Faith, the sacred task of repairing our Nation's founding covenants with our Creator; and having diligently and wholeheartedly sought forgiveness for breaches of said covenants, offensive to God and detrimental to mankind; we now solemnly and mutually, in the Presence of God and one another, combine these founding covenants as one Sacred Consecration of this land, the United States of America and all of its territories, to the Lord Jesus Christ.

And to this combined Declaration of Covenant, and all of our founders' intentions in establishing One Nation under God, with the witness of Heaven and Earth, we do add our agreement that this Land, its people and resources, be entirely consecrated to You. As You have engraved us in the palm of Your hand, we now ask for the Hand of God in marriage, unto whom we promise all submission and due obedience.

In witness whereof we have hereunto subscribed our names in _____ (state) this _____ day of _____, 20_____ :

We, The Beloved of God, and The Lord of All, do by these present make known that we have on this _____ day of _____, 20_____ , by solemn vow:

Covenanted to be forever bound to one another—I the Lord declare, "You will call me husband" (see Hos. 2:16); "I will betroth you to Me forever. I will betroth you in righteousness and justice, in love and compassion. I will betroth you in faithfulness, and you will know the Lord" (see Hos. 2:19-20).

We, the Beloved of God, declare: "We acknowledge You alone"; "You are my God" (see Hos. 2:20,23). It is to You alone that we will be faithful. We will know no other. We, the Beloved of God, do acknowledge and declare: We betroth You in our righteousness and justice, in our love and compassion. It is You, our God, we betroth in faithfulness. We acknowledge You alone as our Bridegroom and our provider (Hos. 2:8). And we will at all times look to You—one with Your heart, in covenant with You for our land. And hereto do we make our sacred promise.

_____

The Church, the Beloved of God

And I do receive it.

_____

The Lord of All

RESOLUTION OF APOLOGY

January 7, 2020

Dr. Negiel Bigpond
All Tribes D.C.
P.O. Box 97
Bixby, OK 74008

Dear Mr. President,

It is with honor that we, All Tribes D.C. founded by Dr. Negiel Bigpond, write to you asking for your assistance in the matter of declaring an apology to Native Americans for the atrocities perpetrated on our people by the U.S. government as recorded in history. A resolution of apology was signed into law on December 19, 2010, but has never been publicly announced. The resolution reads as follows:

S.J. RES 14—111TH CONGRESS

Section 1. Resolution of Apology to
Native Peoples of the United States.

1. (a) Acknowledgment and Apology—The United States, acting through Congress—

    a. (1) recognizes the special legal and political relationship Indian tribes have with the United States and the solemn covenant with the land we share;

    b. (2) commends and honors Native Peoples for the thousands of years that they have stewarded and protected this land;

    c. (3) recognizes that there have been years of official depredations, ill-conceived policies, and the breaking of covenants by the Federal Government regarding Indian tribes;

    d. (4) apologizes on behalf of the people of the United States to all Native Peoples for the many instances of violence, maltreatment, and neglect inflicted on Native Peoples by citizens of the United States;

    e. (5) expresses its regret for the ramifications of former wrongs and its commitment to build on the positive relationships of the past and present to move toward a brighter future where all the people of this land live reconciled as brothers and sisters, and harmoniously steward and protect this land together;

f. (6) urges the President to acknowledge the wrongs of the United States against Indian tribes in the history of the United States in order to bring healing to this land; and

g. (7) commends the State governments that have begun reconciliation efforts with recognized Indian tribes located in their boundaries and encourages all State governments similarly to work toward reconciling relationships with Indian tribes within their boundaries.

2. (b) Disclaimer—Nothing in this Joint Resolution—

a. (1) authorizes or supports any claim against the United States; or

b. (2) serves as a settlement of any claim against the United States.

We ask for the public declaration of this resolution for the healing of our people, many of whom carry the deep wounds of losses greater than we can imagine. The declaration being made public is crucial to:

- Bring healing to the soul of Native Americans;
- Foster unity among the people of this land; and
- Acknowledge the 6.79 million people comprising 573 recognized Native American tribes as human beings deserving of honor and dignity.

Canada is further along in this journey with its public apology on June 11, 2008. A few states have introduced and signed into law resolutions of apology, such as California (2019), Colorado (2014), Virginia (2007),

Alaska (2018), and Kansas (2013). Many more are working on this at the state level.

Mr. President, the public declaration of this apology will establish this resolution in the hearts and minds of our Native Americans, bringing us closer to the fulfillment of the following prophecies delivered to our people to rise up offering friendship and solutions to what ails this land:

> "The Red Nation shall rise again and it shall be a blessing for a sick world; a world filled with broken promises, selfishness and separations; a world longing for light again.
>
> I see a time of Seven Generations when all the colors of mankind will gather under the Sacred Tree of Life and the whole Earth will become one circle again.
>
> In that day, there will be those among the Lakota (and tribes) who will carry knowledge and understanding of unity among all living things and the young white ones will come to those of my people and ask for this wisdom.
>
> I salute the light within your eyes where the whole Universe dwells. For when you are at that center within you and I am at that place within me, we shall be one."

Stated by Crazy Horse (Oglala Lakota Sioux) as he sat smoking the Sacred Pipe with Sitting Bull for the last time. He was assassinated four days later on September 5, 1877.

And:

> "You are a sleeping giant, the original American. You are now awakening. Just around the corner, you may become a spiritual superpower in this country that could change not only America, but the world."

Billy Graham 1975, Albuquerque, N.M.

And:

> "The Lord told me that when the President verbally releases
> the Native American apology, verbally, he's to look to the east
> (to be aligned with Israel, which President Obama wasn't).
> Look to east and the hand of God will come across this
> nation, healing the land and the world."

Dr. Negiel Bigpond (Euchee Chief) December, 2010

All Tribes D.C. has been founded upon the desire to bring healing to
this land and its people, Native and non-Native alike. The principle of forgiveness was publicly proclaimed by Native American leaders on the Washington Mall, October 6, 2016. We are active participants in the Presidential
Prayer Breakfast, the National Day of Prayer, and launching teams to pray at
the Capitol and other sites in D.C.

We are committed to pray for you as you navigate difficult territory and
look forward to hearing from you on this matter.

Most respectfully,

Dr. Negiel Bigpond

Resources

Virginia Senate Joint Resolution No. 332, S.J.Res. 332, 2007 Sess. (Va. 2007) [hereinafter Virginia Resolution].

https://www.gov.ca.gov/2019/06/18/governor-newsom-issues-apology-to-native -americans-for-states-historical-wrongdoings-establishes-truth-and-healing -council/

https://www.krcc.org/post/commemorating-150th-anniversary-sand-creek-governor -hickenlooper-apologizes

https://splinternews.com/its-been-a-historic-wild-week-for-native-americans -in-1829863951

https://blogs.wsj.com/washwire/2009/12/22/us-offers-an-official-apology-to-native -americans/

https://www.govinfo.gov/content/pkg/STATUTE-107/pdf/STATUTE-107 -Pg1510.pdf

http://worldpopulationreview.com/states/native-american-population/

https://indigenous.ku.edu/governor-brownback-issues-proclamation-apologizing -potawatomi-trail-death

BAAL TEACHING FROM DUTCH SHEETS

THROUGH a season of tremendous warfare in November and December, as well as confirmation from many key leaders, God has exposed the spirit of Baal as one of the strongmen—perhaps the strongman—over America.

- Baal is identified as the ruler of the demons (Matthew 12:24: Beelzebub is another name for Baal).

- Baal-hamon, one of Baal's names, means "the lord of wealth or abundance." Chuck Pierce believes, and I agree, that this is the principality warring against the great transfer of wealth to the church. You must war against this spirit to see your inheritance released. Claim Jeremiah 51:44 (Bel in this verse is Baal).

- Baal-berith, another of his names, means "the lord of the covenant." The Hebrew word baal actually means "husband" or "marriage." This spirit always attempted to cause Israel to "divorce" or break covenant with God and "marry" or align with him. Consistent with this, in so many ways America has broken covenant with God and married Baal. This is, I believe, the strongman behind most covenant-breaking.

- Baal is the strongman behind sexual perversion. Homosexuality was and is one of his big strongholds. I believe all of the sexual sin and perversion in America is, to one degree or another, under Baal's orchestration. You will continue to see God expose leaders in the church who aligned themselves with this spirit. Pray for the church to be cleansed and for Baal's hold on America in this area to be broken.

- Baal always goes after the next generation, trying to cut off the extension of God's covenantal purposes. He is a violent spirit and even required human sacrifice. Abortion is under Baal, as is the "cutting" of today's young generation (see 1 Kings 18:28), the vampire and goth movement, and the death culture in general that has so invaded America. Baal is leading the fight to avert the great awakening planned for the young generation of Americans today. Pray against and bind these efforts.

- Witchcraft and occult spirits in general operate under Baal. So does Jezebel.

THE BAAL PRINCIPALITY
(GOD OF 1,000 FACES)

Baal (Sun god): Bel, Apollo, Zeus, Marduk, Ahura-Mazda, Osiris, Tammuz, Dagon, Prometheus, Jupiter, Nimrod, Mithra ("Another Jesus" and "The Anti-Christ"), Ra, Lucetius, Dyaus, Dionysus, Hermes, Adonis, Pan, Hades, Eros, Uranus, Gaea, Assur, Merodach, Ninus, Shamas, Zeus-Belus, Bacchus

Queen of Heaven (Moon and Sun goddess): Mother of Harlots, Mother of God (and child), the Great Mother, Ashtaroth, Artemis, Aphrodite, Juno, Lilith, Minerva, Columbia, Nike, Astarte, Athena, Beltis, Diana, Isis (Horus), Anahita, Inanna, Tanat, Ishtar (Easter), Cybele, Mylitta, Hathor, Kali

Leviathan: Neptune, Poseidon, Tiamet, King of Children of Pride

2 Samuel 21:1-6,14; Matthew 6:9-10; Isaiah 9:7; 2 Chronicles 7:13-14; Ephesians 6:12-13; 2 Corinthians 10:4; 1 Peter 5:8-9; 2 Corinthians 2:11; 11:14-15; Mathew 12:24, 28-29; Jeremiah 51:44; Hosea 2:16-17, 19; 2 Corinthians 11:2-4; Job 31:26-28; Deuteronomy 4:19; Exodus 20:3-6; 1 Corinthians 10:19-21; Romans 1:23; Jeremiah 7:16-18

PRAYER FOR RELEASE FOR FREEMASONS AND THEIR DESCENDANTS

This is an excerpt from Unmasking Freemasonry: Removing the Hoodwink, by Dr. Selwyn Stevens.

IF you were once a member of a Masonic organization or are a descendant of someone who was, we recommend that you pray through this prayer from your heart. Please don't be like the Masons who are given their obligations and oaths one line at a time and without prior knowledge of the requirements. Please read it through first so you know what is involved.

It is best to pray this aloud with a Christian witness present. We suggest a brief pause following each paragraph to allow the Holy Spirit to show any related issues which may require attention.

A significant number of people also reported having experienced physical and spiritual healings as diverse as long-term headaches and epilepsy as the result of praying through this prayer. Christian counselors and pastors in many countries have been using this prayer in counseling situations and seminars for several years, with real and significant results.

Some language could be described as "quaint Old English" and is the real terminology used in the Masonic ritual. The legal renunciation opens the way for spiritual, emotional, and physical healing to take place.

There are differences between British Commonwealth Masonry and American and Prince Hall Masonry in the higher degrees. Degrees unique to Americans are marked with this sign "*" at the commencement of each paragraph. Those of British Commonwealth descent shouldn't need to pray through those paragraphs.

THE PRAYER OF RELEASE

Father God, creator of heaven and earth, I come to You in the name of Jesus Christ Your Son. I come as a sinner seeking forgiveness and cleansing from all sins committed against You, and others made in Your image. I honor my earthly father and mother and all of my ancestors of flesh and blood and of the spirit by adoption and godparents, but I utterly turn away from and renounce all their sins. I forgive all my ancestors for the effects of their sins on me and my children. I confess and renounce all of my own sins, known and unknown. I renounce and rebuke satan and every spiritual power of his affecting me and my family, in the name of Jesus Christ.

True Holy Creator God, in the name of the True Lord Jesus Christ, in accordance with Jude 8-10, Psalm 82:1, and 2 Chronicles 18, I request You to move aside all Celestial Beings, including Principalities, Powers, and Rulers, and to forbid them to harass, intimidate, or retaliate against me and all participants in this ministry today.

I also ask that You prevent these beings of whatever rank to not be permitted to send any level of spiritual evil as retaliation against any of those here, or our families, our ministries, or possessions.

I renounce and annul every covenant made with Death by my ancestors or myself, including every agreement made with Sheol, and I renounce the refuge of lies and falsehoods which they have been hidden behind.

In the name of the Lord Jesus Christ, I renounce and forsake all involvement in Freemasonry or any other lodge, craft, or occultism by my ancestors and myself. I also renounce and break the code of silence enforced by Freemasonry and the occult on my family and myself. I renounce and repent of all pride and arrogance which opened the door for the slavery and bondage of Freemasonry to afflict my family and me. I now shut every door of witchcraft and deception operating in my life and seal it closed with the blood of the Lord Jesus Christ. I renounce every covenant, every blood covenant, and every alliance with Freemasonry or the spiritual powers behind it made by my family or me.

In the name of Jesus Christ, I rebuke, renounce, and bind Witchcraft, the principal spirit behind Freemasonry, and I renounce and rebuke Baphomet, the Spirit of Antichrist, and the spirits of Death and Deception.

I renounce and rebuke the Spirit of Fides, the Roman goddess of Fidelity that seeks to hold all Masonic and occultic participants and their descendants in bondage, and I ask the One True Holy Creator God to give me the gift of Faith to believe in the True Lord Jesus Christ as described in the Word of God.

I also renounce and rebuke the Spirit of Prostitution, which the Word of God says has led members of Masonic and other occultic organizations astray, and caused them to become unfaithful to the One True and Holy God. I now choose to return and become faithful to the God of the Bible, the God of Abraham, Isaac, and Jacob, the Father of Jesus Christ, who I now declare is my Lord and Savior.

I renounce the insecurity; the love of position and power; the love of money, avarice, or greed; and the pride that would have led my ancestors into Masonry. I renounce all the fears that held them in Masonry, especially the fears of death, fears of men, and fears of trusting, in the name of Jesus Christ.

I renounce every position held in the lodge by any of my ancestors or myself, including "Master," "Worshipful Master," or any other occultic title.

I renounce the calling of any man "Master," for Jesus Christ is my only master and Lord, and He forbids anyone else having that title. I renounce the entrapping of others into Masonry, and observing the helplessness of others during the rituals. I renounce the effects of Masonry passed on to me through any female ancestor who felt distrusted and rejected by her husband as he entered and attended any lodge and refused to tell her of his secret activities. I also renounce all obligations, oaths, and curses enacted by every female member of my family through any direct membership of all Women's Orders of Freemasonry, the Order of the Eastern Star, or any other Masonic or occultic organization.

All participants should now be invited to sincerely carry out in faith the following actions:

1. Symbolically remove the blindfold (hoodwink) and give it to the Lord for disposal;

2. In the same way, symbolically remove the veil of mourning, to make way to receive the Joy of the Lord:

3. Symbolically cut and remove the noose from around the neck, gather it up with the cable-tow running down the body, and give it all to the Lord for His disposal;

4. Renounce the false Freemasonry marriage covenant, removing from the 4th finger of the right hand the ring of this false marriage covenant, giving it to the Lord to dispose of it;

5. Symbolically remove the chains and bondages of Freemasonry from your body;

6. Symbolically remove all Freemasonry regalia, including collars, gauntlets, and armor, especially the Apron with its snake clasp, to make way for the Belt of Truth;

7. Remove the slipshod slippers, to make way for the shoes of the Gospel of Peace;

8. Symbolically remove the ball and chain from the ankles.

9. Invite participants to repent of and seek forgiveness for having walked on all unholy ground, including Freemasonry lodges and temples, including any Mormon or any other occultic/Masonic organizations.

10. Proclaim that satan and his demons no longer have any legal rights to mislead and manipulate the person seeking help.

33rd and Supreme Degree

In the name of Jesus Christ, I renounce the oaths taken and the curses and iniquities involved in the supreme Thirty-Third Degree of Freemasonry, the Grand Sovereign Inspector General. I renounce the secret passwords, DEMOLAY-HIRUM ABIFF, FREDERICK OF PRUSSIA, MICHA, MACHA, BEALIM, and ADONAI, and all their occultic and Masonic meanings. I renounce all of the obligations of every Masonic degree, and all penalties invoked.

I renounce and utterly forsake the Great Architect of the Universe, who is revealed in this degree as Lucifer, and his false claim to be the universal fatherhood of God. I reject the Masonic view of deity because it does not square with the revelation of the One True and Holy Creator God of the Bible.

I renounce the cable-tow around the neck. I renounce the death wish that the wine drunk from a human skull should turn to poison and the skeleton whose cold arms are invited if the oath of this degree is violated. I renounce the three infamous assassins of their grand master, law, property, and religion, and the greed and witchcraft involved in the attempt to manipulate and control the rest of mankind.

In the name of God the Father, Jesus Christ the Son, and the Holy Spirit, I renounce and break the curses and iniquities involved in the idolatry, blasphemy, secrecy, and deception of Freemasonry at every level, and I appropriate the Blood of Jesus Christ to cleanse all the consequences of these from my life. I now revoke all previous consent given by any of my ancestors or myself to be deceived.

Blue Lodge

In the name of Jesus Christ, I renounce the oaths taken and the curses and iniquities involved in the First or Entered Apprentice Degree, especially their effects on the throat and tongue. I renounce the Hoodwink blindfold and its effects on spirit, emotions, and eyes, including all confusion, fear of the dark, fear of the light, and fear of sudden noises. I renounce the blinding of spiritual truth, the darkness of the soul, the false imagination, condescension, and the spirit of poverty caused by the ritual of this degree. I also renounce the usurping of the marriage covenant by the removal of the wedding ring. I renounce the secret word, BOAZ, and it's Masonic meaning. I renounce the serpent clasp on the apron and the spirit of Python which it brought to squeeze the spiritual life out of me.

I renounce the ancient pagan teaching from Babylon and Egypt and the symbolism of the First Tracing Board. I renounce the mixing and mingling of truth and error, the mythology, fabrications, and lies taught as truth, and the dishonesty by leaders as to the true understanding of the ritual, and the blasphemy of this degree of Freemasonry.

I renounce the breaking of five of God's Ten Commandments during participation in the rituals of the Blue Lodge degrees. I renounce the presentation to every compass direction, for all the Earth is the Lord's, and everything in it. I renounce the cable-tow noose around the neck, the fear of choking, and also every spirit causing asthma, hay fever, emphysema, or any other breathing difficulty. I renounce the ritual dagger, or the compass point, sword or spear held against the breast, the fear of death by stabbing pain, and the fear of heart attack from this degree, and the absolute secrecy demanded under a witchcraft oath and sealed by kissing the Volume of the Sacred Law. I also renounce kneeling to the false deity known as the Great Architect of the Universe, and humbly ask the One True God to forgive me for this idolatry, in the name of Jesus Christ.

I renounce the pride of proven character and good standing required prior to joining Freemasonry, and the resulting self-righteousness of being good enough to stand before God without the need of a savior. I now pray for healing of (throat, vocal cords, nasal passages, sinus, bronchial tubes, etc.), for healing of the speech area, and the release of the Word of God to me and through me and my family.

Second or Fellow Craft Degree of Masonry

In the name of Jesus Christ, I renounce the oaths taken and the curses and iniquities involved in the Second or Fellow Craft Degree of Masonry, especially the curses on the heart and chest. I renounce the secret words SHIBBOLETH and JACHIN and all their Masonic meaning. I renounce the ancient pagan teaching and symbolism of the Second Tracing Board. I renounce the Sign of Reverence to the Generative Principle. I cut off emotional hardness, apathy, indifference, unbelief, and deep anger from me and my family. In the name of Jesus Christ, I pray for the healing of (the chest/lung/heart area) and also for the healing of my emotions, and ask to be made sensitive to the Holy Spirit of God.

Third or Master Mason Degree

In the name of Jesus Christ, I renounce the oaths taken and the curses and iniquities involved in the Third or Master Mason Degree, especially the curses on the stomach and womb area. I renounce the secret words TUBAL CAIN and MAHA BONE and all their Masonic meaning. I renounce the ancient pagan teaching and symbolism of the Third Tracing Board used in the ritual. I renounce the Spirit of Death from the blows to the head enacted as ritual murder, the fear of death, false martyrdom, fear of violent gang attack, assault, or rape, and the helplessness of this degree. I renounce the falling into the coffin or stretcher involved in the ritual of murder.

In the name of Jesus Christ, I renounce Hiram Abiff, the false savior of Freemasons revealed in this degree. I renounce the false resurrection of this degree, because only Jesus Christ is the Resurrection and the Life!

I renounce the pagan ritual of the "Point within a Circle" with all its bondages and phallus worship. I renounce the symbol "G" and its veiled pagan symbolism and bondages. I renounce the occultic mysticism of the black and white mosaic checkered floor with the tessellated border and five-pointed blazing star.

I renounce the All-Seeing Third Eye of Freemasonry or Horus in the forehead and its pagan and occult symbolism. I rebuke and reject every spirit of divination which allowed this occult ability to operate. (Action: Put your hand over your forehead.) I now close that Third Eye and all occult ability to see into the spiritual realm, in the name of the Lord Jesus Christ, and put my trust in the Holy Spirit sent by Jesus Christ for all I need to know on spiritual matters. I renounce all false communions taken, all mockery of the redemptive work of Jesus Christ on the cross of Calvary, all unbelief, confusion, and depression. I renounce and forsake the lie of Freemasonry that man is not sinful, but merely imperfect, and so can redeem himself through good works. I rejoice that the Bible states that I cannot do a single thing to earn my salvation, but that I can only be saved by grace through faith in Jesus Christ and what He accomplished on the Cross of Calvary.

I renounce all fear of insanity, anguish, death wishes, suicide, and death in the name of Jesus Christ. Death was conquered by Jesus Christ, and He alone holds the keys of death and hell, and I rejoice that He holds my life in His hands now. He came to give me life abundantly and eternally, and I believe His promises.

I renounce all anger, hatred, murderous thoughts, revenge, retaliation, spiritual apathy, false religion, all unbelief, especially unbelief in the Holy Bible as God's Word, and all compromise of God's Word. I renounce all spiritual searching into false religions and all striving to please God. I rest in the knowledge that I have found my Lord and Savior Jesus Christ, and that He has found me.

In the name of Jesus Christ, I pray for the healing of (the stomach, gall bladder, womb, liver, and any other organs of my body affected by Masonry), and I ask for a release of compassion and understanding for me and my family.

York Rite

I renounce and forsake the oaths taken and the curses and iniquities involved in the York Rite Degrees of Masonry. I renounce the Mark Lodge, and the mark in the form of squares and angles which marks the person for life. I also reject the jewel or occult talisman which may have been made from this mark sign and worn at lodge meetings, the Mark Master Degree with its secret word JOPPA, and its penalty of having the right ear smote off and the curse of permanent deafness, as well as the right hand being chopped off for being an imposter.

I also renounce and forsake the oaths taken and the curses and iniquities involved in the other York Rite Degrees, including Past Master, with the penalty of having my tongue split from tip to root, and of the Most Excellent Master Degree, in which the penalty is to have my breast torn open and my heart and vital organs removed and exposed to rot on the dung hill.

Holy Royal Arch Degree

In the name of Jesus Christ, I renounce and forsake the oaths taken and the curses and iniquities involved in the Holy Royal Arch Degree, especially the oath regarding the removal of the head from the body and the exposing of the brains to the hot sun. I renounce the false secret name of God, JAHBULON, and declare total rejection of all worship of the false pagan gods Bul or Baal and On or Osiris. I also renounce the password AMMI RUHAMAH and all its Masonic meaning. I renounce the false communion or Eucharist taken in this degree and all the mockery, skepticism, and unbelief about the redemptive work of Jesus Christ on the cross of Calvary. I cut off all these curses and their effects on me and my family in the name of Jesus Christ, and I pray for (healing of the brain, the mind, etc.).

I renounce and forsake the oaths taken and the curses and iniquities involved in the Royal Master Degree of the York Rite, the Select Master Degree with its penalty to have my hands chopped off to the stumps, to have my eyes plucked out from their sockets, and to have my body quartered and thrown among the rubbish of the Temple.

I renounce and forsake the oaths taken and the curses and iniquities involved in the Super Excellent Master Degree along with the penalty of having my thumbs cut off, my eyes put out, my body bound in fetters and brass, and conveyed captive to a strange land; and also of the Knights or Illustrious Order of the Red Cross, along with the penalty of having my house torn down and my being hanged on the exposed timbers.

I renounce the Knights Templar Degree and the secret words of KEB RAIOTH, and also Knights of Malta Degree and the secret words MAHER-SHALAL-HASH-BAZ.

I renounce the vows taken on a human skull, the crossed swords, and the curse and death wish of Judas of having the head cut off and placed on top of a church spire. I renounce the unholy communion and especially of drinking from a human skull in many rites.

Ancient and Accepted or Scottish Rite

(Only the 18th, 30th, 31st, 32nd, and 33rd degrees are operated in British Commonwealth countries.)

* I renounce the oaths taken and the curses, iniquities, and penalties involved in the American and Grand Orient Lodges, including of the Secret Master Degree, its secret passwords of ADONAI and ZIZA, and their occult meanings. I reject and renounce the worship of the pagan sun god as the Great Source of Light, and the crowning with laurel sacred to Apollo, and the sign of secrecy in obedience to Horus;

* of the Perfect Master Degree, its secret password of MAH-HAHBONE, and its penalty of being smitten to the Earth with a setting maul;

* of the Intimate Secretary Degree, its secret passwords of YEVA and JOABERT, and its penalties of having my body dissected, and of having my vital organs cut into pieces and thrown to the beasts of the field, and of the use of the nine-pointed star from the Kabbala and the worship of Phallic energy;

* of the Provost and Judge Degree, its secret password of HIRUMTITO-CIVI-KY, and the penalty of having my nose cut off;

* of the Intendant of the Building Degree, of its secret password AKAR-JAI-JAH, and the penalty of having my eyes put out, my body cut in two and exposing my bowels;

* of the Elected Knights of the Nine Degree, its secret password NEKAM NAKAH, and its penalty of having my head cut off and stuck on the highest pole in the East;

* of the Illustrious Elect of Fifteen Degree, with its secret password ELIGNAM, and its penalties of having my body opened perpendicularly and horizontally, the entrails exposed to the air for eight hours so that flies may prey on them, and for my head to be cut off and placed on a high pinnacle;

* of the Sublime Knights elect of the Twelve Degree, its secret password STOLKIN-ADONAI, and its penalty of having my hand cut in twain;

* of the Grand Master Architect Degree, its secret password RABBANAIM, and its penalties;

* of the Knight of the Ninth Arch of Solomon or Enoch Degree, its secret password JEHOVAH, it's blasphemous use, its penalty of having my body given to the beasts of the forest as prey, and I also renounce the revelations from the Kabbala in this and subsequent degrees;

* of the Grand Elect, Perfect and Sublime Mason or Elu Degree, its secret password MARAH-MAUR-ABREK and IHUH, the penalty of having my body cut open and my bowels given to vultures for food, and I reject the Great Unknowable deity of this degree;

Council of Princes of Jerusalem

* of the Knights of the East Degree, its secret password RAPH-ODOM, and its penalties;

* of the Prince of Jerusalem Degree, its secret password TEBE-TADAR, and its penalty of being stripped naked and having my heart pierced with a ritual dagger;

Chapter of the Rose Croix

* of the Knight of the East and West Degree, its secret password ABADDON, and its penalty of incurring the severe wrath of the Almighty Creator of Heaven and Earth. I also reject the Tetractys and its representation of the Sephiroth from the Kabbala and its false tree of life. I also reject the false anointing with oil and the proclamation that anyone so anointed is now worthy to open the Book of Seven Seals, because only the Lord Jesus Christ is worthy;

18th Degree

I renounce the oaths taken and the curses, iniquities, and penalties involved in the Eighteenth Degree of Freemasonry, the Most Wise Sovereign Knight of the Pelican and the Eagle, and Sovereign Prince Rose Croix of Heredom. I renounce and reject the false Jesus revealed in this degree because He doesn't point to the light or the truth since the True Lord Jesus Christ is the Light of the World and the Truth. I renounce and reject the Pelican witchcraft spirit, as well as the occultic influence of the Rosicrucians and the Kabbala in this degree.

I renounce the claim that the death of Jesus Christ was a "dire calamity," and also the deliberate mockery and twisting of the Christian doctrine of the Atonement. I renounce the blasphemy and rejection of the deity of Jesus Christ and the secret words IGNE NATURA RENOVATUR INTEGRA and its burning. I renounce the mockery of the communion taken in this degree, including a biscuit, salt, and white wine.

Council of Kadosh

I renounce the inappropriate use of the title "Kadosh" used in these council degrees because it means "Holy" and it is here used in an unholy way.

I renounce the oaths taken and the curses, iniquities, and penalties involved in the Grand Pontiff Degree, its secret password EMMANUEL, and its penalties;

of the Grand Master of Symbolic Lodges or Ad Vitum Degree, its secret passwords JEKSON and STOLKIN, and the penalties invoked, and I also reject the pagan Phoenician and Hindu deities revealed in this degree;

of the Patriarch Noachite or Prussian Knight Degree, its secret password PELEG, and its penalties;

of the Knight of the Royal Axe or Prince of Libanus Degree, its secret password NOAH-BEZALEEL-SODONIAS, and its penalties;

of the Chief of the Tabernacle Degree, its secret password URI-EL-JEHOVAH, and its penalty that I agree the Earth should open up and engulf me up to my neck so I perish, and I also reject the false title of becoming a "Son of Light" in this degree;

of the Prince of the Tabernacle Degree, and its penalty to be stoned to death and have my body left above ground to rot. I also reject the claimed revelation of the mysteries of the Hebrew faith from the Kabbala, and the occultic and pagan Egyptian, Hindu, Mithraic, Dionysian, and Orphic mysteries revealed and worshiped in this degree;

of the Knight of the Brazen Serpent Degree, its secret password MOSES-JOHANNES, and its penalty to have my heart eaten by venomous serpents. I also reject the claimed revelation of the mysteries of the Islamic faith, I reject the insulting misquotations from the Koran, and the gift of a white turban in this degree;

* of the Prince of Mercy Degree, its secret password GOMEL, JEHOVAHJACHIN, and its penalty of condemnation and spite by the entire universe. I also reject the claimed revelation of the mysteries of the Christian religion because there are no such mysteries. I reject the Druid trinity of Odin, Freya, and Thor revealed in this degree. I also reject the false baptism claimed for the purification of my soul to allow my soul to rejoin the universal soul of Buddhism, as taught in this degree;

* of the Knight Commander of the Temple Degree, its secret password SOLOMON, and its penalty of receiving the severest wrath of Almighty God inflicted upon me. I also reject the claimed revelation of the mysteries of Numerology, Astrology, and Alchemy and other occult sciences taught in this degree;

* of the Knight Commander of the Sun, or Prince Adept Degree, its secret password STIBIUM, and its penalties of having my tongue thrust through with a red-hot iron, of my eyes being plucked out, of my senses of smelling and hearing being removed, of having my hands cut off and in that condition to be left for voracious animals to devour me, or executed by lightening from heaven;

* of the Grand Scottish Knight of Saint Andrew or Patriarch of the Crusades Degree, its secret password NEKAMAH-FUR-LAC, and its penalties;

Thirtieth Degree

I renounce the oaths taken and the curses and iniquities involved in the Thirtieth Degree of Masonry, the Grand Knight Kadosh and Knight of the Black and White Eagle. I renounce the secret passwords, STIBIUM ALKABAR, PHARASH-KOH, and all they mean.

Sublime Princes of the Royal Secret
Thirty-First Degree of Masonry

I renounce the oaths taken and the curses and iniquities involved in the Thirty-First Degree of Masonry, the Grand Inspector Inquisitor Commander. I renounce all the gods and goddesses of Egypt which are honored in this degree, including Anubis with the jackal's head, Osiris the Sun god, Isis the sister and wife of Osiris, and also the moon goddess. I renounce the Soul of Cheres, the false symbol of immortality, the Chamber of the dead, and the false teaching of reincarnation.

Thirty-Second Degree of Masonry

I renounce the oaths taken and the curses and iniquities involved in the Thirty-Second Degree of Masonry, the Sublime Prince of the Royal Secret. I renounce the secret passwords PHAAL/ PHARASH-KOL and all they mean. I renounce Masonry's false trinitarian deity AUM, and its parts—Brahma the creator, Vishnu the preserver, and Shiva the destroyer. I renounce the deity of AHURA-MAZDA, the claimed spirit or source of all light, and the worship with fire, which is an abomination to God, and also the drinking from a human skull in many rites.

Shriners (applies only in North America)

* *I renounce the oaths taken and the curses, iniquities, and penalties involved in the Ancient Arabic Order of the Nobles of the Mystic Shrine. I renounce the piercing of the eyeballs with a three-edged blade, the flaying of the feet, the madness, and the worship of the false god Allah as the god of our fathers. I renounce the hoodwink, the mock hanging, the mock beheading, the mock drinking of the blood of the victim, the mock dog urinating on the initiate, and the offering of urine as a commemoration.*

All Other Degrees

I renounce all the other oaths taken, the rituals of every other degree, and the curses and iniquities invoked. These include the Acacia, Allied Degrees, the Red Cross of Constantine, the Order of the Secret Monitor, and the Masonic Royal Order of Scotland.

I renounce all other lodges and secret societies including Prince Hall Freemasonry, Grand Orient Lodges, Mormonism, the Ancient Toltec Rite, the Order of Amaranth, the Royal Order of Jesters, the Manchester Unity Order of Oddfellows and its womens' Order of Rebekah lodges, the Royal Antediluvian Order of Buffaloes, Druids, Foresters, the Loyal Order of Orange, including the Purple and Black Lodges within it, Elks,

Moose, and Eagles Lodges, the Ku Klux Klan, the Grange, the Woodmen of the World, Riders of the Red Robe, the Knights of Pythias, the Order of the Builders, the Rite of Memphiz and Mitzraim, Ordo Templi Orientis (OTO), Aleister Crowley's Palladium Masonry, the Order of the Golden Key, the Order of Desoms, the Mystic Order of the Veiled Prophets of the Enchanted Realm, the women's Orders of the Eastern Star, of the Ladies Oriental Shrine, and of the White Shrine of Jerusalem, the girls' order of the Daughters of the Eastern Star, the International Orders of Job's Daughters, and of the Rainbow, the boys' Order of De Molay, and the Order of the Constellation of Junior Stars, and every university or college fraternity or sorority with Greek and Masonic connections, and their effects on me and all my family. Lord Jesus, because You want me to be totally free from all occult bondages, I will burn all objects in my possession that connect me with all lodges and occultic organizations, including Masonry, Witchcraft, the Occult, and Mormonism, and all regalia, aprons, books of rituals, rings, and other jewelry. I renounce the effects these or other objects of Masonry, including the compass and the square, have had on me or my family, in the name of Jesus Christ.

In the name and authority of Jesus Christ, I break every curse of Freemasonry in my life, including the curses of barrenness, sickness, mind-blinding, and poverty, and I rebuke every evil spirit which empowered these curses.

I also renounce, cut off, and dissolve in the blood of Jesus Christ every ungodly soul-tie I or my ancestors have created with other lodge members or participants in occultic groups and actions, and I ask You to send out ministering angels to gather together all portions of my fragmented soul, to free them from all bondages and to wash them clean in the Blood of Jesus Christ, and then to restore them to wholeness to their rightful place within me. I also ask that You remove from me any parts of any other person's soul which has been deposited within my humanity. Thank You, Lord, for restoring my soul and sanctifying my spirit.

I renounce and rebuke every evil spirit associated with Freemasonry, Witchcraft, the Occult and all other sins and iniquities. Lord Jesus, I ask You to now set me free from all spiritual and other bondages, in accordance with the many promises of the Bible.

In the name of the Lord Jesus Christ, I now take the delegated authority given to me and bind every spirit of sickness, infirmity, curse, affliction, addiction, disease, or allergy associated with these sins I have confessed and renounced, including every spirit empowering all iniquities inherited from my family. I exercise the delegated authority from the Risen Lord Jesus Christ over all lower levels of evil spirits and demons which have been assigned to me, and I command that all such demonic beings are to be bound up into one, to be separated from every part of my humanity, whether perceived to be in the body or trapped in the dimensions, and they are not permitted to transfer power to any other spirits or to call for reinforcements.

I command, in the name of Jesus Christ, for every evil spirit to leave me now, touching or harming no one, and go to the dry place appointed for you by the Lord Jesus Christ, never to return to me or my family, and I command that you now take all your memories, roots, scars, works, nests, and habits with you. I surrender to God's Holy Spirit and to no other spirit all the places in my life where these sins and iniquities have been.

Conclusion

Holy Spirit, I ask that You show me anything else which I need to do or to pray so that I and my family may be totally free from the consequences of the sins of Masonry, Witchcraft, Mormonism, and all related paganism and occultism.

(Pause, while listening to God, and pray as the Holy Spirit leads you.)

Now, dear Father God, I ask humbly for the blood of Jesus Christ, Your Son and my Savior, to cleanse me from all these sins I have confessed and renounced, to cleanse my spirit, my soul, my mind, my emotions, and every part of my body that has been affected by these sins, in the name of Jesus Christ. I also command every cell in my body to come into divine order now, and to be healed and made whole as they were designed to by my loving Creator, including restoring all chemical imbalances and neurological functions, controlling all cancerous cells, reversing all degenerative diseases, and I sever the DNA and RNA of any mental or physical diseases or afflictions that came down through my family blood lines. I also ask to receive the perfect love of God which casts out all fear, in the name of the Lord Jesus Christ.

I ask You, Lord, to fill me with Your Holy Spirit now according to the promises in Your Word. I take to myself the whole armor of God in accordance with Ephesians Chapter Six, and rejoice in its protection as Jesus surrounds me and fills me with His Holy Spirit. I enthrone You, Lord Jesus, in my heart, for You are my Lord and my Savior, the source of eternal life. Thank You, Father God, for Your mercy, Your forgiveness, and Your love, in the name of Jesus Christ, amen.

Since the above is what needs to be renounced, why would anyone want to join?

This information is taken from *Unmasking Freemasonry—Removing the Hoodwink* by Dr. Selwyn Stevens, published by Jubilee Resources, PO Box 36-044, Wellington 6330, New Zealand (ISBN 1877203-48-3).

Notice

Copying of this prayer is both permitted and encouraged provided reference is made to book title, author, publisher, and web address www.jubileeresources.com or www.jubilee.org.nz. This and other similar prayers are available to download freely from our website. Resources on other subjects are also available to educate and equip Christians on a wide range of spiritual deceptions. These prayers will also be in Spanish, Brazilian Portuguese, French, German, Italian, and other languages as can be arranged.

Written testimonies of changed lives also are welcome.

If additional prayer and ministry is required, or information is required about other spiritual deceptions, please contact us on the Jubilee Resources Enquiry page. For reasons of distance, we may refer you to someone based closer to you. We have counseling referrals available in many countries particularly in North America, Australia, and Europe.

HOW TO JOIN THE

Heartland Apostolic Prayer Network

As an organization or an individual who prays and intercedes for God's purpose to save and transform, you can be a part of the growing army of intercessors. To unite with HAPN, visit www.hapn.us/join or:

HAPN
1780 W. Memorial Road
Oklahoma City, OK 73134
PO Box 720006 OKC, OK 73172
(405) 463-4900
HAPN: info@hapn.us | www.hapn.us

HOW TO ORDER

Dr. Benefiel's *Binding the Strongman*

THREE-HOUR TEACHING ON DVD OR CD

- DVD set $30
- CD series $20
- Purchase online at www.hapn.us/bts
- Or, for more information, please contact the audio visual department at (405) 463-4900.

SEND CHECK OR MONEY ORDER TO:

Audio Visual Department
Church on the Rock
P.O. Box 720006
OKC, OK 73172

NOTES

FOREWORD

1. Kim Daniels, *Give It Back* (Lake Mary, FL: Charisma House, 2007), 168.
2. Dutch Sheets, *Authority in Prayer* (Bloomington, MN: Bethany House Publishers, 2006), 20.

CHAPTER 2

1. Cindy Jacobs, *Reformation Manifesto* (Bloomington, MN: Bethany House Publishers, 2008), 13-14.
2. Edwin J. Orr, "Spirit of Revival," *Campus Crusade for Christ,* Special Edition (1999): 30–33.
3. *Random House Unabridged Dictionary*, s.v. "revival," http://dictionary.infoplease .com/revival (accessed March 23, 2009).
4. Ibid., s.v. "awakening," http://dictionary.infoplease.com/awakening (accessed March 23, 2009).
5. Ibid.
6. Charles Grandison Finney, *Lectures on Revivals and Religion,* ed. William G. McLoughlin (Cambridge: Harvard University Press, 1960), 196-197.

7. Huston Hurn, *The Pioneers*, The Old West (Alexandria, VA: Time Life Books, 1974), 49.

8. Jacobs, *Reformation Manifesto,* 18.

9. Jack Utter, *American Indians: Answers to Today's Questions* (Lake Ann, MI: National Woodlands Publishing, 1993), 86.

10. James W. Loewen, *Lies My Teacher Told Me: Everything Your American History Textbook Got Wrong* (New York, NY: Simon & Schuster, 1995), 123–126.

CHAPTER 3

1. Farley, Gloria, *In Plain Sight* (Chelsea, MI: Sheridan Books, Inc., 2007), 64, fig. 4.4.

2. Ibid., 63, fig. 4.2.

3. Ibid., 66, fig. 4.7.

4. Ibid., 249-254.

5. Salvatore Michael Trento, *The Search for Lost America* (Hammondsworth, UK: Penguin Books, 1979).

6. Barry Fell, *America B.C.* (Muskogee, OK: Artisan Publishing, 2006), 59.

7. Ibid., 100–101.

8. Ibid., 159.

9. Marjo C.A. Korpel, "Fit for a Queen—Jezebel's Royal Seal," *Biblical Archeology Review* (March/April 2008), 37.

10. Dennis Bratcher, "Ba'al Worship in the Old Testament," *CRI/Voice Institute,* January 19, 2009, http://www.crivoice.org/baal.html.

CHAPTER 5

1. Brent Staples, "Unearthing a Riot," *New York Times*, December 19, 1999.

2. Ibid.

CHAPTER 11

1. Isabel Kershner, "Deadly Israeli Raid Draws Condemnation," *New York Times,* May 31, 2010.

CHAPTER 12

1. Courtesy James Nesbit, Prepare the Way Ministries.

2. See 1 Kings 14:24, 15:12, 22:46; 2 Kings 23:7; Hosea 4:14 (NIV).

3. See Leviticus 18:21; 20:3–5; 1 Kings 11:7; 2 Kings 23:10; Jeremiah 32:35.

4. Rachel K. Jones, et al., "Abortion in the United States: Incidence and Access to Services, 2005," *Perspectives on Sexual and Reproductive Health* 40, no.1 (2008): 6–16.

5. A.C. de LaRive, *La Femme et l'Enfant dans la Franc-Maconnerie Universelle*, (Paris, France, 1889), 588, quoted in Lady Queenborough, *Occult Theocrasy* (France, 1933) 220-221, http://www.religiouscounterfeits. org/ml_realgod.htm.

6. Heidi N. Moore, "Wall Street Sex Scandals: A Partial History," *Deal Journal,* March 10, 2008.

7. Inés San Martín, "Pope calls idea of declaring Mary co-redemptrix 'foolishness,'" *CRUX,* December 13, 2019, https://cruxnow.com/vatican/2019/12/pope-calls -idea-of-declaring-mary-co-redemptrix-foolishness/.

CHAPTER 15

1. Words and music ©Andy Leong, May 10, 1998, Church on the Rock, Oklahoma City.

2. Words and music ©Andy Leong, 2008, Church on the Rock, Oklahoma City.

CHAPTER 19

1. Erik Walters, "These 6 Corporations Control 90% of the Media in America—NO WONDER!" April 9, 2019, https://www.libertyparkpress.com/these-6-corporations-control-90-of-the-media-in-america.

2. "Who Owns the Media?" Democracy on Deadline, Independent Lens, https://www.pbs.org/independentlens/democracyondeadline/mediaownership.html.

CHAPTER 20

1. Hans Rosling, Olga Rosling, and Anna Rosling Rönnlund, *Factfulness: Ten Reasons We Are Wrong About the World—And Why Things Are Better Than You Think* (New York, NY: Flatiron Books, 2018).

2. Steven Pinker, "Has the Decline of Violence Reversed since *The Better Angels of Our Nature* was Written?" https://stevenpinker.com/files/pinker/files/has_the_decline_of_violence_reversed_since_the_better_angels_of_our_nature_was_written.pdf, accessed May 17, 2020.

3. Steven Pinker, *The Better Angels of Our Nature: Why Violence Has Declined* (New York: Penguin Books, Ltd, 2011).

4. Max Roser and Esteban Ortiz-Ospina, "Global Extreme Poverty," 2013, 2017, 2019, *Our World in Data,* https://ourworldindata.org/extreme-poverty, accessed May 17, 2020.

5. Jon Berkeley, "The world's next great leap forward toward the end of poverty," *The Economist,* June 1, 2013, https://www.economist.com/leaders/2013/06/01/towards-the-end-of-poverty.

6. George Weigel, "Christian Number-Crunching reveals impressive growth," CERC, https://www.catholiceducation.org/en/controversy/common-misconceptions/christian-number-crunching-reveals-impressive-growth.html, accessed May 18, 2020.

7. Tom Phillips, "China on Course to Become World's Most Christian Nation Within 15 Years," *The Telegraph,* https://www.telegraph.co.uk/news/worldnews/asia/china/10776023/China-on-course-to-become-worlds-most-Christian-nation-within-15-years.html, accessed May 18, 2020.

8. Ibid.

9. "The Truth About Islam," *Solomon's Porch,* The Solomon Foundation, https://thesolomonfoundation.org/solomons-porch/the-truth-about-islam, accessed May 18, 2020.

10. Ibid.

ABOUT THE AUTHOR

DR. JOHN BENEFIEL is the founder and Senior Pastor of Church on the Rock, Oklahoma City. He also founded and leads the Heartland Apostolic Prayer Network (HAPN) and the Global Apostolic Prayer Network (GAPN), with a leader and a network in each of the 50 states and 112 nations. The purpose of the networks is to impact the seven mountains of culture—Religion, Family, Education, Government, Media/Arts & Entertainment, Protect & Serve, and Economy—for God's kingdom through our prayers and influence.

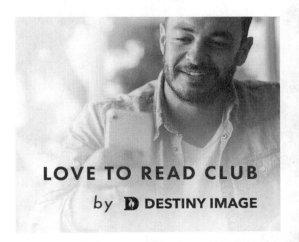